MEASURING AND MANAGING CREDIT RISK

ARNAUD DE SERVIGNY

OLIVIER RENAULT

McGraw-Hill

New York Chicago San Francisco Lisbon London Madrid
Mexico City Milan New Delhi San Juan Seoul
Singapore Sydney Toronto

6 7 8 9 0 DOC/DOC 0 9 8

ISBN 0-07-141755-9

This publication is designed to provide accurate and authoritative information in regard to the subject matter covered. It is sold with the understanding that the publisher is not engaged in rendering legal, accounting, or other professional service. If legal advice or other expert assistance is required, the services of a competent professional person should be sought.
> —From a declaration of principles jointly adopted by a committee of the American Bar Association and a committe of publishers.

McGraw-Hill books are available at special discounts to use as premiums and sales promotions, or for use in corporate training programs. For more information, please write to the Director of Special Sales, Professional Publishing, McGraw-Hill Two Penn Plaza, New York, NY 10011-2298. Or contact your local bookstore.

To Marie and Marion

Library of Congress Cataloging-in-Publication Data

Servigny, Arnaud de.
  Measuring and managing credit risk / by
Arnaud de Servigny and Olivier Renault.
    p. cm.
Includes bibliographical references.
  ISBN 0-07-141755-9 (Hardcover : alk. paper)
  1. Credit—Management—Mathematical models. 2. Risk
management—Mathematical models. 3. Credit ratings. 4. Derivative
securities. 5. Default (Finance) I. Title: Measuring and managing credit risk.
II. Renault, Olivier. III. Title.

HG3751.S47 2004
332.1'068'1—dc22

                                                        2003018949

CONTENTS

FOREWORD

Credit risk, the chance that money owed may not be repaid, is hardly a new concept. There can be little doubt, however, that awareness of credit risk has continued to grow. This has been accompanied by an increasing recognition across many sectors of the economy that credit risk needs to be actively managed. Finally, sometimes as a result of these trends and sometimes as a precursor to them, tools and techniques to manage credit risk have become both increasingly sophisticated and more readily available.

Defaults on credit obligations have always been a fact of economic life, but the world's economies have increasingly seemed to create spikes in default rates that have been truly punishing, not just for banks and bond investors, but for corporations and other institutions as well. That has contributed significantly to heightened awareness of credit risk and the idea that credit risk exposures need to be more actively and effectively managed. For banks, the new Basel regulatory proposals provide an added impetus for a reexamination of their approach to credit risk management. Finally, and most fundamentally, for all types of organizations, the need to use their capital as efficiently as possible— and thus the need to understand how much should properly be allocated to offset credit risk—is a key driver for a renewed focus on credit risk management.

With the increased attention on credit risk comes a growing need to better understand its elements as well as the continuing development of tools and techniques to manage it. Arnaud de Servigny and Olivier Renault do a wonderful job of taking on this challenge. They provide robust explanations of the elements of credit risk and the range of approaches available to analyze and manage it. They cover credit risk analysis from both a qualitative and quantitative perspective, effectively providing insights into the role both can play in an effective credit risk management program. They deal with loss recovery as well as default. They provide a strong foundation for a review of credit portfolio analytics by first reviewing credit correlation issues. They tie all of this effectively to capital allocation. Finally, they recognize the growing trend toward active trading of credit through an examination of the market's treatment of credit risk.

For management of banks, insurers, finance companies, asset managers, corporations, government agencies, and others, understanding the credit risk issue and the available solutions is increasingly one of the keys to their success. *Measuring and Managing Credit Risk* by de Servigny and Renault is an invaluable aid in helping to understand how to do it right.

ROY TAUB

Executive Managing Director
Standard & Poor's Risk Solutions

INTRODUCTION

*M*easuring and Managing Credit Risk presents modern techniques of credit risk management used within banks. Writing a comprehensive book on credit risk is becoming increasingly difficult every day given the exponential growth in knowledge and in techniques that have been developed by the industry and academia. As a result we have had to make choices. In this book we focus on issues that we consider to be crucial, while skipping other topics. In particular we are more focused on credit risk management rather than on credit pricing, which has already received considerable attention in other books.

The clear objective of this book is to blend three types of experiences in a single text. We always aim to consider the topics from an academic standpoint as well as from a banking angle, and from the specific perspective of a rating agency.

Our review goes beyond a simple list of tools and methods. In particular, we try to provide a robust framework regarding the implementation of a credit risk management system. In order to do so, we analyze the most widely used methodologies in the banking community and point out their relative strengths and weaknesses. We also offer insight from our experience of the implementation of these techniques within financial institutions.

Another feature of this book is that it surveys significant amounts of empirical research. Chapters dealing with loss given default or correlations, for example, are illustrated with recent statistics that allow the reader to have a better grasp of the topic and to understand the practical difficulties of implementing credit risk models empirically.

Although the book deals with techniques, it also aims at bringing a high level of understanding of core issues about the strategic management of banks. This specific contribution is devised to bring a perspective on credit risk to the senior management of banks. Bank managers indeed appear to be divided between those who are reluctant to apply quantitative techniques and those who are very keen. We believe that presenting the merits and the limitations of the various techniques in an objective way will help managers understand how these tools can help their bank to control risks and where the strategic insight of managers is most needed.

STRUCTURE OF THE BOOK

This book is divided into 10 chapters. We begin with microeconomics and describe the functions performed by banks as well as the environment in which they operate (Chapter 1). We then focus on ratings developed internally by banks or supplied by rating agencies (Chapter 2). This enables us to describe the value of qualitative assessments for credit purposes. In Chapter 3 we present quantitative techniques to assess the credit quality of firms. We focus in particular on the structural approach to credit risk and on scoring models. We stress some very important elements of default probability models and define robust criteria to evaluate the performance of these models.

In Chapter 4, we consider a rather unexplored territory: recovery rates with a specific empirical and international focus. In Chapter 5, we study default correlation, which has been an active area of empirical and theoretical research. A sound understanding of default dependencies is key to the implementation of modern risk management based on diversification.

Chapter 6 gathers all the building blocks developed in previous chapters to construct portfolio models. Competing approaches (analytical versus simulation-based) are presented and compared. The output of these models is used to compute risk-adjusted performance measures.

In Chapter 7 we consider credit risk management from the point of view of the senior executives of banks. We move away from the bottom-up approach developed in previous chapters and show that this approach has to be complemented by market information and a top-down perspective. In Chapter 8 we introduce the determinants and dynamics of credit spreads, while in Chapter 9 we review credit derivatives and securitization products that are designed to mitigate or isolate credit risk.

Finally, Chapter 10 concludes this book by reviewing credit risk regulation from a practical and a theoretical point of view. Regulatory reform, and in particular the Basel II framework and the new International Accounting Standard rules, have been key drivers in the development of credit risk management tools.

Our hope is that this book will help practitioners and students gain a broad understanding of the key issues and techniques linked to the measurement and management of credit risk.

ACKNOWLEDGMENTS

Our gratitude goes to all those who have helped us in carefully reading this book and providing comments. We would like to thank in particular Ron Anderson, Max Bezard, Regis Blazy, Alain Carron, Fabien Couderc, Michel Crouhy, Jan Ericsson, Julian Franks, Blaise Ganguin, Kai Gilkes, David Hand, Florian Heider, Philippe Henrotte, Jan-Pieter Krahnen, Frédéric Loss, Nancy Masschelein, Janet Mitchell, Franck Moraux, William Perraudin, Mark Salmon, Olivier Scaillet, Dirk Tasche, Ivan Zelenko, and our colleagues at Standard & Poor's Risk Solutions.

ARNAUD DE SERVIGNY

OLIVIER RENAULT

CHAPTER 1

Credit, Financial Markets, and Microeconomics

Most papers, articles, and books on risk management are primarily centered on techniques. This book is no exception, as will be apparent in the next chapters. However, before we get to the techniques, we would like to take a microeconomic point of view and highlight the definition of a bank, as well as the nature of the relationship between banks and industrial firms. These are best described in a microeconomic framework.

The increasing breadth of credit markets in most advanced economies has reduced the role of banking intermediation. The trend toward market-based finance appears to be very strong and even calls into question the reason for having banks. The objective of this chapter is to analyze the underlying microeconomics in order to better understand this change and its consequences and to identify the value brought by banks to the economy. This analysis will help us to better grasp the characteristics of the optimal behavior of banks in a market environment. This will prove particularly valuable when dealing with bank risk management.

At the outset, it is important to mention that the definition of the banking firm, according to microeconomic theory, is a rather narrow one, corresponding more to commercial banking than to investment banking: A bank basically receives deposits and lends money. Loans are not assumed to be tradable in debt markets. In this respect an investment bank that tends to offer services linked with market activities (securities issuance, asset management, etc.) is not considered a bank, but is simply included in the financial markets environment. Other important financial intermediaries such as institutional investors (insurance companies, pension funds, etc.) and rating agencies (acting as delegated monitors) are not yet as well identified. These categories of participants should find a better place in financial theory, in conjunction with their increased role.

According to microeconomic principles, the rationale for the existence of banks is linked with the absence of *Walrasian* financial markets,[1] providing full efficiency and completeness. Such absence can result from either asymmetric information on industrial projects, incompleteness of contracts, or incompleteness of markets.[2] A Walrasian economy is necessary for financial markets to provide *Pareto optimal*[3] adjustments between supply of and demand for money. The "real-world" economy cannot be qualified as Walrasian.

Following Merton's (1995) approach,[4] a bank should be defined by the missions it fulfills for the benefit of the economy. This analysis is shared by many significant contributors to banking theory.[5] A bank is described as the institution, or to rephrase it in microeconomic wording, as *the most adequate—Pareto optimal—coalition of individual agents,* able to perform three major intermediation functions[6]: liquidity intermediation, risk intermediation, and information intermediation.

1. *The liquidity intermediation* function is the most obvious one. It consists of reallocating all the money in excess, saved by depositors, in order to finance companies short of cash and expanding through long-term investment plans. This "asset transformation" activity reconciles the preference for liquidity of savers with the long-term maturity of capital expenditures.

2. *The risk intermediation* function corresponds to all operations whereby a bank collects risks from the economy (credit, market, foreign exchange, interest rate risks, etc.) and reengineers them for the benefit of all economic agents. The growing securitization activity, whereby a bank repackages risks and resells them in the market through new securities with varying degrees of risk, falls into this category.

3. *The information intermediation* function is particularly significant whenever there is some asymmetric information between an entrepreneur (who has better information about the riskiness of his project) and the uninformed savers and investors from whom he is seeking financing. Since the seminal article by

Diamond (1984), banks have been considered as *delegated monitors*. They are seen as able to operate for the benefit of the community of investors in order to set mechanisms for information revelation. Moral hazard and adverse selection[7] can be tackled by them.

To summarize, banks exist because they fulfill intermediation services and fill in gaps in financial markets.

In addition, in a theoretical perfect economy, agents should be indifferent between the two major sources of funding: equity and debt (Modigliani and Miller, 1958). One could then argue that equity raised on financial markets should be sufficient for financing corporations and that bank lending should not be absolutely required. However, just like banking theory, financial theory accounts for the existence of both debt and equity because of imperfect financial markets where there is asymmetric information, incomplete contracts, or frictions such as taxes. With the existence of these different financial products, banks have found a very important role, focusing particularly on the lending business. One of their main characteristics (and a competitive advantage of banks) is that they are focused on debt management. They are in fact the only type of financial institution that manages debt both as resources (through either deposits that are debt-like contracts or money raised on financial markets) and as assets, with loans customized to requirements.

Credit disintermediation has a very strong momentum, and the traditional segregation between debt and equity as well as between the banking firm and financial markets tends to evolve quickly (see Figure 1-1). The main reason behind these dynamics is the increasing level of efficiency of markets.

In the following section of this chapter, we first look at the theory of the firm in order to identify the drivers of capital structure, as well as the role of debt and equity. This review of the microeconomics of the firm helps us to better understand major pitfalls and risk mitigation requirements related to providing external funding. A snapshot of the theory of financial contracts in particular will enable us to properly identify where the added value of the banking industry lies. We then briefly review the theory of the banking firm in order to show more precisely how banks can be a good alternative to markets for debt allocation to companies.

FIGURE 1-1

The Trend Toward Disintermediation

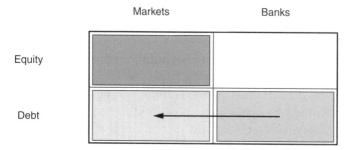

THE ROLE OF DEBT IN THE THEORY OF THE FIRM

The financial world is generally supposed to be subordinated to the "real economy." It provides support to companies that produce goods and services and thus contributes to increased global welfare. Credit markets evolve according to the funding choices of corporate firms.

In making financial decisions, a firm should seek to maximize its value. When the owner and the manager of the company are the same, then maximization of the value of the firm corresponds to maximizing the manager's wealth. But when a manager and various investors share the profits of the firm, the various parties tend to seek their own interest.[8] As the firm is not a perfect market, there is no pricing system that solves conflicts of interest and internal tensions. There is no a priori rationale to ensure that the balancing of individual interests leads to the maximization of the value of the firm. This explains why modern corporate finance theory measures the quality of the capital structure of the firm based on the appropriateness of the financial instruments used[9]: The relevant capital structure should induce agents in control of the firm to maximize its value. This approach is not consistent with the Modigliani-Miller (1958) setting in which the choice of the financial structure of the firm has no bearing on its value.[10] The Modigliani-Miller theorem breaks down because a very important assumption about perfect markets is not fulfilled in practice: the transparency of information.

The funding of a given project will in general be supplied not only by the cash flows of the company, but also by additional debt or equity. Debt and equity offer very different payoff patterns, which trigger different behaviors by the claim holders. More precisely, the equity holder has a convex profile (of payoff as a function of the value of the firm), and the debt holder has a concave one (Figure 1-2). As a result, there are two issues. Each of the stakeholders will have different requirements (cash flow rights) and would make different decisions about the management of the firm (control rights[11]).

Figure 1-2 depicts the payoffs to the debt holder and the equity holder as a function of the value of the firm V at the debt maturity. D is the principal of debt. The payoff to the debt holder is bounded by the repayment of the principal D. If the value of the firm is below the principal ($V < D$), then debt holders have priority over equity holders and seize the entire value of the firm V. Therefore equity holders have a zero payoff. However, if the value of the firm is more than sufficient to repay the debt ($V > D$), the excess value ($V - D$) falls into the hands of equity holders. Clearly, the debt holder is not interested in the firm reaching very high levels $V > > D$ as its payoff is unchanged compared with the situation in which $V = D$. On the contrary, the higher the value of the firm, the better for the equity holder.

Equity holders run the firm and make investment and production decisions. The convexity of their payoff with respect to the value of the firm induces them to take on more risk in order to try and reach very high levels of V. If the project fails, they are protected by limited liability and end up with nothing. If the project succeeds, they extract most of the upside, net of the repayment of the debt.

FIGURE 1-2

Debt and Equity Payoffs

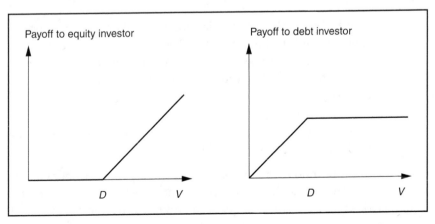

Financial theory shows that optimal allocation of control rights between debt holders and shareholders enables in some cases the maximization of the value of the firm in a comparable way to the entrepreneur who funds capital expenditures from his or her own resources. This second-order optimum requires a fine tuning between equity and debt in order to minimize the following two sources of inefficiency:

- The asymmetry of roles between the uninformed lender and the well-informed entrepreneur
- Market inefficiencies—the incompleteness of contracts, leading both parties to be unable to devise a contract that would express the adequate selection rule as well as the rule for optimized management of the project[12]

We now turn to these inefficiencies in more detail, focusing first on the impact of the asymmetric relationship between entrepreneurs and investors vis-à-vis the value of the firm. We then review the *instrumental* understanding of the capital structure of the firm, given incomplete contracts.

The Impact of the Asymmetric Relationship between Investors and Entrepreneurs

An asymmetric relationship exists between the investor providing funding and the entrepreneur seeking it: asymmetry in initial wealth, asymmetry regarding the management of the funded project, and, of course, asymmetric information. The entrepreneur has privileged private knowledge about the value of the project and how it is managed.

There are two major types of asymmetric information biases in microeconomic theory:

- *Adverse selection.* Because of a lack of information, investors prove unable to select the best projects.[13] They will demand the same interest rate for all projects. This will, in turn, discourage holders of good projects, and investors will be left with the bad ones.
- *Moral hazard.* If an investor cannot monitor the efforts of an entrepreneur, the latter can be tempted to manage the project suboptimally in terms of the value of the firm. This lack of positive incentive is called "moral hazard."

Adverse selection refers to the intrinsic quality of a project, whereas moral hazard relates to how the entrepreneur behaves (whatever the actual intrinsic quality of the project). In addition, adverse selection will occur before a contractual relationship is entered, whereas moral hazard will develop during the relationship.

Adverse Selection

Here we highlight some aspects of the complex impact of adverse selection on good firms and good projects. We mainly consider investors and firms. We show how difficult the selection of companies is for investors. In particular, debt allocation (in essence bank intermediation) is important to support projects and provide a signal to investors.

The Capital Structure of the Firm Can Be Seen as a Signal to Investors, and Surprisingly Not Exactly the Way Common Sense Would Suggest

When there is adverse selection, the financial structure of the firm can be seen as a signal to investors. The two approaches below are about costs of signaling. In Ross (1977), costly bankruptcy is considered. In Leland and Pyle (1977), the focus is on managerial risk aversion, with managers who signal good projects by retaining risky equity.

A reasonably large level of debt could be seen as evidence of the good quality of the firm. Ross (1977) expresses this idea in a particular case, i.e., on the basis of two strong assumptions:

+ The entrepreneur is a shareholder and therefore will benefit from debt leverage since it increases the value of the firm.
+ The entrepreneur will receive a specific penalty if the firm goes bankrupt.[14]

Under such assumptions, only good firms would use debt, because for bad companies, recourse to debt would not maximize the utility function of the entrepreneur, given the increased bankruptcy risk. In this context, debt would operate as a way to segregate good companies from bad ones.

Other models[15] follow the same path, assuming that up to a certain level, debt and leverage can be seen as an expression of robustness of firms, providing a positive signal. Leland and Pyle (1977) come to the same result, but without assigning penalties to the entrepreneur under bankruptcy. The idea behind such models is that if the entrepreneur knows that a given project within the firm is good, he will tend to increase his participation in the company. But because he needs cash to finance the project, he will have to use debt. In the end, increased leverage goes along with increased participation of the entrepreneur as a shareholder, thus providing a good signal.

To Some Extent, the Definition of a Pecking Order of Financial Instruments Can Compensate for Adverse Selection, When a Signal Can Be Sent to Investors
Another element tends to restrain the selection of good projects: the underestimation of the value of the equity by investors due to their limited access to company and project information. If the value of the shares of a firm is significantly undervalued, good new projects that would be suitable for investment[16] may be rejected because of lack of funding. Existing shareholders will not be willing to supply new funding given the low valuation of the firm. They will also refuse to allow new shareholders in since newcomers not only would benefit from the cash flows of the new projects but also would benefit from all existing projects of the firm (dilution effect). This situation of lack of equity funding is clearly suboptimal for the economy. It can be compensated by seeking internal funding based on cash flows. If this option proves impossible, then the company will try to avoid the effect of adverse selection through the use of external debt and in particular of fairly valued low-risk securities with strong collateral (e.g., asset-backed securities on receivables, etc.).

Under strong adverse selection, all companies will be evaluated by investors at a single price, based on average expected return. The average price will play against good companies. In the end, good firms will curtail their investment plans, whereas bad ones will keep on investing by tapping the equity markets. In reality, ways exist to compensate for adverse selection through recourse to funding based on a pecking order.[17] The firm will try to limit its cost of financial funding by choosing instruments based on a ranking: Cash flow comes first, then risk-free debt, then well-secured less risky debt, then unsecured debt, and ultimately equity.

Moral Hazard
Recent crises like Enron in the United States or Vivendi Universal in Europe, where the management of the company has shifted from the initial core business without the clear consent of all stakeholders, stand as a good example of moral hazard. Enron indeed moved from a gas pipeline business to an energy trading activity, while Vivendi Universal evolved from a water and waste management utility to a media and telecom company. Both companies engineered a buoyant communication policy vis-à-

vis the stakeholders that was largely focused on the personality of the top management. This behavior ultimately led to some accounting opacity concealed to some extent by the communication policy.

The investor-entrepreneur relationship can be illustrated using principal-agent theory.[18] Moral hazard supposes that decisions made by the agent that affect the utility function of both the agent and the principal cannot be fully observed by the principal.

In what follows, we first describe the moral hazard problems and then show how banks bring value in solving parts of these issues.

Conflict of Interest between Entrepreneurs and Investors
According to Jensen and Meckling (1976), moral hazard between an entrepreneur and an investor arises from competing interests. The entrepreneur tries to benefit from any new project and to extract value for herself. She does so, for instance, by recourse to additional spending paid by the firm, hence reducing the shareholders' value.

The main types of entrepreneurs' misbehaviors are:

+ Actions driven by private benefits
+ The use of firm resources for private purposes
+ Limited effort
+ Blackmail on early departure from the company
+ Overinvestment to maximize the entrepreneur's utility[19]
+ Disagreement on the decision to terminate the business though it is the optimal decision

Given all these negative incentives, it seems desirable to have entrepreneurs who are also shareholders. However, as entrepreneurs are typically short of cash, a high level of leverage is often required to finance the expansion of the firm, leading the entrepreneurs to resort to large debt. This often results in a new form of moral hazard between shareholders and debt holders. Shareholders indeed benefit from limited liability and have an incentive to maximize leverage and favor riskier projects, while debt holders seek to minimize risk in order to avoid the large downside corresponding to bankruptcy. In other words, shareholders tend to seize parts of the benefits that should accrue to debt holders. As debt holders expect such behavior, they ask for an additional risk premium on issued debt. The value of the firm is thus lessened by agency costs on debt issuance.

Jensen and Meckling (1976) conclude that the balance between debt and equity can be analyzed on a cost-benefit basis. The benefit is linked with the convergence of the utility of the entrepreneur and that of the shareholder (reducing moral hazard between the two). Cost is expressed as agency cost generated by the risk-averse debt holder.

The Debt Contract: The Way to Reduce Such Inefficiencies Carefully specifying covenants in debt contracts can provide a remedy for many inefficiencies. In the situation described above, analyzed by Harris and Raviv (1991), the control of the firm or of its assets will typically be transferred to creditors in case of distress or default.

Several studies have come to the conclusion that a standard debt contract[20] is optimal in a context of asymmetric information. Indeed, revealing the true return of the project to the investor becomes the best choice of the entrepreneur. The standard debt contract can always be improved in order to deal with the problem of limited involvement of the entrepreneur. The best way to do so is to award a bonus[21] that is calibrated on an observable criterion expressing the effort of the manager. This can also be complemented by ongoing surveillance of the entrepreneur through some monitoring of the project's performance.

These developments on optimal contracts do not, however, provide insights regarding the rationale for equity origination. One of the main weaknesses of the previous analysis is that it is static.[22] Diamond (1989) considers a dynamic approach with repeated games and reputational effects. He shows that in a Jensen and Meckling (1976) setup, shareholders and debt holders will pilot the level of risk together in order to establish the reputation of the company and reduce agency costs in the long run, i.e., credit spreads. This analysis is particularly insightful with respect to the debt policy of large companies.

In reality the relationship between creditors and debtors can be more complex. It cannot always be ruled by a customized written contract. As a result, the conceptual framework most frequently used to deal with moral hazard corresponds to the analysis of dynamic interactions between agents in a situation of incomplete contracts.

The Financial Structure of Firms as an Optimal Allocation of Control Rights

About Incomplete Contracts

Moral hazard between the debtor and the creditor is a significant issue. They stand in a conflicting position, challenging each other on the control of the firm in a situation where asymmetric information prevails. Finding a conceptual way to resolve this issue is possible by considering incomplete contracts.

Allocation of Control Rights   The starting point with this approach is to assume that no contract can fully solve the latent conflict of interest between creditors and debtors. In order to obtain a performance as close as possible to the optimum, the best solution is to allocate control to the agent[23] who will follow the most profitable strategy for the firm. Simply put, the efficiency of the performance of the firm will then depend on the optimal allocation of control rights. This allocation process is dynamic and, of course, fully contingent on the current performance of the firm.[24]

The above corresponds to an instrumental view on contracts. This means that such contracts are used in order to distribute control rights appropriately among the entrepreneur, shareholders, and creditors.

The Two Main Types of Contracts   The management policies resulting from debt and equity contracts will be dissimilar:

- Debt contracts typically lead to higher risk aversion, strong governance, and strict control of the entrepreneur.
- Equity contracts, on the other hand, imply lower risk aversion, more flexibility, and freedom for the top management of the firm.

Let us examine a simplified two-period case. Under incomplete contracts, we assume that the initial financial structure of the firm is defined and is reflected in financial contracts with lenders and shareholders. At the end of the first period, the agents (debt holders, shareholders) observe the level of return as well as the involvement and performance of the entrepreneur. Usually, debt contracts will enable the redistribution of control rights. For example, in the case of default or distress, a new negotiation between stakeholders will occur, giving power to creditors. Creditors can decide to liquidate or to reorganize the firm. As a result, the control of creditors will be much tighter.[25]

The Capital Structure Seen as an Optimal Dynamic Management Tool

The model by Dewatripont and Tirole (1994) shows how the capital structure can lead to optimal dynamic management. For instance, the authors explain that a sharp increase in short-term debt will lead to a real risk of default as well as to a potential change of control in favor of creditors.

Because of this threat, entrepreneurs have strong incentive to manage the company appropriately, i.e., taking into account creditors' interests. Since debt is considered a risk for managers, it leads them to conduct business prudently. In addition, problems linked with existing asymmetric information and conflicts of interest among stakeholders are lessened by the necessity to sustain a firm's reputation as a debtor. Large corporate firms reflect this situation well, being continually reviewed by rating agencies that assess their reputation.

Summary

We have seen that all stakeholders involved in a firm have different objectives and risk profiles. We have tried to explain where these differences are coming from, using both payoff analysis and concepts extracted from microeconomic theory (adverse selection and moral hazard). We have also discussed the ability of financial contracts related to the capital structure of the firm to allocate control rights in the most efficient way in order to achieve optimal risk-return performance. Based on this investigation, formulating customized contracts and engaging in active monitoring can prove an interesting solution. It all relates to the role of banks, the subject of the following sections.

BANKING INTERMEDIATION THEORY

Why use banks? This question can be formulated from the point of view of a firm seeking financing: Why choose a bank rather than tap the market in order to raise finance? It can also be considered from the point of view of investors: Why deposit money in a bank account instead of buying a bond directly?

Banking theory is based on intermediation: The institution receives deposits, mainly short-term ones, and lends money for typically fixed long-term maturities (illiquid loans). This maturity transformation activity is a necessary function for the achievement of global economic optimum. Banks act as an intermediary and reduce the deficiencies of markets in three areas: liquidity, risk, and information.

In the next paragraphs we address these various types of intermediation. We particularly focus on the reason why banking intermediation is Pareto optimal, compared with disintermediated markets. The core advantages of banks in this activity are explicitly defined.

Liquidity Intermediation

Providing Liquidity Intermediation

The banking activity reconciles the objectives of two major conflicting agents in the economy:

- *Consumers.* These agents maximize their consumption utility function at a given time horizon (short term). Their needs are subject to random variations. Consumers are averse to volatility and prefer smooth consumption patterns through time. Shocks in purchasing power (due to temporary unemployment or an unexpected expense, for example) could generate reduced utility if the agents were forced to cut their spending. The best way for them to minimize this risk and maintain optimal behavior is to keep a sufficient deposit cushion that absorbs shocks. Bank deposits are similar to liquidity insurance. The insurance premium is reflected in the low interest rate paid on such deposits.

- *Investors.* The bank makes profits in leveraging consumers' deposits and financing long-term illiquid investments. The two core requirements to succeed in such operations are diversification and liquidity stability based on "mutualization." Diversification means that the bank is able to repay deposits because it works on a diversified portfolio of loans (diversified in terms of maturities and credit risk). Liquidity stability suggests that the amount of deposits it holds is fairly stable over time because all depositors will not require cash at the same time.

One of the first models portraying banking intermediation is that of Diamond and Dybvig (1983). The authors show that banking intermediation is Pareto optimal in an economy with two divergent time horizons: the long term of entrepreneurs and the short term of consumers.

Diamond and Dybvig clearly put emphasis on deposits rather than on lending policy.[26] Their bank could have invested in bonds (rather than lend to entrepreneurs) and obtained a sufficient diversification effect. In their very theoretical economy, if consumers directly owned long-term bonds, these instruments would tend to be underpriced. This price gap would correspond to a liquidity option required by these agents in order to cover any sudden liquidity need.

Providing Liquidity Insurance to Firms

When an entrepreneur develops a new project, she knows that she may have to face unexpected financial needs to sustain random shocks on income or expenses. As long as these new financial requirements imply value creation for the firm,[27] there will probably exist an investor to bring additional cash. But the new money needed may not be linked with the value of the firm or the value of the project. It can be a mere cost.[28]

The company has to anticipate such a liquidity risk. Two main options are available:

+ Hold money in reserve, for example through liquid risk-free bonds (government bonds), that can be used for unexpected difficulties.

+ Hold no initial reserve and rely on an overdraft facility obtained from a bank.

Diamond (1997) and Holmström and Tirole (1998) offer interesting insights regarding the second option. When the liquidity risks of different companies are independent, then bank overdrafts become Pareto optimal and supersede the use of liquid bonds. The proof is again based on mutualization: If nothing happens to the project or to the company, then the bonds are unnecessarily held while the money could be invested in the firm. It artificially increases the value of these bonds on financial markets and is costly to the company itself (in terms of yield differential between the riskless investment and an investment in other projects). In contrast, any new customer increases the mutualization and diversification of the bank, thereby improving overdraft lending conditions.

Risk Intermediation

Banks fulfill another very important economic function: bearing, transforming, or redistributing financial risks. For example, the progress achieved in interest rate risk management in the eighties has been accompanied by the boom in derivative markets. Banks have become experts in terms of financial risk management and have begun to sell this expertise to corporate firms. This activity has been predominantly driven by investment banks.

The objective of this section is not to discuss asset and liability management specifically, nor to explain how credit derivatives can be used to manage risks.[29] It is rather to focus on the changing relationship between commercial banks and firms in the context of financial market expansions and credit disintermediation.

Looking at risk management principles from the bank's point of view, and in particular at credit risk, we shed some light on the criteria for decision making: Should a bank hold and manage such risks or sell them?

The Trend toward the Marketing of Credit Risk

In developed economies, credit products are increasingly available in financial markets. In particular, securitization has expanded significantly since the eighties. It has given birth to an enormous market of traded structured bonds (collateralized debt obligations, asset-backed securities, etc.) in the United States and subsequently in Europe. Credit derivatives have enabled synthetic risk coverage, without physical exchange of property rights and without initial money transfer. This trend illustrates a major shift in the role of commercial banks in financial markets. Allen and Santomero (1999) show how important securitization has been in the United States (see Figure 1-3).

As Figure 1-3 shows, credit risk is increasingly brought back to the market by commercial banks. The next step is then to rationalize the decision process within the bank, based on an adequate definition of the risk-aversion profile of the bank. In a similar way as for interest rate risk, the choice will lie somewhere between two extreme options: Either become a broker through complete hedging in financial markets, or become an asset transformer who holds and actively manages risk through diversification and ongoing monitoring of counterparties.[30]

FIGURE 1-3

The Growing Importance of Securitization

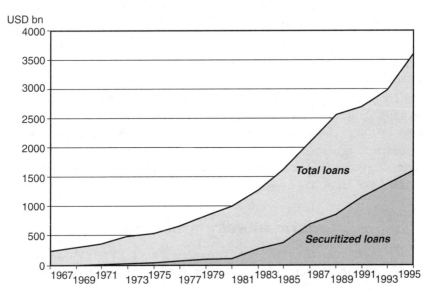

Sell or Hold Credit Risk?

A credit decision involves three components: financial, managerial, and strategic. Risk management consists primarily of reducing earnings volatility and avoiding large losses. For a bank, mastering the stability of its profits is a critical credibility issue, because if the current capital structure of a banking firm is not strong enough, some additional external funding will be required. Such funding can prove costly and dangerous because of agency costs driven by asymmetric information or potential conflicts of interest between managers and investors. As a result, the bank should definitely think about and define its own risk aversion in order to target earnings stability and the robustness of its capital structure.[31] This part of a bank's mission is often understated although it is critical in terms of competitive positioning among peers.

In addition, risk management allows banks to have less costly capital sitting on their balance sheet, while satisfying minimum capital requirements.

From a management point of view, both brokerage (reselling risk) and asset transformation (keeping risk) are possible as long as the underlying assets display sufficient liquidity.[32]

+ In the case of brokerage, the bank's profit is based on marketing and distribution skills.
+ In the case of asset transformation, a gross profit from risk holding is generated. This profit has to be netted with holding costs, such as monitoring costs and costs associated with concentration of the portfolio in a specific sector or region.

Considering these two options, the bank has to draw comparisons and to set limits, based on a return-risk performance indicator. When holding risk is preferred to pure brokerage, the ability to measure appropriately the level of economic capital "consumed" by a specific loan becomes critical, as it is the most important risk component in the evaluation of the performance indicator. This stresses the crucial priority of understanding dependence-correlation patterns in a dynamic way, as diversification is one of the most significant ways to gain economic capital relief (see Chapters 5 and 6).

Information Intermediation

From a strategic perspective, the main question is to understand whether a bank holds a competitive advantage in the lending business compared with markets. Leland and Pyle (1977) were the first to identify that banks have an advantage over investors, based on the privileged information they collect on loans and borrowers. Diamond (1984) and a stream of other articles have established that debtor surveillance and delegated monitoring by banks corresponded to an optimal behavior. It is now clear that the right perimeter for the lending business by banks is that in which the bank retains an informational advantage in terms of credit risk management.

The Bank as an Optimal Monitor

Investment financing takes place in a context where asymmetric information is frequent and significant. The entrepreneur seeking financing obviously knows more about his project than potential investors or their representatives.

Two perverse effects result from asymmetric information as recalled above: adverse selection and moral hazard.

The entrepreneur could try to benefit from asymmetric information and to extract undue value from his project. As mentioned previously, the nature of the lending contract can minimize this risk and provide incentive for the entrepreneur to behave optimally. However, direct surveillance of the manager by the lender can prove very valuable to deter the entrepreneur from concealing information. Diamond (1984) has introduced the concept of monitoring. If the bank (the monitor) observes the evolution of the value of the project carefully and frequently, it can dissuade the entrepreneur from defaulting on his debt by introducing the threat of a liquidation. Most of the time the threat will be sufficient, and the bank can deter the entrepreneur without having to take action. This active monitoring obviously has a cost, but Diamond estimates that it is lower than the expected cost of going into liquidation.

Let us now focus on the reason why banks are best placed to perform monitoring. When the number of projects (n) and the number of lenders (m) get large, the number of required surveillance actions becomes very quickly intractable. There is a strong incentive to delegate monitoring to a bank that will supervise all projects on behalf of investors. The bank faces a single cost of K per project; i.e., the corresponding cost for each lender becomes K/m. This is in fact not exactly true, as lenders must deal with an additional moral hazard problem: how to make sure that the bank is acting appropriately. In order not to have to monitor the bank itself, investors seek insurance to protect their deposits. Diamond shows that the monitoring costs for the bank correspond to nK, plus the cost associated with deposits contract $c(n)$. This global cost is inferior, for a large m, to direct monitoring costs nmK by investors.

On the basis of all the approaches generated by Diamond's (1984) seminal article, we will identify where the advantage of the banks resides in terms of monitoring.

Banks' Competitive Advantage

Theoretical Advantages for Banks Diamond's presentation has been criticized, modified, and broadened. The optimality of standard debt contracts has been tested in various cases,[33] for different types of loans,[34] and for various agents.[35] Other models have been introduced where moral hazard impacts on the level of effort provided by the entrepreneur.

Most of the articles tend not to focus on adverse selection. Gale (1993), however, has mixed delegated monitoring with appropriate screening of entrepreneurs. This type of screening selection requires an additional cost equivalent to a pure monitoring cost. In Gale's model, a too large demand for loans tends to saturate the banking system and to generate credit rationing.[36] In the end Gale suggests adding additional selection criteria, such as asking for an ex ante fee to work on any loan requirement. This reduces the demand for loans and the risk of credit rationing.

Bank Lending Efficiency A bank lends money to a company, having spent time and money on monitoring. To some extent, through this initial investment, the bank has significantly reduced competition. At the same time, it takes a long time for the customer to obtain the positive reputation of "a good debtor" when the maturity of the loan is long enough. In the meantime the bank will be in a position to have the customer overpay on any new loans until his reputation as a reliable borrower is clearly established. Through this mechanism, the bank can generate a secure surplus.[37] This could lead to a too high cost of capital in the economy and to suboptimal investment.

Optimal Split between Banks and Financial Markets It is clear that when there is transparency and when information about companies is widely diffused, the competitive advantage of banks over financial markets tends to decrease.[38] For large firms, monitoring can be performed outside the bank, for example by rating agencies.[39]

For well-rated large companies with good profit prospects, financial markets can fully solve moral hazard issues without recourse to monitoring. The main incentive for such a company is to sustain its good reputation. A rating migration, an increase in the firm's spread level or a period of financial distress can tarnish the firm's reputation, damage investors' confidence, and increase substantially its funding costs. The reputation effect becomes a very strong incentive, capable of restraining debtors.[40] In such a situation financial markets benefit from a strong advantage, as marked-to-market prices tend to reflect all available information and affect all stakeholders. This informational advantage can be seen as a strong positive element in the economy.

Private companies, e.g., smaller or younger companies or companies without any rating or with a low (non-investment-grade) rating, tend to ask for bank loans and ongoing monitoring in order to strengthen their reputation before tapping the bond markets. For such debtors asymmetric information becomes the major issue. We have seen above that banks are most efficient in dealing with this type of problem.

On the particular topic of financing very innovative projects, some studies have shown, however, that market intermediaries such as private equity or leveraged finance specialists are better able to perform selection of entrepreneurs and projects, based on customized contracts.[41]

CONCLUSION

The first conclusion we would like to draw is that although disintermediation is a real phenomenon, the future of banks is not at stake. Their scope of activity has evolved given the increased weight of financial markets, but their activity more than ever is central to the efficiency of the economy.

In addition we have seen that a bank is properly defined by three major intermediation activities: liquidity, risk, and information intermediation. When dealing with credit risk management, it is essential not to forget some very important concepts such as liquidity management and information management. In the recent past it has been increasingly recognized that credit risk management cannot be separated from global risk management. The message we would like to convey here is that global risk management cannot be isolated from liquidity and information management.

APPENDIX 1A

Credit Rationing

Credit rationing is a well-established concept. Jaffee and Modigliani (1969) had already mentioned that in the case of interest rate rigidity, banks would opt for credit rationing. This concept has, for example, been used in macroeconomics to evaluate the impact of a monetary policy on the real economy when investment demand appears to be partially disconnected from interest rates (Bernanke, 1983, 1988).

THE BANK IS "PRICE MAKER"

The seminal article in credit rationing is Stiglitz and Weiss (1981). The authors study the credit market under incomplete information. They show how asymmetric information leads to credit rationing, i.e., a situation where the demand for loans is in excess of offer.

The relation between a bank's expected profit and the offered interest rates is abnormal, being altered by adverse selection and lack of incentive. In such a situation the bank cannot distinguish among various debtors who have private information on the true level of risk of their projects. When banks' competition is limited (the banks are "price makers"), a bank can choose to increase interest rates in order to select the best-performing projects. But contraintuitively such a policy will penalize the best projects first, leading banks to pick worse ones.

An analysis of the behavior of the debtor and the creditor will explain this result. We consider two projects with equal expected returns but different risk levels.

For each project (i), the project return is $X(i)$, the debt level is $B(i)$, and the interest rate is r. From the company standpoint, the manager can expect to make a profit once she has repaid the debt:

$$\Pi(k) = \max[0, X(k) - (1 + r)\, B(k)] \qquad \text{for } k = i, j, \text{ where } E[\Pi(i)] = E[\Pi(j)]$$

This corresponds to writing a call option. But for a call, we know that vega = $\partial\pi/\partial\sigma > 0$, which implies that the riskier the project, the more rewarding it is in terms of call value. For a given expected return, the debtor will prefer the riskier project. This corresponds to moral hazard.

The manager of a risky project will therefore agree to pay a higher interest rate than the manager of a safe project, given the higher level of the upside. Limited liability ensures that the downside is bounded. This mechanism, whereby a bank has incentive to select bad risks ("lemons" as Akerlof, 1970, puts it) and to reject good ones, is called adverse selection. This phenomenon tends to reduce the bank's expected profit. The function that maps interest rates to expected profit has a bell shape. Its maximum is obtained for a level of interest rates where adverse selection reduces the bank's profits enough to offset the increase due to interest rates. This value may not correspond to the full adjustment between the offer of and demand for loans: Credit rationing appears with suboptimality.

The model by Stiglitz and Weiss (1981) is one of the most important reference points in banking theory. It has clarified the effect of asymmetric information in banking. However, the lender has a simplistic behavior, because the lender can only act through the interest rate on loans.

THE BANK IS "PRICE TAKER"

Several articles have tried to illustrate constraints on a "price-taker" bank and the consequences in terms of credit rationing.

In a competitive environment a bank is not able to adjust its interest rates. The adjusted price is based on market equilibrium. Before accepting any project, the bank has to check the following three criteria:

1. On each project the interest rate has to incorporate the default risk on the global portfolio of the bank (Jaffee and Russell, 1976). In the following equation, Φ is the expected profit of the bank, δ the refinancing cost of the bank, Γ the average recovery rate on the bank loan portfolio, B is the loan exposure of the bank, and r the interest rate on loans. The bank maximizes

$$\Phi = \Gamma(1 + r)B - (1 + \delta)B$$

With a minimal equilibrium for $\Phi = 0$ (competition drags expected profits to 0), we have

$$1 + r^* = \frac{(1 + \delta)}{\Gamma}$$

The inability to identify the credit quality of its individual clients implies that the bank has to charge an average interest rate based on the average recovery rate: "Good" borrowers will pay for "bad" ones. There is a mutualization effect. Such a behavior will penalize good borrowers who will have to pay a risk premium independent from the risk of their project. By acting this way, a bank could avoid financing good projects for which market pricing is considered as being incompatible with the bank's internal hurdle rate.

2. On each project there is an adjustment between market interest rate pricing and an optimal interest rate required by the bank:
   - If the interest rate is lower than the optimum defined by the bank, then the project may not be retained.
   - If the interest rate is higher than this optimum, then increasing default risk will reduce expected return. Indeed the bank's expected return follows a concave function of the interest rate (bell curve). The bank can discover the optimal point and understand that too-high interest rates weaken projects and make them riskier in terms of probability of default.

   When market equilibrium interest rates are too far from the optimal rate defined by the bank, then the project is rejected within the bank, i.e., there is credit rationing.

3. On each project the impact of the size of a loan needs to be taken into account. Say the profit of the firm is X. It is supposed to be bounded, with $k < X < K$. The loan is B, and r is the interest rate. One of these three results would be obtained:
   - For small-size loans $[B < k/(1 + \delta)]$, the loan service is inferior to the minimum profit of the firm. The bank can lend just over refinancing cost.
   - If the size of B increases, the probability of default increases equally, but a higher interest rate r is sufficient to compensate for accrual risk.
   - Over a certain B^*, it would be wise to increase interest rates and reduce the size of the loan.

When the bank is price taker, it has to reject some projects because of return requirements. This can lead to credit rationing. These requirements depend on the average default rate in the bank portfolio, the size of the exposure on each project, and the market interest rate compared with the expected return of the bank.

External and
Internal Ratings

In order to assess default risk, it is customary to oppose qualitative tools and quantitative approaches. Ratings are among the best-known forms of qualitative measurements. In this chapter we review rating methodologies and assess their strengths and weaknesses.

Rating agencies[1] fulfill a mission of delegated monitoring for the benefit of investors active in bond markets. The objective of rating agencies is to provide an independent credit opinion based on a set of precise criteria. Their contribution is reflected through rating grades that convey information about the credit quality of a borrower. Rating agencies strive to make their grades consistent across regions, industries, and time. Over the past 20 years, rating agencies have played an increasingly important role in financial markets, and their ratings have had a greater impact on corporate security prices.

It is important to stress that delegated monitoring is also a mission of the banking firm, as noted in Chapter 1. A large part of the competitive advantage of banks lies in their ability to assess risks in a timely manner and accurately, based on relevant information. Ideally banks would like to assign analysts to the monitoring of each of their counterparts. Indeed, who better than a senior industry analyst is able to capture the dynamics of a company's creditworthiness, based on a mix of criteria: financial ratios, business factors, strategic performance, industrial market cyclicality, changes in competitiveness, products innovation, etc.?

Assigning an analyst to every counterpart is, of course, not realistic for cost reasons. The cost of the time spent by an analyst gathering and processing the data may not be recouped (in terms of reduced default losses) for smaller loans. A bank will therefore have to rely on quantitative techniques, such as those detailed in Chapter 3 in particular, for small and midsize enterprises (SMEs).

In this chapter we focus exclusively on borrower ratings and not on facility ratings. We first present the most significant elements regarding the rating methodology and criteria that external agencies use. Then we consider comments and criticisms about ratings and finally turn our attention to internal rating systems.

RATINGS AND EXTERNAL AGENCIES[2]

The Role of Rating Agencies in the Financial Markets

A rating agency is an organization that provides analytical services. These services are based on independent, objective, credible, and transparent assessments. The agency's recognition depends on the investor's willingness to accept its judgment.

Credit Ratings

Rating Scales   A credit rating represents the agency's opinion about the creditworthiness of an obligor with respect to a particular debt security or other financial obligation (*issue-specific credit ratings*). It also applies to an issuer's general creditworthiness (*issuer credit ratings*). There are generally two types of assessment corresponding to different financial instruments: long-term and short-term ones. We should stress that ratings from various agencies do not convey the same information. Standard & Poor's perceives its ratings primarily as an opinion on the likelihood of default of an issuer,[3] whereas Moody's ratings tend to reflect the agency's opinion on the expected loss (probability of default times loss severity) on a facility.

Long-term issue-specific credit ratings and issuer ratings are divided into several categories, e.g., from AAA to D for Standard & Poor's. Short-term issue-specific ratings can use a different scale (e.g., from A-1 to D). Figure 2-1 shows Moody's and S&P's rating scales. Although these grades are not directly comparable as mentioned earlier, it is common to put them in parallel. The rated universe is broken down into two very broad categories: investment grade (IG) and non-investment-grade (NIG), or speculative, issuers. IG firms are relatively stable issuers with moderate default risk, while bonds issued in the NIG category, often called junk bonds, are much more likely to default.

The credit quality of firms is best for Aaa/AAA ratings and deteriorates as ratings go down the alphabet. The coarse grid AAA, AA, A, . . . CCC can be supplemented with pluses and minuses in order to provide a finer indication of risk.

The Rating Process   A rating agency supplies a rating only if there is adequate information available to provide a credible credit opinion. This opinion relies on various analyses[4] based on a defined analytical framework. The criteria according to which any assessment is provided are very strictly defined and constitute the intangible assets of rating agencies, accumulated over years of experience. Any change in criteria is typically discussed at a worldwide level.

FIGURE 2-1

Moody's and S&P's Rating Scales

Description	Moody's	S&P	
Investment grade			
	Aaa	AAA	Maximum safety
	Aa	AA	
	A	A	
	Baa	BBB	
Speculative grade			
	Ba	BB	
	B	B	
	Caa	CCC	
			Worst credit quality

For industrial companies, the analysis is commonly split between business reviews (firm competitiveness, quality of the management and of its policies, business fundamentals, regulatory actions, markets, operations, cost control, etc.) and quantitative analyses (financial ratios, etc.). The impact of these factors depends highly on the industry.

Figure 2-2 shows how various factors may impact differently on various industries. It also reports various business factors that impact on different sectors.

Following meetings with the management of the firm that is asking for a rating, the rating agency reviews qualitative as well as quantitative factors and compares the company's performance with that of its peers. (See the ratio medians per rating in Table 2-1.) After this review, a rating committee meeting is convened. The committee discusses the lead analyst's recommendation before voting on it.

The issuer is subsequently notified of the rating and the major considerations supporting it. A rating can be appealed prior to its publication if meaningful new or additional information is to be presented by the issuer. But there is no guarantee that a revision will be granted. When a

FIGURE 2-2

Examples of Various Possible Determinants of Ratings[5]

Indicative Averages	Retail	Airlines	Property	Pharmaceuticals
Investment and speculative grade (%)	Investment grade: 82% Speculative grade: 18%	Investment grade: 24% Speculative grade: 76%	Investment grade: 90% Speculative grade: 10%	Investment grade: 78% Speculative grade: 22%
Business risk weight	*High*	*Low*	*High*	*High*
Financial risk weight	*Low*	*High*	*Low*	*Low*
Business qualitative factors	• Discretionary vs. nondiscretionary • Scale and geographic profile • Position on price, value, and service • Regulatory environment	• Market position (share capacity) • Utilization of capacity • Aircraft fleet (type, age) • Cost control (labor, fuel)	• Quality and location of the assets • Quality of the tenants • Lease structure • Country-specific criteria (laws, taxation, and market liquidity)	• R&D programs • Product portfolio • Patent expirations

TABLE 2-1

Financial Ratios per Rating (3-Year Medians for 1998–2000), U.S. Firms

	AAA	AA	A	BBB	BB	B	CCC
EBIT int. cov. (x)	21.4	10.1	6.1	3.7	2.1	0.8	0.1
EBITDA int. cov. (x)	26.5	12.9	9.1	5.3	3.4	1.8	1.3
Free oper. cash flow/ total debt (%)	84.2	25.2	15.0	8.5	2.6	(3.2)	(12.9)
Funds from oper./total debt (%)	128.8	55.4	43.2	30.8	18.8	7.8	1.6
Return on capital (%)	34.9	21.7	19.4	13.6	11.6	6.6	1.0
Operating income/sales (%)	27.0	22.1	18.6	15.4	15.9	11.9	11.9
Long-term debt/capital (%)	13.3	28.2	33.9	42.5	57.2	69.7	68.8
Total debt/capital (%)	22.9	37.7	42.5	48.2	62.6	74.8	87.7
Number of Companies	8	29	136	218	273	281	22

rating is assigned, it is disseminated to the public through the news media.

All ratings are monitored on an ongoing basis. Any new qualitative or quantitative piece of information is under surveillance. Regular meetings with the issuer's management are organized. As a result of the surveillance process, the rating agency may decide to initiate a review (i.e., put the firm on credit watch) and change the current rating. When a rating is put on a credit watch list, a comprehensive analysis is undertaken. After the process, the rating change or affirmation is announced.

More recently the "outlook" concept has been introduced. It provides information about the rating trend. If, for instance, the outlook is positive, it means that there is some potential upside conditional to the realization of current assumptions regarding the company. On the flip side, a negative outlook suggests that the creditworthiness of the company follows a negative trend.

A very important fact that the agencies persistently emphasize is that their ratings are mere opinions. They do not constitute any recommendation to purchase, sell, or hold any type of security. A rating in itself indeed says nothing about the price or relative value of specific securities. A CCC bond may well be underpriced while an AA security may be trading at an overvalued price, although the risk may be appropriately reflected by their respective ratings.

The Link between Ratings and Probabilities of Default Although a rating is meant to be forward-looking, it is not devised to pinpoint a precise probability of default, but rather to point to a broad risk bucket. Rating agencies publish on a regular basis tables reporting observed default rates per rating category, per year, per industry, and per region. These tables reflect the empirical average defaulting frequencies of firms per rating category within the rated universe. The primary goal of these statistics is to verify that better (worse) ratings are indeed associated with lower (higher) default rates. They show that ratings tend to have homogeneous default rates across industries,[6] as illustrated in Table 2-2.

Figure 2-3 displays cumulative default rates in S&P's universe per rating category. There is a striking difference in default patterns between investment-grade and speculative-grade categories. The clear link between observed default rates and rating categories is the best support for claims by agencies that their grades are appropriate measures of creditworthiness.

Rating agencies also calculate transition matrices, which are tables reporting probabilities of migrations from one rating category to another. These are reviewed at length in Appendix 2A. They serve as indicators of the likely path of a given credit at a given horizon. Ex post information such as that provided in default tables or transition matrices does not guarantee to provide ex ante insights regarding future probabilities of default or migration. Both the stability over time of default probability in a given rating class and the stability of rating criteria used by agencies also contribute to making ratings forward-looking predictors of default.

COMMENTS AND CRITICISMS ABOUT EXTERNAL RATINGS

We have discussed above the general process that agencies use to determine their ratings, and we have described how these assessments give an appropriate broad ranking of firms in terms of creditworthiness. We now focus on three specific issues related to agency ratings. The first issue deals with the horizon of ratings and their dependence on the business cycle. The second is the consistency of transition matrices across time and regions with particular emphasis on the academic literature on the topic. Finally we consider the documented impact of rating changes on corporate security prices and firm value.

TABLE 2-2

Average 1-Year Default Rates per Industry (in Percent)[*]

	Trans.	Util.	Tele.	Media	Insur.	High tech	Chem.	Build.	Fin.	Ener.	Cons.	Auto.
AAA	0.00	0.00	0.00	0.00	0.00	0.00	0.00	0.00	0.00	0.00	0.00	0.00
AA	0.00	0.00	0.00	0.00	0.06	0.00	0.00	0.00	0.00	0.00	0.00	0.00
A	0.00	0.11	0.00	0.00	0.09	0.00	0.00	0.42	0.00	0.00	0.00	0.00
BBB	0.00	0.14	0.00	0.27	0.67	0.73	0.19	0.64	0.32	0.22	0.17	0.29
BB	1.46	0.25	0.00	1.24	1.59	0.75	1.12	0.89	0.86	0.98	1.77	1.47
B	6.50	6.31	5.86	4.97	2.38	4.35	5.29	5.41	8.97	9.57	6.77	5.19
CCC	19.4	71.4	35.9	29.3	10.5	9.52	21.6	21.9	24.7	14.4	26.0	33.3

[*]Default rates for CCC bonds are based on a very small sample and may not be statistically robust.
Source: S&P CreditPro, 1981–2001.

FIGURE 2-3

Cumulative Default Rates Per Rating Category

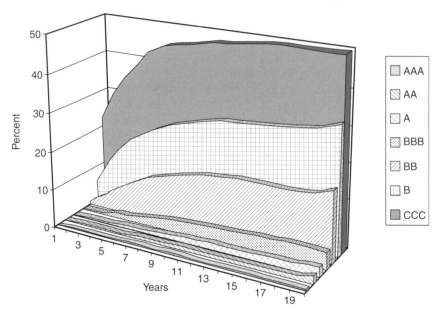

Source: S&P CreditPro, 1981–2001.

Ratings, Related Time Horizon, and Economic Cycles

Time Horizon for External Ratings

Rating agencies are very clear about the fact that issuer credit ratings or long-term issue ratings should not correspond to a mere snapshot of the present situation, but should focus on the long term. The agencies try to factor in the effect of cycles, though they recognize it is not always easy to anticipate them and though cycles are not fully repetitive in terms of duration, magnitude, and dynamics. The confluence of different types of cycles (macroeconomic and industrial, for example) is not unusual and contributes to making the task of rating analysts harder.

A careful assessment of business-risk sensitivity to cycles, for given industry categories, is an important part of the due diligence performed by analysts. Once this has been assessed, analysts try to mitigate the effect of cycles on ratings by incorporating the effect of an "average cycle" in their scenarios. This helps to make the final rating less volatile and less sensitive to expected changes in the business cycle. Rating agencies are therefore associated with "through-the-cycle" ratings.

Figure 2-4 shows how a through-the-cycle rating can filter out cycle effects: A through-the-cycle rating does not fluctuate much with temporary changes in microeconomic conditions (e.g., expected or likely changes in quarter-on-quarter sales) since they are already factored in the rating. However, once the analyst is convinced that a worsening of economic conditions both at the firm level and at the macro level is persistent, then the rating is downgraded on several occasions.

We stated earlier that ratings were broad indicators of probabilities of default (PD) and do not pinpoint a specific PD at a given horizon. This is illustrated in Figure 2-5. The figure shows how a persistent downturn in the economy, such as those observed in the early parts of the 1980s, 1990s and 2000s, significantly raises 1-year default rates within a given rating class. This emphasizes the fact that although the ranking of firms (AAA, AA, etc.) tends to work well on average, the absolute level of riskiness within a rating category fluctuates: Ratings incorporate an average cycle but may overshoot or undershoot when economic conditions deviate too strongly from "average."

FIGURE 2-4

Ratings as Through-the-Cycle Indicators

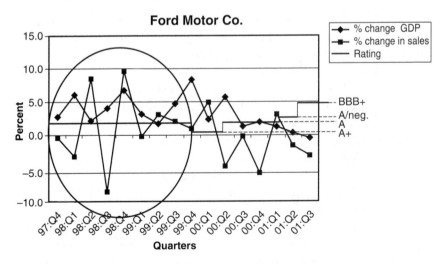

Source: S&P Risk Solutions.

FIGURE 2-5

Impact of Macroeconomic Shock on Default Rates

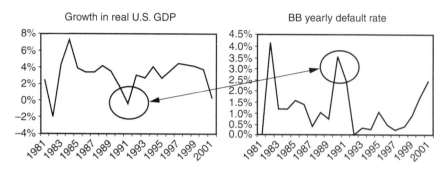

Source: CreditPro and Federal Reserve.

To be fair, Figure 2-5 overstates the real variability of default rates within rating categories for at least two reasons: First, volatility has to be expected at the bottom end of the rating scale (for speculative-grade issuers). If we had considered the AAA category, we would have observed a perfectly consistent zero default rate throughout the period. Furthermore, the small number of firms rated BB also contributes to the volatility and explains, for example, why there was no default at all in this category in 1992.

Quality of Transition Matrices over Time and Regions

In this section, we address the following questions: Are migration probabilities, based on past data, useful to predict future migrations? Are transition matrices stable through time?

Nickell, Perraudin, and Varotto (2000) test the stability of transition matrices, based on several drivers: time, the type of borrower, and the position in the economic cycle. Their study is based on a sample of 6534 issuers[7] over the period from December 1970 to December 1997.[8] The authors first calculate a transition matrix on the whole period unconditional on economic cycles and show that migration volatility is higher for low ratings. The calculated transition matrix is also different from those calculated in a previous study using the same data source but for a different time period (Carty and Fons, 1993).[9] This may come as a surprise, as it means that a single transition matrix, independent from the economic cycle, is not really time stationary even when the averaging is performed on a very long time period.

As a second step, Nickell, Perraudin, and Varotto (2000) carry out an analysis by type of borrower and by geographic area. Their conclusions indicate that transition matrices tend to be stable *within* broad homogeneous economic sectors and by geographic areas. However, differences are noticeable *across* sectors, especially for investment-grade issuers: It can be observed that components from transition matrices by sector tend to differ by more than 5 percent from the global multisectors transition matrix. Major discrepancies tend to occur for best ratings. For example, migration volatility is higher for banks than for corporates (they are more likely to change ratings), but conversely large movements are more frequent in industrial sectors than in the banking industry.

As for regional homogeneity, North American matrices per activity are close to the global one. This is natural given the large share of the region in the global sample. This is not the case for the Japanese sample, which may not be of sufficient size to draw statistically robust inference.

Transition matrices also appear to be dependent on the economic cycle as downgrades and default probabilities increase significantly during recessions.[10] Nickell, Perraudin, and Varotto (2000) classify the years between 1970 and 1997 into three categories (growth, stability, and recession) according to GDP growth for the G7 countries. One of their observations is that for investment-grade counterparts, migration volatility is much lower during growth periods than during recessions. Therefore, their conclusion is that transition matrices unconditional on the economic cycle cannot be considered as Markovian.[11]

In another study based on S&P data, Bangia, Diebold, Kronimus, Schagen, and Schuermann (2002) observe that the more the time horizon of an independent transition matrix increases, the less monotonic[12] the matrix becomes. This point illustrates nonstationarity. Regarding its Markovian property, the authors tend to be less affirmative than Nickell, Perraudin, and Varotto (2000); i.e., their tests show that the Markovian hypothesis is not strongly rejected. The authors, however, acknowledge that one can observe path dependency in transition probabilities. For example, a past history of downgrades has an impact on future migrations. Such path dependency is significant since future PDs can increase up to five times for recently downgraded companies.

The authors then focus on the impact of economic cycles on transition matrices. They select two types of periods (expansion and recession) according to NBER indicators. The major difference between the two matrices corresponds mainly to a higher frequency of downgrades during recession periods. Splitting transition matrices in two periods is helpful; i.e., out-of-diagonal terms are much more stable. Their conclusion is that choosing two transition matrices conditional on the economic cycle gives much better results in terms of Markovian stability than considering only one matrix unconditional on the economic cycle.

In order to investigate further the impact of cycles on transition matrices and credit VaR (value at risk), Bangia, et al. (2002) use a version of CreditMetrics[13] on a portfolio of 148 bonds. They show that the necessary economic capital increases substantially during recessions compared with growth periods (by 30 percent for a 99-percent confidence level of credit VaR, or 25 percent for a 99.9-percent confidence level). Note that the authors ignore the increase in correlation during recessions. We will see in Chapter 5 that this latter factor alone contributes substantially to the increase in portfolio losses during recessions, particularly at higher confidence levels.

Industry and Geography Homogeneity

External rating agencies as well as internal credit departments within banks aim at using the same rating grades to characterize default risk for all countries and for the various asset classes they cover, such as large corporates, financial institutions, municipalities, sovereigns, etc.

Two initial remarks often appear regarding homogeneity and external rating agencies:

- First, because rating agencies have originally developed their methodologies in the United States, there could be differences in performance between U.S. firms and non-U.S. firms. If such a bias existed, it could come from the fact that the rating history outside the United States is much shorter.
- Second, Morgan (1997) shows that the level of consensus among rating agencies is much lower for financial institutions than it is for corporates. The rationale for such differences is often linked with the opacity of financial institutions. As a result, different levels of transparency between sectors could lead to rating heterogeneity.

Nickell, Perraudin, and Varotto (2000), as well as Ammer and Packer (2000), review these two issues. The empirical study of the latter is based on Moody's database between 1983 and 1998. Their conclusion is twofold:

- Geographic homogeneity is not questionable.

♦ For a given rating category, banks tend to show higher default rates than corporates

External rating agencies have recently put a lot of emphasis on ratings homogeneity (Standard & Poor's, 1999). In the light of the Basel II reform (Chapter 10), it is also important that rating agencies provide broadly similar assessments of risk, at least on average. In their "standardized approach," the Basel proposals enable banks to rely on external agency ratings to calculate the risk weights used in calculating capital requirements. Wide discrepancies across agencies would induce banks to select the most lenient rating provider. In order to preclude "agency arbitrage," i.e., to choose the rating agency providing the most favorable rating, the regulators have to ensure that there is no obvious systematic underestimation of risk by authorized agencies.

There have been relatively few empirical studies on comparing agencies' output, probably due to the difficulty of gathering data from all providers. Beattie and Searle (1992) provide a comprehensive analysis of the assessment of eight rating agencies (Figure 2-6). Their results show that larger players (Moody's and S&P) exhibit very similar average assessments. Neither of them exhibits significantly more conservative behavior than the other. However, there are some large differences with more specialized or regional agencies. Unfortunately, Beattie and Searle's (1992) paper is now quite old, and we are not aware of any more recent studies on a similar scale.

Impact of Rating Changes on Corporate Security Prices

If ratings bring information about the credit quality of firms, a change in rating should lead to a reassessment of the firm's risk by market participants and therefore to changes in the prices of corporate securities such as bonds and equity issued by the firm. The impacts of upgrades and downgrades have attracted a lot of academic attention, which we now briefly summarize.

Effect of Rating Changes on Bond Prices

We have seen earlier that rating categories were associated with different default probabilities. The expected sign of the impact of a rating change on bond prices should be and is actually unambiguous. Given that ratings

FIGURE 2-6

Average Rating Difference Compared with S&P's*

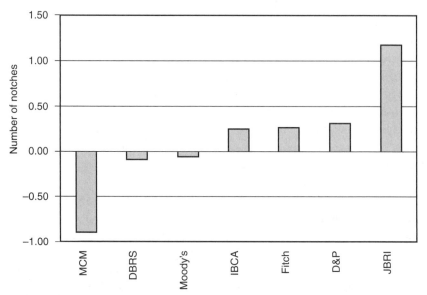

*Notches below zero = more conservative than S&P; notches above zero = more lenient.
Source: Beattie and Searle (1992).

act as a proxy for default probability or expected loss, a downgrade (upgrade) is likely to have a negative (positive) impact on bond prices.

This intuition is supported by most studies on the topic, such as that of Hand, Holthausen, and Leftwich (1992) among many others. Most articles rely on event study methodologies and report a statistically significant underperformance of recently downgraded bonds. Recently upgraded bonds tend to exhibit overperforming returns, but this result is generally less statistically significant. The findings are very sensitive to the frequency of observation (monthly bond return versus daily) and the possible "contamination" of rating changes by other events impacting on bond prices. For example, if a firm is downgraded at the beginning of a month and announces a substantial restructuring during the same month, the negative price impact of the rating may be compensated for by a positive change linked to the restructuring. Overall the price may rise during the observation month although the actual event of interest (downgrade) had the expected negative effect. This may explain the results of early studies, such as that of Weinstein (1977), that do not find a price reaction at the time of rating changes.

The well-documented link between default probability and rating (see, e.g., Figure 2-3) is in itself insufficient for rating changes to have some bearing on prices. It is also important for investors that the information content of ratings not be fully anticipated and previously incorporated in asset prices. Alternatively ratings may influence the supply of and demand for securities and therefore trigger price changes irrespective of informational issues.

A lot of debate has recently focused on whether rating analysts should incorporate more timely market information in their assessment. Ratings have indeed been shown in some cases to lag equity prices in capturing deterioration in credit quality. We will not enter this debate here but want to point out that the value of ratings resides to a large extent in the fact that agency analysts bring new information to the market. If ratings were to mimic market fluctuations, their usefulness would be severely jeopardized. The argument that ratings do not bring information and that the signal brought by ratings is fully anticipated by the market is contradicted by the fact that rating changes do affect corporate security prices.

Supply and demand effects also partly explain why rating changes translate into price shocks. Some market participants such as asset managers often have self-imposed restrictions on the credit quality of the assets they can invest in. In particular, many funds have a policy to invest only in investment grade bonds. A downgrade to speculative grade therefore leads to significant sales by asset managers and contributes to depressing the prices of bonds issued by the downgraded company. Banking regulation also leads to the segmentation of bond markets. Under the current Basel guidelines (whereby all corporate bonds bear a 100 percent risk weight irrespective of the credit quality of their issuer), banks are at a competitive disadvantage compared with funds and insurance companies on the investment-grade market. Banks indeed have to put capital aside to cover potential losses, while other investment houses are not subject to the same constraints. This explains why banks tend not to be the dominant players in the investment-grade market where spreads are too narrow to compensate them for the cost of capital. By making explicit the relationship between regulatory risk weights and ratings in the standardized approach, the purchases and sales of corporate bonds by banks (and their induced price effects) will arguably be more dependent on rating changes and should reinforce the effects of rating changes on bond prices.

Rating triggers, i.e., bond covenants based on the rating of a bond issue, are also instrumental in explaining the underperformance of downgraded bonds in some cases. The most common type of securities with rating triggers is step-up bonds whose coupons increase when the issuer is downgraded below a predefined threshold. While these features may at first seem attractive for bondholders, they are double-edged swords: When a company starts entering into difficulties and gets downgraded, it is further penalized by the rating triggers (higher interest payments). Therefore, not only does the downgraded firm find new funding to be more expensive (because the rating change leads to higher spreads), but its current source of funds becomes more costly as well. This has been shown to lead to vicious-circle effects, with recently downgraded firms more likely to be downgraded again. Rating triggers were particularly popular with telecom issuers, who found them a convenient way to raise reasonably cheap capital in good times.

More recently, credit derivatives have led to price volatility in the corporate bond market. One of the main novelties introduced by credit derivatives has been to allow market participants to sell credit short. The ability of traders to "short" corporate bonds leads to more ample price fluctuations than those that were previously observed. Some of this volatility is generated at times of rating changes as some credit products are based on the rating of an underlying firm or security. The rebalancing of hedging portfolios leads to large purchases and sales of corporate bonds around times of rating changes, which increases price volatility.

The Impact of Rating Changes on Stock Prices

We have seen that the link between the probability of default and rating brings an intuitive connection between rating changes and bond returns. The impact of these events on stock prices is less obvious. If rating changes leave the value of the firm unchanged, equity prices should, of course, jump in the opposite direction to bond prices.

A downgrade due to an increase in firm risk (volatility of assets) can indeed be beneficial to equity holders who own a call on the value of the firm. Kliger and Sarig (2000) find such an overall neutral effect in their experiment. They analyze the impact of Moody's shift from a coarse rating grid to a finer one, which occurred in 1982. This was not accompanied by any fundamental change in issuers' risks but brought a more precise assessment of the default probability. The authors report that the incremental rating information did not affect firm value although individual claims (debt and equity) were affected.

Goh and Ederington (1993) make a distinction between downgrades associated with increases in leverage and those linked to deteriorating financial prospects. While the latter type of downgrades is bad news for bondholders and shareholders alike, the former case corresponds to a wealth transfer from bondholders to shareholders and should be associated with an increase in the price of equity. They find on a sample of Moody's ratings, that downgrades related to falling expectations of the firm's future earnings or sales are associated with stock price falls, whereas downgrades linked to increased leverage do not have any impact. They interpret the latter result as a sign that changes in leverage are generally anticipated by the market.

On the whole there is no reason to believe that rating revisions should not affect the value of the firm. Many articles, (Dichev and Piotroski, 2001; Holthausen and Leftwich, 1986; and Pinches and Singleton, 1978) indeed report falls in the value of equity. Bankruptcy costs, for example, can lead to a drop in the value of the firm as the probability of default increases and some of the value is transferred to third parties (lawyers, etc.). A segmentation of the bond market, particularly between investment-grade and non-investment-grade categories, can also lead to a downgrade being associated with a drop in the overall asset value.

A persistent finding in almost all papers is that downgrades affect stock prices significantly but upgrades do not. Authors disagree on the explanation for this fact. One possibility could be that firms' managers tend to divulge good news and retain bad news so that an upgrade is more likely to be expected than a downgrade. Another alternative would be asymmetric utility functions with downside risk priced more dearly than upside potential.

Given the overwhelming share of the rated universe accounted for by the United States, very few authors have carried out similar studies outside the United States. Two noticeable exceptions are Barron, Clare, and Thomas (1997) and Matolcsy and Lianto (1995), who report results for U.K. and Australian stock returns, respectively, that are broadly similar to the U.S. experience. Both studies are limited to a very small sample (less than 100 observations), and so tests on subsamples such as downgrades should therefore be interpreted with caution.

APPROACHING CREDIT RISK THROUGH INTERNAL RATINGS OR SCORE-BASED RATINGS

Over the past few years, banks have attempted to mirror the rating behavior of external rating agencies. Given that the core business of a bank is not to provide assessments of the creditworthiness of companies but to lend money, it is a natural incentive for a bank's credit analysts to set up processes similar to those that have been thoroughly tested and validated over time by agencies.

Not long ago, the initial question asked by many bank credit committees was whether the creditworthiness of a company was good or bad, leading directly to a yes or no lending decision. To some extent this policy persists in the personal loan business where customers either satisfy a list of criteria and are granted the loan or fail to satisfy one criterion and their application is rejected. The problem with this black-and-white assessment is that there are no distinctions among "good" customers, and so all of them are assigned the same average interest rate based on an average probability of default and recovery rate.

This approach has evolved with time notably because of two major drivers: First, external rating agencies' scales are being used extensively as a common language in financial markets and banks. Second, regulators, in the context of the Basel II new rules, have strongly recommended the use of a relatively refined rating scale to assess credit quality. Such scales make sense from a statistical point of view. Indeed, empirical tests performed on a historical basis show that in a vast majority of cases a default is the consequence of several rating downgrades. Sudden defaults without preliminary downgrades are much rarer (11 percent on average according to a study by Moody's in 1997[14]).

Any internal rating approach, however, raises a lot of questions: the objectivity of qualitative judgments, the validity of the rating allocation process, the quality of forecast information embedded in ratings, the time horizon, the consistency with external ratings, etc.[15] We have listed in Appendix 2C what we have identified as the major biases regarding the elaboration of an internal rating approach.

We will now raise the very important issue of the time horizon associated with internal ratings before turning to the process of building an internal rating system.

Internal Ratings, Scores, and Time Horizons

Internal ratings generally refer to a time-consuming qualitative assessment process devised to identify the credit quality of a firm. They generally use either letter-labeled classes similar to those of rating agencies (e.g., BBB or Baa) or numbers (1, 2, . . .).

Scores tend to use quantitative methodologies based on financial and sometimes nonfinancial information. One of the best-known initial approaches was the Z-score proposed by Altman (1968). It assumes that past accounting variables provide predictive information on the default probability of any firm. Default probability information corresponds to a percentage extracted from the [0 percent, 100 percent] continuous scale.

The link between continuous scales and discrete ones is often built through an internal "mapping" process. Most of the time the continuous scale is split either in buckets reflecting scores or directly in internal rating categories. We should stress that such a mapping between probabilities of default and internal ratings only makes sense if the time horizons corresponding to the two approaches are comparable.

Two Ways to Rate or Score a Company

One way to rate a company is to use an "at-the-point-in-time" approach. This kind of approach assesses the credit quality of a firm over the coming months (generally 1 year). This approach is widely used by banks that use quantitative scoring systems, for example, based on discriminant analysis or logit models (linear, quadratic, etc.). All tools based on arbitrage between equity and debt markets, through to structural models, like KMV Credit Monitor EDFs (expected default frequencies), also fall into the at-the-point-in-time category of default estimates. All these models will be described in Chapter 3.

A second way to rate a company is to use a through-the-cycle approach. As explained earlier, a through-the-cycle approach tries to capture the creditworthiness of a firm over a longer time horizon, including the impact of normal cycles of the economy. A through-the-cycle assessment therefore embeds scenarios about the economy as well as business and financial factors. Because the economic cycle is factored in, such ratings are supposed to be much more stable than at-the-point-in-time estimates.

The Incompatibility of the Two Approaches

In many banks it is common to follow a qualitative process for large corporates, based on a comparison with ratings from rating agencies, and at the same time use a scoring approach for the middle market or SMEs, with a very basic mapping process to revert to the bank's master rating scale. Such a mix may not be optimal, as the same internal rating scale is used to convey at the same time through-the-cycle and point-in-time information. This homogeneity issue corresponds to a real stake for banks' internal rating systems and may lead banks to significant biases regarding their economic capital allocation process. Indeed asset classes rated with through-the-cycle tools would be penalized during growth periods compared with asset classes rated with at-the-point-in-time tools, and vice versa in recessions.

At-the-point-in-time score volatility is much higher than through-the-cycle score volatility.[16] But this volatility is not comparable across the rating scale: Median at-the-point-in-time scores tend to display significant volatility, whereas high and low at-the-point-in-time scores often exhibit a more moderate level of volatility more akin to through-the-cycle ratings.

For these reasons the two approaches are not comparable and should not be mixed. Banks try to build a consistent view of the credit-worthiness of their counterparts for all their asset classes. As a result, they should exercise great care if they use, for example, at-the-point-in-time scores for their SMEs or private corporates and through-the-cycle ratings for their public corporates at the same time.

A practical way to observe the differences is to calculate 1-year transition matrices for a typical scoring system and compare them to those of an external rating agency. A transition matrix is devised to display average 1-year migrations for all scores or ratings, i.e., probabilities to move from one rating category to another. Considering both Standard & Poor's rating universe and a common scored universe (see Figure 2-7[17]), we observe that an AA trajectory is very different from a "2" trajectory although their mean 1-year PD may be similar: The probability of an AA firm to remain an AA a year after is between 80 and 90 percent, whereas the probability of a 2 to remain a 2 one year after is only between 30 and 40 percent. Therefore these two creditworthiness indicators are not comparable.

Two results are found persistently when analyzing transition matrices derived from scores: The weight on the diagonal (the probability of remaining in the same rating) is (1) fairly low and (2) nonmonotonic as a function of score level. In contrast, rating transition matrices are heavily concentrated on the diagonal and exhibit lower volatility as one reaches higher grades.

Attempts to Extract Through-the-Cycle Information from At-the-Point-in-Time Scores

From a risk-mitigation standpoint, it is not only default risk for today or tomorrow that has to be forecast. For buy-and-hold strategies (typical of banks' lending books) what matters is default risk at any time until the horizon of the underlying credit instruments. As a result an appropriate credit assessment should in theory not just be limited to a probability of default at a given horizon but also reflect its variability through time and its sensitivity to changes in the major factors affecting a given company. One needs to consider not only a short-term PD, but also the estimated *trajectory* of this PD over a longer horizon.

Most quantitative analysts trying to build a scoring system tend to face a difficult dilemma: Either target the highest level of predictive

FIGURE 2-7

Scoring versus Rating Transition Matrix

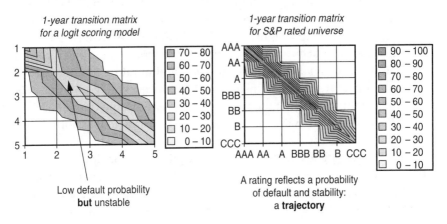

1-year transition matrix for a logit scoring model

	70 – 80
	60 – 70
	50 – 60
	40 – 50
	30 – 40
	20 – 30
	10 – 20
	0 – 10

Low default probability
but unstable

1-year transition matrix for S&P rated universe

	90 – 100
	80 – 90
	70 – 80
	60 – 70
	50 – 60
	40 – 50
	30 – 40
	20 – 30
	10 – 20
	0 – 10

A rating reflects a probability
of default and stability:
a trajectory

power at a given horizon and fail to obtain a stable through-the-cycle system, or reduce the level of predictive power in order to increase stability. The obtained trade-off is in general not fully satisfactory.

Chassang and de Servigny (2002) propose a way to extract through-the-cycle predictive default information from financial input. They show that with a sufficiently large history of past short-term PDs, it is possible to obtain through-the-cycle equivalent ratings, thanks to a mapping exercise based on the estimation of appropriate rating buckets defined on a mean, variance, skewness (of PDs) space. The main underlying idea is that a through-the-cycle rating is the combination of at-the-point-in-time PD information and a range of different trajectories along time, which are representative of a given rating category. This approach is described in Appendix 2B.

Löffler (2002) tries another interesting way to capture the through-the-cycle information, using a Kalman filter. His approach relies on the underlying assumption that a Merton-type distance to default is the single driver for creditworthiness.

How to Build an Internal Rating System?

Using Rating Templates to Mirror the Behavior of External Agencies Ratings

As mentioned above, one way for banks to obtain an internal rating system is to try and mirror the behavior of rating agencies' analysts. This is particularly necessary for asset classes where default observations are very scarce,[18] for example for financial institutions, insurance, or project finance. Such methodology is very straightforward, as it consists of identifying the most meaningful ratios and risk factors (financial or nonfinancial ones) and assigning weights to each of them in order to derive a rating estimate close to what an analyst from a rating agency would calculate. Of course, the agency analyst does not use a model to rate a company, but a model can integrate the most meaningful factors considered by this analyst. The weights on each of the factors can either be defined qualitatively, based on discussions with the analysts, or be extracted quantitatively through various statistical methodologies.

Rating templates allow banks to calibrate their internal rating process. They also enable them to use, in a consistent manner, rating agencies' transition matrices for portfolio management matters. Figure 2-8 is an illustrative example of a summarized template. The analyst would enter his opinion on all relevant variables in the form of a score. All scores are then weighted to obtain a global score that is mapped to a rating category. Obviously, the choice of weight is crucial, and weights need to be calibrated on a fairly large sample and back-tested regularly. The usual way to check the appropriateness of weights is to compare external ratings with internal ones on a sample of firms. If a systematic difference (overestimation or underestimation of risk) is observed, the weights should be amended.

FIGURE 2-8

Example of an Internal Rating Template

	Weighting	Scoring	
Corporate Credit Score	A	C	(B × C)
	Weight (%)	Score (0 – 100)	Weighted Score
1. Industry characteristics			
2. Market position			
3. Management			
Total score* for business profile			
4. Financial policy			
5. Profitability			
6. Cash flow			
7. Capital structure			
8. Financial flexibility			
Total score* for financial profile			
Total score			

Calibrating and Back-Testing a Rating System Requires a Long Time Horizon

When banks build their internal rating system, their objective is twofold. First they want to assess the creditworthiness of companies during the loan application process. Second they want to use rating information to feed their portfolio management tools designed to produce regulatory capital or economic capital measures. As a result, banks have to devise links between their internal rating scale and tables displaying cumulative probabilities of default at horizons ranging from 1 year to the longest maturity of the debt instruments they hold.

When banks define their internal scale, they have no track record of default rates per rating category, per industry, or per region. They may also have a rated universe that is by construction too small to provide strong statistics about empirical default rates.[19]

The second step for banks, just as for rating agencies, is to test the stability of their internal transition matrices. If this assumption is found to be acceptable, then and only then should banks be entitled to devise a link between internal ratings and probabilities of default. Some banks might find that they need to build different transition matrices that are specific to their different asset classes or to the economic cycle. The question then is how many years should be required to perform such a complete analysis?

Based on Moody's database, Carey and Hrycay (2001) estimate that a historical sample between 11 and 18 years should be necessary[20] in order to test the validity of internal ratings. Based on Standard & Poor's universe, we think that a time period of 10 years should be considered as a minimum for investment-grade securities, while 5 years should be enough to back-test non-investment-grade issues. Figure 2-9 is calculated from a sample of defaulted firms and reports the average time it took for firms in a given rating grade to drift down to default.[21]

In many banks we are still far from ex post statistical testing, because the rating history is in general too short.[22] In the future many banks will probably discover that their internal rating system is weaker than they expected.

Banks using at-the-point-in-time tools as the backbone of their internal rating system have two options, each associated with a specific risk. One option is to stick to probabilities of default, without using any internal rating scale. Such an approach will convey an accurate measure of the creditworthiness of the bank's counterparts. The associated risk is procyclicality since changes in the credit quality of the portfolio can evolve very quickly. If, on the contrary, banks using at-the-point-in-time

FIGURE 2-9

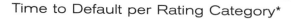

Time to Default per Rating Category*

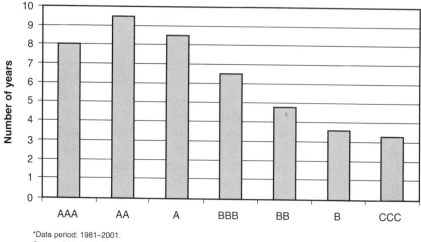

*Data period: 1981–2001.
Source: S&P Credit Pro.

methodologies revert to an internal rating scale, the main risk is providing highly unstable transition matrices and no guidance for the long term.

Impact of Internal Models at the Macro Level

So far we have only considered the impact of PD measures on banks but have ignored their systemic or macroeconomic effects.

Procyclicality is a topic that is becoming a central issue with Basel II regulation. It is the fact that linking capital requirements to PDs may induce all banks to overlend in good times and underlend in bad times, thereby reinforcing credit and economic cycles. Many academics and practitioners have recently considered this issue.[23] One of the major dangers with the procyclical effects of the new techniques that banks use to evaluate their economic or regulatory capital requirement lies in the risk of a sudden liquidity crisis affecting the whole economy.

Procyclicality could affect even more those banks that have chosen to set their internal credit limits in terms of expected loss[24] rather than exposure. Expected loss will be very volatile due to the high volatility of PDs calculated using at-the-point-in-time methods. Consequently, during a recession period, short-term PDs will increase sharply and the bank will have to reduce significantly its loan exposures in order to maintain stable expected losses. If such types of PD measures are used by a majority of banks, then firms will face liquidity shortages because of unexpected credit rationing (all their lending banks may simultaneously refuse to grant them further credit). As a consequence, real economic cycles may be amplified.

Another type of cyclical effect comes from the use of at-the-point-in-time measures of risk in economic capital calculations and in the lending process. These models tend to underevaluate risk during growth periods (and overestimate it in recessions). Because defaults take some time to materialize, banks lack incentives to adjust their credit policy before entering into recession: The last years have shown few defaults in their portfolio, and their model (calibrated on previous years' data) still reports low probabilities of default for most firms. After 1 or 2 years (when the economy is in a trough), the number of cases of financial distress increases significantly, and lending conditions are tightened by banks. As a result, the credit cycle tends to lag the economic cycle. Credit rationing may result as a consequence of the contraction of the lending activity by banks. This will in turn exacerbate economic downturn. Credit rationing will impact first and foremost asset classes that are highly dependent on banks because they are too small or have not yet established sufficient reputation to tap financial markets. In particular, the SME sector is very sensitive to banks' lending policies.

Finally, at-the-point-in-time measures of risk present another risk for the aggregate economy. Short-term PD measures tend to bias loan procedures in favor of short-term projects. The selection of short-term projects can lead to suboptimal investment decisions.[25]

Granularity of Rating Scales

There has recently been intense discussion comparing the output of external rating agencies with the output of structural models, such as the KMV Credit Monitor. The core topics discussed focused on the reactivity of structural models versus the stability of ratings. The acquisition of KMV by Moody's has in fact given practical evidence of the complementarity of the two approaches. But the question of the appropriate rating scale[26] to reflect such reactivity is still an open one within banks.

In this respect, a bank and an external rating agency may not share the same objectives. For the latter, communication to investors is dominant. A downgrade or an upgrade is an important event, with various consequences. Having a discrete scale with a limited level of granularity reinforces the informational impact of any migration, sending a strong signal reflecting substantial changes in firms.[27] Banks do not use their internal ratings for external communication and, provided they have enough data and are sufficiently confident in their own systems, they could choose a more granular approach.

Consequences

This approach of evaluating default risk through ratings migration is quite attractive because of its simplicity. Its robustness is undoubtedly very good for investment grade (IG) counterparts. Regarding non-investment-grade (NIG) counterparts, banks and rating agencies are usually very cautious because migration volatility is strongly related to the economic cycle.

Recent history has shown on many occasions how high-yield markets can be volatile and unpredictable. The split between IG and NIG universes may seem unfair to companies crossing the fence, given its impact in terms of bond spreads. But from a global standpoint, it really seems to correspond to different firms' behavior, different credibility, and different risk profiles. It is also meaningful in terms of segmentation of the demand for such products: Investors in investment-grade and non-investment-grade bonds exhibit very different risk-aversion profiles.

CONCLUSION

Rating agencies have developed very precise methodologies to assess the creditworthiness of companies. The stability over time of their approach and of their criteria is key to their success. The main challenge for rating agencies is to convey through-the-cycle information (i.e., about the trajectory of an issuer's creditworthiness) while maintaining a sufficient level of reactivity in order to incorporate early warning predictive power.

The task related to internal ratings assigned to banks in the Basel II accord is very challenging. Banks have to rate a very large universe corresponding to most of the asset classes they are dealing with. For most banks it is a new task that they have to perform. They suffer from a lack of data history, and it will take years before they have sufficient results to back-test their methodologies. Many are at the stage of choosing their approaches for the various asset classes: A qualitative approach (internal rating) is generally adopted for larger positions, and a scoring model deals with smaller exposures. The next step will be to integrate the two approaches consistently in a portfolio model.

A P P E N D I X   2 A

Transition Matrices

Transition matrices are matrices reporting the probabilities of migrating from a given rating to another rating over a chosen time period. Let us consider a rating system with n non-default states ordered such that 1 is the best credit quality, 2 is the second best, and n is the worst. $n + 1$ is the default state.

S&P's 1-year transition matrix is shown in Table 2A-1. It has $n = 7$ and is such that the first rating category is AAA while the nth is CCC. D denotes default. It can be read as follows: The first row tabulates first the probability of remaining in AAA, then of migrating from the AAA rating to the AA, etc. The second row reports the migration probabilities from the AA class to all ratings, and so on.

Transition matrices can be obtained in discrete time, i.e., for a finite number of terminal dates t or in continuous time, where transition probabilities can be calculated for any horizon h.

T A B L E   2A-1

1-Year Transition Matrix (Percents)—United States, All Industries (1981–2001)

Initial Rating	End Rating							
	AAA	AA	A	BBB	BB	B	CCC	D
AAA	93.57	5.84	0.47	0.08	0.04	0	0	0
AA	0.6	91.79	6.77	0.63	0.07	0.09	0.03	0.01
A	0.07	2.14	91.8	5.21	0.48	0.18	0.05	0.06
BBB	0.04	0.26	4.78	89.26	4.49	0.72	0.17	0.29
BB	0.03	0.08	0.47	6.67	82.57	8.01	0.89	1.28
B	0	0.1	0.28	0.35	5.33	83.14	4.18	6.61
CCC	0.14	0	0.29	0.86	1.86	9.89	58.17	28.8

Source: S&P CreditPro.

Discrete-Time Transition Matrices

The traditional transition matrices provided by rating agencies are in discrete time, typically with a 1-year horizon ($h = 1$). Information at only two dates for each year of data is necessary to calculate such a transition matrix. We start by gathering data about the rated universe at the beginning of the period (we assume that there are n rating classes). Let us use N_t^i to denote the number of firms rated i at the beginning of period t and use $T_t^{i,j}$ to denote the number of firms rated i at the beginning of period t and j at the end of the period.

The transition probabilities for period t can thus be estimated as

$$p_h^{i,j}(t) = \frac{T_t^{i,j}}{N_t^i} \qquad \text{for } i = 1, \ldots, n \text{ and } j = 1, \ldots, n$$

Note that this method of calculating transition matrices leaves out some potentially relevant information such as when transitions take place during the period. It also ignores rating actions that have been reversed during the same period. Assume, for example, that a BBB firm is downgraded at the beginning of a given year and upgraded back to BBB at the end of the same year. The transition matrix as calculated above would record "no move," as both the initial and terminal ratings are the same. We will return to these issues in a later section.

If we have a sample with several periods, say k (rating agencies typically have over 20 years of data), then we can calculate unconditional probabilities as

$$p_h^{i,j} = \sum_{t=1}^{k} w_t^i \frac{T_t^{i,j}}{N_t^i} \qquad \text{for } i = 1, \ldots, n \text{ and } j = 1, \ldots, n \text{ and } \sum_{t=1}^{k} w_t^i = 1$$

Unconditional probabilities are just weighted averages of individual period probabilities, with weight w_t^i. The weights are generally chosen such that $w_t^i = 1/k$ (each period is equally weighted), or

$$w_t^i = \frac{N_t^i}{\sum_{s=1}^{k} N_s^i}$$

(each period is weighted by its relative size in terms of observations). The latter approach is retained by S&P.

More generally, the transition matrix for a given horizon h therefore can be written as

$$
\Pi(h) = \begin{bmatrix} p_h^{1,1} & p_h^{1,2} & \cdots & p_h^{1,n+1} \\ \cdots & \cdots & & \cdots \\ p_h^{n,1} & p_h^{n,2} & \cdots & p_h^{n,n+1} \\ 0 & 0 & \cdots & 1 \end{bmatrix}
$$

The last row is added such that the matrix is square. Its interpretation is that default is an absorbing state; i.e., a firm in default has 100 percent probability of remaining in default. In actuality, some bonds (sometimes called phoenix bonds) emerge from default, and so there should be some small probability outside the default state. But these events are rare, and the assumption of absorbing default is convenient for calculation purposes.

Adjusting for Withdrawn Ratings

Some firms that had a rating at the beginning of a given period may no longer have one at the end. This may be due to the fact that the issuer has not paid the agency's fee or that it has asked the agency to withdraw its rating. These events are not rare and account for about 4.5 percent of transitions in the investment-grade class and 10 percent in the speculative-grade category over a given year.

When calculating migration probabilities, one needs to adjust them to take into consideration the possibility of a withdrawn rating. Otherwise the sum of transition probabilities to the n ratings would be less than 1. The unadjusted transition matrix using the same data as in Table 2A-1 is given in Table 2A-2.

The adjustment is performed by ignoring the firms that have their rating withdrawn during a given period. The underlying assumption is that the withdrawal of a rating is a neutral event; i.e., it is not associated with any information regarding the credit quality of the issuer. One could, however, argue that firms that expect a downgrade below what they perceive is an acceptable level ask for their ratings to be withdrawn, while firms that are satisfied with their grade generally want to maintain it.

It is difficult to get information about the motivation behind a rating's withdrawal, and therefore the above adjustment is generally considered acceptable.

TABLE 2A-2

1-Year Transition Matrix (Percents)—United States, All Industries (1981–2001), Unadjusted

Initial Rating	End Rating							
	AAA	AA	A	BBB	BB	B	CCC	D
AAA	89.41	5.58	0.44	0.08	0.04	0	0	0
AA	0.58	88.28	6.51	0.6	0.07	0.09	0.03	0.01
A	0.07	2.05	87.85	4.99	0.46	0.17	0.05	0.06
BBB	0.04	0.24	4.52	84.4	4.24	0.68	0.16	0.27
BB	0.03	0.07	0.43	6.1	75.56	7.33	0.82	1.17
B	0	0.09	0.25	0.32	4.78	74.59	3.75	5.93
CCC	0.13	0	0.25	0.75	1.63	8.67	51.01	25.25

Source: S&P CreditPro.

CONTINUOUS TIME

The transition matrices considered above are calculated in discrete time. In order to compute them, we consider cohorts starting at the beginning of a calendar year and track the migrations at the end of each year. The outcome is a transition matrix for a fixed horizon, generally 1 year, which is the required input in credit portfolio models (see Chapter 6). For some applications, however, a fixed number of years may not be the desired horizon. For example, for pricing a credit derivative with 2 months to maturity or a 2.5-year bond, we need a greater variety of horizons. This is achieved by calculating continuous-time transition matrices.

A continuous-time transition matrix with horizon h can be obtained from its generator Λ through the equation

$$Q(h) = \exp(h\Lambda) = \sum_{k=0}^{\infty} (h\Lambda)^k/k! \qquad (2A-1)$$

The generator is a matrix with the same dimension as the transition matrix:

$$\Lambda = \begin{bmatrix} \lambda_1 & \lambda_{1,2} & \cdots & \lambda_{1,n+1} \\ \cdots & \cdots & & \cdots \\ \lambda_{n,1} & \lambda_{n,2} & \cdots & \lambda_{n,n+1} \\ 0 & 0 & \cdots & 0 \end{bmatrix} \qquad (2A\text{-}2)$$

where

$$\lambda_{i,j} \geq 0 \qquad \text{for all } i \text{ and } j$$

and

$$\lambda_i = -\sum_{i=1, i \neq j}^{n+1} \lambda_{i,j} \qquad \text{for } i = 1 \ldots n + 1$$

Calculating the Generator from a Discrete-Time Matrix

Λ can be estimated by inverting Equation (2A-1)[28] and using, for example, a 1-year transition matrix $Q(1)$ as calculated in the previous section. Once Λ is known, a transition matrix for any horizon can be computed using Equation (2A-1).

Duration-Based Estimators

Cohort methods presented in the previous section ("Discrete-Time Transition Matrices") ignore some potentially valuable information:

- When transitions take place during the calendar year
- How many changes (if any) have led to a given rating at the end of the year (2 one-notch upgrades from BBB to A and then to AA, for example, yield the same result as 1 two-notch upgrade from BBB directly to AA)

They are also affected by the choice of observation times: the beginning and end of each calendar year in the sample. Consider, for example, a firm that is rated AAA in January of year 1. It is downgraded to BBB in October of the same year and finally defaults in March of year 2. The cohort matrix would record one transition in year 1 (AAA to BBB) and one in year 2 (BBB to D). It would not however, reflect the fact that an AAA firm defaulted within a 12-month period (between October of year 1 to March of year 2).

Alternative estimation methods that do not suffer from these limitations have been proposed by Kavvathas (2000) and Lando and Skødeberg (2002) among others. These are based on the times (durations) between rating changes, i.e., the time spent by issuers in a given rating class. The simplest maximum-likelihood estimator for the constituents of the generator is

$$\hat{\lambda}_{i,j} = \frac{T^{i,j}(h)}{\int_0^h N^i(s)\, ds} \qquad (2A\text{-}3)$$

where $T^{i,j}(h)$ is the number of transitions from rating i to rating j during the period h and $N^i(s)$ is the number of firms in rating i at time s. Intuitively, the estimator counts the number of transitions from i directly to j (numerator) and also considers the total time spent by firms in a given rating i (denominator). Table 2A-3 is the 1-year matrix computed by applying Equation (2A-3) to the same data used to generate Table 2A-1. One can observe that continuous-time matrices tend to yield higher default probabilities for the best ratings.

TABLE 2A-3

1-Year Continuous-Time Transition Matrix (Percents)—
United States, All Industries (1981–2001)

	End Rating							
	AAA	**AA**	**A**	**BBB**	**BB**	**B**	**CCC**	**D**
AAA	93.2173	6.0306	0.6519	0.0492	0.0446	0.0057	0.0007	0.0002
AA	0.5370	91.9710	6.6712	0.6166	0.1066	0.0725	0.0193	0.0059
A	0.0957	2.0738	91.8381	5.1772	0.5418	0.2320	0.0196	0.0218
BBB	0.0430	0.3073	5.1703	88.3310	4.8415	1.0056	0.0975	0.2037
BB	0.0221	0.1246	0.8173	6.2201	82.8938	8.1124	0.7898	1.0198
B	0.0047	0.0879	0.3539	0.6095	5.0942	83.7310	4.6957	5.4231
CCC	0.0703	0.0089	0.3510	0.5017	1.2398	8.1386	55.3077	34.3821

Source: S&P CreditPro data.

Lando and Skødeberg (2002) also propose an estimator for a time-inhomogeneous transition matrix (i.e., the transition matrix changes with time, for example with economic fluctuations). They show that the assumption of time homogeneity is rejected statistically. Confidence intervals for continuous-time estimators are provided in Christensen and Lando (2002).

Jafry and Schuermann (2003) compare the three approaches on S&P transition data. They develop a statistical framework to test the differences between matrices calculated using the cohort approach as well as the time-homogeneous and -inhomogeneous continuous-time methods. Their main finding is that ignoring the continuous nature of transitions can have a substantial impact on credit portfolio risk measures and the price of credit derivatives. Incorporating inhomogeneity does not appear to bring any substantial benefit in their examples.

FROM HISTORICAL TO RISK NEUTRAL

All our discussion so far has focused on historical transition matrices, that is, probabilities estimated directly on transition data. For pricing purposes, one requires "risk-neutral" probabilities (see Appendix 8B in Chapter 8). A risk-neutral transition matrix can be extracted from the historical matrix and a set of corporate bond prices.

We will use $Q(h)$ to denote the risk-neutral transition matrix with horizon h:

$$
Q(h) = \begin{bmatrix}
q_h^{1,1} & q_h^{1,2} & \cdots & q_h^{1,K+1} \\
\cdots & \cdots & & \cdots \\
q_h^{K,1} & q_h^{K,2} & \cdots & q_h^{K,K+1} \\
0 & 0 & \cdots & 1
\end{bmatrix}
\tag{2A-4}
$$

All components of the matrix (q probabilities) take the same interpretation as p above but are under the risk-neutral measure.

In the original Jarrow-Lando-Turnbull (JLT) paper (Jarrow, Lando, and Turnbull, 1997), the authors impose the following specification for the risk premium adjustment allowing us to compute risk-neutral probabilities from historical ones:

$$
q^{i,j}(t,t+1) = \begin{cases}
\pi_i(t)p^{i,j} & \text{for } i \neq j & (2\text{A-}5a) \\
1 - \pi_i(t)(1 - p^{i,j}) & \text{for } i = j & (2\text{A-}5b)
\end{cases}
$$

Note that the risk premium adjustments π_i are deterministic and do not depend on the terminal rating but only on the initial one. This assumption enables JLT to obtain a (inhomogeneous) Markov chain for the transition process under the risk-neutral measure.

Risk-neutral default probabilities are obtained as follows: Assuming that the recovery in default is a fraction δ of a Treasury bond $B(t,T)$ with the same maturity T, the price of a risky zero-coupon bond at time t with rating i is

$$P^i(t,T) = B(t,T) \times [1 - q^{i,n+1}(1 - \delta)] \tag{2A-6}$$

Thus, we have

$$q^{i,n+1} = \frac{B(t,T) - P^i(t,T)}{B(t,T)(1 - \delta)} \tag{2A-7}$$

and thus the 1-year risk premium is

$$\pi_i(t) = \frac{B(t,t + 1) - P^i(t,t + 1)}{B(t,t + 1)(1 - \delta)q^{i,n+1}} \tag{2A-8}$$

The JLT specification is easy to implement but often leads to numerical problems because of the very low probability of default by investment-grade bonds at short horizons. In order to preclude arbitrage, the risk-neutral probabilities must indeed be nonnegative. This constrains the risk premium adjustments to be in the interval

$$0 < \pi_i(t) \le \frac{1}{1 - p^{i,i}} \qquad \text{for all } i \tag{2A-9}$$

In practice, when calibrating these risk premiums on credit spread data, the upper bound is often violated.

Kijima and Komoribayashi (1998) propose another risk premium adjustment that guarantees the positivity of risk-neutral probabilities in practical implementations. They replace Equations (2A-5a) and (2A-5b) with

$$\pi_{i,j}(t) = l_i(t) \qquad \text{for } j \ne n + 1$$

$$q^{i,j}(t,t + 1) = \begin{cases} l_i(t)p^{i,j} & \text{for } j \ne n + 1 \tag{2A-10a} \\ 1 - l_i(t)(1 - p^{i,n+1}) & \text{for } j = n + 1 \tag{2A-10b} \end{cases}$$

where $l_i(t)$ are deterministic functions of time. Although this adjustment looks minor, it is a major practical improvement, as it enables us to avoid "negative prices" for credit derivatives, particularly in investment-grade ratings.

EXTENSIONS

In this section we briefly mention other contributions in the field of the estimation of transition matrices. This list is mainly for completeness, and the interested reader can refer to the cited articles for more details.

Most models for pricing credit derivatives or for credit risk management assume that the transition process is Markovian.[29] This greatly simplifies calculations, but this assumption is generally invalidated in practice. In particular, the "rating momentum" is a well-documented empirical fact: A firm that has recently been downgraded is more likely to be downgraded again than other firms in the same rating category.

Bahar and Nagpal (2000) have recognized this fact and incorporated the rating momentum in a discrete-time model of transition.[30] Their model is still Markovian, but they extend the state space by a factor of 3. They argue that the transition from, say, a BBB to BB cannot be considered Markovian, but if we break down BBB into BBB_u, BBB_s, and BBB_d,[31] then the Markov assumption is valid empirically. A similar idea is pursued by El Karoui, Faracci-Steffan, and Sismail (2001) in the continuous-time setup.

Finally, Frydman and Kadam (2002) propose an extension to the continuous-time inhomogeneous model mentioned above to incorporate population heterogeneity in terms of the age of bonds (time since issuance). They show that young bonds indeed exhibit a much lower propensity to change ratings and therefore to default.

APPENDIX 2B

From a Scoring Model to a Rating System

Chassang and de Servigny (2002) propose a methodology to extract rating information from scoring methodologies. The input of their model is a time series of probabilities of default per issuer. They suggest three options to obtain such a history of PDs:

Option 1. This option consists of four steps:

Step 1. Select relevant credit factors that convey high predictive power, like financial ratios (free cash flow over debt, return on assets, etc.).

Step 2. Estimate the time-series model for those variables using a multivariate ARCH framework that integrates both past and current values of the ratios as well as past and current values of a synthetic macroeconomic index.

Step 3. Calibrate a simple autoregressive model for the macroeconomic index.

Step 4. Simulate short-term probabilities of default over the next 5 years.

Option 2. Apply the methodology described in option 1 to probabilities of default directly rather than to the underlying credit factors.

Option 3. Rely on a sufficiently long history of probabilities of default from a scoring model (3 to 4 years are a minimum) and use these data directly.

Once the PD history is obtained, buckets are defined. They represent the PD trajectory corresponding to a rating category. The main drivers that are used to classify companies in the buckets are the first three moments (mean, variance, and skewness) of their probability of default (see Figure 2B-1).

Based on empirical analysis, the type of parametric surfaces considered by the authors satisfy the following functional form:

$$\mu + \alpha\sqrt{(1 + \beta S)} \times (\sigma^2 - \gamma)^2 = \delta\sqrt{\eta - S} + \lambda$$

where μ is the mean, σ is the standard deviation, and S is the skewness. All the other letters correspond to parameters that have to be estimated.

Two cases are possible:

Regarding options 1 and 2, the mean of future PDs defines an average creditworthiness over the next years. The variance defines the volatility around the mean. The higher the volatility, the lower the rating. The skewness parameter enables us to integrate the trend in the evolution of the PDs.

Regarding option 3, instead of looking at forward information, we look at backward information. The mean PD is calculated using decreasing weights for older data.

FIGURE 2B-1

Rating Buckets

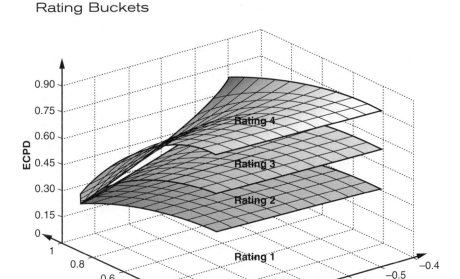

An additional step is to use a fuzzy bucket approach in order to reject changes from one rating category to another that are due to the model's uncertainty. As a result, a rating will be changed if the change is material with a given confidence level. Based on this methodology, a new creditworthiness classification is obtained that really includes trajectory information in addition to mean PD.

Let us consider an example. The three transition matrices shown in Tables 2B-1 to 2B-3 correspond to the same sample of firms. The matrix in Table 2B-1 corresponds to the usual S&P transition matrix calculated on this specific sample (AAA = 1, AA = 2, and so on). The matrix shown in Table 2B-2 is calculated directly on the scoring model, and the one in Table 2B-3 is calculated on the transformed model using the methodology described above. Obviously, the matrix in Table 2B-3 is much more akin to S&P's matrix. It incorporates at the same time information about PDs and about the dynamics of migrations.

TABLE 2B-1

S&P Ratings Transition Matrix (in Percent)

Initial Rating	Rating at Year-End						
	1	2	3	4	5	6	7
1	93.3	6.2	0.4	0.1	0.0	0.0	0.0
2	0.6	91.6	7.0	0.5	0.1	0.1	0.0
3	0.1	2.2	91.8	5.3	0.4	0.2	0.1
4	0.0	0.3	4.6	89.5	4.4	0.8	0.5
5	0.0	0.1	0.4	6.3	83.1	7.6	2.5
6	0.0	0.1	0.3	0.4	5.4	82.8	11.0
7	0.1	0.0	0.3	0.8	1.8	10.1	87.0

TABLE 2B-2

1-Year Transition Matrix for a Simple Score System (in Percent)

Initial Rating	Rating at Year-End						
	1	2	3	4	5	6	7
1	39.9	36.7	16.7	4.9	1.3	0.5	0.0
2	18.6	37.6	29.2	10.5	3.3	0.7	0.1
3	4.6	21.7	38.1	27.1	6.2	2.2	0.1
4	0.7	6.3	21.1	43.7	22.6	4.8	0.6
5	0.2	1.9	6.2	30.1	43.9	13.2	4.5
6	0.1	0.4	1.8	10.1	34.5	38.4	14.6
7	0.1	0.4	2.3	5.8	13.2	32.6	45.5

T A B L E 2B-3

1-Year Transition Matrix for Trajectory Ratings (in Percent)

Initial Rating	Rating at Year-End						
	1	2	3	4	5	6	7
1	81.0	14.0	5.0	0.0	0.0	0.0	0.0
2	13.0	63.0	16.0	6.0	1.0	0.0	0.0
3	4.0	11.0	69.0	12.0	5.0	1.0	0.0
4	1.0	3.0	16.0	63.0	13.0	4.0	0.0
5	0.0	1.0	8.0	11.0	63.0	15.0	3.0
6	0.0	0.0	2.0	5.0	13.0	71.0	8.0
7	0.0	0.0	2.0	2.0	4.0	19.0	72.0

In addition, the performance of each of the rating[32] categories over longer horizons is consistent with the S&P approach as shown in the graph in Figure 2B-2, where the 1-to-7 categories have been matched to S&P rating grades.

F I G U R E 2B-2

Cumulative Default Rates

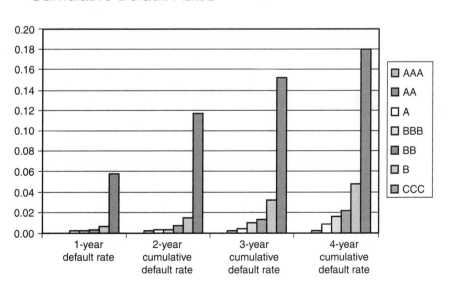

APPENDIX 2C

Important Biases

This appendix lists several important biases that may affect the internal rating system of a bank:

1. *Time horizon bias.* Mixing at-the-point-in-time and through-the-cycle ratings

2. *Homogeneity bias.* Not obtaining consistency of rating methodologies across industries, countries, or asset classes

3. *Principal agent bias.* Not managing the potential conflict of interest between risk and salespeople within a bank

4. *Information bias.* Insufficiency of information to assign a rating

5. *Criteria bias.* Having no clear-cut and stable criteria for allocating ratings

6. *Scale bias.* Not keeping a stable rating scale through time

7. *Bias arising from lack of back testing.* Bank analysts trusting blindly the theoretical mapping between their rating classes and effective default rates without validating it regularly on ex post default data

8. *Distribution bias.* Bias in the outcome of the PD model resulting from the choice of a specific distribution (often the normal distribution) to model explanatory factors

CHAPTER 3

Default Risk: Quantitative Methodologies

In the previous chapter we analyzed agency and internal ratings. We stressed that banks were increasingly trying to replicate the agencies' process in order to rate their largest counterparts. It is, however, impossible to allocate an analyst to each of the numerous smaller exposures on a bank's balance sheet. One needs statistical approaches for segregating "good borrowers" from "bad borrowers" in terms of their creditworthiness in an automated way. The techniques used for retail and SME loans are typically scoring models. For publicly listed corporates, it is also possible to rely on equity-based models of credit risk.

Credit scoring is often perceived as not being highly sophisticated. At first sight it seems that the banking industry considers that nothing significant has been discovered since Altman's (1968) Z-score. One gathers information on a small set of key financial variables and inputs them in a simple model that separates the good firms from the bad firms. The reality is totally different: Credit scoring is a very little piece of the large data-mining jigsaw. Data mining—and in particular, statistical pattern recognition—is a flourishing research area. For example, Jain, Duin, and Mao (2000) perform a short survey including most significant and recent contributions in the area of statistical pattern recognition. They list more than 150 recent working papers and published articles. Since then, a lot of new fields, such as support vector machines, have been investigated more in depth. From a practical viewpoint, this means that most current statistical models applied to credit risk are lagging far behind state-of-the-art methodologies. As a consequence, we anticipate that banks will be catching up in the coming years with the integration of nonparametric techniques and machine learning methods.

Credit scoring models apply to any type of borrower. For the largest corporates (those with listed equity), structural models may be an appealing alternative. Structural models, also called Merton-type models, are becoming very widespread in the banking community. Two major reasons account for their popularity: They tend to convey early warning information, and they also reflect the idea of a marked-to-market assessment of the credit quality of obligors.

In this chapter we first discuss the merits and the shortcomings of structural models of credit risk. We then turn to the main types of credit scoring models and discuss at length the measures that may be used to assess the performance of a scoring model, either in absolute terms or relative to other models.

ASSESSING DEFAULT RISK THROUGH STRUCTURAL MODELS

Structural, or firm-value-based, models of credit risk describe the default process as the explicit outcome of the deterioration of the value of the firm. Corporate securities are seen as contingent claims (options) on the value of the issuing firm. Once a model for the value of the firm process has been assumed and the capital structure of the firm is known, it is possible to price equity and debt using option pricing formulas.

Conversely, it is possible to extract some information about the value of the firm from the price of the quoted equity. Once this is achieved, an equity-implied probability of default can be calculated, thereby replacing the probability of default of traditional scoring models.

Structural models have gained wide recognition among professionals and have become a market standard in the field of default risk. One of the great features of this class of models is their ability to provide a continuous marked-to-market assessment of the creditworthiness of listed firms. Unfortunately, the underlying assumptions necessary to obtain simple formulas for probabilities of default are sometimes heroic. In this section we present the classic Merton (1974) model and discuss its insights and limitations. We then provide a nonexhaustive list of the refinements brought to the Merton approach in the credit pricing field.

We also discuss how these models have been applied by practitioners to assess probabilities of default and extract early warning information about troubled companies.

The Merton Model

In their original option pricing paper, Black and Scholes (1973) suggested that their methodology could be used to price corporate securities. Merton (1974) was the first to use their intuition and to apply it to corporate debt pricing. Many academic extensions have been proposed, and some commercial products use the same basic structure.

The Merton (1974) model is the first example of an application of contingent claims analysis to corporate security pricing. Using simplifying assumptions about the firm's value dynamics and the capital structure of the firm, the author is able to give pricing formulas for corporate bonds and equities in the familiar Black and Scholes (1973) paradigm.

In the Merton model a firm with value V is assumed to be financed through equity (with value S) and pure discount bonds with value P and maturity T. The principal of the debt is K. At any $t \leq T$, the value of the firm is the sum of the values of its securities: $V_t = S_t + P_t$. In the Merton model, it is assumed that bondholders cannot force the firm into bankruptcy before the maturity of the debt. At the maturity date T, the firm is considered solvent if its value is sufficient to repay the principal of the debt. Otherwise the firm defaults.

The value of the firm V is assumed to follow a geometric Brownian motion[1] such that[2] $dV = \mu V \, dt + \sigma_v V \, dZ$. Default occurs if the value of the firm is insufficient to repay the debt principal: $V_T < K$. In that case bondholders have priority over shareholders and seize the entire value of the firm V_T. Otherwise (if $V_T \geq K$) bondholders receive what they are due: the principal K. Thus their payoff is $P(T,T) = \min(K,V_T) = K - \max(K-V_T,0)$ (see Figure 3-1).

Equity holders receive nothing if the firm defaults, but profit from all the upside when the firm is solvent; i.e., the entire value of the firm net of the repayment of the debt $(V_T - K)$ falls in the hands of shareholders. The payoff to equity holders is therefore $max(V_T - K,0)$ (see Figure 3-1).

Readers familiar with options will recognize that the payoff to equity holders is similar to the payoff of a call on the value of the firm struck at K. Similarly, the payoff received by corporate bondholders can be seen as the payoff of a riskless bond minus a put on the value of the firm.

FIGURE 3-1

Payoff of Equity and Corporate Bond at Maturity T

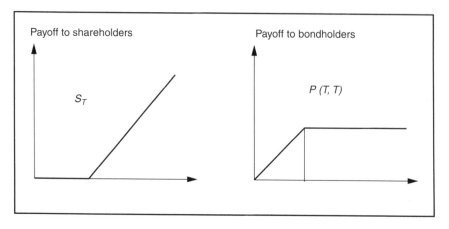

Merton (1974) makes the same assumptions as Black and Scholes (1973), and the call and the put can be priced using option prices derived in Black-Scholes. For example, the call (equity) is immediately obtained as

$$S_t = V_t N(k + \sigma_V \sqrt{T - t}) - Ke^{-r(T-t)} N(k)$$

where

$$k = \frac{\log(V_t/K) + (r - \frac{1}{2}\sigma_V^2)(T - t)}{\sigma_V \sqrt{T - t}}$$

and where $N(.)$ denotes the cumulative normal distribution and r the riskless interest rate.

The Merton model brings a lot of insight into the relationship between the fundamental value of a firm and its securities. The original model, however, relies on very strong assumptions:

- The capital structure is simplistic: equity + one issue of zero-coupon debt.
- The value of the firm is assumed to be perfectly observable.
- The value of the firm follows a lognormal diffusion process. With this type of process, a sudden surprise (a jump), leading to an unexpected default, cannot be captured. Default has to be reached gradually, "not with a bang but with a whisper," as Duffie and Lando (2001) put it.

- Default can only occur at the debt maturity.
- Riskless interest rates are constant through time and maturity.
- The model does not allow for debt renegotiation between equity and debt holders.
- There is no liquidity adjustment.

These stringent assumptions may explain why the simple version of the Merton model struggles in coping with empirical spreads observed on the market. Van Deventer and Imai (2002) test empirically the hypothesis of inverse co-movement of stock prices and credit spread prices, as predicted by the Merton model. Their sample comprises First Interstate Bancorp 2-year credit spread data and the associated stock price. The authors find that only 42 percent of changes in credit spread and equity prices are consistent with the directions (increases or decreases) predicted by the Merton model.

Practical difficulties also play a part in hampering the empirical relevance of the Merton model:

- The value of the firm is difficult to pin down because the marked-to-market value of debt is often unknown. In addition, all that relates to goodwill or to off-balance-sheet elements is difficult to measure accurately.
- The estimation of assets volatility is difficult due to the low frequency of observations.

A vast literature has contributed to extend the original Merton (1974) model and lift some of its most unrealistic assumptions. To cite a few, we can mention:

- Early bankruptcy and liquidation costs introduced by Black and Cox (1976)
- Coupon bonds, e.g., Geske (1977)
- Stochastic interest rates, e.g., Nielsen, Saa-Requejo, and Santa-Clara (1993) and Shimko, Tejima, and Van Deventer (1993)
- More realistic capital structures (senior, junior debt), e.g., Black and Cox (1976)
- Stochastic processes including jumps in the value of the firm, e.g., Zhou (1997)
- Strategic bargaining between shareholders and debt holders, e.g., Anderson and Sundaresan (1996)
- The effect of incomplete accounting information analyzed in Duffie and Lando (2001) (see Appendix 3A)

For a more detailed discussion on credit spreads and the Merton model, see Chapter 8.

KMV Credit Monitor Model
and Related Approaches

Although the primary focus of Merton (1974) was on debt pricing, the firm-value-based approach has been scarcely applied for that purpose in practice. Its main success has been in default prediction.

KMV Credit Monitor applies the structural approach to extracting probabilities of default at a given horizon from equity prices. Equity prices are available for a large number of corporates. If the capital structure of these firms is known, then it is possible to extract market-implied probabilities of default from their equity price. The probability of default is called expected default frequency (EDF) by KMV.

There are two key difficulties in implementing the Merton-type approach for firms with realistic capital structure. The original Merton model only applies to firms financed by equity and one issue of zero-coupon debt: How should we calculate the strike price of the call (equity) and put (default component of the debt) when there are multiple issues of debt? The estimation of the firm value process is also difficult: How should we estimate the drift and volatility of the asset value process when this value is unobservable? KMV uses a rule of thumb to calculate the strike price of the default put, and it uses a proprietary undisclosed methodology to calculate the volatility.

KMV assumes that the capital structure of an issuer consists of long debt (i.e., with maturity longer than the chosen horizon) denoted LT (long term) and short debt (maturing before the chosen horizon) denoted ST (short term). The strike price default point is then calculated as a combination of short- and long-term debt: "We have found that the default point, the asset value at which the firm will default, generally lies somewhere between total liabilities and current, or short term liabilities" (Modeling Default Risk, 2002). The practical rule chosen could be the following:

$$\text{Default value } X = ST + 0.5\ LT \qquad \text{if } LT/ST < 1.5$$

$$\text{Default value } X = ST + (0.7 - 0.3\ ST/LT)\ LT \qquad \text{otherwise}$$

The rule of thumb above is purely empirical and does not rest on any solid theoretical foundation. Therefore there is no guarantee that the same rule should apply to all countries and jurisdictions and all industries. In addition, little empirical evidence has been shown to provide information about the confidence level associated with this default point.[3]

In the Merton model, the probability of default[4] is

$$PD_t = N\left(-\frac{[\log(V_t) - \log(X) + (\mu - \sigma_V^2/2)(T-t)]}{\sigma_V\sqrt{T-t}}\right)$$

where:

$N(.)$ = the cumulative Gaussian distribution

V_t = the value of the firm at t

X = the default threshold

σ_V = the asset volatility of the firm

μ = the expected return on assets

Example

Consider a firm with a market cap of $3 billion, an equity volatility of 40 percent, ST liabilities of $7 billion and LT of $6 billion. Thus $X = 7 + 0.5 \times 6 = \$10$ billion. Assume further that we have solved for $A_0 = \$12.511$ billion and $\sigma_V = 9.6$ percent. Finally $\mu = 5$ percent, the firm does not pay dividends, and the credit horizon is 1 year. Then

$$\frac{\log(V_t/X) + (\mu - \sigma_V^2/2)}{\sigma_V} = 3$$

And the "Merton" probability of default at a 1-year horizon is

$$N(-3) = 0.13\%$$

The EDF takes a very similar form. It is determined by a distance to default:

$$EDF_t = \Xi\left(-\frac{(\log(V_t) - \log(X) + (\mu - \sigma_V^2/2)(T-t))}{\sigma_V\sqrt{T-t}}\right)$$

Distance to default DD

Unlike Merton, KMV does *not* rely on the cumulative normal distribution $N(.)$. Default probabilities calculated as $N(-DD)$ would tend to be much too low due to the assumption of normality (too thin tails). KMV therefore calibrates its EDF to match historical default frequencies recorded on its databases. For example, if historically 2 firms out of 1000 with a DD of 3 have defaulted over a 1-year horizon, then firms with a DD of 3 will be assigned an EDF of 0.2 percent. Firms can therefore be put in "buckets" based on their DD. What buckets are used in the software is not transparent to the user. In the formula above, we use $\Xi(.)$ to denote the function mapping the DD to EDFs.

Figure 3-2 is a graph of the asset value process and the interpretation of EDF.

Once the EDFs are calculated, it is possible to map them to a more familiar grid such as agency rating classes (see Table 3-1). This mapping, while commonly used by practitioners, is questionable for reasons explained in the previous chapter: EDFs are at-the-point-in-time measures of credit risk focused on default probability at the 1-year horizon. Ratings

FIGURE 3-2

Relating Probability of Default and Distance to Default

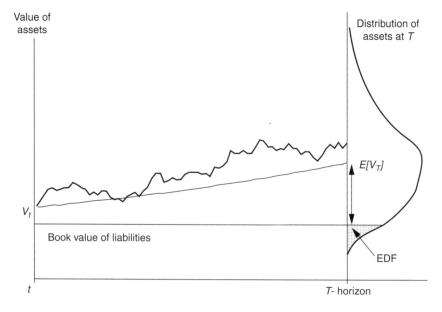

are through-the-cycle assessments of creditworthiness—they cannot, therefore, be reduced to a 1-year PD.

TABLE 3-1

EDFs and Corresponding Rating Class

EDF	S&P
0.02–0.04%	AAA
0.04–0.10%	AA/A
0.10–0.19%	A/BBB+
0.19–0.40%	BBB+/BBB−
0.40–0.72%	BBB−/BB
0.72–1.01%	BB/BB−
1.01–1.43%	BB−/B+
1.43–2.02%	B+/B
2.02–3.45%	B/B−

Source: Crouhy, Galai, and Mark (2000).

Figure 3-3 is an empirical illustration of the structural approach to default prediction. It reports the 1-year PD and associated rating category for France Telecom stock, using a model similar to Merton or Credit Monitor. The effect of the collapse of the telecom bubble since March 2000 is clearly reflected in the probability of default of France Telecom.

Uses and Abuses of Equity-Based Models for Default Prediction

Equity-based models can be useful as an early warning system for individual firms. Crosbie (1997) and Delianedis and Geske (2001) study the early warning power of structural models and show that these models can give early information about ratings migration and defaults.

There have undoubtedly been many examples of successes where structural models have been able to capture early warning signals from the equity markets. These examples, such as the WorldCom case, are heavily publicized by vendors of equity-based systems. What the vendors do not mention is that there are also many examples of false starts: A general fall in the equity markets will tend to be reflected in increases in all EDFs and many "downgrades" in internal ratings based on them,

F I G U R E   3-3

France Telecom 1-Year PD from Merton-Type Model

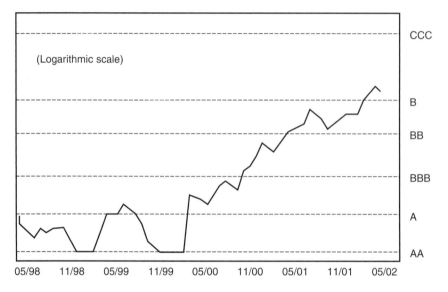

although the credit quality of some firms may be unaffected. False starts are costly, as they induce banks to sell their position in a temporary downturn and therefore at an unfavorable price.

Conversely, in a period of booming equity markets such as 1999, these models will tend to assign very low probabilities of default to almost all firms. In short, equity-based models are prone to overreaction due to market bubbles.

At the portfolio level this overreaction can be problematic. Economic capital linked to PDs calculated on the basis of equity-based models will tend to be very volatile. As a result, these models are unlikely to be favored by the top management of banks. The generalized usage of this kind of model by banks in a Basel II context would lead to a much increased volatility of regulatory capital (see Chapter 10) and to increased procyclicality in the financial sector. Equity-based models are indeed much more procyclical than through-the-cycle ratings because stock markets tend to perform well in growth periods and badly in recessions: Banks are therefore encouraged to lend more in good times and less when the economy needs it most.

To sum up, Merton-type models have become very popular among practitioners. Many banks have developed their own systems to extract early warning information from market variables. Many variants can be found that extract the volatility of the firm from either equity time series, implied volatilities in options markets, or even spreads. Vendors also supply their own interpretation of the structural approach. Equity-based models reflect the market's view about the probability of default of specific issuers and can therefore provide valuable early warning signals. Unfortunately, they are no panacea, as they also reflect all the noise and bubbles that affect equity markets. Overall they can be seen as a useful complement to an analysis of a firm's fundamentals.

CREDIT SCORING

The structural models presented above are based on equity information. They are therefore useful for listed companies but do not extend easily to smaller and private firms. For that purpose banks generally rely on credit scoring. In this section we provide a brief overview of the history of credit scoring. We proceed with an analysis of traditional scoring approaches and more recent developments and then discuss extensively the various performance measures that have been proposed to assess the quality of credit scoring models.

Scoring Methodologies

We begin by reviewing the history of credit scoring. We then turn our attention to an analysis of traditional scoring approaches, and finally we focus on more recent developments.

A Brief Retrospective on Credit Scoring

Quantitative models rely on mathematical and statistical techniques whose development leads the applications to credit scoring. Fitzpatrick (1932) initially established the dependence between the probability of default and individual characteristics for corporate credits. In the same period, Fisher (1936) introduced the concept of discriminant analysis between groups in a given population. Subsequently an NBER study by Durand (1941) used discriminant analysis techniques to segregate good and bad consumer loans. After the Second World War, large companies would use such techniques for marketing purposes.

A major breakthrough in the use of quantitative techniques occurred with the credit card business in the 1960s. Given the size of the population using such cards, automated lending decisions became a requirement. Credit scoring was fully recognized with the 1975 and 1976 Equal Opportunity Acts (implemented by the Federal Reserve Board's Regulation B). These acts stated that any discrimination in the granting of credit was outlawed except if it was based on statistical assessments. Originally methods were based on what was called the "5 Cs": character (reputation), capital (amount), capacity (earnings volatility), collateral, and condition (economic cycle).

In terms of methodology, the 1960s brought serious improvements. The use of credit scoring techniques was extended to other asset classes and in particular to the population of SMEs. Myers and Forgy (1963) compared regression and discriminant analysis in credit scoring applications, then Beaver (1967) came with pioneering work on bankruptcy prediction models, and Altman (1968) used multiple discriminant credit scoring analysis (MDA). This technique enables one to classify the quality of any firm, assigning a Z-score to it. Martin (1977), Ohlson (1980), and Wiginton (1980) were the first to apply logit analysis to the problem of bankruptcy prediction.

All these approaches focused both on the prediction of failure and on the classification of credit quality. This distinction is very important, as it is still not clear in the minds of many users of scores whether classification or prediction is the most important aspect to focus on. This will typically translate into difficulties when selecting criteria for performance measures.

Credit scoring has now become a widespread technique in banks. The Federal Reserve's November 1996 Senior Loan Officer Opinion Survey of Bank Lending Practices showed that 97 percent of U.S. banks were using internal scoring models for credit card applications and 70 percent for small business lending. These figures have increased over the past 5 years, in particular with the Basel II focus on probabilities of default. In 1995 the largest U.S. provider of external models, Fair, Isaac and Company, introduced its first Small Business Credit Scoring model[5] using data from 17 and then 25 banks. Today there are several providers of credit models and credit information services in the market.

The major appeal of scoring models is related to a competitive issue. They enable productivity growth by providing a credit assessment in a limited time frame with reduced costs. Allen (1995) reports that based on credit scoring, the traditional small-business loan approval process averages about 12 hours per loan, a process that took up to 2 weeks in the past.

Berger, Frame, and Miller (2002) review the impact of scoring systems on bank loans to the lower end of the SME business[6] in the United

States over the period 1995–1997. They show that the use of scoring systems within banks is positive in the sense that it tends to increase the appetite of banks for that type of risk and that it reduces adverse selection by enabling "marginal borrowers" with higher risk profiles to be financed more easily, but at an appropriate price. Interestingly, Berger, Frame, and Miller were unable to confirm the real benefit of scoring systems for larger loans (between $100,000 and $250,000), but their database is more limited over that range.

The most widespread current credit scoring technologies consist of four multivariate scoring models: the linear regression probability model, the logit model, the probit model, and the multiple discriminant analysis model. These models are fairly simple in terms of structure and will be reviewed in the next section together with newer, more advanced models.

Choosing the optimal model, based on an existing data set, remains a real challenge today. Galindo and Tamayo (2000) have defined five requisite qualities for the choice of an optimal scoring model:

1. *Accuracy*. Having low error rates arising from the assumptions in the model
2. *Parsimony*. Not using too large a number of explanatory variables
3. *Nontriviality*. Producing interesting results
4. *Feasibility*. Running in a reasonable amount of time and using realistic resources
5. *Transparency and interpretability*. Providing high-level insight into the data relationships and trends and understanding where the output of the model comes from

The Common Range of Credit Scoring Models

In this section we analyze the most popular models used in credit scoring. We also describe newer methodologies that are being introduced to credit scoring problems. We believe that some of these techniques will progressively be implemented in more sophisticated banks.

Figure 3-4 is an overview of the various classes of models we consider in this section. This classification is inspired by Jain, Duin, and Mao (2000).

In statistical pattern recognition, it is common to find a distinction between supervised and unsupervised classification. The difference between the two approaches is that in the first case, we know according to which criteria we want to classify firms between groups. In the second

FIGURE 3-4

Classification of Pattern Recognition Approaches

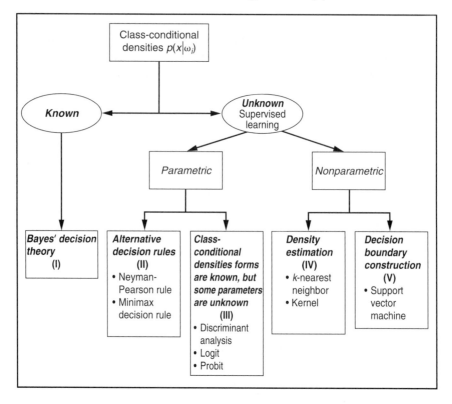

case, in contrast, the model builder seeks to learn the groupings themselves from the model. In the section that follows, we only consider
supervised classification.

The models listed in parts (I) and (II) of Figure 3-4 will be
described later in the chapter, as part of the performance measure
framework. The reason for this is that the underlying rules to which
they correspond do matter when defining optimal classification or optimal prediction.

In this section we focus on four different approaches (with corresponding references in Figure 3-4):

♦ Fisher linear discriminant analysis (III)

♦ Logistic regression and probit (III)

- ◆ *k*-nearest neighbor classifier (IV)
- ◆ Support vector machine classifier (V)

These four approaches encompass the most widely used techniques in the credit scoring arena. Many other techniques exist, such as neural networks, tree induction methods, and genetic algorithms. These are treated in statistical pattern recognition books such as Webb (2002).

The first two types of classifiers we mention (discriminant and logit/probit) will often be used as front-end tools[7] because they are easy to understand and to implement. Their main strength corresponds above all to classification accuracy and ease of use. The last two (nearest neighbor and support vector machines) are often seen as back-end tools, because they require longer computational time. Their value is based on high predictive performance standards.

Fisher (1936) Linear Discriminant Analysis

The principal aim of discriminant analysis is to segregate and classify a heterogeneous population in homogeneous subsets. In order to obtain such results, various decision criteria are used to determine a relevant decision rule.

The idea is quite simple: We first select a number of classes C in which we want to segregate the data. In the case of a credit scoring model, there can be, for example, two classes: default and nondefault. Then, we look for the linear combination of explanatory variables which separates the two classes most.

Before we can get into the details of the models, we need to introduce some notations:

n is the number of data points to be separated—for example, the number of borrowers of a bank.

p is the number of variables available for each data point. In the case of credit scoring, the variables[8] would be, for example, plain amounts like EBIT, total assets, liabilities, or ratios like gearing.

$x = (x_1, x_2, ..., x_p)$ is the vector of observations of the random variables $X = (X_1, X_2, ..., X_p)$.

C denotes the number of categories in which the data will be classified. In the case of a good loan–bad loan separation, there are only two categories: $C = 2$.

μ_i denotes the mean of the variables in class i.

Σ is the between-class covariance matrix.

Let us now consider the Fisher approach to separate two classes ω_1 and ω_2 such as "good borrowers and bad borrowers." Fisher's idea is to look for the linear combination of explanatory variables which leaves the maximum distance between the two classes.

His selection criterion can be written as maximizing

$$F = \frac{|w^T (\mu_1 - \mu_2)|^2}{w^T \Sigma w}$$

where w is the vector of weights that needs to be found. The numerator is the global covariance, and the denominator is the variance.

The maximum is obtained by differentiating F with respect to the vector of weights and setting the differential equal to zero:

$$\frac{\partial F}{\partial w} = 0.$$

The unique solution is

$$w = \Sigma^{-1}(\mu_1 - \mu_2).$$

A pattern x (i.e., a borrower in the case of credit scoring) is then assigned to group ω_1 if $w^T x + \alpha > 0$ and to group ω_2 if $w^T x + \alpha < 0$.

Maximizing F does not, however, provide a rule to determine α, i.e., the cutoff point separating classes ω_1 and ω_2. In general, it has to be chosen by the user.

The most famous application of discriminant analysis to credit scoring is Altman's (1968) Z-score. Explanatory variables used in this model include working capital/assets, retained earnings/assets, EBIT/assets, net worth/liabilities, and sales/assets.

Example

The comparison between the conditional probability of default $P(D|L)$ and the a priori default probability P_D enables us to qualify the riskiness of a company for which the score belongs to L. If $P(D|L) > P_D$, then there is high risk; otherwise no. The more significant the difference, the higher the risk (Figure 3-5).

Parametric Discrimination   Assume that $S(x) = w^T x + \alpha$, is the score function. Once α is chosen, Fisher's rule provides a clear-cut segregation between ω_1 and ω_2. It does not provide probabilities of being

FIGURE 3-5

Separating Companies Using a Discriminant Ratio

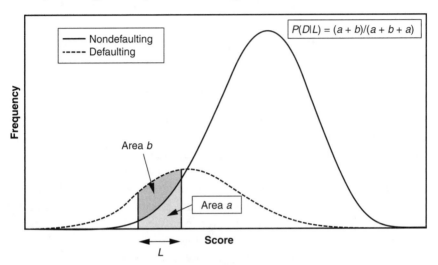

in one class or another, conditional on observing realizations of the variables.

In most cases the choice will not be as simple as being either in class ω_1 or in class ω_2, and one would need probabilities of being in a given class. A very crude approach would be to apply a simple linear regression and say that $S(x) = p(\omega_2 \mid x)$, this means that the probability of being in class ω_2 (for example, default) conditional on observing realizations of the variables x (for example, financial ratios[9]), is simply equal to the score. This is not adequate, as the probability should be between 0 and 1, whereas the score is generally not bounded.

One way to get around this problem is to apply a transformation to the score in order to obtain a probability that lies in the interval [0,1].

Linear Logit[10] and Probit

Let us first consider that the score has the following relationship with the probability:

$$S(x) = w^T x + \alpha = \log \left(\frac{p(x \mid \omega_1)}{p(x \mid \omega_2)} \right) \qquad (3\text{-}1)$$

Then it can be shown that

$$p(\omega_2 \mid x) = \frac{1}{1 + \exp{(w^T x + \beta)}} = \frac{1}{1 + \exp\left(\sum\limits_{i=1}^{p} w_i x_i + \beta\right)} \quad (3\text{-}2)$$

where β is a constant that reflects the relative proportion of firms in the two classes:

$$\beta = \alpha + \log{[p(\omega_1)/p(\omega_2)]}.$$

Equation (3-2) gives the conditional probability of the firm being in class ω_2 (defaulting) conditional on a realization of its variables (financial ratios). The probability follows a logistic law, hence the name logit model. Other transformations are possible, such as using the normal distribution, leading to the normit model—more commonly known as the probit model. In both cases the estimation of the parameters is performed by maximum likelihood. The main difference between the two approaches is linked to the fact that the logistic distribution has thicker tails than the normal distribution (see Figure 3-6). However, this will not make a huge difference in practical applications as long as there are not too many extreme observations in the sample.

The decision rule for classifying patterns (borrowers) remains as simple as in the linear discriminant case: Assign a borrower with observed financial ratios x to class ω_1 if $w^T x + \beta > 0$; otherwise assign it to ω_2. The estimation of w is performed using maximum-likelihood techniques. The larger the training sample on which the weights are estimated, the closer it is from the unknown true value.

Engelmann, Hayden, and Tasche (2003) provide an empirical comparison of the logit model and Altman's Z-score (discriminant analysis) on a large sample of SMEs. They show a very significant outperformance of the logit model in terms of rank ordering (the ROC coefficient[11]).

Example

In regard to the weights on factors using a logit model on a set of SME companies (Figure 3-7). These weights have been determined using a maximum-likelihood approach on a training sample.

Nonlinear Logit

Linear logit models assume by definition a linear relationship between the score and the variables. More complex relationships such as nonmonotonicities are ignored factors. Let us take an anecdotal example of a variable that has been shown to exhibit a nonmonotonic relationship

FIGURE 3-6

Logistic and Normal Cumulative Distribution Functions

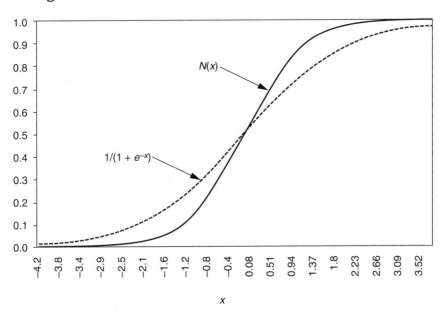

x

FIGURE 3-7

Example Parameters of a Logit Model

Constant	-2.62
Age of the company	-0.847
Assets	-0.2371
Profit on ordinary activities/total debt	-2.551
Solvency ratio	-1.825
Current assets/current liabilities	-0.6154
Gross interest cover	-2.948

with the probability of financial distress in the SME market: the age of the manager.

When the manager of a small firm is very young, she is inexperienced and often not risk averse. Young age will therefore tend to be associated with a high riskiness of the firm. Then as the manager becomes more mature, she will have gained experience, may have a mortgage and a family and therefore be more prudent. However, as she approaches retirement, her potential successors may start fighting for power, or her heir, who has no notion of the business, may be about to take over. Therefore old age also tends to be associated with high risk. The relationship between age and riskiness is thus U-shaped and not monotonic. It cannot be described satisfactorily by a linear function.

Laitinen and Laitinen (2000) suggest applying a nonlinear transformation to the factors $T(x)$ such that

$$S(x) = w^T T(x) + \alpha = \log \left(\frac{p(x \mid \omega_1)}{p(x \mid \omega_2)} \right)$$

where the data transformation could be the Box-Cox function:

$$T_i(x_i) = \frac{(x_i)^{\lambda_i} - 1}{\lambda_i}$$

where λ_i is a convexity parameter: If $\lambda_i < 1$, the transformation is concave; if $\lambda_i > 1$, it becomes convex.[12]

Many other transformations are possible, including the quadratic logit model. It is an immediate extension of the linear logit model presented above. Instead of considering only the first-order terms, the quadratic logit model also includes second-order terms:

$$F(y) = \frac{1}{1 + \exp \left(\beta + \sum_{i=1}^{p} \delta_i x_i + \sum_{i=1}^{p} \sum_{j=1}^{p} \gamma_{ij} x_i x_j \right)}$$

where β is a constant and δs and γs are the weights. It has the advantage of not only including the possibility of a nonlinear relationship between the score and each explanatory variable but also incorporating interactions between variables via the product $x_i x_j$.

These models have more parameters and will therefore tend to provide a better fit and have more predictive power than simple linear models. They remain relatively simple to estimate on the data.

Nonparametric Discrimination: The k-Nearest Neighbor Approach[13]   The k-nearest neighbor (kNN) classifier is one of the easiest approaches to obtaining a nonparametric classification.

In spite of (or thanks to) this simplicity, it has been widely used because it performs well when a Bayesian classifier[14] is unknown. The entire training set is the classifier.

The kNN technique assesses the similarities between the input pattern x and a set of reference patterns from the training set. A pattern is classified to a class of the majority of its k-nearest neighbor in the training set. The classification is based on a basic idea expressed by Dasarathy (1991): " Judge a person by the company he keeps."

Figure 3-8 is a simple graphical example of kNN classification. We want to classify good firms (those that won't default) and bad firms (those that will) using two explanatory variables: return on assets (ROA) and leverage. Clearly, the higher the ROA and the lower the leverage, the less risky the firm. A set of good firms and bad firms has been identified in a training sample, and we want to classify a new firm. We choose $k = 6$. Looking at the six nearest neighbors of the new firm (those within the

FIGURE 3-8

k-Nearest Neighbor Classification

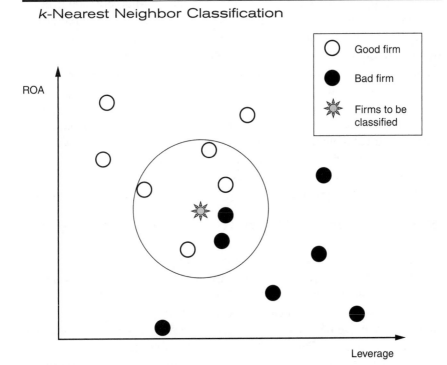

circle), we can see that four of them are good firms and only two are bad firms. The new borrower will therefore be classified as good.

The distance chosen to identify the nearest neighbors is crucial for the results. Several options have been proposed, and the choice of distance metric has been one of the avenues of research taken to improve the performance of this methodology. The most frequently used is the Euclidean distance. Assume that we have values for p variables (in the example above, $p = 2$, corresponding to leverage and ROA) of a given firm we want to classify: $x_1, x_2, ..., x_p$ and that the corresponding values for a firm in the training set are $y_1, y_2, ..., y_p$. The Euclidian distance between the two firms is

$$\left(\sum_{j=1}^{p} (x_j - y_j)^2 \right)^{\frac{1}{2}}$$

One of the main drawbacks of the kNN technique is that it can prove time consuming when the sample size becomes large. Indeed if we consider a training set of n patterns, $n(n - 1)/2$ distances should be calculated in order to determine the nearest neighbors (the number of variables p may be large as well). For a reasonable data set of SMEs of 10,000 firms, it involves the calculation of nearly 50 million distances. Manipulations of the patterns in the training set to reduce the time and space complexity have therefore been introduced by several authors.

The choice of k (the number of neighbors to consider) is also important. For example, if we had chosen $k = 3$ in the example above, we would have assigned the new borrower to the class of bad firms. In case k is too small, the classification may be unstable. Conversely, if it is really too large, some valuable information may be lost. Enas and Choi (1986) give a rule of $k \approx n^{1/4}$, but there is no generally accepted best k.

Hand and Henley (1997) discuss the implementation of a kNN credit rating system with particular emphasis on the choice of distance metrics.

Support Vector Machines[15] Support vector machines[16] (SVMs) have been introduced by Cortes and Vapnik (1995). They have received a lot of interest because of their good performance and their parsimony in terms of parameters to specify. The main idea is to separate the various classes of data using a "best" hyperplane.

We first examine a linear support vector machine (LSVM). Assume that, as above, we have two types of borrowers (good and bad) and that we want to classify them according to two variables (ROA and leverage). If the data are linearly separable (i.e., if one can "draw a straight line" to separate good firms and bad firms), there are often many ways to perform this segregation. In Figure 3-9a we draw two lines[17] A and B that separate the data.

LSVM provides a rule to select among all possible separating hyperplanes: The best separating hyperplane (BSH) is the hyperplane for which the distance to two parallel hyperplanes on each side is the largest. Figure 3-9b shows the BSH that separates the data optimally. Two parallel hyperplanes with the same distance to the BSH are tangent to some observations in the sample. These points are called support vectors (SV on the graph).

The Case Where Data Are Linearly Separable

Points x on the best separating hyperplane satisfy the equation $w^T x + w_0 = 0$. If we consider a set of training observations x_i, where $i \in \{1,...,n\}$, an observation x_i will be assigned to class ω_1 according to the rule $w^T x_i + w_0 > 0$ and to class ω_2 according to the rule $w^T x_i + w_0 < 0$.

FIGURE 3-9a

Two Arbitrary Separations of the Data

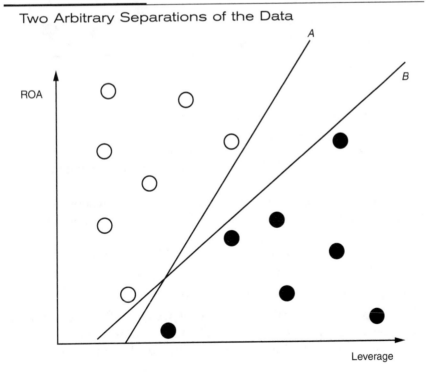

FIGURE 3-9*b*

Best Separating Hyperplane

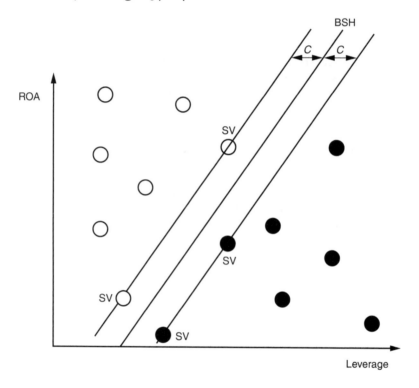

The rule can be expressed synthetically as $y_i(w^T x_i + w_0) > 0$ for all i, where $y_i = 1$ if $x_i \in \omega_1$ and -1 otherwise.

The BSH does not provide the tightest separation rule. This is provided by the two hyperplanes that are parallel to the BSH and tangent to the data.

One can thus use a stricter rule: $y_i(w^T x_i + w_0) \geq c$, where c is the distance from the BSH to the tangent hyperplanes (called canonical hyperplanes).

Parameters of the hyperplanes are found by minimizing[18] $||w||$, subject to $y_i(w^T x_i + w_0) \geq c$. This is a standard mathematical problem.

The Case Where the Data Are Not Linearly Separable

The case considered above was simple, as we could find a straight line that would separate good firms from bad firms. In most practical cases, such straightforward separation will not be possible. In Figure 3.10 we have added only one observation, and the data set is no longer separable by a straight line.

We can still use linear support vector machines but must modify the constraints slightly. Instead of the strict rule $w^T x_i + w_0 > 0$ that lead to being assigned to ω_1, we use $w^T x_i + w_0 > 1 - F_i$, where F_i is a *positive* parameter that measures the degree of fuzziness or slackness of the rule.

Similarly, the slack rule will classify a firm in category ω_2 if $w^T x_i + w_0 < -1 + F_i$.

A firm will then be assigned to the wrong category by the LSVM if $F_i > 1$. The optimization program should include a cost function that penalizes the misclassified observations. Given that misclassification implied large values of F_i, we can adopt a simple rule such as, for example, to make the cost proportional to the sum of adjustments $(\sum_i F_i)$.

FIGURE 3-10

Nonlinearly Separable Data

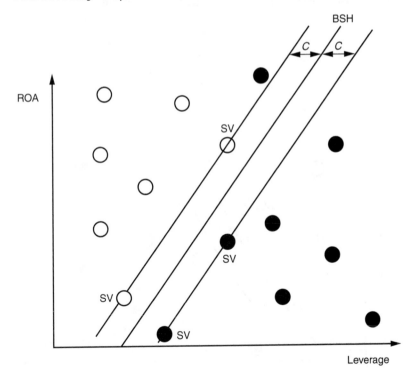

Nonlinear Support Vector Machine

Another way to deal with nonlinearly separable data is to use a nonlinear classifier $h(x)$. The decision rule is similar but substitutes $h(x)$ for x. Thus we obtain $y_i[w^T h(x_i) + w_0] > 0$ for all i. This defines now the best separating surface.

The term $h(x_i)^T h(x_j)$ arises in the determination of the optimal parameter vector w. This term can be replaced by a kernel $K(x_i, x_j)$ function.

Some popular choices for kernels are the Gaussian kernel: $K(x_i, x_j) = \exp(-\frac{1}{2}|x_i - x_j|^2/\sigma^2)$ and the polynomial kernel of order p: $K(x_i, x_j) = (1 + x_i^T x_j)^p$. For most kernels it is generally possible to find values for the kernel parameter for which the classes are separable, but there is a risk of overfitting the training data.

Figure 3-11 shows an example of how a nonlinear classifier can separate the data.

FIGURE 3-11

Nonlinear Kernel Support Vector Machine

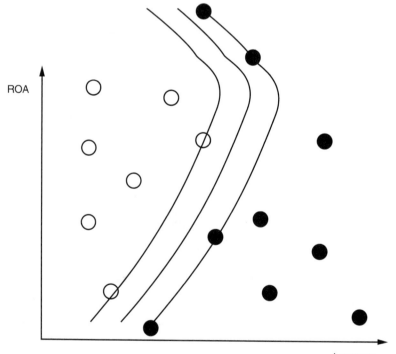

Practical Implementations

Support vector machines are not only theoretically interesting; they are really applied by practitioners to credit data. For example, Standard & Poor's CreditModel uses a fast class of SVMs called *proximal* support vector machines to obtain rating estimates for nonrated companies (see Friedman, 2002).

Model Performance Measures

The objective of this section is to introduce the various performance measures used to assess scoring models. A more detailed treatment of performance measurement can be found, for instance, in Webb (2002). This section follows some of its structure.

Performance measurement is of critical importance in many fields such as computer sciences, medical diagnosis, shape, and voice and face recognition. In credit analysis the stability of a bank may be at stake if the bank relies on a flawed credit model that persistently underestimates the risk of the bank's counterparts.

The architecture of this section is organized according to Figure 3-12. We first describe performance measures that are widespread in statistical pattern recognition (classification tools). Second we review prediction tools that are particularly important for credit scoring. Then, before segregating the two approaches, we build on a common platform related to decision rules. In particular, we put emphasis on the description of a Bayesian framework, as it is the most common language for parametric and nonparametric modeling.

Definition of Decision Rules

Here we introduce decision methodologies used to classify patterns. The space (the set of all possible combinations of variables) is divided into decision regions separated by decision boundaries. We first examine cases where class-conditional distributions and a priori distributions are identified.

If x is a vector that corresponds to a set of measurements obtained through observation and C is the number of different classes, then C is partitioning the space Ω in regions Ω_i for $i = 1,...,C$. If an observed measurement x is in Ω_i, then it is said to belong to class ω_i. The probability of each class occurring is known: $p(\omega_1),..., p(\omega_C)$.

FIGURE 3-12

Classification of Performance Measures

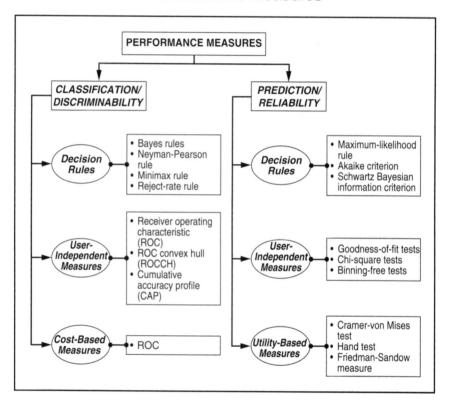

In credit terms, x would be the observed variables for a given firm (leverage, return on assets, profit and loss, and so on).

The "Minimum-Error" Decision Rule   If we want to classify a firm with no prior information except the probability of a firm being in a given risk class ω_k, we would assign it to the most probable class, i.e., class j defined as $p(\omega_j) = \max_k [p(\omega_k)]$ for $k = 1,...,C$.

Thus if the only information available is that there are two-thirds of good firms and one-third of bad firms, any new firm will be classified as good because it maximizes the unconditional (or a priori) probability.

If we have some data x about the explanatory variables, then the decision rule to assign x to class Ω_j (and thereby the firm to ω_j) is given by

$$p(\omega_j \,|\, x) = \max_k [p(\omega_k \,|\, x)] \quad for \; k = 1,...,C$$

$p(\omega_j | x)$ is the conditional probability of being in class ω_j, knowing x, also called a posteriori probability.

Using Bayes' theorem, we can express the a posteriori $p(\omega_j | x)$ with a priori probabilities $p(\omega_j)$ and the class-conditional density functions $p(x | \omega_j)$:

$$p(\omega_j | x_j) = \frac{p(x | \omega_j)p(\omega_j)}{p(x)}$$

This can also be read as

$$\text{Posterior probability} = \frac{\text{likelihood function} \times \text{prior belief}}{\text{evidence}}$$

The conditional decision rule can then be rewritten as

$$p(x | \omega_j)p(\omega_j) = \max_k [p(x | \omega_k)p(\omega_k)] \qquad \text{for } k = 1,\ldots,C$$

It is called Bayes' rule for minimum error.

And the Bayes' error is defined as

$$E_B = 1 - \int \max_k [p(x | \omega_k)p(\omega_k)] \, dx$$

Regarding the choice between two classes a and b (such as between good borrowers and bad borrowers), the decision rule boils down to allocating the firm to class ω_a if

$$p(x | \omega_a)p(\omega_a) > p(x | \omega_b)p(\omega_b)$$

and to class ω_b otherwise. The rule is illustrated in Figure 3-13.

It can also be expressed as a likelihood ratio: x assigned the firm to class ω_a if

$$L(x) = \frac{p(x | \omega_a)}{p(x | \omega_b)} > \frac{p(\omega_b)}{p(\omega_a)}$$

and to ω_b otherwise. $p(\omega_b)/p(\omega_a)$ is the threshold.

The "Minimum-Risk" Decision Rule

Other decision rules exist, such as minimum risk. The minimum-error rule consisted in selecting the class for which a posteriori $p(\omega_j | x) = \max_j [p(\omega_k | x)]$ was the greatest.

A different rule can be chosen which minimizes the expected loss, i.e., the risk of misclassification. The costs of misclassification often have

FIGURE 3-13

Bayes' "Minimum-Error" Decision Rule

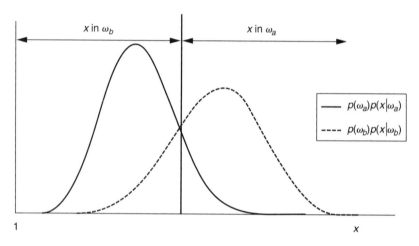

to be considered precisely. For instance, it can be more damaging to the bank to lend to a company that is falsely considered to be sound than to wrongly avoid lending to a sound company.

In order to reflect misclassification, a loss matrix C is defined whose elements c_{ab} are the cost of assigning a pattern x to ω_b instead of ω_a. The matrix will have to be defined by the user of the model according to the user's own utility function. This task is often difficult to achieve because these costs are highly subjective.

Bayes' expected loss or risk is then defined as

$$R_B = \int_x \min_{b=1,\dots C} \sum_{a=1,\dots,C} c_{ab}\, [p(x \mid \omega_a)p(\omega_a)]\, dx$$

The Neyman-Pearson Decision Rule This classification rule applies to two-class problems, such as good and bad firms. With two classes, four types of events can occur, including two possible misclassification errors (E_I and E_{II}):

- The firm is bad and is classified as bad: right detection $(1 - E_I)$.
- The firm is bad and is classified as good: wrong detection of default E_I

- The firm is good and is classified as good: right detection $(1 - E_{II})$.
- The firm is good and is classified as bad: false alarm E_{II}.

More formally, the two types of misclassification errors are
Type I error

$$E_I = \int_{\Omega_2} p(x \mid \omega_1) \, dx \qquad \text{corresponding to the false nondefaulting companies}$$

Type II error

$$E_{II} = \int_{\Omega_1} p(x \mid \omega_2) \, dx \qquad \text{corresponding to the false defaulting companies}$$

Being a false nondefaulting company is more dangerous than being a false defaulting company, because a loan will be granted to the former and not to the latter. A Type I error damages the wealth of the bank, given its utility function, whereas a Type II error is only a false alarm.

The Neyman-Pearson rule minimizes E_I, with E_{II} remaining constant. The solution is the minimum of

$$R = \int_{\Omega_2} p(x \mid \omega_1) \, dx + \mu \left[\int_{\Omega_1} p(x \mid \omega_2) \, dx - \overline{E}_{II} \right]$$

where μ is a Lagrange multiplier and $\overline{E}_{II}$ is the specified false alarm rate chosen by the user.

The rule will be to allocate the firm to region Ω_1 if

$$L(x) = \frac{p(x \mid \omega_1)}{p(x \mid \omega_2)} > \mu$$

and to Ω_2 otherwise. The threshold μ is implied by the choice of $\overline{E}_{II}$.

The Minimax Decision Rule
The "minimax" concept refers to the objective of a maximum error or a maximum risk that is targeted to be minimum. To minimize the maximum error in a two-class environment, the minimax procedure consists of choosing the partitions Ω_1 and Ω_2 and minimizing:

$$\text{Max} \left[\int_{\Omega_2} p(x \mid \omega_1) \, dx, \int_{\Omega_1} p(x \mid \omega_2) \, dx \right]$$

The minimum is obtained when

$$\int_{\Omega_2} p(x \mid \omega_1) \, dx = \int_{\Omega_1} p(x \mid \omega_2) \, dx$$

That is, the regions Ω_1 and Ω_2 are chosen so that the probabilities of the two types of error are the same.

Performance Measures: Targeting Classification Accuracy

Now that we have surveyed the various decisions rules, we turn next to the subject of the different tools available, either for classification performance measures or for prediction performance measures. Appendix 3C reports practical issues regarding the assessment of credit scoring models.

Measuring Classification: The ROC Approach   The

ROC receiver operating characteristic measure and the Gini coefficient, described later, are probably the most commonly used approaches to measuring credit scoring performance.[19] Figure 3-14 illustrates how to calculate the ROC coefficient. We assume that we have the output of a scoring model calibrated on a population with D defaults out of N firms.

FIGURE 3-14

The ROC Curve

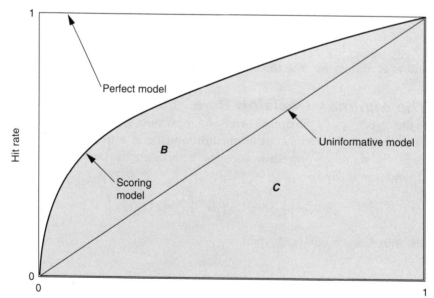

A score s_i and a probability of default p_i are assigned to each firm i = 1,...,N, and the analyst chooses a cutoff level T such that the firm is considered bad if $p_i > T$ and good if $p_i \leq T$.

For each firm, four cases are possible:

1. It defaults, and the model had classified it as bad (appropriate classification).
2. It defaults, and the model had classified it as good (Type I error).
3. It does not default, and the model had classified it as bad (Type II error, false alarm).
4. It does not default, and the model had classified it as good (appropriate classification).

We use as C_T and F_T to denote, respectively, the number of firms correctly and wrongly classified as bad (note that they depend on the cutoff level T). Then the hit rate H and false alarm rate F are:

$$H_T = \frac{C_T}{D} \quad , \quad F_T = \frac{W_T}{N-D}$$

The ROC curve is a plot of H_T against F_T. The steeper the ROC curve, the better, as it implies that there are few false alarms compared with correctly detected bad firms. On Figure 3-14 the perfect model is a vertical line going from (0,0) to (0,1) and then a vertical line linking (0,1) to (1,1). An uninformative model would on average have as many false alarms as correct detections and would result in a diagonal (0,0) to (1,1) ROC curve. Credit scoring models will produce intermediate ROC curves.

The ROC curve can also be seen as a trade-off between Type I (E_I) and Type II (E_{II}) errors. H_T indeed corresponds to $1 - E_I$ and E_{II} to F_T.

The ROC curve is also related to the minimum loss or minimum cost as defined above (see Figure 3-15). One starts by defining iso-loss lines whose slope is $p(\omega_2)/p(\omega_1)$, the ratio of ex ante probabilities. By definition, any point on a given line corresponds to the same loss. The minimum loss point will be at the tangency between the ROC curve and the lowest iso-loss line.

The area below the ROC curve (either B or $B + C$) is widely used as a measure of performance of a scoring model. The ROC measure, however, suffers from several pitfalls. First, ROC is focused on rank ordering and thus only deals with *relative* classification. In credit terms, as long as the model produces a correct ranking of firms in terms of probabilities of default, it will have a good ROC coefficient, irrespective of whether all

FIGURE 3-15

Finding the Minimum-Loss Point

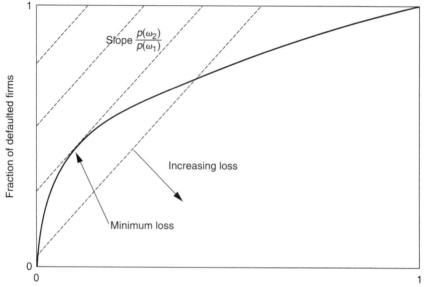

Fraction of all firms (from riskiest to safest)

firms are assigned much lower (or higher) probabilities than their "true" values. Therefore one may have a model that underestimates risk substantially but still has a satisfactory ROC coefficient.

Second, ROC is an acceptable measure as long as class distribution is not skewed. This is the case with credit, where the nondefaulting population is much larger than the defaulting one. ROC curves may not be the most adequate measure under such circumstances.

In order to tackle the latter criticism, it is possible to include differing costs for Type I and Type II errors. Appendix 3D shows why it may be useful and how it affects the minimum-cost point.

Measuring Classification: The Gini/CAP Approach

Another commonly used measure of classification performance is the Gini curve or cumulative accuracy profile (CAP). This curve assesses the consistency of the predictions of a scoring model (in terms of the ranking of firms by order of default probability) to the ranking of observed defaults. Firms are first sorted in descending order of default probability as produced by the scoring model (the horizontal axis of Figure 3-16). The vertical axis displays the fraction of firms that have actually defaulted.

FIGURE 3-16

The CAP Curve

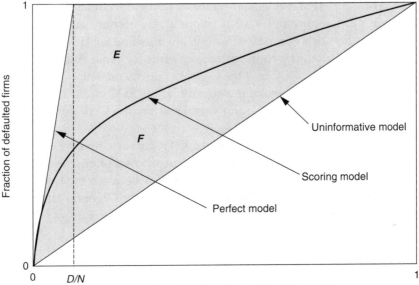

Fraction of all firms (from riskiest to safest)

A perfect model would have assigned the D highest default probabilities to the D firms that have actually defaulted out of a sample of N. The perfect model would therefore be a straight line from the point $(0,0)$ to point $(D/N,1)$ and then a horizontal line from $(D/N,1)$ to $(1,1)$. Conversely, an uninformative model would randomly assign the probabilities of defaults to high-risk and low-risk firms. The resulting CAP curve is the diagonal from $(0,0)$ to $(1,1)$.

Any real scoring model will have a CAP curve somewhere in between. The Gini ratio (or accuracy ratio), which measures the performance of the scoring model for rank ordering, is defined as $G = F/(E + F)$, where E and F are the areas depicted in Figure 3-16. This ratio lies between 0 and 1; the higher this ratio, the better the performance of the model.

The CAP approach provides a rank-ordering performance measure of a model and is highly dependent on the sample on which the model is calibrated. For example, any model that is calibrated on a sample with no observed default and that predicts zero default will have a 100 percent Gini coefficient. However, this result will not be very informative about the true performance of the underlying models. For instance, the same model can exhibit an accuracy ratio under 50 percent or close to 80 percent, according to the characteristic of the underlying sample. Comparing different models on the basis of their accuracy ratio, calculated with different samples, is therefore totally nonsensical.

When the costs of misclassification are the same for Type I and Type II errors (corresponding to the minimum-error Bayesian rule), the summary statistics of the ROC and the CAP are directly related: If A ($= B + C$ on Figure 3-14) is the value of the area under the ROC curve and G is the Gini coefficient or accuracy ratio calculated on the CAP curve,[20] then $G = 2(A - 0.5)$.

In this case the ROC curves and CAP curves convey exactly the same information. When a specific structure of costs of misclassification is introduced in the calculation of ROC, the link between the two curves is lost. ROC can probably be considered as more general than CAP because it allows for differing costs to be selected by the user.

Overall:

- ♦ The CAP curve provides valuable information if the user considers that misclassification costs are equal and provided the size of the defaulting subsample is somehow comparable with the non-defaulting one.[21] If this is not the case, then another type of measure should complement the comparison of the performance of different models.

- ♦ Since bankers and investors are usually risk averse and would tend to avoid Type I errors more than Type II errors, CAP curves or Gini coefficients are not best suited to assess the performance of credit scoring models.

- ♦ The ROC measure is broader than the CAP measure because it enables the users of the model to incorporate misclassification costs or their utility function. If the objective is to assess the ability of the model to classify firms, then ROC, and in particular ROCCH[22] is an attractive measure.

- ♦ A significant weakness of both the ROC and CAP approaches is that they are limited to rank ordering. This is a weak measure of performance in the area of credit where not only the relative riskiness but also the level of risk is crucial.

Performance Measures: Targeting Prediction Reliability

Until now we have discussed the ability to split a sample into subgroups such as good and bad borrowers. The focus was on the ability to discriminate between classes of firms, but not on the precise assessment of the probability of default. This is what prediction measurement is about: measuring how well the posterior probability of group membership is estimated by the chosen rule. Prediction reliability is a particularly important requirement in the credit universe, because a price (interest rate) may be associated with the output of a credit scoring model. If the bank's credit scoring model underestimates risk systematically, it will charge too low interest rates and will thus, on average, make a loss.

The Maximum-Likelihood Decision Rule

Geometric mean probability (GMP) is a measure similar to maximum likelihood that is easy to estimate. It is defined as

$$\text{GMP} = e^{\frac{1}{N} \sum_{i=1}^{N} y_i \log[p(x_i)] + (1-y_i) \log[1-p(x_i)]}$$

Given a model tested on a sample of N observations, the first term of the GMP focuses on truly defaulting companies i (where $y_i = 1$), for which a probability of default $p(x_i)$ is assigned by the model. The second term of the GMP targets truly nondefaulting companies (where $y_i = 0$), for which a probability of default $p(x_i)$ is assigned by the model.

When comparing two different models on the same data set, the model with a higher GMP will be said to perform better than the other one. An ideal model would assign $p(x_i) = 100$ percent to all defaulting companies and $p(x_i) = 0$ percent to all nondefaulting companies. Therefore GMP would be 100 percent.

From an economic standpoint, likelihood maximization can be seen as a measure of wealth maximization for a user of the scoring model. However, the underlying assumption is that the user of the model does not consider asymmetric payoffs. For the user, this means that all types of errors (E_I, E_{II}) have the same weight and impact on his wealth. Therefore likelihood measures can appear insufficient in the area of financial scoring where asymmetric payoffs matter.

What is interesting about likelihood is that it is primarily a simple aggregated measure of performance, whereas more complex well-established measures such as CAP and Gini focus more on misclassification and rank ordering.

There exist several additional criteria, based on likelihood, devised to compare different models. They tend to consider both likelihood and the number of parameters required to fit the model. The ultimate objective is to include what is called the "minimum description length" principle, which advantages the model having the shortest or more succinct computational description.

There are among others:

The Akaike (1974) information criterion (AIC):
$\mathrm{AIC} = -2 \log L(\hat{\theta}_k) + 2k$.

The Schwartz (1978) Bayesian information criterion (BIC):
$\mathrm{BIC} = -2 \log L(\hat{\theta}_k) + k \log N$, where k is the number of parameters, N the size of the sample, and $\hat{\theta}$ the k-dimensional vector of parameter estimates. $L(.)$ is the likelihood function.

The best model is supposed to minimize the selected criterion. Both BIC and AIC penalize models with many parameters and thereby reduce overfitting.

Some other tests exist such as Hand's criterion.[23]

Measuring Prediction: Goodness-of-Fit Tests[24]   As with likelihood decision rules, the goodness-of-fit tests are devised to measure the deviation of a random sample from a given probability distribution function. In the following sections, the tests reviewed will be either distribution-free or adaptable to any type of distribution. We split between two types of tests, those that are applied to binned data and those that are applied to bins-free samples.

An Example of a Test Dependent on Binning: The Chi-Square Test

The purpose of the chi-square test is to analyze how close a sample drawn from an unknown distribution is to a known distribution. The chi-square test measures a normalized distance.

Assume that we have a large sample of N events that are distributed in K classes, according to a multinomial distribution with probabilities p_i. Using N_i to denote the number of observations in class $i = 1, \ldots, K$ (e.g., rating classes), we obtain

$$D_N = \sum_{i=1}^{K} \frac{(N_i - Np_i)^2}{Np_i}$$

which follows asymptotically a χ^2 distribution with $K - 1$ degrees of freedom.[25]

The probability α of a Type I error is related to the chi-square distribution by $F_{K-1}(\chi_0^2) = 1 - \alpha$. It defines a level χ_0^2 that determines the rejection of the null hypothesis H_0. H_0 (i.e., the hypothesis according to which the data sample follows the identified probability distribution function) is rejected at the α confidence level if $\chi^2 > \chi_0^2$.

An Example of the Use of a Chi-Square Test to Define Whether an Internal Scoring Model of a Bank Is Performing Well in Comparison with Expected Default

Let us consider a scoring system with 10,000 scores classified in 10 rating classes, 1 being the best class and 10 being the worst. Suppose 200 companies have actually defaulted. The null hypothesis is that the internal ratings classify in a satisfactory way, compared with the expected default rate per rating category.

The null hypothesis is H_0: The model appropriately replicates the expected default rate.

We have the following observations:

	Rating Class									
	1	2	3	4	5	6	7	8	9	10
Empirical number of defaults per class	5	10	10	15	30	20	15	25	25	45
Expected number of defaults per class (Np_j)	5	7	9	10	12	15	19	25	38	60

The chi-square statistic is 41.6. The 95th percentile for a chi-square distribution with $K - 1 = 9$ degrees of freedom is 16.9. As the latter is significantly inferior to the statistic, it means that the hypothesis of the scoring system replicating the expected default rate satisfactorily should be rejected.

This test is easy to implement. It shows, however, some limitations:

♦ It depends highly on the choice of classes (binning).
♦ It assumes independent classes.
♦ It is accurate only when there is a reasonable trade-off between the number of events and the number of classes.
♦ It considers all deviations with the same weight.

An Example of Binning-Free Tests: The Kolmogorov-Smirnov Test

The test above relied on a specific bucketing (binning) of firms in risk classes. A way to avoid the impact of binning is to compare the empirical with the theoretical distribution.

The empirical distribution on a data sample with N observations is constructed as follows. We first rank the observations X_i in ascending order so that $X_1 < X_2 < \ldots < X_N$. An empirical step distribution function is then built:

$$F_N(x) = \begin{cases} 0 & \text{for } x < X_1 \\ \dfrac{i}{N} & \text{for } X_i \le x < X_{i+1} \\ 1 & \text{for } X_N \le x \end{cases}$$

which is the fraction of observations below x.

Binning-free tests compare this empirical cumulative distribution with a theoretical distribution $F(x)$ such as the normal distribution. The null hypothesis of the test is that the two distributions are identical.

The observed distance between the theoretical and empirical distribution is $D(x) = F_N(x) - F(x)$.

The Kolmogorov difference is the maximum absolute difference:

$$D_{\text{Kol}} = \max_x [\, |\, D(x)\, |\,]$$

The Kolmogorov-Smirnov test is based on the Kolmogorov difference. The null hypothesis [$F_N(x)$ corresponds to $F(x)$] is rejected if the Kolmogorov distance is sufficiently large: $D_{\text{Kol}} > D_0(\alpha)$. $D_0(\alpha)$ is the cutoff value that depends on the confidence level α chosen for the test.

Measuring Prediction: Considering the Utility Function of the Model User

Over the past years, some financial institutions have tried to consider credit scoring, more with the perspective of maximizing profit than minimizing risk. The term used to refer to this approach is "profit scoring." Profit scoring can, however, prove a difficult task to achieve, for several reasons:

- ◆ Solving data warehousing problems in order to take into account all elements that make up the profit
- ◆ Deciding between transaction profit and customer profit
- ◆ Selecting an appropriate time horizon to consider profit
- ◆ Including economic variables in profit scoring

- ◆ Understanding better current and future customers' behavior (attrition rate, expected profit on future operations, etc.)

The choice among default scoring, risk scoring, and profit scoring will often be very specific to each financial institution. It reflects different governance profiles, i.e., different utility functions. In this section we will focus on utility maximization. We could have chosen to put more emphasis on cost minimization, but the maximization of a utility function under a cost constraint is equivalent to minimizing costs under a utility constraint.

From a practical standpoint, we know that spelling out the costs of misclassification is difficult. We have intuitively observed that these costs were specific to the user of the models: the investor, the banker, or, as in the example of Appendix 3D, the tourist and the patient.

In order to make the measure of performance user-specific, we introduce a utility function and describe the approach by Friedman and Sandow (2002). Their approach can be seen as an extension of the model selection with cost functions presented in Appendix 3D. The main difference is that instead of assigning costs (or payoffs) to misclassified firms (Type I and Type II errors), they assign a payoff to every outcome based on the utility function[26] of the model user. For simplicity, we focus on the case of discrete payoffs, but their measure also works in the continuous case.

Assume that an investor invests his wealth on N assets, with b_y denoting the proportion of wealth invested in asset $y = 1,...,N$. Naturally

$$\sum_y b_y = 1$$

Each asset will return a payoff of O_y.[27] The true probability of each payoff to be received by the investor is denoted as p_y. It is unknown but can be estimated by the empirical probability $\bar{p}_y$. The investor's view of the true probability (i.e., the probability derived from his model) is q_y.

The true and estimated maximum expected utilities the investor will derive from his investment are, respectively,[28]

$$\sum_y p_y U\left[b_y^*(q)O_y\right]$$

and

$$\sum_y \bar{p}_y U\left[b_y^*(q)O_y\right]$$

where b^* denotes the optimal investment weights corresponding to the allocation rule that maximizes the utility of the investor. This allocation is based on the output (q) of the model.

Now consider two models (i.e., two sets of probabilities) q^1 and q^2. The relative expected utility can be calculated as

$$\Delta U(q^1, q^2, O) = \sum_{y=1}^{N} \bar{p}_y \left[U(b_y^*(q^2)O_y) - U(b_y^*(q^1)O_y) \right]$$

Then the selection rule is that $\Delta U(q^1, q^2, O) > 0$, which implies that model 2 outperforms model 1.

The preferred class of utility function considered in Friedman and Sandow (2002) is the logarithmic family:

$$U(W) = \alpha \log (W + \gamma) + \beta$$

where W corresponds to the wealth of the investor.

The three parameters α, γ, and β allow for a lot of flexibility in the shape of the function. This class of utility function has the added advantage that it makes the model performance measure independent from the payoff structure.[29]

This approach is not limited to the logarithmic class of utility functions, but this class has several nice properties:

- It makes the relative performance measure above independent of the odds ratio.
- The model classification corresponds to the intuitive maximization of likelihood.
- It approximates the results obtained under other popular utility functions—very well in many cases.
- The classification rule takes an economic interpretation: maximization of the rate of growth in wealth.

Measuring Prediction: Pitfalls about Model Calibration and Reliability

We have shown in the previous section that the performance of a model is not only linked with its classification ability, but also with its predictive power. This is particularly important for banks that trade risk for return and need a reliable measure of performance for each of their obligors.

Regarding the performance of scoring systems, rank-ordering performance is not sufficient, and the calibration[30] of a model can be unreliable, although its ability to discriminate may be satisfactory. We now review some common pitfalls of credit scoring systems:

♦ Scoring models frequently rely on parametric assumptions regarding the shape of the distribution of PDs, scores, and ratings in the firms' sample. The models are designed to produce score distributions that are roughly bell-shaped (like a normal distribution) or at least "unimodal." If the true data distribution is indeed unimodal, then calibrating the mean and the variance may provide a satisfactory fit to the data. Figure 3-17*a* shows the result of the calibration of a scoring model around a mean on the S&P rated universe. The scoring model classifies firms in 18 risk classes and correctly calibrates the mean probability of default. The parametric assumption about the data distribution, however, strongly biases the results since Standard & Poor's universe rating distribution appears to have two peaks: one around the A grade and one around the B+ grade (see Figure 3-17*b*).

♦ Another doubtful assumption is the idea of a central tendency. According to this a priori assumption, the distribution of scores is a function of a driving parameter (the central tendency), which is linked to the economic cycle. The central tendency plays the role of a mean around which the distribution of scores is centered: When the economy is in recession, all the distribution is "shifted" toward the right (bad scores), and conversely in expansion. This again is contradicted by Standard & Poor's experience as low ratings are much more volatile than high ratings.[31] Therefore, a simple shift around a central tendency cannot replicate the impact of the business cycle on the distribution of scores or ratings: Both the mean and the volatility change. As a result, calibrations based on the idea of central tendency adjustment would typically underestimate the impact of the cycle on the non-investment-grade universe and penalize investment-grade obligors.

Some Observations about Performance Measures

In many sectors where statistical pattern recognition is applied, classification measures may be sufficient. This is not the case for credit scoring

FIGURE 3-17a

Scoring Model Distribution

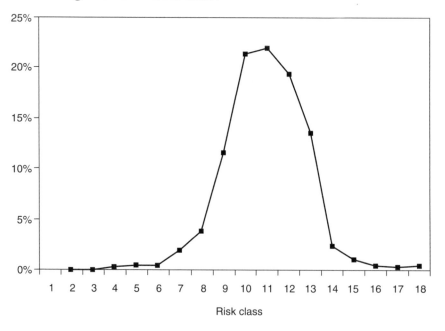

Risk class

where the assessment of the default risk of an obligor or a loan is associated with its pricing. The question is not how well a specific company is doing compared with some others, but what the probability is of this company defaulting over a given horizon and what would be the impact of this default on the profit of the bank.

Is classification worthless? The answer is no, because classification measures, and ROC in particular, give good insight into Type I and Type II errors. This piece of information matters for bankers and investors for several reasons, such as defining the default cutoff point or enabling them to compare Type I errors for different models—in other words, to assess the rank-ordering accuracy of different models.

Is classification sufficient? No again, because a credit scoring model with good rank-ordering accuracy can prove very imprecise in prediction and seriously damage the profit of the user. Classification measures should therefore be complemented by maximum likelihood or techniques including the utility function of the user.

FIGURE 3-17b

Standard & Poor's Rating Universe

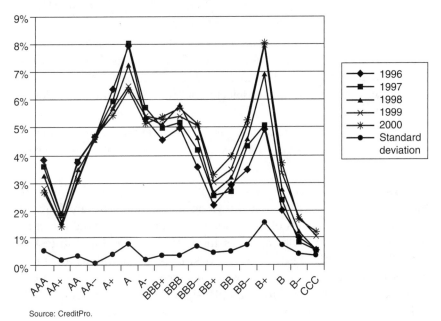

Source: CreditPro.

How to Select a Class of Models?

Fifteen years ago the level of sophistication of credit scoring models was fairly low. One would typically have hesitated between a logit model and a linear discriminant model. With the development of many new techniques and tools such as those reviewed in this chapter, the choice now becomes more complex.

Several factors are important to the choice of a particular class of model over another:

- *Performance*—the primary factor. A more complex model should provide significantly improved detection or classification of risky firms over a naïve rule. Defining classification or prediction as the goal will have an impact on the choice.

- *Data availability and quality.* Many models perform well in the laboratory but do not cope with practical difficulties such as missing values or outliers. A simpler but more robust model may be preferable to a state-of-the-art system on patchy data sets.[32]

+ *Understanding by users.* Users of the scoring models should understand perfectly how the model works and what drives the results. Otherwise they will not be able to spot systematic bias or to understand the limits of their model.

+ *The robustness of the model to new data.* Some models trained on a given data set will provide very different results if the data set is increased slightly. This instability should be avoided, as it may mean that the model is detecting local optima rather than global optima.

+ *The time required to calibrate* or *recalibrate a model.* This also matters, depending on what frequency the user wants to use to run the model.

It is always advisable not to trust a single model blindly but to run the estimations on the same data set using several models. Significant differences in the outcomes of the different methodologies should lead the user to reassess the performance of the preferred model and to test for potential systematic biases or model risk. Back-testing the results of the model is also very important. Frequently, scoring models will be calibrated on a growth period for example, significantly underestimating the risk of the scored universe in times of recession. Note that, as shown above, ROC or CAP measures will not necessarily detect this because the rank ordering of the model may remain satisfactory. The models should therefore be estimated on a sufficiently long history of data with as many different economic conditions as possible, and the user should use several performance measures based on both classification and prediction.

CONCLUSION

Default risk analysis is obviously the cornerstone of credit risk measurement and management. The quality of the quantitative tools used to perform creditworthiness assessments is critical in order to minimize model risk and to improve the performance of banks.

Being able to develop, update, and improve such quantitative tools is becoming a key requirement for banks, and as we saw in this chapter, there have been significant recent developments in the field of statistical pattern recognition. In addition to the current methodological race, banks are facing data issues. The quality of any system is indeed highly correlated with the value of the related input information. Optimizing and filtering the breadth of the information flow available for modeling is the second pillar for a predictive tool.

APPENDIX 3A

The Effect of Incomplete Information

Duffie and Lando (2001) stress the fact that structural models are based on accounting information. To investors, this information can be somewhat opaque and sometimes insufficient, as we have observed during 2002–2003 with Enron, Worldcom, Parmalat, and others. In addition, accounting practices lead to the release of data with a time lag and in a discrete way. For all these reasons, part of the information used as input in structural models is imperfect.

Duffie and Lando (2001) suggest that if the information available to investors were perfect, then observed credit spreads would be closer to theoretical ones, as predicted by the Merton models. However, as the information available in the financial markets is not complete, observed spreads exhibit significant differences (see Figure 3A-1).

FIGURE 3A-1

Credit Spreads and Information

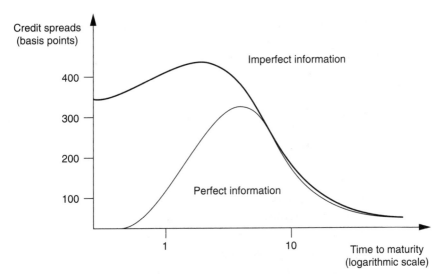

Source: Duffie and Lando (2001).

APPENDIX 3B

A Recipe for an Optimal Selection of Credit Factors in a Linear Logit Scoring Model with Overfitting Regularization

1. Gather a large data set of companies, including the companies' identifier, the date of financial statements, the date of default if applicable, financial statements, and nonfinancial quantitative information.

2. Transform the data in order to treat outliers appropriately.

3. Build as many credit factors as possible (from 50 to 100). Favor ratios that make economic sense.

4. Do a first cut of credit factors by eliminating, one by one, ratios that contribute the least to the predictive power (GMP) or the accuracy (Gini coefficient) of the 100-factor model. Select the best 20 to 30 factors.

5. Reduce the number of credit factors again. The objective is to limit the list to only 10 factors, taking into consideration their correlation, economic sense, and monotonicity at the same time. The process is as follows:

    a. Fit a model based on the best 20 to 30 credit factors, and calculate the PDs for each observation.

    b. Group and order the selected ratios into seven main categories:
    - Leverage
    - Asset utilization
    - Profitability
    - Liquidity
    - Size
    - Efficiency
    - Structure of balance sheet

    c. At the end of the selection process, check to be sure that there are credit factors in at least five different categories.

6. Based on the analysis of monotonicity and correlation, reduce the number of factors to 10 by eliminating nonmonotonic or nonsensical credit factors and those that are highly correlated to others.

7. Run the new model with the 10 factors using the whole sample of transformed factors, and compare with the previous using both GMP and Gini.

8. Review the signs of the weights for each credit factor, and check for economic nonsensicality.

Key Empirical Considerations about Performance Assessment

Screening in three directions should be performed prior to any formal performance assessment: *data issues, discriminability,* and *stability.*

DATA ISSUES

Before looking at sophisticated measurement formulas for the performance of a model, it is very important to assess the quality of the underlying data. Several criteria have to be looked at and reviewed carefully. Four are crucial:

- Use of a large data set
- Availability of a sufficiently high number of defaulted companies
- Presence of a limited number of missing values among selected credit factors
- Recourse to a transparent and "noninvasive" procedure regarding the elimination of outliers

PRACTICAL DISCRIMINABILITY

This concept refers to how well a scoring system classifies unseen data. Practically, the main issue is to maximize the divergence or separation between categories such as default/nondefault. The main problem is to obtain an error rate independent from the set on which it is calculated.[33] The error rate will tend to differ when calculated on a training set or a testing set.[34] There are four common types of procedures for deriving error rates:

+ *The holdout estimate method.* The sample is split in two exclusive sets. The training set is used for training (minimization of in-sample error), and the testing set is used for performance calculation (calculation of out-of-sample error). This estimate is pessimistically biased: It will typically overestimate the true level of error, as shown in Figure 3C-1. In this respect the size of the training set is important to reduce the bias. The speed of convergence will typically vary with the kind of scoring model used. Defining the appropriateness of a scoring model like a logit, rather than any others such as a probit or a k-nearest neighbor, will depend on the highest obtained speed of convergence, given the fixed amount of data available.

+ *The n-fold cross-validation technique.* This consists of splitting the sample in n sets. The training is performed on $n - 1$, and the testing is performed on the remaining one. This is repeated as each set is withheld in turn.

+ *The jackknife.* This procedure is used to reduce the bias of the apparent error rate.[35]

FIGURE 3C-1

In-Sample and Out-of-Sample Performance versus Sample Size

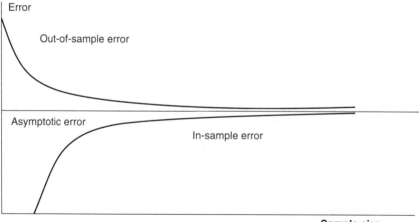

♦ *The bootstrap technique.*[36] This type of procedure provides nonparametric estimates of the bias and variance of the error rate estimator, thanks to new sets of observation generated by the technique. Bootstrap estimates can display a lower variance than other methods.

Golfarelli, Maio, and Maltoni (1997) consider a reject rate corresponding to a classification made with a confidence level that is too low. The classifier is generally not doing very well when the observed case falls close to the decision-rule boundary, the region where the two classes overlap. Therefore, instead of assigning the case to one of the categories, introducing a reject option reduces the error rate. The larger the reject rate, the smaller the error rate. A good way to define an optimal reject rate is to consider the trade-off, and related costs, between reject and incorrect decision.

STABILITY

This concept is related to optimization. When a user develops a model, either parametric or nonparametric, she will try to obtain unique optimal results, independent from the data set on which it is used.

♦ For parametric models, this means selecting the most meaningful classes or credit factors. This means also allocating optimal weights to the selected factors. Being able to reach a clear, unique optimal result—and not just a local optimal solution—is a very important issue that requires specific testing.

♦ For parametric and nonparametric models, this means reviewing carefully the treatment and the impact of outliers on the model. Very straightforward methods exist, such as removing all extreme data that are outside the homogeneous sample, i.e., at a distance of more than two or three times the standard deviation.[37] Another technique, called "winsorisation," consists of bringing back extreme values at a defined level mentioned above. More sophisticated mathematical methods, using the properties of wavelets, have recently been developed. They seem to apply more to large time series at the moment, but they could be used in a cross-sectional way. See Struzik and Siebes (2002).

A P P E N D I X   3 D

Incorporating Costs of Misclassification

We have seen that Bayes' rule for classification allocated the same cost to Type I and Type II errors. An observation x will be assigned to class ω_1 (good firm) if

$$\frac{p(x \mid \omega_1)}{p(x \mid \omega_2)} > \frac{p(\omega_2)}{p(\omega_1)}$$

and to ω_2 (bad firms) otherwise.

Figure 3-15 showed how the minimum-loss point could be found— as the point at which the ROC curve is tangential to the iso-loss line with slope $p(\omega_2) / p(\omega_1)$.

ROC is also able to deal with asymmetric misclassification costs. The classification rule is changed to

$$\frac{p(x \mid \omega_1)}{p(x \mid \omega_2)} > \frac{c_{21}p(\omega_2)}{c_{12}p(\omega_1)}$$

where c_{ij} is the cost of assigning x to ω_j when it is in ω_i. In the case of a credit risk model, c_{12} (the cost of not detecting a defaulting firm) is likely to be much higher than c_{21} (the cost of wrongly classifying a good firm in the bad category).

The equation of the iso-loss line is given by $L = c_{21} p(\omega_2) E_{II} + c_{12} p(\omega_1) E_I$, where $p(\omega_i)$ corresponds to the ex ante belief. The slope of the iso-loss curves is now

$$\frac{c_{21}p(\omega_2)}{c_{12}p(\omega_1)}$$

The minimum-loss solution is still the point at which the ROC curve and one of the iso-loss lines are tangential.[38] Figure 3D-1 illustrates how the move from weighting Type I and Type II errors equally to different costs changes the minimum-loss point.

FIGURE 3D-1

Minimum-Loss Points When Costs Change

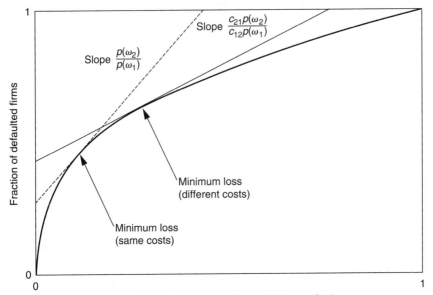

Fraction of all firms (from riskiest to safest)

A PRACTICAL EXAMPLE ABOUT THE IMPORTANCE OF MISCLASSIFICATION COSTS

Let us consider two travelers with different utility functions using the same airline company. They have to go through the same security control process. This security control process corresponds to the classifier and has to select genuine travelers from criminals.

We consider four models or classifiers:

+ Model M1 is performing well in terms of minimum error: low Type I error and low Type II error.

+ Model M2 is not performing well: high Type I error and high Type II error.

+ Model M3 has mixed performance: high Type I error and low Type II error.

✦ Model M4 also has mixed performance: low Type I error and high Type II error.

The security systems have a trade-off between speed of processing (i.e., reducing the length of time the passengers will have to wait before boarding) and accuracy in selection (spotting all potential weapons). Type I error corresponds to letting potential criminals through, while Type II error is stopping genuine tourists for further investigation. Models with high Type I errors (M2 and M3) will be unsafe, and models with high Type II errors (M2 and M4) will induce large delays.

The two passengers we consider are one tourist and one patient going for an urgent heart operation. Table 3D-1 summarizes the payoffs for the two passengers.

From this example we see that it is very difficult to evaluate the performance of the four models independently from the requirement of the users. Obviously M1 will be preferred by both travelers, and M2 will be the least popular choice. However, the choice between M3 and M4 which corresponds to the choice between more Type I errors and more Type II errors depends on the utility of the user.

This shows that ROC curves will not provide sufficient information to qualify fully the performance of any model. The characteristics (cost-benefit) of the user of the models have to be expressed and integrated into the performance measurement.

TABLE 3D-1

	Models			
	M1	**M2**	**M3**	**M4**
	Processing is fast	*Processing is slow*	*Processing is fast*	*Processing is slow*
Payoff for the tourist	He catches his flight and is safe	He misses his flight and may be at risk	He catches his flight and may be at risk. **It is not worth it.**	He misses his flight
Payoff for the patient	He catches his flight and is safe	He misses his flight and may be at risk	He catches his flight but may be at risk. **It is worth it.**	He misses his flight

CHAPTER 4

Loss Given Default

The second key input in a credit risk analysis, besides the probability of default, is the recovery rate, or loss given default (defined as 1 minus the recovery rate). The recovery rate corresponds to the amount of money, expressed as a percentage of the par amount that can be recovered on defaulted loans or bonds. Unlike the probability of default, which typically summarizes the creditworthiness of a *company*, the recovery rate is most of the time specifically defined at a *facility* level.

While probabilities of default have received considerable attention over the past 20 years as we have seen earlier, the issue of recoveries remains to a large extent unexplored, especially outside the United States. And for many asset classes for which a secondary market does not exist, information is not easily available even in the United States. The Basel II banking regulation emphasizes loss given default (LGD) and provides strong incentives for a more accurate measurement of recoveries (see Appendix 4D).

The main difference between probabilities of default and loss given default is that LGD is, as we will see, better represented by a distribution than by a single figure. Uncertainty about recovery depends not only on quantifiable facts, but also on more fuzzy factors such as the bargaining power of debtors and creditors. We will therefore focus on the microeconomics of recovery whenever required.

The objective of this chapter is to review the major issues about recovery, including core drivers such as the level of seniority of underlying loans or constraints like local jurisdiction. The chapter is organized as follows. We first introduce some definitions related to default and LGD. We then review what measures of recovery are available and which are appropriate for use in a portfolio credit risk model. Next we identify the key determinants of loss given default: the seniority of the instrument, the industry of the issuer, the business cycle, the availability of collateral or guarantees, the bargaining power of debt holders, and the jurisdiction of the issue. We show some empirical findings that have been reported on various data sets and highlight the impact these factors have on realized recovery. We also discuss a potential link between recovery rates and probabilities of default that has recently been documented in the literature and may have a significant bearing on credit losses. In addition, we explain how to extract recovery information in the case of nontraded debt.

Next we illustrate through an example the importance of taking into consideration the random nature of recoveries and show how failure to do so may lead to a substantial underestimation of extreme losses in a bond portfolio. Most credit risk portfolio models incorporate such stochastic recoveries. They typically assume that LGD follows a parametric distribution and calibrate it on the empirical mean and variance of observed recovery rates. We then review this procedure and provide an alternative (nonparametric) way to estimate loss distributions for many industrial sectors. A new parametric model capturing the entire distribution of recoveries is also presented.

The final part of this chapter is devoted to extracting recovery rates from the prices of financial instruments.

SOME DEFINITIONS

In a simple setup such as the Merton (1974) model, for instance, bond recovery is fully determined by the value of the firm. The issuer defaults if the value of the firm is below the principal of the debt at maturity. In that case bondholders seize the entire value of the firm (the recovery) and equity holders are left with nothing. This analytical framework is intuitively appealing but too simplistic to estimate recovery rates in practice. It makes two key underlying assumptions about the recovery process:

◆ First the absolute priority rule[1] holds; i.e., debt has priority over equity and senior debt over subordinated.

◆ Second there are no bankruptcy or liquidation costs.

Practically speaking, another limitation of the Merton approach is that it only applies to quoted companies (since the value of the firm is estimated from the equity price). Most defaults on a bank's book, however, occur within middle-market companies where public information is limited. We will see later that the recovery process is not the same for bank loans and traded bonds. We first focus on nonperforming *loans*, and then on nonperforming *bonds*.

Bank Loans

Bank loans are often granted under nonstandard terms. First the bank will usually perform a careful review of the creditworthiness of the firm. Then a negotiation will occur regarding the optimal way to mitigate risks via covenants and collateral. In order to make accurate decisions, the bank must have a good understanding of the firm and will have to perform active ongoing monitoring on a regular basis. A bank will therefore often be in a position to anticipate any significant difficulty faced by the firm. When such difficulties are observed, the relationship banker within the branch will transfer the case to a more centralized rescue unit dealing with difficult situations. The firm is placed in "intensive care."

Before being formally in default, a company facing difficulties with its debt is said to be in distress. Distress can materialize in specific events, such as a breach in covenants. The state of distress can also be derived from the subjective appreciation of the banker based, for example, on a breach of overdraft limits or on deteriorating balance sheet ratios. In some cases a distressed company can be rescued through a renegotiation of debt with its creditors. In other cases distress may be followed by a default of payment. The bank may not always be in a position to observe a formal state of distress, and default sometimes can occur directly without any such intermediate phase.

There is still much uncertainty in the financial community about what default should correspond to. In particular, a default event is not always defined in the same way by all stakeholders:

- The market definition for default is related to financial instruments. It corresponds to principal or interest past due.
- The Basel II definition considers a default event based on various alternative options such as past due 90 days on financial instruments or provisioning. It can also be based on a judgmental assessment of a firm by the bank.
- The legal definition is linked with the bankruptcy of the firm. It will typically depend on the legislation in various countries.

The difficulty in grasping default may arise because of these definition issues. More importantly it comes from the fact that a default is not the logical consequence of a unique, well-defined process. It can derive from many reasons such as a sudden and unexpected shock to a company or a failed negotiation between the entrepreneur of a distressed firm and his creditors.

All stakeholders in the distressed firm may not share the same interests either and may not be willing to trigger default at the same time. For example, an entrepreneur will try to run his company as long as possible, retaining control of the firm. The state may wait and face a high level of unpaid taxes to avoid unemployment. Trade creditors may try to avoid triggering default, knowing that their expected recovery rate will be low, as trade creditors are typically junior to banks and to the state. Bankers, on the other hand, may decide to force the firm quickly into liquidation in order to maximize their recovery on secured loans. For banks the optimal default point could then be the date when the value of collateral equals the value of loans plus the costs of realization.

The steps from default to bankruptcy and liquidation also depend very much on the insolvency legislation enacted in each country. We will review the case of the United States, United Kingdom, France, and Germany later in this chapter.

The general context of bank loan insolvency can be summarized in the graph in Figure 4-1. This graph makes it clear that not all distressed companies become defaulting companies and that not all defaulting companies go into liquidation. We will see later in the chapter that in the United Kingdom more than 50 percent of distressed companies do not go into formal bankruptcy. In Figure 4-1, only 25 percent of the companies do so.

In addition to resulting from a delicate assessment, the state of default on bank loans may not lead to a simple and straightforward recovery process.

FIGURE 4-1

Example of the Distress/Default Process*

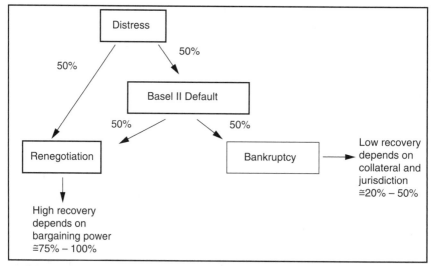

*Figures are for illustrative purposes.

As we saw in Chapter 1, banks generally face contractual incompleteness. The nature of lending contracts and the existence of collateral and guarantees have a significant impact on the behavior of banks and on loan recovery rates. The effective recovery process may deviate from efficiency.

In the literature, four factors are usually considered that may lead to inefficient behaviors and to suboptimal loan recovery rates:

+ The debt structure of the firm itself can be a driver of inefficiencies. In particular, there is a risk of "creditors' run" in the absence of creditors' coordination.

+ The bargaining power of the debtor who tries to extract concessions from creditors can result in inefficient behaviors.

+ The high level of seniority or the recourse to excessive control rights by the main creditor can damage a firm. Based on his dominant position, such a creditor may reduce his monitoring of the firm. This behavior is often called "lazy banking"[2] and will lead to both premature and too frequent bankruptcies.

+ Bank control of firms can damage the performance of firms. This issue is often related to the particular phenomenon of "house banks."

These types of behaviors have been extensively described[3] and modeled from a theoretical standpoint, but seldom tested empirically. Most empirical studies in the United States consider a sample of large quoted companies or are based on public records at bankruptcy level only. The most significant studies we have come across on this topic have recently been produced on a U.K.[4] and on a German sample[5] based on banks' private information. The studies conclude that in these countries none of the four suboptimal behaviors described above has been observed empirically with statistical significance.

Based on our discussion so far, it is clear that any attempt to build a model simulating recovery rates for bank loans will have to be based on at least four major drivers:

+ A very clear definition of the default event

+ The bank's behavior in terms of debt renegotiation with debtors, which will be country-specific

+ The quality of collateral attached to loans

+ The comparative level of seniority of the bank loans vis-à-vis state liabilities, trade credit, etc.

Traded Bonds

In LGD studies, bonds are frequently classified in terms of seniority and allocated collateral. Seniority captures the order of priority of claimants over the assets of the defaulted firm, while collateralization measures the allocation of specific assets as guarantees for the facility in case of default. Table 4-1 summarizes the possible combinations of seniority and collateral levels. Most firms not only will have traded bonds on their balance sheet, but also will have bank loans. Bank loans are often highly collateralized and with high priority.

Market participants are assumed to have similar levels of information about bonds. The monitoring of the quality of bonds is performed both by investors and by rating agencies. The setup described in the previous subsection, where banks can adopt various definitions of default, no longer applies, and a default event is much more formalized, usually corresponding to missed payment.

Recent controversies about credit default swap contracts and the related definition of default events come, however, as a reminder that market participants sometimes still disagree on a common definition (see Chapter 9).

The occurrence of default events itself depends on insolvency regulation and related contractual procedures. The dependence of the recovery rate of defaulted bonds will be discussed further in the chapter. For instance, the debtor-friendly option to file for Chapter 11 in the United States, without having to prove insolvency, may induce different behaviors from those observed in Europe. As a consequence, default and recovery rates will be related, and both depend on legislative issues. This impact of the insolvency regime on both default time and recovery procedures will make bond recovery rates country-specific.[6] Furthermore the

TABLE 4-1

Collateral and Priority Order

Pecking Order	Collateral		
	Secured	Unsecured	Subordinated
Senior	✔	✔	✔
	-	-	✔
Junior	-	-	✔

existence or otherwise of deep and liquid markets for nonperforming bonds, i.e., the existence of buyers such as "vulture funds," will have a significant bearing on recovery rates in various countries.

Even at a country level, controversy exists over state mandatory procedures[7] opposed to private efficient contracts. Franks and Torous (1994), for example, have compared the result of informal private debt renegotiation in the United States with formal procedures such as Chapter 11 and liquidation under Chapter 7. Their finding is that informal reorganization leads to lower costs and higher recovery rates. What is more important is that state mandatory procedures lead to larger deviations from absolute priority, in particular in favor of shareholders and unsecured creditors.

WHAT MEASURE OF RECOVERY SHOULD ONE USE?

There are two commonly used measures of the level of recovery in default: the ultimate recovery—which is the amount that the debt holder will eventually recover after the default is settled[8] —and the price of debt just after default. Both have their advantages and drawbacks. In all the discussion below, LGDs and recovery rates are expressed as a fraction of the par amount of the loan or bond.

The *post-default price* is only available for the fraction of debt that is traded and for which a distressed debt market exists. Its scope is therefore very limited in some instances (often restricted to bonds). When available, the post-default price has the advantage of providing a measure of recovery shortly after the default event.

Measuring *ultimate recoveries,* on the other hand, is often very hard when bankruptcy claims are not settled in cash but in terms of securities (substitute debt, equity, or various assets) with illiquid or no secondary market. This is, however, the only way to measure recovery rates for illiquid bank loans. Ultimate recoveries are usually discounted to reflect the time value of money.

Bahar and Brand (1998) have carried out an extensive study on over 500 recoveries on U.S. bonds. They compare the price of the defaulted securities immediately after default[9] with the price just prior to emergence from default or liquidation. Recoveries for senior bonds tend to be much higher in absolute terms at emergence than just after default. Bahar and Brand (1998) report an average time between default and emergence or liquidation of 2.5 years, which raises the issue of the appropriate risk-adjusted discounting.

Table 4-2 displays recent comparative figures about ultimate versus trading price recovery. It shows that there is, on average, some financial incentive to go through the recovery process internally. The level of internal rate of return (IRR, around 20 percent) is fairly high but the related standard deviation is over 60 percent. Thus both nonperforming loan trading and vulture fund activity are therefore high-return, high-risk businesses.

HISTORY AND DETERMINANTS OF RECOVERY RATES

Let us first take a broader look at average LGDs on rated bonds before focusing on the main determinants of recoveries.[10]

Historical Perspective

Figure 4-2 is a graph of mean recovery rates for U.S. defaulted bonds from 1982 to 1999. The recovery rates are market-based prices immediately after default. The thin solid line is obtained as the simple average of the recoveries of all bonds available in the database in a given year, irrespective of their industry and seniority. The dashed line corrects for the potential bias generated by the changes in the composition of each year's sample in terms of number of events per industry and per seniority level.

This adjusted average is calculated as follows. We regress the entire sample on dummy variables representing seniority levels and industries. We then calculate each year's average recovery as the standard mean

TABLE 4-2

Recoveries at Emergence from Default (Ultimate) and Just after Default (Trading)

1988–3Q 2002	Trading Price Recovery	Nominal Ultimate Recovery	Internal Rate of Return
Bank debt	60.6%	88.9%	20.0%
Senior secured notes	50.2%	76.5%	20.5%
Senior unsecured notes	37.9%	54.9%	23.0%
Senior suborndinated notes	30.2%	38.2%	7.7%

Source: Standard & Poor's LossStats Database: 1975 defaulted loans and bond issues that defaulted between 1987 and 2002. Standard & Poor's Trading Price Database: 758 defaulted loans and bond issues that defaulted between 1988 and 3Q 2002.

FIGURE 4-2

U.S. Historical Average Recovery Rate

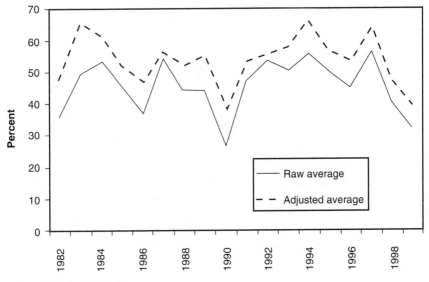

Source: Standard & Poor's data.

adjusted for the industry and seniority effects. The reported average corresponds to the average recovery on a senior unsecured bond in the energy & natural resources sector. Parameter values for the dummy variables representing each industry and seniority are provided in Table 4-3. They can be interpreted as the average difference in recovery rate in a given seniority level and industry compared with a senior unsecured bond of the energy & natural resources industry. For example, a senior secured bond in the utility sector will have an average recovery 16.9 percent (= 15.6 percent + 1.3 percent) higher than that of a senior unsecured bond of the energy & natural resources industry.

In the United States the mean value of recovery rates has not exhibited any significant long-term trend, though Figure 4-2 shows obvious recovery cycles. For the period 1900–1943, Hickman (1958) reports a through-the-cycle average of 40 percent of par, with more precisely 43 percent for firms rated as investment grade 5 years prior to default and 35 percent for others. Interestingly, the 1982–1999 data plotted in Figure 4-2 displays a very similar through-the-cycle average of 42 percent. The standard deviation around this central indication is nonetheless quite large, with data ranging in [25 percent, 65 percent].

TABLE 4-3

Industry and Seniority Effects

	Coefficients (%)	t-Stat
Intercept	53.1	15.8
Utility	15.6	3.4
Insurance and real estate	−7.7	−1.5
Telecommunications	−25.0	−3.8
Transportation	−12.8	−2.7
Financial institutions	−19.2	−3.4
Health care/chemicals	−8.4	−1.4
High technology/computers/office equipment	3.4	0.5
Aerospace/automotive/capital goods	−5.5	−1.4
Forest and building products/homebuilders	−5.7	−1.2
Consumer/service sector	−9.1	−2.6
Leisure time/media	−2.9	−0.8
Senior secured	1.3	0.4
Junior	−12.0	−4.9
Junior subordinated	−12.5	−4.9

Impact of Seniority

For traded debt, seniority is one of the key determinants of the level of recovery. Table 4-4 gathers average recovery rates per broad seniority class using S&P's (1988–2002) and Moody's (1977–1998) databases. Results from these studies are broadly comparable.

Average figures confirm the intuitive relationship between recovery rates and the level of seniority. We can also observe from Table 4-4 that recovery rates are highly volatile, as shown by their large standard deviation. We will show later that taking this into consideration is critical in capturing the full extent of potential losses due to LGD uncertainty.

Keisman and Van de Castle (1999) focus on a more continuous measure of seniority called the debt cushion.[11] The debt cushion expresses in a synthetic way the impact of the debt structure of the firm on the level of recovery associated with a bond. The more debt is junior to a given bond, the higher the recovery rate on this bond. In fact, instead of looking at the relative position of the bond in the pecking order, the debt cushion measure focuses more on the amount of debt that is ranked junior to the

TABLE 4-4

Recovery per Seniority

The 1988–2002 Period

Seniority Class	Mean Recovery	Std. Dev.	Observations
Bank debt	81.0%	29.7%	678
Bank secured notes	66.6%	33.0%	218
Bank unsecured notes	46.4%	36.3%	367
Senior subordinated notes	33.3%	33.6%	327
Subordinated notes	31.2%	35.1%	343
Junior subordinated notes	22.6%	34.0%	42

Source: Standard & Poor's LossStats Database.

The 1998–2002 Stress Period

Seniority Class	Mean Recovery	Std. Dev.	Observations
Bank debt	74.1%	32.4%	331
Bank secured notes	45.8%	36.5%	42
Bank unsecured notes	36.8%	35.1%	198
Senior subordinated notes	21.3%	30.8%	116
Subordinated notes	15.0%	24.7%	55
Junior subordinated notes	2.5%	4.1%	4

Source: Standard & Poor's LossStats Database.

1977–1998

Seniority Class	Mean (%)	Std. Dev. (%)
Bank loan	70.26	21.33
Senior secured	55.15	24.31
Senior unsecured	51.31	26.30
Senior subordinated	39.05	24.39
Subordinated	31.66	20.58
Junior subordinated	20.39	15.36

Source: Keenan, Hamilton, and Berthault (2000).

bond. For U.S. leveraged loans, Keisman and Van de Castle (1999) show that when the debt cushion is 75 percent or more, then 89 percent of loans have a present value of recoveries of over 90 percent. And when the debt cushion is under 20 percent, 40 percent of loans show a present value of recoveries of under 60 percent.

The concept of seniority with clearly defined layers of debt being repaid in strict order is simplistic for most firms. In many countries most corporates raise their capital from banks rather than in the markets. There are therefore multiple commitments from a corporate to repay many creditors with the same seniority. This blurs further the assessment of potential recovery rates. We will return to recoveries of bank loans later in the chapter.

Impact of Industry

Recovery rates are ultimately driven by the value of assets that can be seized in case of default. The value of liquidated assets is in turn dependent on the industry of the issuer. Firms in some sectors (e.g., utilities) have large quantities of real assets that can be sold on the market, while other sectors are more labor-intensive and may see their workforce leave when the company enters into financial distress. Some industries such as European coal mining suffer from a structural lack of demand in their region or lack of competitiveness and therefore will command lower recovery rates.

Industry should thus intuitively be a determinant of recoveries. Segregating the effect of industry on recovery rates from that of collateral is, however, not easy. Most recent internal studies by Standard & Poor's Risk Solutions tend to show that the impact of industries on recovery is overstated. According to these studies, collateral and the balance sheet structure are the primary drivers of recovery. These factors are intimately linked to industry sectors. For instance, services rely extensively on immaterial investments; they typically offer weaker collateral than utilities or heavy industry. In the remainder of this section, we will report results on the impact of industry on recoveries. The studies mentioned hereafter do not take into consideration collateral or balance sheet structure. What may appear as an industry effect may actually reflect differences in collateral quality offered by firms in various industries.

The most extensive recovery study to date has been carried out by Altman and Kishore (1996). They calculate the mean and standard deviation of recovery rates per industry and report very large variations across industries and within a given industry. Not surprisingly (see Table 4-5), public utilities come at the top of mean recoveries. This result has been reported in many other studies about recovery rates and is also one of our findings, discussed a little later in this chapter.

Izvorski (1997) identifies three characteristics as the most important factors in industry differences: physical asset obsolescence, industry growth, and industry concentration. More competitive industries (as measured by higher Herfindahl index H^{12}) are associated with stronger recoveries. Assets that can be readily reused by another party have higher liquidation values and help increase recovery rates.

We will come back to industry differences later when we consider the entire distribution of recovery rates on another data set. Once again, however, note in Table 4-5 the very large variability of recovery rates, with standard deviations in the region of 20 percent as in previous tables.

To give a practical example and illustrate the dependence of LGD on industries and on the business cycle, let us quote a few sentences extracted from the Dow Jones News wire:

> In late December, the court had authorized Winstar to sell most of its operating assets to IDT Corp. (IDT) for about $42.5 million. When Winstar filed for Chapter 11 on April 18, 2001, it listed assets of $4.98 billion and debts of $5 billion.

TABLE 4-5

Recoveries per Industry

Industry	Mean (%)	Std. Dev. (%)
Public utilities	70.47	19.46
Chemicals, ...	62.73	27.10
Machinery, ...	48.74	20.13
Services	46.23	25.03
Food	45.28	21.67
Wholesale and retail	44.00	22.14
Divers. manufacturing	42.29	24.98
Casino, hotel, ...	40.15	25.66
Building material, ...	38.76	22.86
Transportation	38.42	27.98
Communication	37.08	20.79
Financial institutions	35.69	25.72
Mining and petroleum	33.02	18.01
Lodging, hospitals, ...	26.49	22.65

Source: Altman and Kishore (1996).

"With telecom, Internet, even bio-genetics firms, you either have a lot of value or none, but you don't have any in between" said Martin Zohn, a bankruptcy attorney with Proskauer Rose LLP. "When many of these companies failed, they failed in a big way."

And it is not just Winstar, Net2000 Communications Inc., Zephion Networks Inc., eGlobe Inc., and others all turned to Chapter 7 after either selling the bulk of their assets or finding virtually no interest for them.

Zohn said the downturn in the economy is partly to blame. "Things have been in the bust phase long enough that it's tough to find buyers" he said. "That's the trend we'll be seeing until a lot of entrepreneurs come back." (Becker, 2002)

Impact of Macroeconomic and Business Cycle Factors

Recovery amounts are linked with the issuer's asset values and are therefore sensitive to changes in economic conditions. Allen and Saunders (2002) survey cyclical effects on the various components of credit risk. They point out that although intuition and some empirical evidence indicate that LGDs should be cyclical, this has not yet been incorporated in most commercial portfolio credit risk packages where LGDs are typically assumed to be exogenously determined.

GDP growth, industrial production, or any other proxy for the business cycle correlate strongly with average recovery rates. Interest rates such as the Treasury bill yield and Treasury yield curve should also impact directly on recovery rates as measured by prices just after default. Higher interest rates should lead *ceteris paribus* to lower discounted values of future recovered assets. Therefore one can expect higher interest rates to be associated with higher LGD.

Figure 4-3 is an example of the impact of macroeconomic factors on recovery rates. It uses data on bank recovery rates in Germany during the 1991 crisis and in the years before. A significant drop is observable in 1991, when short-term interest rates were dramatically increased to stem inflation.

The joint dependence of PDs and LGDs on the same macroeconomic variables can also explain the recently documented link between PDs and LGDs, which we now review in more detail.

The Link between Default and Recovery Rates

Probabilities of default and recovery rates have usually been treated as independent quantities in practitioners' credit risk models.[13] They are,

FIGURE 4-3

Gross Debt Recovery on Bank Lending (Germany)

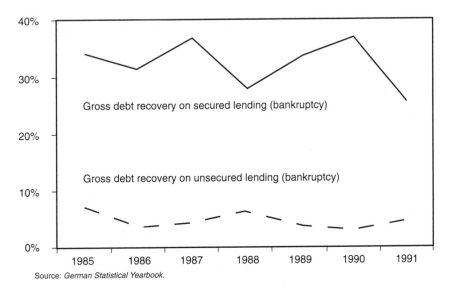

Source: *German Statistical Yearbook.*

however, influenced to some extent by the same macroeconomic variables, and it would seem natural to assume that they may exhibit some co-movement. The study by Altman, Resti, and Sironi (2001) documents the link between default and recovery rates and shows that high default rates tend historically to be associated with low recovery rates (see Figure 4-4[14]). This is quite intuitive: As the economy enters into recession, default rates increase. This leads to a large quantity of assets being liquidated on the market at a time when investment and demand are low. The liquidated assets therefore tend to fetch lower prices than during growth periods. Figure 4-5 illustrates this using S&P data. The recession period in 1990–1991 is clearly associated with higher than average probabilities of default and LGDs.

Frye (2000a, 2000b) models the recovery process in the context of a factor model of credit risk (see Chapters 5 and 6 for a more thorough description). Firms' asset values and bond LGDs are driven by a systematic factor that can serve as a proxy for the state of the economy and a firm-specific factor. The author finds evidence that the systematic factor affects both the asset value (which is inversely related to the probability of default) and the recovery rate positively and therefore that a negative relationship exists between PD and LGD.

FIGURE 4-4

Link between Average U.S. Default Rate and Recovery Rate

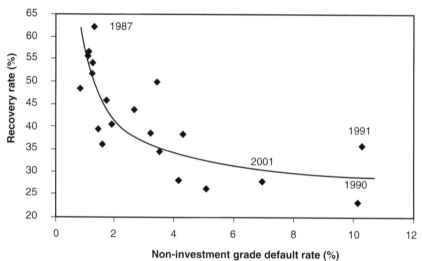

Source: Altman, Resti, and Sironi (2001).

FIGURE 4-5

U.S. Average LGD and Default Rate

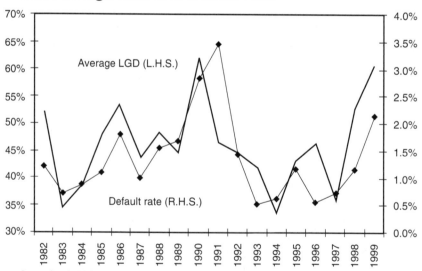

Source: Standard & Poor's.

At the industry level, although it is not documented in the above studies, this link should be even stronger. The default experience in the telecom industry in 2001 is a good example: A substantial number of firms in the telecom sector defaulted in that year due to overcapacity and falling growth regarding demand. The very large influx of telecom assets being liquidated further increased the imbalance between supply and demand and depressed the value of these assets in the market.

If we measure recovery rates as defaulted bond prices rather than the liquidation value of assets (as implied previously), we would obtain the same result (Figure 4-5). The distressed bond market is held by specialist funds, sometimes called "vulture capitalists." These funds have a limited ability to absorb larger than usual quantities of defaulted debt and therefore tend to offer lower prices for distressed debt in times of high default frequency.

At the portfolio level, taking into account a link between recovery rate and default frequency will have a significant impact on the amount of capital necessary to cover credit losses in a recession. This has not yet been recognized by most providers of the major credit risk portfolio models.

Impact of Collateral

Collateral consists of assets serving as a guarantee in case of default on a facility. Lenders often require collateral as a condition for granting a loan. Collateral comes typically in the form of portfolios of assets (stocks and bonds) and real estate. For smaller corporates, personal guarantees (i.e., the personal assets of the manager of the firm) are the most common form of collateral.[15]

Collateral, however, should not lead to complacency, as shown in Appendix 4C, for at least two reasons: It may have an adverse impact on bank monitoring, and the value of the collateral may drop when the economy enters a downturn and firms start defaulting in greater numbers.[16]

Frye (2000a) shows that the link between LGDs and PDs is partly due to the fact that the value of collateral falls in recessions, when probabilities of default are high. Recovery rates on collateralized facilities therefore decline as a result of the fall in the value of their collateral. This sends a clear message to "lazy banking" practices that may lead to monitoring heavily collateralized loans less tightly. The safety net provided by collateral may break at the very moment when it is most needed i.e., in an economic downturn. The still ongoing Japanese banking crisis and overuse of real estate collateral is a good example of such risk.

Collateral does not guarantee full recovery as shown on Table 4-6, built on the S&P-PMD LossStats data set of U.S. defaulted bonds from 1982 to 1999. Depending on the type of assets posted as collateral, recoveries can fluctuate substantially.

Jurisdiction

When defaults end up in bankruptcy, the recovery can be determined either by a court or by a private receiver or practitioner that was appointed by the main secured creditors. International differences in insolvency legislation are therefore key to understanding the differences in recovery rates and in times to recovery. Bankruptcy proceedings in the United States and United Kingdom typically take between 18 months and 3 years, while it is not infrequent to see them reach 10 years in continental Europe.

Kaiser (1996) explains that in all countries, irrespective of bankruptcy law, there are two main options: Either facilitate liquidation, or encourage reorganization of the distressed company. What will vary across countries is the weighting of these two general targets as well as their accessibility. Assessing the comparative efficiency of different codes is not easy. Obviously, the control of costs of financial distress is a common objective, but the way to achieve this goal remains open to debate: Should the system aim at maximizing the number of successfully reorganized firms whatever the cost for creditors, or should it aim at maximizing the creditors' recovery rate? We will see that the different approaches across countries tend to blend these objectives to various degrees.

Franks, Nyborg, and Torous (1996) analyze three insolvency codes, those of the United Kingdom, Germany, and the United States. The authors consider that efficiency should be measured at three stages in order to analyze the process of diffusion of information to stakeholders:

TABLE 4-6

The Value of Collateral

Collateral Type	Recovery, %
All assets or current assets	89.8
Most assets	54.0
Noncurrent assets	75.5
Capital stock	70.5
Second lien	58.8

Source: Derived from Keisman and Van de Castle (1999).

+ First, *ex ante* when the company is not yet in distress
+ Second, at the *interim* stage when all stakeholders have different information about the distressed firm and its future
+ Last, *ex post* when all stakeholders share the same information

They then set a list of key questions as the relevant criteria for a valuable comparison between different codes:

+ Does the code preserve promising enterprises while liquidating uneconomic ones?
+ Does it allow the firm to be reorganized or liquidated at minimum possible cost?
+ Does it permit innovations in debt contracts to improve the insolvency process?

And as a result of their conclusion, a fourth criterion (not mentioned initially) is worth adding:

+ Is the process generally speedy or lengthy?

No insolvency framework appears to dominate the others in all these respects. It explains why in the United States, the United Kingdom, Germany, and France, bankruptcy codes are revised roughly every 10 to 15 years in order to achieve marginal improvement.

A detailed table of the impact of insolvency regimes on recovery rates is provided in Appendix 4B.

Impact of Investors' Bargaining Power

In the case of multiple creditors, recovery will be the outcome of a bargaining process.

Let us first focus on the issue of private debt renegotiation versus public debt renegotiation. Public debt holders are less flexible than private ones. As a result, in the case of public debt no efficient renegotiation may be possible, leading to difficulties in turning around distressed firms. Gertner and Scharfstein (1991) show that, in the United States, even in the case where public debt can be renegotiated, investment inefficiencies still remain.

Considering the relationship between creditors and the debtor, we find that, in every country, there are prespecified rights called "control rights" that are used when a firm enters the insolvency process. These rights tend to create tensions among the different classes of creditors. Franks, Nyborg, and Torous (1996) show that these tensions appear in particular with secured creditors who may try to extract value at the expense of other creditors or the entrepreneur. Control rights, however, have some positive aspects: They provide incentives for banks to finance companies and projects by mitigating the banks' risk. In this respect, empirical studies[17] report evidence supporting the view that the right of creditors to dismiss the manager and to take over the firm as a going concern[18] or to extend the maturity of the debt in default plays a key role in facilitating the lending process by enforcing the repayment of debt.

In the wake of Myers (1977), Franks and Sanzhar (2002) investigate how financially distressed firms are able to raise significant amounts of equity without transferring the value of new projects financed by the new financing back to the existing debt holders (the debt overhang problem). In particular, they analyze, using a sample of 111 firms, how much debt forgiveness has been granted to distressed companies that have raised new equity. Surprisingly most of the companies in the sample have obtained no or little concession from creditors. It seems, however, that the level of net present value (NPV) of the going concern is an important criterion. Highly leveraged firms with low NPV could obtain concessions from banks, whereas firms with higher NPV typically would not.

From a practical standpoint, many default settlements occur outside courts of justice and are negotiated among the claim holders.[19] It is obvious that a bank holding a substantial share of the claims on the firm's assets and facing other much smaller claimants will have more bargaining power and will in many cases extract more value than dispersed investors. LGDs are impacted by the structures and rights of debt holders, which can only be assessed on a case-by-case basis and are in many instances difficult to determine.

RECOVERY ON NONTRADED DEBT
General Principles

Traded debt may only represent a small share of the total debt of a firm. In continental Europe, for example, corporate financing has traditionally been bank-based, and seniority issues therefore do not apply in such a clear-cut way as described in the previous section. Information about recovery, including informal renegotiation, is held within banks on a proprietary basis, and it is difficult to assess what the market price of liquidated assets would be. In most cases banks only have a rather imprecise view of recovery rates at the facility level. And some of them were more prone to track recovery at a client level before Basel II requirements, particularly when the jurisdiction allows cross-collateralization.

The estimation of recovery rates on bank loans is therefore more difficult than in the case of traded bonds. In rare cases a market value of defaulted loans can be obtained, and recovery rates can then be proxied by the market value of the distress debt market as above (see, e.g., the study on bank loan LGD by Carty, Gates, and Gupton, 2000).

However, most defaulted loans do not have a secondary market, and the only available measure will be ultimate recovery. A common formula for the nominal value of the ultimate recovery rate is

$$1 - \text{LGD} = \frac{R + M + S - C}{P + I}$$

where:

R = cash recovered from the borrower and security
M = instruments received whose market value can be estimated
S = security received in a reorganization
C = cost attributable to the facility
P = principal outstanding at the default date
I = interest owing but unpaid at the default date

This formula has an intuitive interpretation. The ultimate recovery rate is defined as the ratio of all value recovered in terms of cash or securities net of the costs to the nominal value of unpaid interest and principal.

This loss rate needs to be discounted in order to take into account the time value of money. There is no universally accepted rate to discount defaulted loans. One possibility is to use the original interest rate on the facility.

The Case of The United Kingdom

Franks and Sussman (2002) describe the experiences of distressed U.K. SMEs borrowing money from three major banks. The sample comprises 542 English firms.

They show that a distressed company will generally follow a two-step process. Step 1 is a rescue phase that is handled in a "business support unit" and lasts on average 7.5 months. Step 2 is a proper recovery period that is managed in the "debt recovery unit." This first observation shows us how difficult the identification of the Basel II default point is, as it is probably located at some time during the intensive care in the business support unit. The precise default event may not be obvious, and some banks may have different views about it, leading ultimately to different measured recovery rates.

Once a company has entered into a rescue process, there are four possible strategies for the bank:

+ Have the distressed firm repay its debt to its current bank and change bank.
+ Turn around the troubled company and return to the "good book."
+ Sell the company as a going concern.
+ Liquidate the bankrupt company.

Practically, the level of recovery will depend on the path followed by each company. In the United Kingdom, SME bank loans are highly collateralized, with about or more than 80 percent secured by both fixed and floating charges. This explains a high net recovery rate of around 75 percent in the case of liquidation or sale of the bankrupt company. But banks face high receivership costs (approximately one-fourth of proceeds). Interestingly, the incentive for banks either to follow a turnaround or to let companies go to another bank is higher as they normally obtain recovery close to 100 percent.

These figures as well as the average time to recovery, which is particularly short in the United Kingdom, show that banks experience a recovery rate above 50 percent and frequently between 70 percent and 85 percent, depending on the effective cut-off point retained by the bank in its understanding of the Basel II default definition. This level of recovery is particularly high and not necessarily representative of what occurs in various other countries.

THE IMPORTANCE OF STOCHASTIC RECOVERY RATES

We have seen that most empirical studies above report both the average and the standard deviation of the recovery rates. The large standard deviations observed in many cases are an indication of the importance of acknowledging the random nature of recovery rates. Figure 4-6 shows what a significant difference stochastic recovery rates can have on portfolio losses.[20]

We simulate a very granular portfolio of 3000 identical positions of $1 each with 3 percent pairwise correlation, 5 percent probability of default, and a mean recovery rate of 50 percent. In the first case we assume that the recovery rate is constant, while in the second case it is

FIGURE 4-6

Impact of Recovery Assumption on Credit VaR

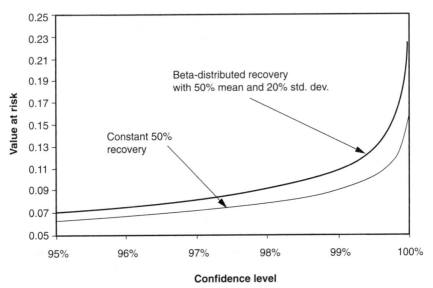

assumed to be beta-distributed (see the next section) with 20 percent standard deviation.[21] We then compute the credit values at risk for various levels of confidence from 95 to 99.9 percent. In this example, assume stochastic recovery rates increases the VaR by 11 percent at the 95 percent level and up to over 50 percent further in the tail.

Arvanitis, Browne, Gregory, and Martin (1998) perform a similar experiment on a swap portfolio and report an increase of 25 percent in economic capital when one includes stochastic recovery rates with reasonable parameter assumptions.

FITTING RECOVERY FUNCTIONS

Using the Beta Distribution

Most portfolio credit risk models, including Portfolio Manager, Portfolio Risk Tracker, and CreditMetrics, assume that the recovery rate follows a beta distribution.[22] This type of parametric distribution is very appealing, as it offers a lot of flexibility. It only requires the mean and the variance for calibration. However, as we will see later, the assumption of beta recovery distributions suffers from two major weaknesses:

◆ The models cannot cope with the point masses at 0 and 100 percent that can be observed when ultimate recoveries are considered.

◆ Bimodal distributions are beyond the scope of beta distributions but have been reported in empirical studies.

The probability density function of the beta distribution can be written as

$$f_{a,b}(x) = \frac{1}{\beta(a,b)} \, x^{a-1} (1-x)^{b-1} \, 1_{[0,1]}(x)$$

where $\beta(a,b)$ is the beta function, a and b are the two parameters of the distribution, and $1_{[0,1]}$ is the indicator function taking the value 1 if $x \in [0,1]$ and 0 otherwise. The latter term ensures that the support of the distribution lies in the interval between 0 and 1. The beta distribution is therefore particularly convenient for modeling recovery rates, which, by definition, share the same support. The parameters a and b enable the calibration of the mean and the variance of the distribution.

Figure 4-7 illustrates various shapes that can be obtained by specific choices of the parameters. One can observe that the beta distribution is quite versatile, as it can capture asymmetry, concavity, or convexity. The beta distribution collapses to the uniform when $a = b = 1$.

FIGURE 4-7

Various Shapes of the Beta Distribution

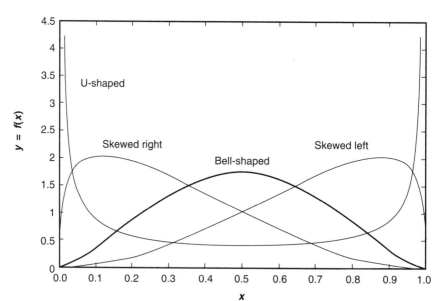

The beta distribution is calibrated in empirical work by using the empirical mean $\hat{m}$ and variance $\hat{v}$ of the recovery rates and using the following mapping between the first two moments of the distribution and its parameters:

$$\hat{b} = \frac{\hat{m}(\hat{m} - 1)^2}{\hat{v}} + \hat{m} - 1$$

$$\hat{a} = -\frac{\hat{b} \times \hat{m}}{\hat{m} - 1}$$

These are method-of-moments estimates of the true parameters a and b using the first two empirical moments. If data are available, we should rather use maximum likelihood, which yields asymptotically unbiased estimates with minimum variance.[23] In practice, however, using our sample described below, we did not find a significant difference between the results of the maximum-likelihood versus the method-of-moment estimators.

Kernel Modeling

Although the beta distribution is quite flexible as mentioned above, it does not necessarily ensure a good fit of the "true" recovery distribution. Figure 4-8 plots a bimodal distribution and the beta distribution with the same mean and variance. Obviously in that case[24] the fit is very poor, and assumption of a beta distribution will lead to a significant underestimation of the probability of a very low recovery.

To tackle this issue, nonparametric techniques have been proposed by Hu and Perraudin (2002) and Renault and Scaillet (2003). Appendix 4A reviews the basics of kernel estimation. Standard kernel estimators such as those described in the appendix typically use probability density functions such as the Gaussian p.d.f., which have nonbounded support. This implies that they assign probability to events outside the [0,1]; i.e., that they will lead to density estimates where negative recoveries as well as recoveries above 100 percent are possible. To be consistent with observed data, we therefore need to rely on nonstandard kernel estimation. One way to do this is to transform the recovery data so that they have $(-\infty, +\infty)$ support and then to perform the estimation using a standard kernel on the transformed data. We then apply the inverse transformation to obtain a [0,1] density as desired.

Renault and Scaillet (2003) use another approach that relies on beta kernels.[25] These estimators are very similar to those described in Appendix 4A but use the beta probability density function as the kernel.

FIGURE 4-8

Beta versus "True" Bimodal Distributions

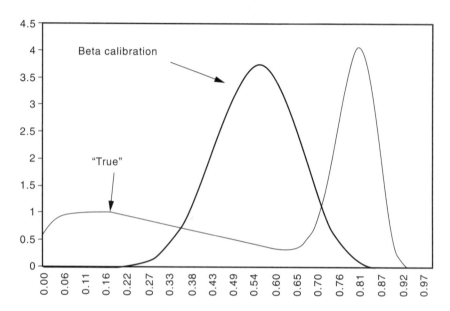

FIGURE 4-9

Beta, "True," and Kernel-Fitted Distributions

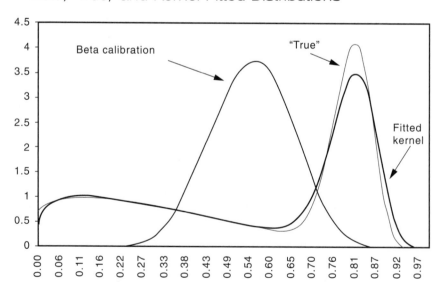

This ensures that the estimated density will lie in the appropriate [0,1] range and does not require transformation of the data. Returning to our example, we may now apply this nonparametric estimator to our bimodal distribution. The choice of bandwidth is crucial for kernel estimation. There is, however, no universally accepted method for selecting the appropriate window width. Using the rule of thumb $h = \hat{\sigma}T^{-2/5}$, where $\hat{\sigma}$ is the sample standard deviation and T is the number of observations, we obtain the result plotted in Figure 4-9. We can observe that although imperfect, the kernel estimate captures the general shape of the distribution much better than a simple calibration of the beta distribution.[26]

Figure 4-10 shows a group of recovery distributions fitted using a beta distribution and a beta kernel estimator. Figure 4-10a provides the fitted distributions per seniority (across all industries). We can observe that the distribution for senior secured recoveries is strongly skewed toward high levels, while that of junior subordinated bonds is concentrated on low rates of recoveries. Figure 4-10b and 4-10c reports similar results for all industries with no distinction of seniority. The data are extracted from the S&P-PMD database.

Conditional Recovery Modeling

Friedman and Sandow (2003) use an alternative parametric methodology to estimate the optimal[27] probability density functions for *ultimate* recovery, conditional on several explanatory variables. Their approach relies on relative entropy minimization over a broad class of models.

Let $p(r \mid x)$ denote the probability of recovering r conditional on a vector x of explanatory variables. The model can be conditioned on any meaningful variables but is most commonly implemented with:

♦ Collateral quality
♦ Debt below class
♦ Debt above class
♦ Aggregate default rate

The main novelty of Friedman and Sandow's (2003) approach is to allow for the computation of the entire distribution of the recovery (and not just the mean and confidence intervals) conditional on multiple factors.

Ultimate recoveries in the S&P LossStats database used in the paper are mostly between 0 and 120 percent, with a large concentration of occurrences at exactly 0 percent and 100 percent recovery (between 10 and 20 percent of observations). The authors tackle this issue by splitting the distribution into density functions for recoveries in the range [0, 120 percent] plus probability masses at LGD = 0 percent and LGD = 100 percent.

FIGURE 4-10*a*

Nonparametric and Beta-Fitted Distributions per Seniority

Source: Renault and Scaillet (2003).

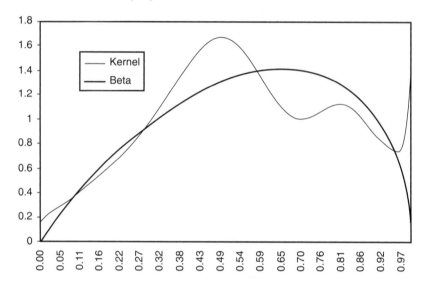

Senior secured

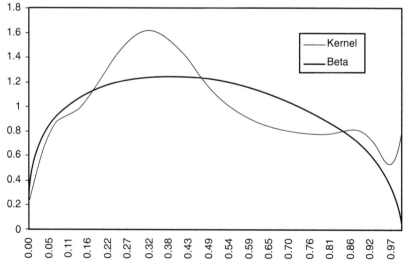

Senior unsecured

FIGURE 4-10a

(continued)

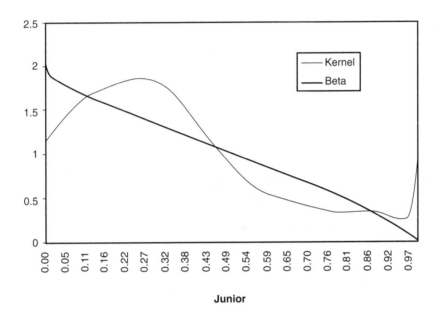

Junior

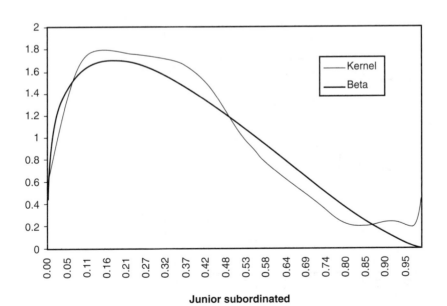

Junior subordinated

F I G U R E   4-10*b*

Nonparametric and Beta-Fitted Distributions per Industry

Source: Renault and Scaillet (2003).

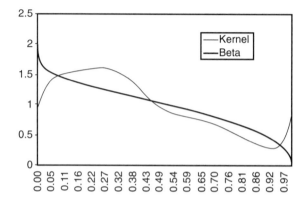

Insurance/real estate

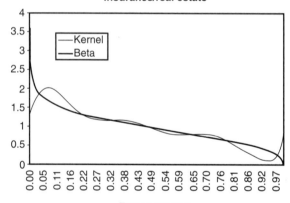

Transportation

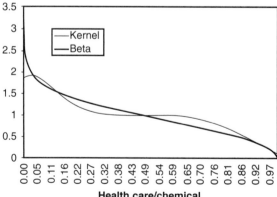

Health care/chemical

FIGURE 4-10*b*

(continued)

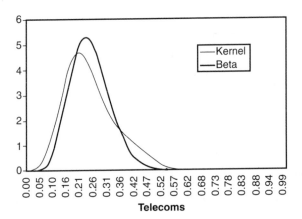

Telecoms

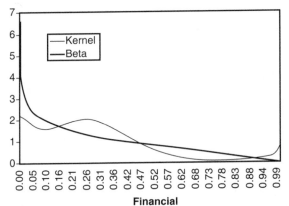

Financial

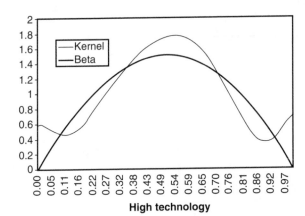

High technology

FIGURE 4-10c

Nonparametric and Beta-Fitted Distributions per Industry

Source: Renault and Scaillet (2003).

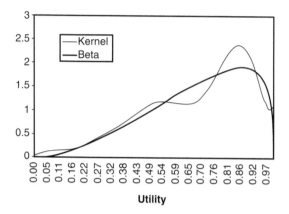

Utility

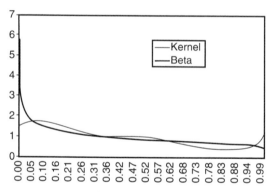

Forest/building

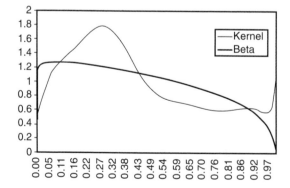

Leisure time/media

FIGURE 4-10c

(*continued*)

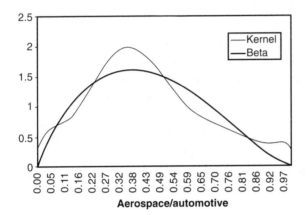

Aerospace/automotive

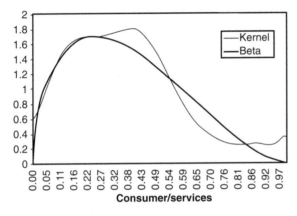

Consumer/services

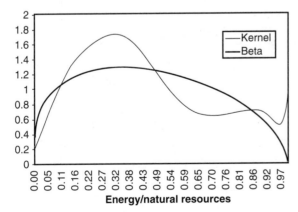

Energy/natural resources

The two steps of the modeling process are:

1. Choose the probability density function out of a very broad class that minimizes relative entropy with a chosen prior distribution.

2. Impose constraints on several moments (covariances between recoveries and explanatory factors). The model's moments are allowed to deviate from empirical moments, but a penalty is associated with the deviation. This prevents overfitting.

Figure 4-11 shows an example of the recovery (RGD = 1 − LGD) probability density function (ignoring the point masses) conditional on the collateral calculated on the U.S. LossStats database. Figure 4-12a shows average RGD and collateral quality. Figure 4.12b shows RGD and debt below class.

FIGURE 4-11

Distribution (PDF) of Recovery versus Collateral Quality

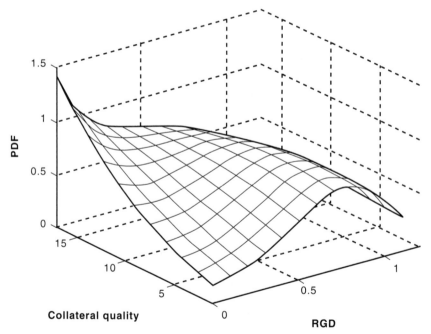

Source: Standard & Poor's.

F I G U R E   4-12a

Recovery versus Collateral Quality

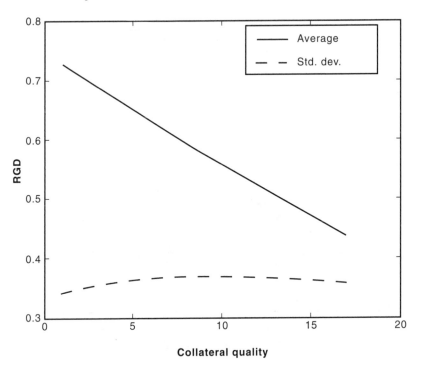

Collateral quality

Source: Standard & Poor's.

EXTRACTING RECOVERIES FROM SECURITY PRICES

Recovery assumptions in pricing models have often been driven by practical requirements rather than by the quest for accuracy. Many closed-form solutions for corporate bond or credit derivative prices are indeed obtained thanks to an appropriate choice of recovery function. Broadly speaking, three main types of assumptions have been made: the recovery of a (random) fraction of par, the recovery of a fraction of predefault value, and the recovery of a fraction of a Treasury bond with the same maturity of the corporate bond one is trying to price.

The latter assumption (fractional recovery of the Treasury bond) is particularly convenient. Assume we want to price at time t a defaultable zero-coupon bond with maturity T. In case of default, the bondholder recovers a fraction δ of an equivalent Treasury bond $B(.,.)$. Then the price of the bond is given by (see Chapter 8):

FIGURE 4-12b

Recovery versus Debt Below Class

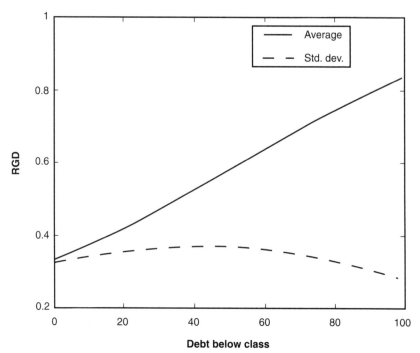

Debt below class

Source: Standard & Poor's.

$$P(t,T) = E_t^Q\left[\left(e^{-\int_t^\tau r_s ds}\right)\delta \times B(\tau,T)1_{\tau \le T} + \left(e^{-\int_t^T r_s ds}\right)1_{\tau > T}\right]$$

where τ is the default time and r is the instantaneous riskless rate. $t > T$ means that the issuer does not default during the life of the bond. Now the price at time τ of a T-maturity Treasury bond is

$$B(\tau,T) = E_\tau^Q\left[e^{-\int_\tau^T r_s ds}\right]$$

Combining the two equations and assuming that default probabilities and the riskless rate are independent, we obtain (using as q to denote the risk-neutral probability of default from t to T):

$$P(t,T) = E_t^Q\left[\left(e^{-\int_t^\tau r_s ds}\right)\delta \times \left(e^{-\int_\tau^T r_s ds}\right)1_{\tau > T} + \left(e^{-\int_\tau^T r_s ds}\right)1_{\tau > T}\right]$$

$$= E_t^Q\left[e^{-\int_t^T r_s ds}\right] \times E_t^Q\left[\delta 1_{\tau \le T} + 1_{\tau > T}\right]$$

$$= E_t^Q \left[e^{-\int_t^T r_s ds} \right] \times \left(1 - q \left(1 - \delta \right) \right)$$

$$= B(t,T) \times \left(1 - q \left(1 - \delta \right) \right)$$

The interpretation is quite intuitive: The risky bond is equal to the riskless bond minus the expected (risk-neutral discounted) loss. Other assumptions in terms of recovery rates will lead to different pricing formulas, some of which will not allow closed-form solutions to be obtained.

It is clear from the formula above that observing the price of risky and riskless bonds allows us to extract the loss rate but not its individual constituents: probability of default and recovery rate.

Jarrow (2001) proposes a way to separate the two components by introducing equity in the pricing model. For that purpose equity can be seen as the most subordinated debt with zero recovery in default. Pinning down the recovery rate for one security then enables us to extract the probability of default of the issuer and then back out the recovery rates for all the other instruments in the capital structure.

Bakshi, Madan, and Zhang (2001) test empirically what recovery assumptions can be supported by corporate bond price data in a reduced-form framework. They build flexible bond pricing models that can embed all three recovery assumptions mentioned above (fractional recovery of par, fractional recovery of Treasury, and fractional recovery of market value). On a sample of BBB-rated corporate bonds, they find that the assumption of recovery of a fraction of discounted face value (Treasury recovery assumption) has better empirical support than the other two specifications: lower average error and substantially lower standard deviation.

CONCLUSION

Loss given default is the second building block of a credit risk measurement system. Although as important as probabilities of default, LGDs have received less attention and are currently measured with less accuracy. Measuring LGDs is a difficult task, complicated by the fact that substantial parts of a firm's debt are not traded and that they are impacted by factors that are difficult to quantify, such as the bargaining power of creditors and debtors.

In addition, the off-the-shelf portfolio management tools that treat LGD as independent of PD will in our view be increasingly criticized as they may lead to an underestimation of credit risk at the portfolio level.

From a regulatory standpoint, it is interesting to note that the Basel II committee has chosen to retain little relief for some types of collateral (e.g., real estate).[28] Such an approach will enable one to play down the procyclical effect of correlated default and recovery rates when a downturn appears.

From a quantitative standpoint, a purely statistical approach to the distribution of LGDs is often adopted in practice. It consists of fitting a beta distribution using the empirical mean and variance of LGDs in a given industry and class of seniority. This simple approximation provides a good fit in many cases, as we have shown, but is limited to unimodal distributions. Nonparametric estimators can also be used to obtain a better calibration, but they require a complete data set of LGDs and not just their mean and variance.

APPENDIX 4A

An Introduction to Kernel Density Estimation

In this appendix we review the basics of density estimation using kernel methods. A more thorough exposition of this topic can be found in Pagan and Ullah (1999). A survey of applied nonparametric methods is provided in Härdle and Linton (1994).

Assume that we have a sample of n observations for X_i, $i = 1,...,n$, whose underlying density f is unknown and has to be estimated. Kernel estimates can be seen as smooth histograms. In a standard histogram each observation is weighted equally: Either it is in a specific bin and it receives a weight of $1/n$, or it is outside the bin and has zero weight in this bin. Kernel estimators allocate different weights to each observation. A kernel estimator of a density at a given point x will allocate weight to all observations in the sample. The weight is decreasing in the distance between the observation and the point at which the density is estimated. More formally the density estimate at x is:

$$\hat{f}(x) = \frac{1}{nh} \sum_{i=1}^{n} K\left(\frac{x - X_i}{h}\right)$$

A kernel is a piecewise continuous function satisfying the property

$$\int_{-\infty}^{+\infty} K(x)\, dx = 1$$

$K(.)$ is most frequently (but not always) chosen to be a symmetric probability density function such as the Gaussian density. h is called the bandwidth or the window width. It determines the degree of smoothness of the estimation—the larger the bandwidth, the smoother the estimation.

APPENDIX 4B

Bonds and Loans Insolvency Regimes

Financial Debt	United States	United Kingdom[a]	Germany	France[b]
Most recent insolvency legislation	1978, reformed in 1994	1985,1986, new regime discussed in 2003	New regime from 1999[c]	1984–1985, modified in 1994
Insolvency control rights	Balanced between debtor and secured creditors before Chapter 11; then debtor and court	Secured creditor in control	Historically creditors' committee in control. More balanced since 1999	Debtor and then court
Private procedure (P)	(P) + (S)	(P)	(S)	(S)
State-driven procedure (S)	Two procedures: ♦ Chapter 7—liquidation (~75%) ♦ Chapter 11—reorganization (~25%)	4 procedures: ♦ Receivership ♦ Administration[d] ♦ CVA[e] ♦ Winding up	Single gateway: court-appointed receiver	Single gateway, three procedures: ♦ Negotiated settlement[f] ♦ Judicial arrangement (RJ) ♦ Judicial liquidation (LJ)[g]
Pro debtor (D) / pro creditor (C)	(P) => (C) Informal procedure (S) => (D) Chapter 11 (S) => (C) Chapter 7	(C) The creditor keeps control of assets through floating and fixed charges	(C) The creditors' assembly is powerful (either Creditors' meeting or Creditors' committee); Senior creditors vote liquidation on a majority basis	(D) The financial creditor comes behind other preferential creditors (state, etc.)

Control on securities — preservation of seniority	Main securities: • Over current assets • Surety or unconditional performance guarantee • Mortgage on fixed assets Security well established but challenged by claims priorities of payment	Main securities: • Fixed charges • Floating charges Seniority preserved; No court involvement required to enforce rights	Main securities: • Mortgage over property • Assignments on assets such as inventory or shares Security available to creditors	For turnaround: The court determines how and when creditors will be paid, despite securities For liquidation: Some securities are easily enforceable; others not because of change of priority order Security difficult to exercise
Who puts together the reorganization plan ?	Exclusive right of the debtor for 120 days, then debtor or any creditor	Receiver / administrative receiver	The insolvency practitioner or borrower	Judicial administrator appointed by the court
Statute of bond or loan creditors compared with other creditors	Unsecured creditors bargain with secured one under threat of borrower going into Chapter 11 The order of priority is very clear under Chapter 7	Priority order well established Priority over trade credit	The principal of preferential creditors abolished Vote on reorganization plan including secured and unsecured creditors	Seniority often not preserved Come after preferential creditors such as state, salaries, claims arising after commencement of proceedings, etc.

(continues)

Financial Debt	United States	United Kingdom[a]	Germany	France[b]
New financing in reorganization—superpriority	New financing can relatively easily be accommodated because it has priority over existing claims (superpriority)	Constrained because new financing will probably come from senior creditors and is junior to existing claims	New financing can be arranged Creditors active after proceedings are priority creditors	New financing can relatively easily be accommodated because it has priority over existing claims (superpriority)
Who accepts the rescue?	Creditors vote but "cramdown" by court possible	Creditors by simple majority of creditors present	Creditor vote and approved by the court	Court decides
Time to emergence (liquidation or going concern)	6 to 36 months	6 to 18 months	Can take more than 3 years	Can take more than 3 years
Direct cost of liquidation	Quite high because of long periods and a court is extensively involved in the process	Around 25% of total recoveries	9% flat	Quite high because of long periods and a court is extensively involved in the process
Specific risks	Intensive litigation	The validity of security can be challenged by receiver (12 months before beginning of insolvency procedure); Scarcely used	Any rehabilitation plan needs to be approved by several actors; It can be a lengthy process	"période suspecte": 18-months-backward period, before ceasing payments where actions can be questioned by the court

Gross average recovery rate on defaulted secured loans	From 60 to 80% for bank loans[h]	From 70 to 85% for SME bank loans[i]	From 40 to 70% for SME bank loans[j]	From 20% for unsecured to 50% for secured for SME bank loans[k]
Ratio (%): liquidation / turnaround + liquidation	Around 80%	Around 75%	Over 90%	Over 90%[l]
Legal penalty on the entrepreneur	No	No	Yes; Related to directors' obligations	Yes for 23% of liquidated companies,[m] but 99% of entrepreneurs of reorganized firms remain in control[n]
Main focus when insolvency	Chapter 11 new loans, insolvency costs, salaries, and then secured loans	Insolvency costs and handling existing contracts	Secured creditors and insolvency costs	Salaries and employment
Incentive to go to informal restructuring	Often initiated by debtor	High as banks succeed in obtaining close to 100% recovery through informal restructuring	Creditors in a strong position both at informal and at formal stage	Very high

(continues)

[a]Franks and Sussman (2002).

[b]Blazy and Combier (1997)

[c]With the new code, imminent insolvency can also trigger bankruptcy. See Elsas and Krahnen (2002).

[d]Administration for large companies.

[e]Company voluntary arrangement.

[f]Very rarely used in practice.

[g]Around 80 percent of firms move directly to liquidation.

[h]Keenan, Hamilton, and Berthault (2000).

[i]Based on Franks and Sussman (2002).

[j]Average recovery on bankruptcy for secured loans for the period 1985–1971: 32 percent (*German Statistical Yearbook*), but bankruptcy is not a good proxy for default.

[k]Recovery on insolvency: 20 percent on the Blazy-Combier (1997) sample and 40 percent on the Robert (1994) sample. Estimated recovery on the post-default, prebankruptcy negotiation around 70 percent.

[l]94 percent in 1994 according to Kaiser (1996).

[m]Blazy and Combier (1997).

[n]Saint-Alary (1990).

THE PARTICULAR CASE OF GERMANY

Elsas and Krahnen (2002) observe a sample of 128 German middle-market companies that have been within banks' workout (Figure 4B-1). They show that, on this sample, 85 percent of companies will go into private restructuring without facing court procedures. This level of private renegotiation is probably one of the highest worldwide. Spain also tends to exhibit such levels, and even higher ones.

FIGURE 4B-1

Financial Distress Process in Germany

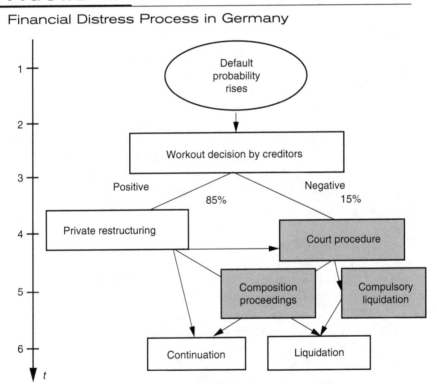

Recovery in Germany: a very high level of restructuring

Source: Elsas and Krahnen (2002).

The Role of Collateral in the Recovery Process

In several countries like the United States, the United Kingdom, Germany, and the Scandinavian countries, collateral plays a significant role in secured lending, for both loans and bonds. There is a general understanding that such collateral can help to reduce LGD significantly. A loan fully covered by collateral could even theoretically be seen as equivalent to a riskless loan despite the probability of default of the underlying debtor. This approach has been widely criticized for many reasons, such as the correlation between LGD and PD, the volatility of the value of collateral with the economic cycle, and the cost of recovery associated with nonperforming loans. Until recently, however, there existed little evidence to document all these issues.

The traditional concept of loan to value is commonly monitored in the banking industry. The loan-to-value ratio is defined as the face value of the debt divided by the current value of the collateral. Guidelines regarding the maximum value of the ratio allowed within each bank will typically be defined internally by the banks themselves or in some cases imposed externally by regulators.[29] A loan-to-value ratio of 80 percent, used, for instance, for housing collateral, will mean that a collateral haircut of 20 percent will have to be considered on the value of the real estate and that 80 percent of its value is set as a cap for any authorized loan. The value of the haircut will typically depend on the volatility of the value of the collateral, given the economic cycle.

Schmit and Stuyck (2002) have recently performed an interesting study[30] on recoveries in the leasing industry in Europe[31] over a period of 26 years. This study provides valuable information about the effective value of assets as debt collateral. The authors focus on three sectors: automotive, equipment, and real estate. The type of recovery they compute is the ratio of the recovery on resale of the asset divided by the outstanding debt at default. Obviously the mean recovery they obtain depends on the amortization profile of the lease (Table 4C-1b). What we are primarily interested in is in the standard deviation (Table 4C-1a).

The tables show that collateral haircut policy should be significantly conservative in terms both of overcollateralization and of a through-the-cycle approach, in order to provide a real hedge on the effective recovery, with a significant confidence level.

TABLE 4C-1a

Asset-Based Leasing Recovery Exhibits
Significant Volatility

Discounted* Recovery Rate on Resale	Automotive Sector (Standard Deviation)	Equipment Sector (Standard Deviation)	Real Estate (Standard Deviation)
Austria	110.3%	39%	43.3%
Belgium	40.4%	53.9%	4.5%
France	39.8%	29.4%	n.a.[†]
Italy	39.4%	31%	63.4%
Luxembourg	25.6%	42.1%	n.a.
Sweden	23.9%	41.5%	n.a.
Average std. dev.	66%	33%	52%

*Discount rate is 10 percent.
[†]Given extremely long recovery procedures.

TABLE 4C-1b

Asset-Based Leasing Average Recovery Rate
Proves Quite Low

Discounted* Recovery Rate on Resale	Automotive Sector (Mean)	Equipment Sector (Mean)	Real Estate (Mean)
All six countries average	68%	40%	68%

*Discount rate is 10 percent.

Further investigation would, however, be required for each type of collateral in order to assess its idiosyncratic versus systematic risk. It seems, for example, that the behavior of automotive collateral is largely idiosyncratic (see Schmit, 2002) . Conversely, commercial real estate collateral is usually considered to be significantly correlated to systematic factors. If collateral volatility is idiosyncratic, it will tend to vanish thanks to portfolio diversification. If it corresponds to systematic risk, it will contribute to an increase in the riskiness of the portfolio.

Recoveries and Basel II

The current proposals for banking regulation (Basel II) emphasize loss given default. The general formula for capital requirement (K) can be summarized as

$$K = \text{LGD} \times F(\text{PD})$$

where $F(.)$ is the function mapping the probability of default to the Basel risk weights. This function is concave as depicted on Figure 4D-1. Therefore an increase by 1 percent at high levels of default probabilities has relatively less impact on capital than the same increase at low levels.

The first term in the capital requirement (K) calculation refers to the LGD and is linear (Figure 4D-2). Thus an increase in LGD raises capital requirements by a similar factor irrespective of the initial level of LGD. At high levels of PDs (e.g., non-investment grade), the relative impact on capital requirements of an increase in the LGD term is stronger than for the PD term.

F I G U R E   4D-1

PD Factor in Basel II Capital Calculation

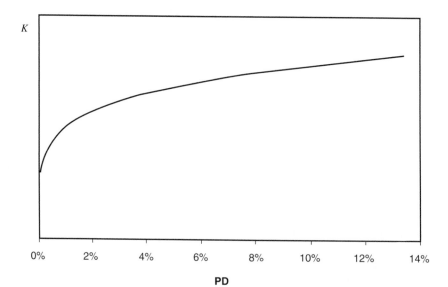

FIGURE 4D-2

LGD Factor in Basel II Capital Calculation

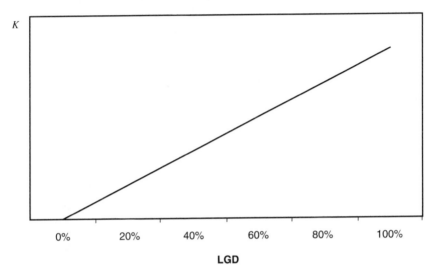

CHAPTER 5

Default Dependencies

In Chapters 2, 3, and 4 we considered default probabilities and recovery rates for individual obligors. At the portfolio level, individual PDs and LGDs are important but insufficient to determine the entire distribution of losses. The portfolio loss distribution is not the sum of distributions of individual losses because of diversification effects.

In this chapter we introduce multivariate effects, i.e., interactions between facilities or obligors. Portfolio measures of credit risk require measures of dependency across assets. Dependency is a broad concept capturing the fact that the joint probability of two events is in general not simply the product of the probabilities of individual events.

The most common measure of dependency is linear correlation.[1] Figure 5-1 illustrates the impact of correlation on portfolio losses.[2] When the default correlation is zero, the probability of extreme events (large number of defaults or zero default) is low. However, when the correlation is significant, the probability of very good or very bad events increases substantially. Given that risk managers focus a lot on tail measures of credit risk such as value at risk and expected shortfall (see the next chapter), correlations are of crucial importance.

For most marginal distributions, however, the linear correlation is only part of the dependency structure and is insufficient to construct the joint distribution of losses. In addition, it is possible to construct a large set of different joint distributions from identical marginal distributions.

FIGURE 5-1

Effect of Correlations on Portfolio Losses

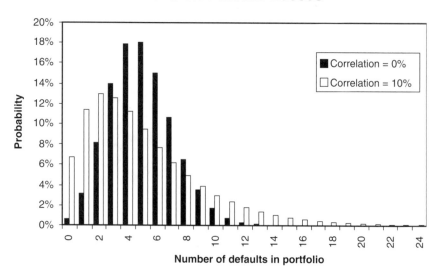

Correlation is therefore a weaker concept than dependency, except in particular cases. A large section of this chapter will be dedicated to alternative dependency measures.

Dependency also includes more complex effects such as the comovement of two variables with a time lag, or causality effects. In a time-series context, correlation provides information about the simultaneity of events, but not on which event triggered another. It ignores contagion and infectious events (see, e.g., Davis and Lo, 1999a, 1999b).

SOURCES OF DEPENDENCIES

In this chapter, we will focus primarily on *measuring* default dependencies rather than on *explaining* them. Before doing so, it is worth spending a little time on the sources of joint defaults.

Defaults occur for three main types of reasons:

♦ *Firm specific reasons.* Bad management, fraud, large project failure, etc.

♦ *Industry-specific reasons.* Entire sectors sometimes get hit by shocks such as overcapacity or a rise in the prices of raw materials.

♦ *General macroeconomic conditions.* Growth and recession, interest rate changes, and commodity prices affect all firms to various degrees.

Firm-specific causes do not lead to correlated defaults. Defaults triggered by these idiosyncratic factors tend to occur independently. In contrast, macroeconomic and sector-specific shocks do lead to increases in the default rates of entire segments of the economy and push up correlations.

Figure 5-2 depicts the link between macroeconomic growth (measured by the growth in gross domestic product) and the default rate of non-investment-grade issuers. The default rate appears to be almost a mirror image of the growth rate. This implies that defaults will tend to be correlated since they depend on a common factor.

Figure 5-3 shows the impact of a sector crisis on default rates in the energy and telecom sectors. The surge in oil prices in the mid-eighties and the telecom debacle starting in 2000 are clearly visible. Commercial models of credit risk presented in Chapter 6 incorporate sector, idiosyncratic, and macroeconomic factors.

FIGURE 5-2

U.S. GDP Growth and Aggregate Default Rates

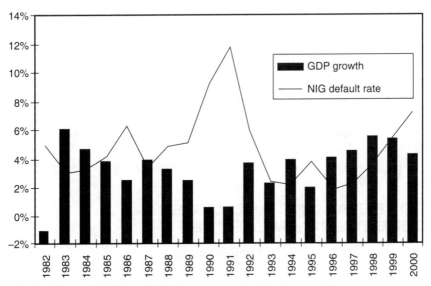

Source: S&P and Federal Reserve Board.

FIGURE 5-3

Default Rates in the Telecom and Energy Sectors

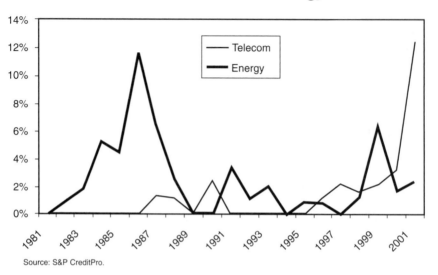

Source: S&P CreditPro.

We begin this chapter with a review of useful statistical concepts. We start by introducing the most popular measures of dependency (covariance and correlation) and show how to compute the variance of a portfolio from individual risks.

Next we use several examples to illustrate that correlation is only a partial and sometimes misleading measure of the co-movement or dependency of random variables. We review various other partial measures and introduce copulas, which fully describe multivariate distributions.

These statistical preliminaries are useful for understanding the last section in the chapter, which deals with credit-specific applications of these dependency measures. Various methodologies have been proposed to estimate default correlations. These can be extracted directly from default data or derived from equity or spread information.

CORRELATIONS AND OTHER DEPENDENCY MEASURES

Definitions

The covariance between two random variables X and Y is defined as

$$\text{Cov}(X,Y) = E(XY) - E(X)E(Y) \tag{5-1}$$

where $E(.)$ denotes the expectation. It measures how two random variables move together.

The covariance satisfies two useful properties:

♦ $Cov(X,X) = var(X)$, where $var(X)$ is the variance
♦ $Cov(aX,bY) = ab\ cov(X,Y)$

In the case where X and Y are independent, $E(XY) = E(X)E(Y)$, and the covariance is 0.

The correlation coefficient conveys the same information about the co-movement of X and Y but is scaled to lie between -1 and $+1$. It is defined as the ratio of X and Y covariance to the product of their standard deviations:

$$Corr(X,Y) = \rho_{XY} = \frac{cov(X,Y)}{std(X)std(Y)} \tag{5-2}$$

$$= \frac{E(XY) - E(X)E(Y)}{\sqrt{\{E(X^2) - [E(X)]^2\}\{E(Y^2) - [E(Y)]^2\}}} \tag{5-3}$$

In the particular case of two binary $(0,1)$ variables A and B, taking value 1 with probability p_A and p_B, respectively, and 0 otherwise and with joint probability p_{AB}, we can calculate $E(A) = E(A^2) = p_A$, $E(B) = E(B^2) = p_B$, and $E(AB) = p_{AB}$.

The correlation is therefore

$$Corr(A,B) = \frac{p_{AB} - p_A p_B}{\sqrt{p_A(1 - p_A)\,p_B(1 - p_B)}} \tag{5-4}$$

This formula will be particularly useful for default correlation because defaults are binary events. Later in the chapter we will explain how to estimate the various terms in the above equation.

Calculating Diversification Effect in a Portfolio

Two-Asset Case

Let us first consider a simple case of a portfolio with two assets X and Y with proportions w and $1 - w$, respectively. Their variances and covariance are σ_X^2, σ_Y^2, and σ_{XY}.

The variance of the portfolio is given by

$$\sigma_P^2 = w^2\sigma_X^2 + (1 - w)^2\sigma_Y^2 + 2w(1 - w)\sigma_{XY} \tag{5-5}$$

The minimum variance of the portfolio can be obtained by differentiating Equation 5-5 and setting the derivative equal to 0:

$$\frac{\partial \sigma_P^2}{\partial w} = 0 = 2w\sigma_X^2 - 2\sigma_Y + 2w\sigma_Y^2 + 2(1 - 2w)\sigma_{XY} \qquad (5\text{-}6)$$

The optimal allocation w^* is the solution to Equation (5-6):

$$w^* = \frac{\sigma_Y^2 - \rho_{XY}\sigma_X\sigma_Y}{\sigma_X^2 + \sigma_Y^2 - 2\rho_{XY}\sigma_X\sigma_Y} \qquad (5\text{-}7)$$

We thus find the optimal allocation in both assets that minimizes the total variance of the portfolio. We can immediately see that the optimal allocation depends on the correlation between the two assets and that the resulting variance is also affected by the correlation. Figures 5-1 and 5-2 illustrate how the optimal allocation and resulting minimum portfolio variance change as a function of correlation. In this example, $\sigma_X = 0.25$ and $\sigma_Y = 0.15$.

In Figure 5-4 we can see that the allocation of the portfolio between X and Y is highly nonlinear in the correlation. If the two assets are highly positively correlated, it becomes optimal to sell short the asset with highest variance (X in our example); hence w^* is negative. If the correlation is "perfect" between X and Y, i.e., if $\rho = 1$ or $\rho = -1$, it is possible to create a riskless portfolio (Figure 5-5). Otherwise the optimal allocation w^* will lead to a low but positive variance.

Figure 5-6 shows the impact of correlation on the joint density of X and Y, assuming that they are standard normally distributed. It is a snapshot of the bell-shaped density seen "from above." In the case where the correlation is zero (left-hand side), the joint density looks like concentric circles. When nonzero correlation is introduced (positive in this example), the shape becomes elliptical: It shows that high (low) values of X tend to be associated with high (low) values of Y. Thus there is more probability in the top-right and bottom-left regions than in the top-left and bottom-right areas. The reverse would have been observed in the case of negative correlation.

Multiple Assets

We can now apply the properties of covariance to calculate the variance of a portfolio with multiple assets. Assume that we have a portfolio of n instruments with identical variance σ^2 and covariance $\sigma_{i,j}$ for $i, j = 1,...,n$.

The variance of the portfolio is given by

FIGURE 5-4

Optimal Allocation versus Correlation

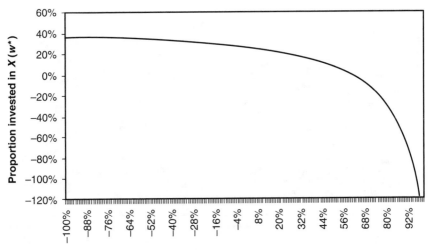

Correlation between X and Y

FIGURE 5-5

Minimum Portfolio Variance versus Correlation

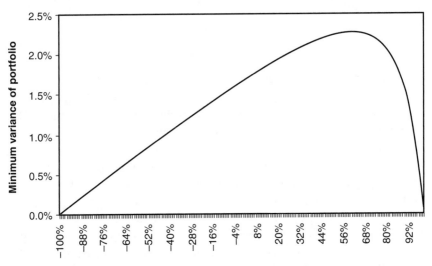

Correlation between X and Y

FIGURE 5-6

Impact of Correlation on the Shape of the Distribution

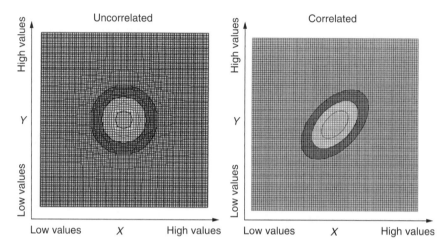

$$\sigma_P^2 = \sum_{i=1}^{n} x_i^2 \sigma^2 + \sum_{i=1}^{n} \sum_{\substack{j=1 \\ j \neq i}}^{n} x_i x_j \sigma_{i,j} \tag{5-8}$$

where x_i is the weight of asset i in the portfolio.

Assuming that the portfolio is equally weighted: $x_i = 1/n$, for all i, and that the variance of all assets is bounded, the variance of the portfolio reduces to:

$$\sigma_P^2 = \frac{\sigma^2}{n} + \frac{n(n-1)}{n^2} \overline{\text{cov}} \tag{5-9}$$

where the last term is the average covariance between assets.

When the portfolio becomes more and more diversified, i.e., when $n \to \infty$, we have $\sigma_P^2 \to \overline{\text{cov}}$. The variance of the portfolio converges to the average covariance between assets. The variance term becomes negligible compared with the joint variation.

For a portfolio of stocks, diversification benefits are obtained fairly quickly: For a correlation of 30 percent between all stocks and a volatility of 30 percent, we are within 10 percent of the minimum covariance with n around 20. For a pure default model (i.e., when we ignore spread and transition risk and assume 0 recovery) the number of assets necessary to reach the same level of diversification is much larger. For example, if the probability of default and the pairwise correlations for all obligors are

2 percent, we need around 450 counterparts to reach a variance that is within 10 percent of its asymptotic minimum.

Deficiencies of Correlation

As mentioned earlier, correlation is by far the most used measure of dependency in financial markets, and it is common to talk about correlation as a generic term for co-movement. We will use it a lot in the section of this chapter on default dependencies and in the following chapter on portfolio models. In this section we want to review some properties of the linear correlation that make it insufficient as a measure of dependency in general—and misleading in some cases. This is best explained through examples.[3]

- Using Equation (5-2), we see immediately that correlation is not defined if one of the variances is infinite. This is not a very frequent occurrence in credit risk models, but some market risk models exhibit this property in some cases.

  Example. See the vast financial literature on α-stable models since Mandelbrot (1963), where the finiteness of the variance depends on the value of the α parameter.

- When specifying a model, one cannot choose correlation arbitrarily over $[-1,1]$ as a degree of freedom. Depending on the choice of distribution, the correlation may be bounded in a narrower range $[\underline{\rho}, \bar{\rho}]$, with $-1 < \underline{\rho} < \bar{\rho} < 1$.

  Example. Suppose we have two normal random variables x and y, both with mean 0 and with standard deviation 1 and σ, respectively. Then $X = \exp(x)$ and $Y = \exp(y)$ are lognormally distributed. However, not all correlations between X and Y are attainable. We can show that their correlation is restricted to lie between

  $$\underline{\rho} = \frac{e^{-\sigma} - 1}{\sqrt{(e-1)(e^{\sigma^2} - 1)}} \quad \text{and} \quad \bar{\rho} = \frac{e^{\sigma} - 1}{\sqrt{(e-1)(e^{\sigma^2} - 1)}}$$

  See Embrecht, McNeil, and Strautmann (1999a) for a proof.

- Two perfectly functionally dependent random variables can have zero correlation.

Example. Consider a normally distributed random variable X with mean 0 and define $Y = X^2$. Although changes in X completely determine changes in Y, they have zero correlation. This clearly shows that while independence implies zero correlation, the reverse is not true!

♦ Linear correlation is not invariant under monotonic transformations.

Example. (X,Y) and $[\exp(X), \exp(Y)]$ do not have the same correlation.

♦ Many bivariate distributions share the same marginal distributions and the same correlation but are not identical.

Example. See the section in this chapter on copulas.

All these considerations should make it clear that correlation is a partial and insufficient measure of dependency in the general case. It only measures linear dependency. This does not mean that correlation is useless. For the class of elliptical distributions, correlation is sufficient to combine the marginals into the bivariate distribution. For example, given two normal marginal distributions for X and Y and a correlation coefficient ρ, we can build a joint normal distribution for (X,Y).

Loosely speaking, this class of distribution is called elliptical because when we project the multivariate density on a plane, we find elliptical shapes (see Figure 5-6). The normal and the t-distribution, among others, are part of this class.

Even for other nonelliptical distributions, covariances (and therefore correlations) are second moments that need to be calibrated. While they are insufficient to incorporate all dependency, they should not be neglected when empirically fitting a distribution.

Other Dependency Measures: Rank Correlations

Many other measures have been proposed to tackle the problems of linear correlations mentioned above. We only mention two here, but there are countless examples.

♦ *Spearman's rho.* This is simply the linear correlation but applied to the ranks of the variables rather than on the variables themselves.

♦ *Kendall's tau.* Assume we have n observations for each of two random variables, i.e., (X_i, Y_i), where $i = 1...n$.

We start by counting the number of concordant pairs, i.e., pairs for which the two elements are either both larger or both lower than the elements of another pair. Call that number N_c.

Then Kendall's tau is calculated as

$$\tau_K = (N_c - N_D)/(N_c + N_D)$$

where N_D is the number of discordant (nonconcordant) pairs.

Kendall's tau shares some properties with the linear correlation: $\tau_K \in [-1,1]$ and $\tau_K(X,Y) = 0$ for X,Y independent. However, it has some distinguishing features that make it more appropriate than the linear correlation in some cases. If X and Y are comonotonic,[4] then $\tau_K(X,Y) = 1$; while if they are countermonotonic, $\tau_K(X,Y) = -1$. τ_K is also invariant under strictly monotonic transformations. To return to our example above, $\tau_K(X,Y) = \tau_K[\exp(X),\exp(Y)]$.

In the case of the normal distribution, the linear and rank correlations can be linked analytically:

$$\tau_K(X,Y) = \frac{2}{\pi} \arcsin [\rho (X,Y)] \qquad (5\text{-}10)$$

These dependency measures have nice properties but are much less used by finance practitioners. Again they are insufficient to obtain the entire bivariate distribution from the marginals. The function that achieves this task is called a copula. We now turn to this important statistical concept and will come back to Spearman's rho and Kendall's tau when we express them in terms of the copula.

Modeling the Entire Multivariate Distribution: The Copula

A copula is a function that combines univariate density functions into their joint distribution. A comprehensive analysis of copulas is beyond the scope of this book,[5] but we just want to provide sufficient background to understand the applications of copulas to credit risk that will be discussed below. Applications of copulas to risk management and the pricing of derivatives have soared over the past few years.

Definition and Sklar's Theorem

Definition. A copula with dimension n is an n-dimensional probability distribution function defined on $[0,1]^n$ that has uniform marginal distributions.

One of the most important and useful results about copulas is
known as Sklar's theorem (Sklar, 1959). It states that any group of random variables can be joined into their multivariate distribution using a
copula. More formally: If X_i, for $i = 1...n$, are random variables with
respective marginal distributions F_i, for $i = 1...n$, and multivariate probability distribution function F, then there exists an n-dimensional copula
such that

$$F(x_1,...,x_n) = C[F_1(x_1),...,F_n(x_n)] \quad \text{for all } (x_1,...,x_n) \quad (5\text{-}11a)$$

and

$$C(u_1,...,u_n) = F[F_1^{-1}(u_1),...,F_n^{-1}(u_n)] \quad (5\text{-}11b)$$

Furthermore, if the marginal distributions are continuous, then the
copula function is unique.

Looking at Equation (5-11a), we clearly see how to obtain the joint
distribution from the data. The first step is to fit the marginal distributions
F_i, $i = 1...n$, individually on the data (realizations of X_i, $i = 1...n$). This yields
a set of uniformly distributed random variables $u_1 = F_1(x_1), ..., u_n = F_n(x_n)$.

The second step is to find the copula function that appropriately
describes the joint behavior of the random variables. There is a plethora
of possible choices that make the use of copulas sometimes impractical.
Their main appeal is that they allow us to separate the calibration of the
marginal distributions from that of the joint law. Figure 5-7 is a graph of
a bivariate Frank copula (see below for an explanation).

Properties of the Copula

Copulas satisfy a series of properties including the four listed below.
The first one states that for independent random variables, the copula
is just the product of the marginal distributions. The second property is
that of invariance under monotonic transformations. The third property provides bounds on the values of the copula. These bounds correspond to the values the copula would take if the random variables were
countermonotonic (lower bound) or comonotonic (upper bound).

FIGURE 5-7

Shape of a Bivariate Copula

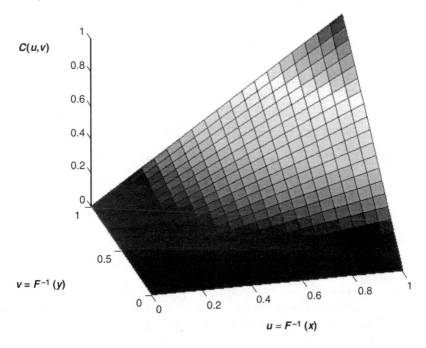

Finally the fourth one states that a convex combination of two copulas is also a copula.

Using similar notations as above where X and Y denote random variables and u and v stand for the uniformly distributed margins of the copula, we have:

1. If X and Y are independent, then $C(u,v) = uv$.
2. Copulas are invariant under increasing and continuous transformations of marginals.
3. For any copula C, we have $\max(u + v - 1, 0) \le C(u,v) \le \min(u,v)$
4. If C_1 and C_2 are copulas, then $C = \alpha C_1 + (1 - \alpha)C_2$, for $0 < \alpha < 1$, is also a copula.

We now briefly review two important classes of copulas which are most frequently used in risk management applications: elliptical (including Gaussian and student-t) copulas and Archimedean copulas.

Important Classes of Copulas

There are a wide variety of possible copulas. Many but not all are listed in Nelsen (1999). In what follows, we introduce elliptical and Archimedean copulas. Among elliptical copulas, Gaussian copulas are now commonly used to generate dependent random vectors in applications requiring Monte-Carlo simulations (see Wang, 2000, or Bouyé, Durrelman, Nikeghbali, Riboulet, and Roncalli, 2000). The Archimedean family is as convenient as it is parsimonious and has a simple additive structure. Applications of Archimedean copulas to risk management can be found in Schönbucher (2002) or Das and Geng (2002), among many others.

Elliptical Copulas: Gaussian and t-Copulas Copulas, as noted above, are multivariate distribution functions. Obviously the Gaussian copula will be a multivariate Gaussian (normal) distribution.

Using the notations of Equation (5-11b), we can write C_Σ^{Gau}, the n-dimensional Gaussian copula with covariance matrix Σ:

$$C_\Sigma^{\text{Gau}}(u_1,...,u_n) = N_\Sigma^n[N^{-1}(u_1),...,N^{-1}(u_n)] \tag{5-12}$$

where N_Σ^n and N^{-1} denote, respectively, the n-dimensional cumulative Gaussian distribution with covariance matrix Σ and the inverse of the cumulative univariate standard normal distribution.

In the bivariate case, assuming that the correlation between the two random variables is ρ, Equation (5-12) boils down to

$$C_\rho^{\text{Gau}}(u,v) = N_\rho^2[N^{-1}(u), N^{-1}(v)]$$

$$= \frac{1}{2\pi(1-\rho^2)} \int_{-\infty}^{N^{-1}(u)} \int_{-\infty}^{N^{-1}(v)} \exp\left(-\frac{g^2 - 2\rho\,gh + h^2}{2(1-\rho^2)}\right) dg\,dh$$

$$\tag{5-13}$$

The t-copula (bivariate t-distribution) with v degrees of freedom is obtained in a similar way. Using evident notations, we have

$$C_{\rho,\nu}^t(u,v) = t_{\rho,\nu}^2\,[t_\nu^{-1}(u),t_\nu^{-1}(v)] \tag{5-14}$$

Archimedean Copulas The family of Archimedean copulas is the class of multivariate distributions on $[0,1]^n$ that can be written as

$$C^{\text{Arch}}(u_1,...,u_n) = G^{-1}[G(u_1) + ... + G(u_n)] \tag{5-15}$$

where G is a suitable function from $[0,1]$ to $]0,\infty[$ satisfying $G(1) = 0$ and $G(0) = \infty$. $G(.)$ is called the generator of the copula.

Three examples of Archimedean copulas used in the finance literature are the Gumbel, the Frank, and the Clayton copulas, for which we provide the functional form now. They can easily be built by specifying their generator (see Marshall and Olkin, 1988, or Nelsen, 1999).

Example 1   The Gumbel Copula (Multivariate Exponential)

The generator for the Gumbel copula is

$$G_G(t) = (-\log t)^\theta \qquad (5\text{-}16)$$

with inverse

$$G_G^{[-1]}(s) = \exp(-s^{1/\theta})$$

AU: brackets are the same size

and $\theta \geq 1$.

Therefore using Equation (5-15), the copula function in the bivariate case is

$$C_G^\theta(u,v) = \exp(-[(-\log u)^\theta + (-\log v)^\theta]^{1/\theta}) \qquad (5\text{-}17)$$

Example 2   The Frank Copula

The generator is

$$G_F(t) = -\log\left(\frac{e^{-\theta t} - 1}{e^{-\theta} - 1}\right) \qquad (5\text{-}18)$$

with inverse

$$G_F^{[-1]}(s) = \frac{-1}{\theta} \log[1 - e^s(1 - e^\theta)]$$

and $\theta \neq 0$.

The bivariate copula function is therefore

$$C_F^\theta(u,v) = \frac{-1}{\theta} \log\left(1 + \frac{(e^{-\theta u} - 1)(e^{-\theta v} - 1)}{(e^{-\theta} - 1)}\right) \qquad (5\text{-}19)$$

Example 3   The Clayton Copula

The generator is

$$G_C(t) = \frac{1}{\theta}(t^{-\theta} - 1) \qquad (5\text{-}20)$$

with inverse

$$G_C^{[-1]}(s) = (1 + \theta s)^{-1/\theta}$$

and $\theta > 0$.

The bivariate copula function is therefore

$$C_C^\theta(u,v) = \max\left[(u^{-\theta} + v^{-\theta} - 1)^{-1/\theta}, 0\right] \qquad (5\text{-}21)$$

Calculating a Joint Cumulative Probability Using a Copula

Assume we want to calculate the joint cumulative probability of two random variables X and Y: $P(X < x, Y < y)$. Both X and Y are standard normally distributed. We are interested in looking at the joint probability depending on the choice of copula and on the parameter θ.

The first step is to calculate the margins of the copula distribution: $v = P(Y < y) = N(y)$ and $u = P(X < x) = N(x)$. For our numerical example, we assume $x = -0.1$ and $y = 0.3$. Hence $u = 0.460$ and $v = 0.618$.

The joint cumulative probability is then obtained by plugging these values into the chosen copula function [Equations (5-17), (5-19), and (5-21)]. Figure 5-8 illustrates how the joint probabilities change as a function

FIGURE 5-8

Examples of Joint Cumulative Probabilities Using Archimedean Copulas

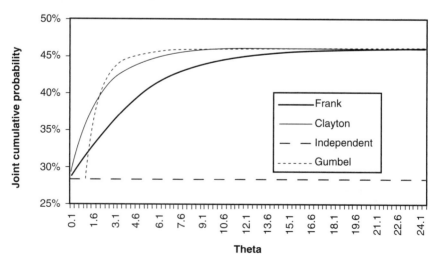

of θ for the three Archimedean copulas presented above. The graph shows that different choices of copulas and theta parameters lead to very different results in terms of joint probability.

Copulas and Other Dependency Measures

Recall that earlier in the chapter we introduced Spearman's rho and Kendall's tau as two alternatives to linear correlation. We mentioned that they could be expressed in terms of the copula. The formulas linking these dependency measures to the copula are

♦ Spearman's rho:

$$\rho_S = 12 \int_0^1 \int_0^1 C(u,v) - uv\, du\, dv \tag{5-22}$$

♦ Kendall's tau:

$$\tau_K = 4 \int_0^1 \int_0^1 C(u,v)d^2C(u,v) - 1 \tag{5-23}$$

Thus once the copula is defined analytically, we can immediately calculate rank correlations from it. Copulas also incorporate tail dependency. Intuitively, tail dependency will exist when there is a significant probability of joint extreme events. Lower (upper) tail dependency captures joint negative (positive) outliers.

If we consider two random variables X_1 and X_2 with respective marginal distributions F_1 and F_2, the coefficients of lower (LTD) and upper tail dependency (UTD) are

$$\text{UTD} = \lim_{z \to 1} \text{Pr}\ [X_2 > F_2^{-1}(z) \mid X_1 > F_1^{-1}(z)] \tag{5-24}$$

and

$$\text{LTD} = \lim_{z \to 0} \text{Pr}\ [X_2 < F_2^{-1}(z) \mid X_1 < F_1^{-1}(z)] \tag{5-25}$$

Figure 5-9 illustrates the asymptotic dependency of variables in the upper tail, using t-copulas. The tail dependency coefficient shown corresponds to UTD.

This section completes our introduction to correlation, copulas, and other dependency measures. We have shown that, although overwhelmingly used by finance practitioners, correlation is a partial indicator of joint behavior. The most general tool for that purpose is the copula, which provides a complete characterization of the joint law. But which copula to

FIGURE 5-9

Upper-Tail Dependency Coefficients for Gaussian and
t-Copulas for Various Asset Correlations

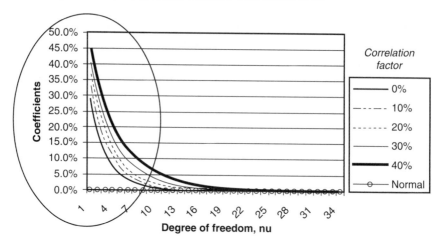

use? This is a difficult question to address in practice, and choices are often (always?) driven by practical considerations rather than any theoretical reasons. The choice of one family of copulas against another or even of a specific copula over another in the same class may lead to substantial differences in the outcome of the model, be it an option price or a tail loss measure such as value at risk.

DEFAULT DEPENDENCIES—EMPIRICAL FINDINGS

Calculating Empirical Correlations[6]

In Equation (5-4) we have derived the correlation formula for two binary events A and B. These two events can be joint defaults or joint downgrades, for example. Consider two firms originally rated i and j, respectively, and let D denote the default category. The marginal probabilities of default are p_i^D and p_j^D, while $p_{i,j}^{D,D}$ denotes the joint probability of the two firms defaulting over a chosen horizon. Equation (5-4) can thus be rewritten as

$$\rho_{i,j}^{D,D} = \frac{p_{i,j}^{D,D} - p_i^D p_j^D}{\sqrt{p_i^D(1 - p_i^D)\, p_j^D(1 - p_j^D)}} \tag{5-26}$$

Obtaining individual probabilities of default per rating class is straightforward. These statistics can be read off transition matrices (we have discussed this at length in Chapter 2). The only unknown term that has to be estimated in Equation (5-26) is the joint probability.

Estimating the Joint Probability

Consider the joint migration of two obligors from the same class i (say, a BB rating) to default D. The default correlation formula is given by Equation (5-26) with $j = i$, and we want to estimate $p_{i,i}^{D,D}$.

Assume that at the beginning of a year t, we have N_i^t firms rated i. From a given set with N_i^t elements, we can create $N_i^t(N_i^t - 1)/2$ different pairs. Using $T_{i,D}^t$ to denote the number of bonds migrating from this group to default D, we can create $T_{i,D}^t(T_{i,D}^t - 1)/2$ defaulting pairs. Taking the ratio of the number of pairs that defaulted to the number of pairs that could have defaulted, we obtain a natural estimator of the joint probability. Considering that we have n years of data and not just 1, the estimator is

$$p_{i,i}^{D,D} = \sum_{t=1}^{n} w_i^t \frac{T_{i,D}^t(T_{i,D}^t - 1)}{N_i^t(N_i^t - 1)} \tag{5-27}$$

where w is the weight representing the relative importance of a given year.

Among possible choices for the weighting schemes, we can find

$$w_i^t = \frac{1}{n} \tag{5-28a}$$

or

$$w_i^t = \frac{N_i^t}{\sum_{s=1}^{n} N_i^s} \tag{5-28b}$$

or

$$w_i^t = \frac{N_i^t(N_i^t - 1)}{\sum_{s=1}^{n} N_i^s(N_i^s - 1)} \tag{5-28c}$$

Equation (5-27) is the formula used by Lucas (1995) and by Bahar and Nagpal (2001) to calculate the joint probability of default. Similar formulas can be derived for transitions to and from different classes. Both papers rely on Equation (5-28c) as the weighting system.

Although intuitive, estimator (5-27) has the drawback that it can generate spurious negative correlation when defaults are rare. Taking a specific year, we can indeed check that when there is only one default, $T(T-1) = 0$. This leads to a zero probability of joint default. However, the probability of an individual default is $1/N$. Therefore, Equation (5-26) immediately generates a negative correlation since the joint probability is 0 and the product of marginal probabilities is $(1/N)^2$.

De Servigny and Renault (2003) therefore propose to replace Equation (5-27) with

$$p_{i,i}^{D,D} = \sum_{t=1}^{n} w_i^t \frac{(T_{i,D}^t)^2}{(N_i^t)^2} \tag{5-29}$$

This estimator of joint probability follows the same intuition of comparing pairs of defaulting firms with the total number of pairs of firms. The difference lies in the assumption of drawing pairs with replacement. de Servigny and Renault (2003) use the weights (5-28*b*). In a simulation experiment, they show that formula (5-29) has better finite sample properties than (5-27); i.e., for small samples (small N) using (5-29) and (5-26) provides an estimate that is on average closer to the true correlation than using (5-27) and (5-26).

Empirical Correlations

Using the Standard & Poor's CreditPro database that contains about 10,000 firms and 22 years of data (from 1981 to 2002), we can apply formulas (5-29) and (5-26) to compute empirical default correlations. The results are shown in Table 5-1.

The highest correlations can be observed in the diagonal, i.e., within the same industry. Most industry correlations are in the range of 1 to 3 percent. Real estate and, above all, telecoms stand out as exhibiting particularly high correlations. Out-of-diagonal correlations tend to be fairly low.

Table 5-2 illustrates pairwise default correlations per class of rating.[7] From these results we can see that default correlation tends to increase substantially as the rating deteriorates. This is in line with results from various studies of structural models and intensity-based models of credit risk that we consider below.

We will return to this issue later in this chapter when we investigate default correlation in the context of intensity models of credit risk.

TABLE 5-1

1-Year Default Correlations, All Countries, All Ratings, 1981–2002 (×100)

	Auto	Cons	Energ	Finan	Build	Chem	Hi tec	Insur	Leis	R.E.	Tele	Trans	Utility
Auto	2.44	0.87	0.68	0.40	1.31	1.15	1.55	0.17	0.93	0.71	2.90	1.08	1.03
Cons	0.87	1.40	−0.42	0.44	1.45	0.96	1.07	0.27	0.79	1.93	0.34	0.95	0.20
Energ	0.68	−0.42	2.44	−0.37	0.01	0.19	0.27	0.26	−0.37	−0.27	−0.11	0.17	0.29
Finan	0.40	0.44	−0.37	0.60	0.55	0.22	0.30	−0.05	0.52	1.95	0.30	0.23	0.23
Build	1.31	1.45	0.01	0.55	2.42	0.95	1.45	0.31	1.54	1.92	2.27	1.65	1.12
Chem	1.15	0.96	0.19	0.22	0.95	1.44	0.84	0.12	0.67	−0.15	1.03	0.78	0.23
High tech	1.55	1.07	0.27	0.30	1.45	0.84	1.92	−0.03	0.94	1.27	1.25	0.89	0.20
Insur	0.17	0.27	0.26	−0.05	0.31	0.12	−0.03	0.91	0.28	0.47	0.28	0.72	0.48
Leisure	0.93	0.79	−0.37	0.52	1.54	0.67	0.94	0.28	1.74	2.87	1.61	1.49	0.85
Real Est.	0.71	1.93	−0.27	1.95	1.92	−0.15	1.27	0.47	2.87	5.15	−0.24	1.38	0.71
Telecom	2.90	0.34	−0.11	0.30	2.27	1.03	1.25	0.28	1.61	−0.24	9.59	2.36	3.97
Trans	1.08	0.95	0.17	0.23	1.65	0.78	0.89	0.72	1.49	1.38	2.36	1.85	1.40
Utility	1.03	0.20	0.29	0.23	1.12	0.23	0.20	0.48	0.85	0.71	3.97	1.40	2.65

Source: Standard & Poor's CreditPro.

TABLE 5-2

1-Year Default Correlations, All Countries,
All Industries, 1981–2002 (×100)

Rating	AAA	AA	A	BBB	BB	B	CCC
AAA	NA	NA	NA	NA	NA	NA	NA
AA	NA	0.16	0.02	−0.03	0.00	0.10	0.06
A	NA	0.02	0.12	0.03	0.19	0.22	0.26
BBB	NA	−0.03	0.03	0.33	0.35	0.30	0.89
BB	NA	0.00	0.19	0.35	0.94	0.84	1.45
B	NA	0.10	0.22	0.30	0.84	1.55	1.67
CCC	NA	0.06	0.26	0.89	1.45	1.67	8.97

Source: Standard & Poor's CreditPro.

Correlation over Longer Horizons

So far we have only considered the 1-year horizon. This corresponds to the usual horizon for calculating VaR but not to the typical investment horizon of banks and asset managers. Tables 5-3 and 5-4 shed some light on the behavior of correlations as the horizon is lengthened. A marked increase can be observed when we extend the horizon from 1 to 3 years (Tables 5-1 and 5-3). Correlations seem to plateau between 3 and 5 years (Tables 5-3 and 5-4).

One explanation for this phenomenon can be that at the 1-year horizon, defaults occur primarily for firm-specific reasons (bad management, large unexpected loss, etc.) and therefore lead to low correlations. However, when the horizon is 3 to 5 years, industry and macroeconomic events start entering into effect, thereby pushing up correlations.

Similar calculations could be performed using downgrades rather than defaults. This could be achieved simply by substituting the number of downgrades for T in Equation (5-29). Correlations of downgrades would benefit from a much larger number of observations and would arguably be more robust estimates. They, however, raise new questions. Should one treat a two-notch downgrade as a one-notch downgrade? As two one-notch downgrades? Is a downgrade from an investment-grade rating to a speculative rating equivalent to any other downgrade? There are no simple answers to all these questions.

TABLE 5-3

3-Year Default Correlations, All Countries, All Ratings, 1981–2002 (×100)

	Auto	Cons	Energ	Finan	Build	Chem	Hi tec	Insur	Leis	R.E.	Tele	Trans	Utility
Auto	**4.81**	1.84	1.57	0.67	2.68	3.65	3.11	0.67	2.06	2.40	7.04	3.56	2.39
Cons	1.84	**2.51**	−1.41	0.83	2.36	1.60	1.69	0.52	2.01	6.03	2.49	2.56	1.31
Energ	1.57	−1.41	**4.74**	−0.50	−0.49	0.94	0.75	0.75	−1.63	−0.20	−0.44	−0.28	0.05
Finan	0.67	0.83	−0.50	**1.39**	1.54	0.52	0.73	−0.03	1.88	6.27	−0.04	1.03	0.67
Build	2.68	2.36	−0.49	1.54	**3.81**	2.09	2.78	0.41	3.64	7.32	3.85	3.29	1.78
Chem	3.65	1.60	0.94	0.52	2.09	**3.50**	2.34	0.41	2.12	0.91	5.21	2.61	1.30
High tech	3.11	1.69	0.75	0.73	2.78	2.34	**3.01**	0.47	2.45	3.83	4.63	2.82	1.67
Insur	0.67	0.52	0.75	−0.03	0.41	0.41	0.47	**0.96**	0.10	0.46	0.50	1.08	0.22
Leisure	2.06	2.01	−1.63	1.88	3.64	2.12	2.45	0.10	**4.07**	9.39	3.51	3.40	1.48
Real Est.	2.40	6.03	−0.20	6.27	7.32	0.91	3.83	0.46	9.39	**13.15**	−1.14	4.78	2.21
Telecom	7.04	2.49	−0.44	−0.04	3.85	5.21	4.63	0.50	3.51	−1.14	**16.72**	5.63	4.33
Trans	3.56	2.56	−0.28	1.03	3.29	2.61	2.82	1.08	3.40	4.78	5.63	**3.85**	1.99
Utility	2.39	1.31	0.05	0.67	1.78	1.30	1.67	0.22	1.48	2.21	4.33	1.99	**2.07**

Source: Standard & Poor's CreditPro.

T A B L E 5-4

5-Year Default Correlations, All Countries, All Ratings, 1981–2002 (×100)

	Auto	Cons	Energ	Finan	Build	Chem	Hi tec	Insur	Leis	R.E.	Tele	Trans	Utility
Auto	3.04	0.51	1.94	1.35	1.52	2.62	1.49	1.25	1.43	4.18	5.00	1.59	1.25
Cons	0.51	2.40	−3.24	1.02	2.08	1.12	0.35	0.54	2.50	6.53	2.71	1.58	1.13
Energ	1.94	−3.24	7.46	−0.13	−1.63	0.00	1.28	1.62	−3.13	1.11	−0.88	−0.56	−0.26
Finan	1.35	1.02	−0.13	2.08	2.16	1.15	1.19	−0.12	3.10	7.38	1.00	1.45	1.02
Build	1.52	2.08	−1.63	2.16	3.75	1.78	1.69	0.22	4.82	8.25	3.24	2.40	1.60
Chem	2.62	1.12	0.00	1.15	1.78	3.46	0.54	0.38	2.02	1.65	6.18	1.35	1.19
High tech	1.49	0.35	1.28	1.19	1.69	0.54	2.06	0.29	1.76	5.61	1.71	1.32	0.98
Insur	1.25	0.54	1.62	−0.12	0.22	0.38	0.29	1.21	−0.30	−0.27	1.18	0.96	0.21
Leisure	1.43	2.50	−3.13	3.10	4.82	2.02	1.76	−0.30	6.97	12.67	3.80	3.31	1.89
Real Est.	4.18	6.53	1.11	7.38	8.25	1.65	5.61	−0.27	12.67	16.99	−2.01	5.49	2.98
Telecom	5.00	2.71	−0.88	1.00	3.24	6.18	1.71	1.18	3.80	−2.01	15.40	3.55	2.57
Trans	1.59	1.58	−0.56	1.45	2.40	1.35	1.32	0.96	3.31	5.49	3.55	2.48	1.22
Utility	1.25	1.13	−0.26	1.02	1.60	1.19	0.98	0.21	1.89	2.98	2.57	1.22	1.12

Source: Standard & Poor's CreditPro.

Equity Correlations and Asset Correlations

An alternative approach to deriving empirical default correlations is proposed by Gordy and Heitfield (2002). It relies on a maximum-likelihood estimation of the correlations using a factor model of credit risk. In this section we introduce this important class of credit risk models.[8]

In a factor model, one assumes that a latent variable drives the default process: When the value A of the latent variable is sufficiently low (below a threshold K), default is triggered. It is customary to use the term "asset return" instead of "latent variable," as it relates to the familiar Merton-type models where default arises when the value of the firm falls below the value of liabilities.

Asset returns for various obligors are assumed to be functions of common state variables (the factors) and of an idiosyncratic term ε_i that is specific to each firm i and uncorrelated with the factors. The systematic and idiosyncratic factors are usually assumed to be normally distributed and are scaled to have unit variance and zero mean. Therefore the asset returns are also standard normally distributed. In the case of a one-factor model with systematic factor denoted as C, asset returns at a chosen horizon (say, 1 year) can be written as

$$A_i = \rho_i C + \sqrt{1 - \rho_i^2}\, \varepsilon_i \tag{5-30a}$$

$$A_j = \rho_j C + \sqrt{1 - \rho_j^2}\, \varepsilon_j \tag{5-30b}$$

such that

$$\rho_{ij} \equiv \mathrm{corr}(A_i, A_j) = \rho_i\, \rho_j \tag{5-31}$$

In order to calculate default correlation using Equation (5-26), we need to obtain the formulas for individual and joint default probabilities. Given the assumption about the distribution of asset returns, we have immediately

$$\begin{aligned} p_i^D &= P(A_i \le K_i) \\ &= N(K_i) \end{aligned} \tag{5-32a}$$

and

$$\begin{aligned} p_j^D &= P(A_j \le K_j) \\ &= N(K_j) \end{aligned} \tag{5-32b}$$

where $N(.)$ is the cumulative standard normal distribution. Conversely, the default thresholds can be determined from the probabilities of default by inverting the Gaussian distribution: $K = N^{-1}(p)$.

Figure 5-10 illustrates the asset return distribution and the default zone (the area where $A \leq K$). The probability of default corresponds to the area below the density curve from $-\infty$ to K.

Assuming further that asset returns for obligors i and j are bivariate normally distributed,[9] the joint probability of default is obtained using

$$p_{i,j}^{D,D} = N_2(K_i, K_j, \rho_{ij}) \tag{5-33}$$

Equations (5-32a and b) and (5-33) provide all the necessary building blocks to calculate default correlation in a factor model of credit risk.

Figure 5-11 illustrates the relationship between asset correlation and default correlation for various levels of default probabilities, using Equations (5-33) and (5-26). The lines are calibrated such that they reflect the 1-year probabilities of default of firms within all rating categories.[10]

It is very clear from the picture that as default probability increases, *default* correlation also increases for a given level of *asset* correlation. This implies that some of the increase in default correlation reported in Tables 5-2 to 5-4 will be captured by a factor model simply because default probabilities increase with the horizon. We will discuss below whether this effect is sufficient to replicate the empirically observed increase in correlations as the horizon is extended.

Lopez (2002) reports that asset correlations decrease in the probability of default. The overall impact of the horizon is therefore unclear in the context of a factor-based model: On the one hand, according to equity-based models, *default* correlations[11] increase in the probability of default (which grows with the horizon), but on the other hand, Lopez claims that *asset* correlations decrease in the probability of default, which should lead to a fall in *default* correlations.

Are Equity Correlations Good Proxies for Asset Correlations?

We have just seen that the formula for pairwise default correlation is quite simple but relies on asset correlation, which is not directly observable. It has become market practice to use equity correlation as a proxy for asset correlation. The underlying assumption is that equity returns should reflect the value of the underlying firms, and therefore that two firms with highly correlated asset values should also have high equity correlations.

FIGURE 5-10

Asset Return Distribution

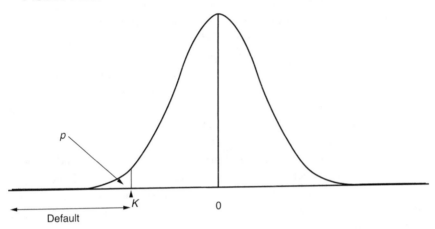

FIGURE 5-11

Default Correlation versus Asset Correlation

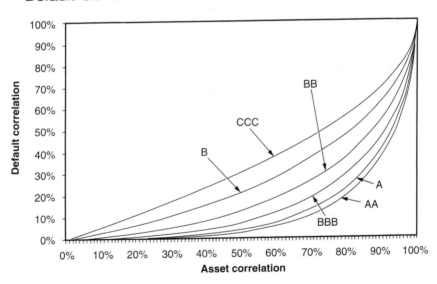

To test the validity of this assumption, de Servigny and Renault (2003) have gathered a sample of over 1100 firms for which they had at least 5 years of data on the ratings, equity prices, and industry classification. They then computed average equity correlations across and within industries. These equity correlations were inserted in Equation (5-33) to obtain a series of default correlations extracted from equity prices. They then proceeded to compare default correlations calculated in this way with default correlations calculated empirically using Equation (5-29).

Figure 5-12 summarizes their findings. Equity-driven default correlations and empirical correlations appear to be only weakly related, or, in other words, equity correlations provide at best a noisy indicator of default correlations. This casts some doubt on the robustness of the market standard assumption and also on the possibility of hedging credit products using the equity of their issuer.

Although disappointing, this result may not be surprising. Equity returns incorporate a lot of noise (bubbles, etc.) and are affected by supply and demand effects (liquidity crunches) that are not related to the firms' fundamentals. Therefore, although the relevant fundamental correlation information may be incorporated in equity returns, it is blended with many other types of information and cannot easily be extracted.

We mentioned earlier that empirical default correlation tends to increase substantially between 1 year and 3 to 5 years. We have also argued that a factor-based model will automatically generate increasing default correlation as the horizon increases. de Servigny and Renault

FIGURE 5-12

Empirical versus Equity-Driven Default Correlations

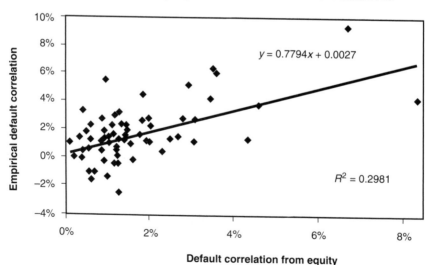

(2003) show on their data set that a constant *asset* correlation cannot replicate the extent of this increase by the simple mechanical effect of the
increase in default probabilities. In order to replicate the empirically
observed increase, one needs to increase substantially the level of asset
correlation in accordance with the chosen horizon.

In conclusion, using equity correlation without adjusting for the
horizon is insufficient. One needs either to take into account the term
structure of correlations or to calibrate a copula. The parameter of such
a copula driving the fatness of the tail would be linked to the targeted
horizon.

Correlations in an Intensity Framework

We have seen earlier in Chapter 4 that intensity-based models of credit
risk were very popular among practitioners for pricing defaultable bonds
and credit derivatives. We will return to these models in later chapters on
spreads and credit derivatives. This class of model, where default occurs
as the first jump of a stochastic process, can also be used to analyze
default correlations.

In an intensity model, the probability of default over [0,t] for a firm
i is

$$PD_i(t) = P_0[\tau_i \leq t] = 1 - E_0\left[\exp\left(-\int_0^t \lambda_s^i \, ds\right)\right] \tag{5-34}$$

where λ_s^i is the intensity of the default process, and τ_i is the default time
for firm i. The linear default correlation (5-26) can thus be written as

$$\rho(t) = \frac{E(y_t^1 y_t^2) - E(y_t^1)E(y_t^2)}{\sqrt{E(y_t^1)[1 - E(y_t^1)]E(y_t^2)[1 - E(y_t^2)]}} \tag{5-35}$$

where

$$y_t^i = \exp\left(-\int_0^t \lambda_s^i \, ds\right) \quad \text{for } i = 1,2 \tag{5-36}$$

Testing Conditionally Independent Intensity Models

Yu (2002b) implements several intensity specifications belonging to the
class of conditionally independent models including those of Driessen
(2002) and Duffee (1999) using empirically derived parameters. These

models are similar in spirit to the factor models described in Appendix 5A except that the factor structure is imposed on the intensity rather than on asset returns.

The intensities are functions of a set of k state variables $X_t = (X_t^1,...,X_t^k)$ defined below. Conditional on a realization of X_t, the default intensities are independent. Dependency therefore arises from the fact that all intensities are functions of X_t.

Common choices for the state variables are term structure factors (level of a specific Treasury rate, slope of the Treasury curve), other macroeconomic variables, firm-specific factors (leverage, book-to-market ratio), etc.

For example, the two state variables in Duffee (1999) are the two factors of a riskless affine term structure model (see Duffie and Kan, 1996). Driessen (2002) also includes two term structure factors and adds two further common factors to improve the empirical fit.

In most papers including those mentioned above, the intensities λ_s^i are defined under the risk-neutral measure (see the definition in Chapter 8), and they therefore yield correlation measures under that specific probability measure. These correlation estimates cannot be compared directly with empirical default correlations as shown in Tables 5-1 to 5-4. The latter are indeed calculated under the subjective historical measure.

Yu (2002b) relies on results from Jarrow, Lando, and Yu (2001), who prove that asymptotically in a very large portfolio, average intensities under the risk-neutral and historical measures coincide. Yu argues that given that the parameters of the papers by Driessen and Duffee are estimated over a large and diversified sample, this asymptotic result should hold. He then computes default parameters from the estimated average parameters of intensities reported in Duffee (1999) and Driessen (2002) using Equations (5-35) and (5-36).

These results are reported in Tables 5-5 and 5-6. The model by Duffee (1999) tends to generate much too low default correlations compared with other specifications.

Tables 5-7 and 5-8 are presented for comparative purposes. As Tables 5-6 and 5-8 show, Driessen (2002) yields results that are comparable to those of Zhou (2001).

Both intensity-based models exhibit higher default correlations as the probability of default increases and as the horizon is extended.

Yu (2002b) notices that the asymptotic result by Jarrow, Lando, and Yu (2001) may not hold for short bonds because of tax and liquidity effects reflected in the spreads. He therefore proposes an ad hoc adjustment of the intensity:

TABLE 5-5

Default Correlations Inferred from Duffee (1999), in Percent

	1 Year			2 Years			5 Years			10 Years		
	Aa	A	Baa	Aa	A	Baa	Aa	A	Baa	Aa	A	Baa
Aa	0.00	0.00	0.00	0.01	0.01	0.01	0.02	0.02	0.03	0.03	0.03	0.05
A	0.00	0.00	0.00	0.01	0.01	0.01	0.02	0.03	0.04	0.03	0.06	0.06
Baa	0.00	0.00	0.01	0.01	0.01	0.02	0.02	0.04	0.06	0.05	0.06	0.09

Source: Yu (2002b).

TABLE 5-6

Default Correlations from Driessen (2002), in Percent

	1 Year			2 Years			5 Years			10 Years		
	Aa	A	Baa	Aa	A	Baa	Aa	A	Baa	Aa	A	Baa
Aa	0.04	0.05	0.08	0.17	0.19	0.31	0.93	1.04	1.68	3.16	3.48	5.67
A	0.05	0.06	0.10	0.19	0.32	0.35	1.04	1.17	1.89	3.48	3.85	6.27
Baa	0.08	0.10	0.15	0.31	0.35	0.56	1.68	1.89	3.05	5.67	5.67	10.23

Source: Yu (2002b).

TABLE 5-7

Average Empirical Default Correlations [Using Equation (5-29)], in Percent

	1 Year			2 Years			5 Years			10 Years		
	AA	A	BBB	AA	A	BBB	AA	A	BBB	AA	A	BBB
AA	0.16	0.02	−0.03	0.16	−0.03	−0.07	0.48	0.12	0.09	0.79	0.54	0.60
A	0.02	0.12	0.03	−0.03	0.20	0.23	0.12	0.32	0.23	0.54	0.54	0.61
BBB	−0.03	0.03	0.33	−0.07	0.23	0.78	0.09	0.23	0.82	0.60	0.61	1.17

Source: S&P CreditPro—over 21 years.

TABLE 5-8

Default Correlations from Zhou (2001), in Percent

	1 Year			2 Years			5 Years			10 Years		
	Aa	A	Baa	Aa	A	Baa	Aa	A	Baa	Aa	A	Baa
Aa	0.00	0.00	0.00	0.00	0.00	0.01	0.59	0.92	1.24	4.66	5.84	6.76
A	0.00	0.00	0.00	0.00	0.02	0.05	0.92	1.65	2.60	5.84	7.75	9.63
Baa	0.00	0.00	0.00	0.01	0.05	0.25	1.24	2.60	5.01	6.76	9.63	13.12

Source: Zhou (2001).

$$\lambda_t^{\text{adj}} = \lambda_t - \frac{a}{b+t}$$

where t is time and a and b are constants obtained from Yu (2002a).

Tables 5-9 and 5-10 report the liquidity-adjusted tables of default correlations. The differences with Tables 5-5 and 5-6 are striking. First, the level of correlations induced by the liquidity-adjusted models is much higher. More surprisingly, the relationship between probability of default and default correlation is inverted: The higher the default risk, the lower the correlation.

Modeling Intensities under the Physical Measure

The modeling approach proposed by Yu (2002b) relies critically on the result by Jarrow, Lando, and Yu (2001) about the equality of risk-neutral and historical intensities which only holds asymptotically. If the assumption is valid, then the risk-neutral intensity calibrated on market spreads can be used to calculate default correlations for risk management purposes.

Das, Freed, Geng, and Kapadia (2002) take a different approach and avoid extracting information from market spreads. They gather a large sample of historical default probabilities derived from the RiskCalc model for public companies from 1987 to 2000. Falkenstein (2000) describes this model that provides 1-year probabilities for a large sample of firms.

Das, Freed, Geng, and Kapadia (2002) start by transforming the default intensity into average intensities over 1-year periods. Using Equation (5-34) and an estimate of default probabilities, they obtain a monthly estimate of default intensity by

$$\lambda^i = -\log\left[1 - PD_i(1)\right] \tag{5-37}$$

The time series of intensities are then split into a mean component $\overline{\lambda^i}$ and a zero-mean stochastic component ε_t^i:

$$\lambda_t^i = \overline{\lambda^i} + \varepsilon_t^i \tag{5-38}$$

Das, Freed, Geng, and Kapadia (2002) study the correlations between ε_t^i and ε_t^j for two firms i and j. Table 5-11 reports their results for various time periods and rating classes. These results cannot be directly compared with those presented above because they are correlations of intensities and not of default events.

Other specifications for the intensity processes are also tested by the authors, including an autoregressive process and a model with asymmet-

TABLE 5-9

Liquidity-Adjusted Default Correlations Inferred from Duffee (1999), in Percent

	1 Year			2 Years			5 Years			10 Years		
	Aa	A	Baa	Aa	A	Baa	Aa	A	Baa	Aa	A	Baa
Aa	0.08	0.07	0.05	0.17	0.14	0.11	0.29	0.23	0.20	0.30	0.22	0.23
A	0.07	0.08	0.05	0.14	0.15	0.10	0.23	0.24	0.17	0.22	0.30	0.18
Baa	0.05	0.05	0.03	0.10	0.11	0.07	0.20	0.17	0.14	0.23	0.18	0.17

Source: Yu (2002b).

TABLE 5-10

Liquidity-Adjusted Default Correlations Inferred from Driessen (2002), in Percent

	1 Year			2 Years			5 Years			10 Years		
	Aa	A	Baa	Aa	A	Baa	Aa	A	Baa	Aa	A	Baa
Aa	1.00	1.12	0.63	3.11	2.98	1.90	11.78	9.58	7.48	28.95	21.92	20.03
A	1.12	1.29	0.72	2.98	2.90	1.84	9.58	7.87	6.12	21.92	16.68	15.22
Baa	0.63	0.72	0.40	1.90	1.84	1.17	7.48	6.12	4.77	20.03	15.22	13.91

Source: Yu (2002b).

TABLE 5-11

Average Correlations between Intensities

Group	Jan. 87 to Apr. 90		May 90 to Dec. 93		Jan. 94 to Apr. 97		May 97 to Oct. 2000	
Aaa to A3	0.62	0.86	0.18	0.63	0.05	0.54	0.58	0.90
Baa1 to Ba3	0.35	0.73	0.20	0.63	0.02	0.52	0.35	0.74
B1 to C	0.17	0.61	0.19	0.61	0.00	0.50	0.29	0.69

Source: Das, Freed, Geng, and Kapadia (2002).

ric correlation structure (different correlations for increases and decreases in default intensities). These are also used in the model we now present about applying copulas to default dependencies.

Applying Copulas to Joint Intensity Modeling

Das and Geng (2002) perform an extensive empirical analysis of alternative specifications of the joint distribution of defaults. Their approach differs from that of Yu (2002b) in that they rely on copula functions and thus estimate marginal distributions separately from the multivariate distribution.

The authors proceed in three steps:

♦ The first step consists of modeling the dynamics of the mean default rate for each rating group (they divide the Moody's rating scale into six rating categories such that rating $i + 1$ corresponds to a higher default probability than rating i). Two specifications are tested: a jump process and a regime-switching (high probability, low probability) model.

♦ Then individual default probabilities (marginal distributions) are calibrated using one of three alternative probability laws: Gaussian, student-t, or skewed double exponential. The parameters of these distributions are estimated by maximum likelihood, and statistical tests are performed to determine which distribution is better able to fit each time series of default probability. Their data are the same as in Das, Freed, Geng, and Kapadia (2002).

♦ Finally, copula functions are used to combine marginal distributions into one multivariate distribution and are constrained to match pairwise correlations between obligors. Four specifications of the copula functions are tested: Gaussian, Gumbel, Clayton, and t-copulas (see the section on correlations and other dependency measures earlier in this chapter).

While standard test statistics are available to identify the marginal distribution fitting the data most closely, multivariate distribution tests in order to calibrate copulas are less widespread. Das and Geng (2002) therefore develop a goodness-of-fit metric that focuses on several criteria.

Goodness of Fit   Das and Geng (2002) choose three features of the multivariate distribution that they think are the most important to calibrate:

♦ *The level of intensity correlation.* The copula should permit the calibration of empirically observed correlations.

- *Correlation asymmetry.* It should allow for different levels of correlations depending on the level of PD.
- *Tail dependency.* The dependency in the lower and upper tails is also a desirable property to calibrate (see the section presented earlier on the copula).

These three features can be measured on a graph of exceedance correlation (Figure 5-13). A correlation at an exceedance level ξ is the correlation ρ^ξ between two random variables X and Y conditional on both variables registering increases or decreases of more than ξ standard deviations from their means. For X and Y centered and standardized, it is defined as

$$\rho^\xi = \begin{cases} \text{corr}(X,Y \mid X > \xi, Y > \xi) & \text{if } \xi \geq 0 \\ \text{corr}(X,Y \mid X < \xi, Y < \xi) & \text{if } \xi \leq 0 \end{cases}$$

The variable of interest (for which we consider exceedance) is the total hazard rate THR_t defined as the sum of the default intensities of all firms at a point in time t. The sample of PDs is then split into categories corresponding to the exceedance levels:

$$\xi \in \{-1.5, -1.0, -0.5, 0, 0, 0.5, 1, 1.5\}$$

FIGURE 5-13

The Asymmetric Correlation Structure

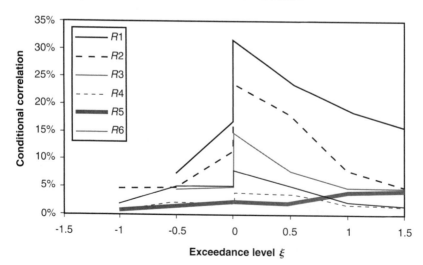

i.e., PDs that are more than 1.5, 1, or 0.5 standard deviation below or above their mean, etc.

Figure 5-13 incorporates all three features of interest. The level of correlation is immediately visible (level of the curves). The asymmetry is also obvious: We observe much higher correlations for positive changes in intensity. The level of tail dependency can be measured by the slope of the lines. As we go further in the tails, the slope decreases, which reflects tail dependency.[12]

The metric used by Das and Geng (2002) to gauge the quality of the fit of the copula is the average of the squared deviations between the exceedance empirically observed correlations (as shown in Figure 5-13) and those produced by the copula. The idea is therefore to minimize

$$q = \sqrt{\frac{1}{48} \sum_{k=1}^{6} \sum_{\xi=-1.5}^{1.5} \left(\rho_k^{\xi} - \rho_k^{\xi*} \right)^2}$$

where k denotes the rating and ξ denotes the exceedance level. Starred correlations are those produced by the copula.

Results   The main results of this extensive empirical study are the following:

- The regime-switching model (high probability, low probability) performs better than the jump model in fitting the mean default rates.
- The skewed double-exponential distribution seems an appropriate choice for the marginal distribution.
- Combined with the Clayton copula, the skewed double-exponential distribution provides the best fit to the data.
- The calibration of marginal distributions is not indifferent to the outcome of the copula to fit the joint distribution.

The last point deserves a little more explanation. The use of copulas is often motivated by the fact that one can separate the task of estimating marginal distributions from that of fitting the multivariate distribution. While this is true, this empirical study shows that the choice of marginal distributions does impact on the choice of the best copula and therefore on the shape of the multivariate distribution. This result is probably dependent on the metric used to select the appropriate specification.

On the whole this broad study sheds some light on many issues of interest to credit portfolio managers. The results reported above are difficult to compare with others, as the empirical literature on applications of copulas to credit risk is very thin. It would, for example, be interesting to check the sensitivity of the conclusions to the choice of metric or to the frequency of data observations.

C O N C L U S I O N

In this chapter we have discussed default dependencies. We have shown that although a partial measure of joint variations, correlations still play a primordial role in financial applications. We have introduced the concept of copula, which proves a promising tool for capturing dependency in credit markets. However, the appropriate choice of a specific copula function remains an open issue.

As far as empirical results are concerned, some stylized facts clearly emerge: Correlations increase markedly in the horizon and appear to be time-dependent. Depending on the choice of model, correlations will either increase or decrease in the probability of default. Empirical correlations increase in default probability, as do correlations implied by an equity-type model of credit risk. On the other hand, intensity-based models tend to generate decreasing correlations as credit quality deteriorates.

We believe that three avenues of research will yield interesting results in the coming years. The first one involves a careful analysis of the common factors driving correlations. Up to now, empirical analyses of default correlations have considered obvious choices such as macroeconomic or industry factors. No convincing systematic study of potential determinants has yet been published to our knowledge.

Second, contagion models are still in their infancy. Davis and Lo (1999a, 1999b) and Yu (2002b) provide interesting insights, but more sophisticated models will no doubt be proposed. Biomedicine researchers have developed an extensive literature on contagion that has not yet been taken on board by financial researchers.

Finally, we have seen several attempts to model correlations under the physical probability measure. Few of these have yet taken the direct approach of modeling joint durations between rating transitions or defaults. This will doubtless be a research direction in the near future.

A P P E N D I X   5 A

Conditionally Independent Models of Credit Risk

The basic setup of a one-factor model of credit risk involves the modeling of asset returns A at a chosen horizon T as a sum of a systematic factor C and an idiosyncratic factor ε:

$$A = \rho C + \sqrt{1 - \rho^2}\ \varepsilon \tag{5A-1}$$

where A, C, and ε are assumed to follow standard normal distributions.

The probability of default p is the probability that the asset return is below a threshold K:

$$p = P(A < K)$$

$$= N(K)$$

Conditional on a specific realization of the factor $C = c$, the probability of default is

$$p(c) = P(A < K \mid C = c)$$

$$= N\left(\frac{K - \rho c}{\sqrt{1 - \rho^2}} \right) \tag{5A-2}$$

Furthermore, conditional on c, defaults become independent, which enables simple computations of portfolio loss probabilities.

Assume that we have a portfolio of H obligors with the same probability of default and the same factor loading ρ. Out of these obligors, one may observe $X = 0, 1, 2$ or up to H defaults before the horizon T. Using the law of iterated expectations, the probability of observing exactly h defaults can be written as the expectation of the conditional probability:

$$P[X = h] = \int_{-\infty}^{+\infty} P[X = h \mid C = c]\phi(c)\ dc \tag{5A-3}$$

where $\phi(.)$ is the standard normal density.

Given that defaults are conditionally independent, the probability of observing h defaults conditional on a realization of the systematic factor will be binomial such that

$$P[X = h \mid C = c] = \binom{H}{h} \left\{ p(c)^h \, [1 - p(c)]^{H-h} \right\} \tag{5A-4}$$

Using Equations (5A-2) and (5A-3), we then obtain the cumulative probability of observing less than m defaults:

$$P[X \le m] = \sum_{h=0}^{m} \binom{H}{h} \int_{-\infty}^{+\infty} \left[N \left(\frac{K - \rho c}{\sqrt{1 - \rho^2}} \right) \right]^h \left[1 - N \left(\frac{K - \rho c}{\sqrt{1 - \rho^2}} \right) \right]^{H-h} \phi(c) \, dc$$

$$\tag{5A-5}$$

The graph in Figure 5A-1 is a plot of $P[X = h]$ for various assumptions of factor correlation from $\rho = 0$ percent to $\rho = 10$ percent. The probability of default is assumed to be 5 percent for all $H = 100$ obligors.

The mean number of defaults is 5 for all three scenarios, but the shape of the distribution is very different. For $\rho = 0$ percent, we observe a roughly bell-shaped curve centered on 5. When correlation increases, the likelihood of joint bad events increases, implying a fat right-hand tail. The likelihood of joint good events (few or zero defaults) also increases, and there is a much larger chance of 0 defaults.

FIGURE 5A-1

Impact of Correlation on Portfolio Loss Distribution

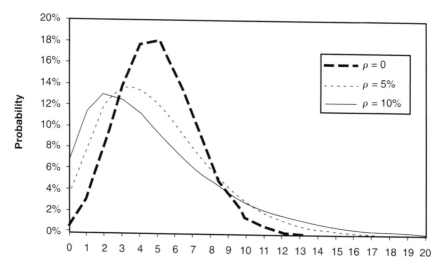

Number of defaults in portfolio

APPENDIX 5B

Calculating Default Correlation in a Structural Credit Risk Model

In Chapter 3 we discussed the simple Merton (1974) model of credit risk. One of the weaknesses of this model was that default is only allowed at the maturity of the debt T.

The Merton framework has been extended to include an early default barrier by Black and Cox (1976) and many subsequent authors. Zhou (2001) was the first to derive a formula for default correlation in a structural model with a barrier. Using Equation (5-30), we need to derive the formulas for univariate and bivariate default probabilities of default: p_i^D, p_j^D, and $p_{i,j}^{D,D}$. Univariate probabilities of default correspond to the probability that the value of firm 1 or firm 2 hit their default barriers (see Figure 5B-1). The default times are denoted as τ_1 and τ_2.

The probabilities of default $p_i^D = P(\tau_i \leq T)$ and $p_j^D = P(\tau_j \leq T)$ correspond to the probability that a geometric Brownian motion (the firm value process) hits an exponentially drifting boundary (the default threshold) before some time T. This formula can be found in textbooks such as Harrison (1985) or Musiela and Rutkowski (1998).

The main contribution of Zhou (2001) is to derive the complex joint probability

$$p_{i,j}^{D,D} = P(\tau_i \leq T, \tau_j \leq T)$$

FIGURE 5B-1

First Passage Times of Firms *i* and *j* to Default
Boundary

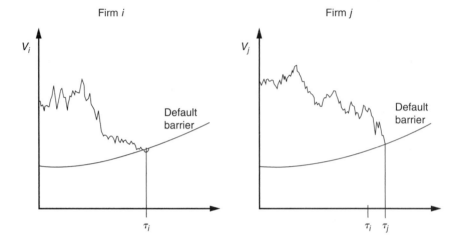

CHAPTER 6

Credit Risk Portfolio Models

Chapters 2 to 5 detailed the three major drivers of portfolio credit risk: the probability of default extracted from qualitative or quantitative approaches, loss given default, and correlations. We have so far treated all these factors in isolation. This chapter brings these building blocks together to derive important indicators such as economic capital or portfolio loss measures.

We start the chapter by explaining why we need a credit risk portfolio model (CRPM). Next we look at the common architecture of the main commercial models and distinguish between an analytical approach and a simulation-based approach. We then turn our attention to the main part of this chapter: a review of five of the most popular models commercially available—CreditMetrics, CreditPortfolioView, Portfolio Risk Tracker, CreditRisk+, and Portfolio Manager—and a discussion of their relative strengths and weaknesses. After that, we focus on the most recent methodologies designed to obtain quick approximations based on analytical shortcuts (the saddle point method and the fast Fourier transform), and we discuss stress testing. Finally, we present risk-adjusted performance measures (RAPMs).

CREDIT RISK PORTFOLIO MODELS: WHAT FOR?

Most commercial models fit in a bottom-up approach to credit risk. The idea is to aggregate the credit risk of all individual instruments in a portfolio. The output is a portfolio credit risk measure that is *not* the sum of risks of individual positions thanks to the benefits of diversification.

One of the main difficulties of dealing with credit-risky assets is that their profit and loss distributions are far from normal (see Figure 6-1). They are frequently characterized by a limited upside, as in the case for loans, but suffer from large potential downside because of high probabilities of large losses due to default (fat tail).

The development of portfolio management tools for market risk in the 1980s and early 1990s has enabled banks to better understand and control that risk. Since then, banks have worked actively to achieve a similar degree of sophistication in their credit risk management systems. This exercise was complicated by the nonnormality of credit loss distributions and the lack of reliable credit data for many asset classes. Four main reasons have driven banks to undertake the development or improvement of their credit portfolio tools:

- ◆ *Regulatory purposes.* CRPMs are useful and will become part of the reporting in the Basel II context (see Chapter 10). Regulatory capital will be tied to the riskiness, maturity, and diversification of the bank's portfolio.

- ◆ *Economic capital calculation and allocation.* Beside regulatory capital, portfolio risk measures are used in banks to determine

FIGURE 6-1

Typical Profit and Loss Profile for a Credit Portfolio

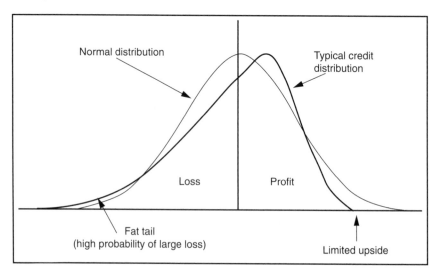

reserves based on economic capital calculations. The split of economic capital consumed by the various loans can also be used to set credit limits to counterparts or to select assets based on risk-return trade-offs, taking into account diversification benefits specific to the constitution of the bank portfolio.

♦ *Pricing purposes.* Some financial instruments can be seen as options on the performance of a portfolio of assets. This is the case, for example, with collateralized debt obligations (CDOs) whose payoffs rely on cash flows generated by a pool of credit instruments. Measuring the risk of a portfolio of credit-risky assets can therefore also be useful both for pricing purposes and for the rating of such instruments by rating agencies (see Chapter 9).

♦ *Fund management.* Asset managers can also benefit from a portfolio credit risk model for asset allocation. The selection of facilities to include in a portfolio or a fund is better determined when a global view on aggregate risk and diversification is available.

A good credit risk portfolio model ideally should capture all facets of credit risk. The most obvious one is default risk (the probability of default and LGD) at the facility level and aggregated in the portfolio. Credit risk also encompasses changes in prices due to credit events. A CRPM therefore should, although in practice it rarely does, incorporate both downgrade and spread risk for the constituents of the portfolio. Finally, we have seen the crucial impact of correlations in the tails of loss distributions: A good portfolio model should also be in a position to reflect diversification or concentration effects accurately.

CLASSES OF MODELS

Here we describe the main architecture of portfolio models. They can be split into two categories: analytical models and simulation-based models.

Analytical Models

Analytical models provide "exact" solutions to the loss distribution of credit assets, given some simplifying assumptions. The first step is to group homogeneous assets in subportfolios for which the homogeneity assumption allows us to derive analytical solutions for the loss distribution. Aggregate losses at the portfolio level are then obtained by a simple addition.

The main advantage of analytical models is that we can obtain results very quickly. Unfortunately, analytical solutions often come at the cost of many stringent assumptions on the drivers of default. The CreditRisk+ model reviewed below belongs to the analytical category.

Simulation-Based Models

Simulation-based models do not yield closed-form solutions for the portfolio loss distribution. The idea underlying this category of models is to approximate the true distribution by an empirical distribution generated by a large number of simulations (scenarios). This process enables gains in flexibility and can accommodate complex distributions for risk factors. The main drawback of this approach is that it is computer-intensive

Figure 6-2 describes the general process of a simulation-based model. The necessary inputs are assessments of probabilities of default, losses given default (mean and standard deviation), and asset correlations for all facilities. Using a Monte Carlo engine, we can use these inputs to simulate many scenarios for asset values which translate into correlated migrations. Conditional on terminal ratings at the end of the chosen horizon, values for each asset are computed and compared with their initial value, thereby providing a measure of profit or loss. The inputs and steps needed to implement a simulation-based model are explained in more detail in the CreditMetrics section that follows.

REVIEW OF COMMERCIAL MODELS

In this section we examine five credit risk portfolio models developed by practitioners: CreditMetrics, PortfolioManager, Portfolio Risk Tracker, CreditPortfolioView, and CreditRisk+. The last one belongs to the analytical class, whereas the first four are simulation-based.

In a survey of 41 large international banks, Brannan, Mengle, Smithson, and Zmiewski (2002) report that more than 80 percent of banks use one of the products listed above as their credit portfolio risk model. Table 6-1 displays the various features of the models: the credit events captured by the models (defaults, transitions, and changes in spreads), the factors driving risk, the type of transition matrices used, the way that correlation is embedded, the specification adopted for LGD, as well as the category of model (analytical versus simulation-based).

FIGURE 6-2

Simulation Framework

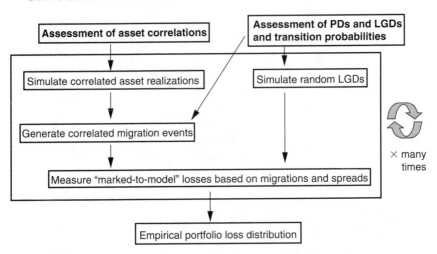

CreditMetrics

CreditMetrics is the credit risk portfolio tool of RiskMetrics. It is a one-period rating-based model enabling the user to calculate credit value at risk via the simulation of multiple normally distributed risk factors. We review in detail below the various steps leading to the calculation of portfolio losses. A more exhausitive description of the model can be found in the technical documents (JP Morgan, 1997). These documents also discuss the important issues of exposure measurement for nonstandard instruments such as derivatives.

Step 1: Gathering the Inputs

Most inputs for credit risk portfolio models (PDs, LGDs, and correlations) have been studied at length in Chapters 2 to 5. We just briefly review them here and refer the reader to relevant chapters for more details.

CreditMetrics relies on many different inputs[1]:

- PDs and transition probabilities
- Mean and standard deviation of recovery rates per industry and seniority
- Factor correlations and how each obligor is related to them (factor loadings)
- Riskless yield curve

TABLE 6-1

Comparative Structure of the Main Models

	CreditMetrics	Credit Portfolio View	Portfolio Risk Tracker	Portfolio Manager	CreditRisk+
Definition of risk	Δ Market value	Δ Market value or default losses only	ΔMarket value	Default losses	Default losses
Credit events	Downgrade/ default	Downgrade/ default	Downgrade/ default and spread changes*	Default	Default
Includes interest rate risk	No	No	Yes	No	No
Risk drivers	Country and industry factors	Macro factors	Country and industry factors	Factors through asset values	Default rates
Transition probabilities	Constant	Driven by macro factors (state dependent transition matrices)	Constant	Constant	N/A
Correlation of credit events	Standard multivariate normal equity returns	Arises due to common dependence on same macro factors	Standard multivariate normal asset returns	Standard multivariate normal asset returns	N/A
Recovery rates	Random (beta distribution)	Random	Random (beta distribution)	Random (beta distribution)	Loss given default (constant)
Numerical approach	Simulation	Simulation	Simulation	Simulation	Analytic

* Asset managers' version of the model.

- ♦ Risky yield curves per rating class
- ♦ Individual credit exposure profiles

Before reviewing the calculation methodology, we first spend some time discussing the various inputs.

PDs and Transition Probabilities   CreditMetrics is a rating-based model. Each exposure is assigned a rating (e.g., BBB). A horizon-specific probability of transition is associated with every rating category. It can be obtained from transition matrices (see Chapter 2).

Each obligor is matched with a corresponding distribution of asset returns. This distribution of asset returns is then "sliced" (Figure 6-3) such that each tranche corresponds to the probability of migration from the initial rating (BBB in this example) to another rating category. The largest area is, of course, that of BBB, because an obligor is most likely to remain in its rating class over a (short) horizon. Thresholds delimiting the various classes can be obtained by inverting the cumulative normal distribution.

For example, the default threshold is obtained as $T_D = N^{-1}(p)$, where p is the probability of default of a BBB bond over the horizon and $N^{-1}(.)$ is the inverse of the cumulative normal distribution. The threshold delimiting the CCC and B classes is calculated as

$$T_{CCC} = N^{-1}(p + p_{CCC})$$

where p_{CCC} is the probability of migrating to CCC, etc.

LGD Data   CreditMetrics draws random beta-distributed recovery rates and assigns the random values to defaulted facilities. Recovery rates on various defaulted counterparts are assumed not to be correlated with one another nor with probabilities of default or other risk factors in the model. Appendix 6A shows how to draw random numbers from an arbitrary distribution.

The beta distribution is specific to a given industry, country, and seniority level. Figure 6-4 is an example of the beta distribution fitted to the mean and volatility of recovery rates in the "machinery" sector across seniorities using U.S. data from Altman and Kishore (1996).

Factor and Asset Correlations   Several approaches can be employed to simulate correlated asset returns. The most straightforward is to simulate them directly by assuming a joint distribution function and

FIGURE 6-3

Splitting the Asset Return Distribution
on Rating Buckets

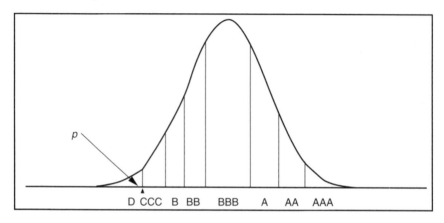

D CCC B BB   BBB   A   AA   AAA

FIGURE 6-4

Density of Recovery Rate Calibrated
to "Machinery" Sector

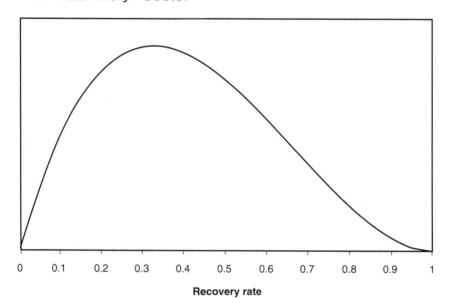

Recovery rate

calculating a correlation matrix for all assets. This can be done when the number of lines N in the portfolio is small but becomes intractable for realistic portfolio sizes. The size of the correlation matrix is indeed $N \times N$.

The traditional approach, employed by CreditMetrics, is to reduce the dimensionality of the problem by assuming that a limited number $n \ll N$ of factors F_i drive the asset returns. Let A_j denote the asset return for firm j at the chosen horizon:

$$A_j = \alpha_{1,j} F_1 + \alpha_{2,j} F_2 + \dots + \alpha_{n,j} F_n + \varepsilon_j \qquad (6\text{-}1)$$

Systematic factors[2] F_i and the idiosyncratic term ε_j follow normal distributions, and so does A_j.

The CreditMetrics model thus requires input of the correlation matrix of the factors F_i as well as the variance of the idiosyncratic terms. It also requires factor loadings α_{ij} which reflect the sensitivity of a given obligor j to the various factors i.

An example of how to calculate the correlation between two firms' asset returns and their default correlation is given in Appendix 6B.

Yield Curves

CreditMetrics considers losses arising both from defaults and from migration. Transition losses are more complex to incorporate in a model than default losses. They require the computation of the future values of all instruments in the portfolio conditional on all possible migrations, as will be shown below.

Future expected values for debt instruments can be computed from the forward interest rate curves. An important input for that purpose is therefore a collection of forward curves (Figure 6-5) for all rating categories.

From the yield curves in Figure 6-5, one can extract forward rates per class of risk at the horizon of the model, typically 1 year. Let $Y_i(0,T)$ denote the yield at time 0 of a T-maturity zero-coupon bond in rating class i. Forward rates 1 year ahead $f_i(0,1,T)$ are obtained using the following relationship:

$$[1 + Y_i(0,T)]^T = [1 + Y_i(0,1)] [1 + f_i(0,1,T)]^{T-1} \qquad (6\text{-}2)$$

Equation (6-2) means that the return obtained from an investment at the rate Y_i at time 0 for T years should be equal to an investment for 1 year reinvested for $T-1$ years at an agreed-upon rate at time 0. The agreed rate is the 1-year forward rate for rating category i: $f_i(0,1,T)$.

FIGURE 6-5

U.S. Industrial Bond Yield Curves (March 11, 2002)

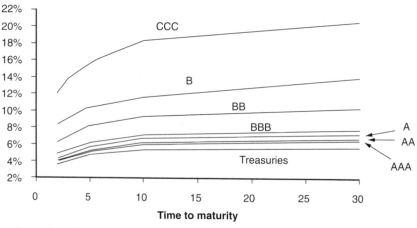

Source: Riskmetrics.

Exposures Most of the inputs discussed so far are not specific to a given bank's portfolio. Obviously the most important input in the model is the identification of the instruments that belong to the portfolio. This comprises the size of each exposure, their rating, their sensitivity to the factors (factor loadings were discussed above), etc.

For plain vanilla loans the definition of the exposure is quite simple, but for optional instruments or swaps the exposure is not constant but depends, for example, on the evolution of interest rates. CreditMetrics assumes that a calculation of the average exposure has been performed elsewhere by the user of the model. The use of such "loan-equivalent" approximations is not fully satisfactory.

Step 2: Generating Correlated Migration Events

Once the user has collected all the necessary input variables (step 1), CreditMetrics can start calculating portfolio losses. As a ratings-based model, the primary purpose of the simulation engine is to generate migration events with the appropriate correlation structure.

Figure 6-6 illustrates the impact of asset correlations on the joint migration of obligors, assuming that there are two nondefault states (investment grade, or IG, and non-investment grade, or NIG) and an absorbing default state D.

FIGURE 6-6

Probabilities of Joint Migrations for Various Levels of Asset Correlation ρ

$\rho = 0\%$

	IG/IG	IG/NIG	IG/D	NIG/NIG	NIG/D	D/D
IG/IG	95.9%	3.9%	0.2%	0.0%	0.0%	0.0%
IG/NIG	3.6%	89.2%	5.2%	1.8%	0.2%	0.0%
IG/D	0.0%	0.0%	97.9%	0.0%	2.0%	0.1%
NIG/NIG	0.1%	6.7%	0.4%	82.8%	9.7%	0.3%
NIG/D	0.0%	0.0%	3.7%	0.0%	91.0%	5.3%
D/D	0.0%	0.0%	0.0%	0.0%	0.0%	100.0%

$\rho = 20\%$

	IG/IG	IG/NIG	IG/D	NIG/NIG	NIG/D	D/D
IG/IG	96.0%	3.7%	0.2%	0.1%	0.0%	0.0%
IG/NIG	3.7%	89.2 %	5.1%	1.7%	0.3%	0.0%
IG/D	0.0%	0.0%	97.9%	0.0%	2.0%	0.1%
NIG/NIG	0.3%	6.7%	0.1%	83.0%	9.3%	0.6%
NIG/D	0.0%	0.0%	3.7%	0.0%	91.0%	5.3%
D/D	0.0%	0.0%	0.0%	0.0%	0.0%	100.0%

$\rho = 50\%$

	IG/IG	IG/NIG	IG/D	NIG/NIG	NIG/D	D/D
IG/IG	96.2%	3.3%	0.1%	0.3%	0.1%	0.0%
IG/NIG	3.7%	89.6%	4.7%	1.4%	0.7%	0.1%
IG/D	0.0%	0.0%	97.9%	0.0%	2.0%	0.1%
NIG/NIG	0.8%	5.8%	0.0%	84.1%	8.0%	1.3%
NIG/D	0.0%	0.0%	3.7%	0.0%	91.0%	5.3%
D/D	0.0%	0.0%	0.0%	0.0%	0.0%	100.0%

The experiment uses a one-factor model such as that described in Chapter 5, Equation (5-30). Similar results would be obtained in the multi-factor setup described in Equation (6-1). The tables are bivariate transition matrices for various levels of asset correlation ρ under the assumption of joint normality of asset returns and using aggregate probabilities of transition extracted from CreditPro.[3] In order to reduce the size of the tables, we have assumed that the pair IG/NIG is identical from a portfolio point of view to the pair NIG/IG. Thus each bivariate matrix is 6 x 6 instead of 9 x 9.

Taking, for example, the case of two non-investment-grade obligors (line NIG/NIG), we can observe that as the correlation increases, the joint default probability (as well as the joint probability of upgrades) increases significantly.

Multivariate transition probabilities cannot be computed for portfolios with reasonable numbers of lines. In a standard rating system with 8 categories, a portfolio with N counterparts would imply an $8^N \times 8^N$ transition matrix that soon becomes intractable.

CreditMetrics simulates realizations of the factors F_i and the idiosyncratic components ε_j [Equation (6-1)]. Given that firms all depend on the same factors, their asset returns are correlated and their migration events also exhibit co-movement.

Joint downgrades for two obligors 1 and 2 will occur when the simulations return a low realization for both asset returns A_1 and A_2. This will be more likely when these asset returns are highly correlated than in the independent case.

Step 3: Measuring "Marked-to-Model" Losses

In step 2, CreditMetrics simulates all the terminal ratings of the obligors in the portfolios. Step 3 calculates the profits or losses arising from these transitions including defaults. For all defaulted assets, a random value for the recovery rate is drawn from the beta distribution, with mean and variance corresponding to the issuer's industry and seniority. For "surviving" obligors, the terminal values of the assets are calculated using the forward curves as observed at the time of the calculations.

Measuring "Marked-to-Model" Losses: Example for a Straight Bond Consider a 5-year straight bond with a current rating of BBB and an annual coupon of 7 percent. We assume that a coupon has just been paid, so that the first cash flow will be paid in exactly 1 year. We have extracted the 1-year forward rates for all rating classes from AAA to CCC using Equation (6-2). Some of the rates are reported in Table 6-2.

From the forward curves computed in Table 6-2, we can calculate the forward values of the bond at our credit horizon (assumed to be 1 year) conditional on the bond terminating in a given rating. At the end of the horizon, the bond will have only 4 years left to maturity.

If it does not default, the bond will have a rating of AAA, AA, ..., or CCC.

TABLE 6-2

1-Year Forward Rates

Time to Maturity	AAA	...	A	...	B	...	CCC
1 year		...	0.0476	...	0.0893		...
2 years		...	0.0510	...	0.0919		...
3 years		...	0.0564	...	0.1020		...
4 years		...	0.0618	...	0.1115		...

For example, if the obligor is upgraded to A, its forward price will be

$$V_A(t + 1) = 7 + 7/(1.0476) + 7/(1.0510)^2 + 7/(1.0564)^3 + 107/(1.0618)^4$$
$$= 110.15$$

However, if it is downgraded to B, the forward price will be

$$V_B(t + 1) = 7 + 7/(1.0893) + 7/(1.0919)^2 + 7/(1.1020)^3 + 107/(1.1115)^4$$
$$= 94.63$$

The forward price must be computed for all seven possible terminal ratings. Hence for each asset in the portfolio, CreditMetrics calculates all possible terminal values.

Step 4: Calculating the Portfolio Loss Distribution

For each realization of risk factors F_i, we have calculated in step 2 the terminal rating of each security. Using the calculation described in step 3, we know what the forward prices of the facilities are, conditional on their terminal ratings.

Step 4 consists of summing up all forward values of the facilities and comparing the discounted sum (terminal value of the portfolio) with the current value of the portfolio. For each simulation run, we obtain a realization of credit profit and loss conditional on the specific value of the risk factors.

The above procedure is repeated a very large number of times, e.g., 1 million times, to obtain an entire distribution of portfolio losses. The distribution can then be used to calculate value at risk, expected shortfall, or any other risk statistic.

Portfolio Manager

KMV's Portfolio Manager is very similar to CreditMetrics. However, unlike CreditMetrics, it is a one-factor model focusing on default losses only. Bohn and Kealhofer (2001) provide an introduction to this model.

The main difference between Portfolio Manager and a simple one-factor version of CreditMetrics lies in the inputs for Portfolio Manager. We first briefly explore the basic structure of the model (which is identical to the CreditMetrics setup) and then discuss the necessary inputs.

Basic Structure

The Portfolio Manager model is based on the multivariate normal distribution: Asset values for all firms are assumed to have normally distributed returns.[4] Just as in CreditMetrics, when asset returns are low, the firm defaults. Transitions to other ratings are ignored.

The model therefore consists of:

1. Drawing many replications of the multivariate normal distribution
2. For each run of simulations, recording which firms default
3. Summing up the losses assuming beta-distributed loss given default
4. Calculating portfolio loss distribution and VaR

Inputs

Since the model relies on the normal distribution, only two types of inputs are necessary: the probabilities of default for all obligors at the chosen horizon and asset correlations.

Instead of using probabilities of default extracted from the rating category of the debt issuer (as in CreditMetrics), Portfolio Manager relies on expected default frequencies (EDFs). EDFs are probabilities of default extracted from a Merton-type model of credit risk (see Chapter 3).

The first input in the model is therefore a set of EDFs. Given that Portfolio Manager is a one-factor model, correlations are driven by only one-factor loading. The general setup can be written as

$$A_j = \rho_j F_j + \varepsilon_j \qquad (6\text{-}3)$$

The careful reader will have noticed that the factor also has subscript j, which means that it is specifically built for firm j. More specifically, it is obtained as

$$F_j = \sum_{i=1}^{I} \beta_{ji} C_i + \sum_{k=1}^{K} \gamma_{ki} S_i \qquad (6\text{-}4)$$

$$\sum_{i=1}^{I} \beta_{ji} = 1 \qquad (6\text{-}5)$$

$$\sum_{k=1}^{K} \gamma_{ki} = 1 \qquad (6\text{-}6)$$

C_i are the indexes for the countries to which the firm is exposed, and S_i are the sectors in which the firm operates.[5]

Equation (6-3) can be estimated from a time series of asset values. The R^2 of the regression determines the balance between systematic and unsystematic risks and therefore the correlation between asset values.

The user of the model can override the R^2 calculated this way and choose to fix it arbitrarily without any reference to a composite index. This flexibility is one of the rare degrees of freedom available to the user in this model. The remainder of the model is identical to CreditMetrics, and the reader can refer to the previous section for details on the calculations in a CreditMetrics-type framework.

Portfolio Risk Tracker

Portfolio Risk Tracker (PRT) is Standard & Poor's rating-based model. While the two products we have discussed so far are static (i.e., they focus exclusively on realizations of risk factors at a chosen horizon), PRT is dynamic. When choosing a 5-year horizon for example, risk factors are simulated at the end of each of the 5 years before the horizon. This allows Portfolio Risk Tracker to tackle products such as credit derivatives and CDOs in the calculation of credit value at risk. Unlike CreditMetrics and Portfolio Manager, PRT includes stochastic interest rates and is therefore able to deal with floating-rate notes and other interest rate–sensitive instruments, without having to rely on loan equivalence. Details of the methodology can be found in de Servigny, Peretyatkin, Perraudin, and Renault (2003).

Portfolio Risk Tracker also includes stochastic spreads,[6] which makes it the only model out of the five discussed in this section to capture the three sources of credit risk: defaults, transitions, and changes in spreads.

Additional novelties embedded in this product include (among others):

♦ The possibility to choose between correlation matrices extracted from spreads, equities, or empirical default correlations

♦ The modeling of sovereign ceilings (the rating of corporates is capped at the level of the sovereign), which enables contagions in specific countries

♦ The modeling of the correlation between PD and LGD (see Chapter 4)

♦ The possibility to include equities, Treasury bonds, and interest rate options

Figure 6-7 is an example of the loss distribution computed with PRT. It clearly displays the asymmetric and fat-tailed shape of credit losses.

CreditPortfolioView

The main difference between CreditPortfolioView (CPV) and the three models presented above is that it explicitly makes transition matrices

FIGURE 6-7

Distribution of Terminal Portfolio Value, Combining
Market and Credit Risk

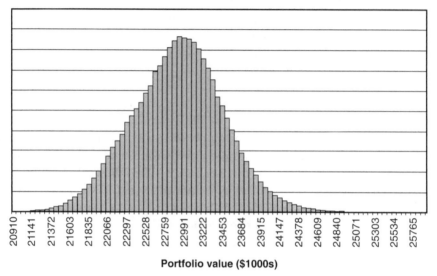

Portfolio value ($1000s)

Source: S&P.

dependent on the economic cycle. Default and migration rates in a given
country and industry at the chosen horizon are conditional on the future
values of macroeconomic variables. This idea is intuitive and supported
by empirical evidence (see Chapter 2). Macroeconomic variables are the
key drivers of default rates through time. Figure 6-8 illustrates this statement using U.S. data: Industrial production changes are clearly reflected
in fluctuations in probabilities of default (the survival probability is
defined as 1 minus the annual default rate across all industries).

CPV estimates an econometric model for a macroeconomic index
which drives sector default rates. Simulated default rates subsequently
determine which transition matrix (expansion or recession) is used over
the next time step. By simulating random paths for the macro index at a
given horizon, the model enables the user to approximate a distribution
of portfolio losses. The main references for this model are three works by
Wilson (1997a, 1997b, 1997c).

The Input

Any macroeconomic variable can be used as the driver of default rates.
The choice is left to the user, who may decide (or preferably test) what fac-

FIGURE 6-8

Survival Probability and Industrial Production Growth

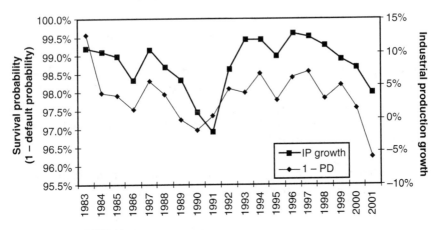

Source: S&P and NBER data.

tors are the most relevant to explain changes in default rates. The set of variables may include:

- GDP or industrial production growth
- Interest rates
- Exchange rates
- Savings rate
- Unemployment rate

The *explanatory* variables above are easily available from public sources such as central banks or national statistics bureaus. The *explained* variables are the default rates per industry and country. They are available from rating agencies for long time series in the United States but not always in the rest of the world. Bankruptcy rates (often at the country level) are sometimes available to compensate for missing information in regions where the rated universe is too small or the time-series history too short.

Other necessary inputs are, as usual, details about the specific exposures included in the portfolio as well as transition matrices and recovery rate statistics.

Model Specification and Calibration

In a given country and industrial sector, CPV proceeds in three steps to calculate the default rate.

- Step one first makes an assumption about the dynamics of the n selected macroeconomic variables X_i that will enter into the macroeconomic index. They are chosen to follow autoregressive processes so that the value at time t of variable X_i is given by

$$X_{i,t} = \alpha_0 + \sum_{j=1}^{m} \alpha_j X_{i,t-j} + e_{i,t} \quad \text{for } i = 1\ldots n \qquad (6\text{-}7)$$

where $e_{i,t}$ are identically independently distributed (i.i.d) normal error terms that can be correlated across variables. The number of lags (m) to include should be determined by likelihood ratio tests, although CPV uses two lags for all variables. The parameters are estimated, and the residual covariance matrix is saved.

♦ Second, the macroeconomic variables are aggregated into sector indexes Y_t^s according to the following specification:

$$Y_t^s = \beta_0^s + \sum_{i=1}^{n} \beta_i^s X_{i,t} + \varepsilon_t^s \qquad (6\text{-}8)$$

where ε_t^s are also i.i.d. normal disturbance terms and s denotes the sector. Each index reflects the health of the economy of a given sector. The macroeconomic indexes above take values in $(-\infty, +\infty)$.

♦ The final step applies the logistic transformation to Y in order to obtain a default rate (DR) that lies in $[0,1]$:

$$DR_t^s = \frac{1}{1 + e^{-Y_t^s}} \qquad (6\text{-}9)$$

Thus as $Y \to +\infty$, DR $\to 1$ and as $Y \to -\infty$, DR $\to 0$.

The estimation of the parameters and residuals in Equations (6-7) and (6-8) can be performed using standard econometric techniques. In order to estimate Equation (6-8) one first needs to invert Equation (6-9) to obtain implied values of the index from observed default rates in each sector. For a given sector s, the index is obtained from

$$Y_t^s = -\log \left(1/DR_t^s - 1\right) \qquad (6\text{-}10)$$

Let us pause and summarize the process. We want to estimate the macroeconomic drivers of the default rate DR_t^s in a given sector s. Intuitively we want to link this default rate to a macroeconomic index that would incorporate all macro variables. This index is Y_t^s and determines the default rate via Equation (6-9). The index is a weighted sum of individual macro variables $X_{i,t}$ [Equation (6-8)] that are assumed to follow a simple autoregressive process [Equation (6-7)].

Simulating the Factors and Calculating Portfolio Losses

The previous section consisted of specifying the dynamics of default rates and estimating the parameters (α, β) on historical data. We now move on to the main goal of the CPV model, which is to use the dynamics calibrated on past default rates to simulate future possible realizations of default rates at various horizons.

Future default rates will be linked to future realizations of macro variables. The simulation engine generates random variables that are used to simulate paths for the macro variables and therefore for the credit index and ultimately for the probabilities of default per industry.

1. The first step is to generate a large number K of vectors of correlated random variables $(e_{i,t+1}, e_{i,t+2}, e_{i,t+3}, ...)$ and $(\varepsilon^s_{t+1}, \varepsilon^s_{t+2}, \varepsilon^s_{t+3}, ...)$ where the length is the time corresponding to the chosen horizon. For example, if the chosen horizon is 1 year and Equations (6-7) and (6-8) have been estimated on quarterly data, the simulated paths should have four time steps. In order to simulate these paths, we need to draw correlated normal random variables with a covariance matrix chosen to correspond to that estimated in the previous section (see Appendix 6A for more information on simulation).

2. These random values are then plugged into Equations (6-7) and (6-8) to obtain K realizations of the macroeconomic index.

3. Then the macroeconomic index realizations are transformed into K realizations of the default rate P(default) using Equation (6-9).

4. For each simulation run, if P(default) is below its long-term average, the sector is assumed to be in expansion and we would choose an expansion transition matrix. But if P(default) is above its average, we would choose a recession matrix for the sector.

In CPV, the correlation arises across sectors due to the fact that sector default probabilities all depend on the same macro factors.

We consider M_h and M_l, the transition matrices associated with high states (growth) and low states (recessions), respectively, in the economic cycle. The significant difference between those two matrices is discussed, for example, in Bangia, Diebold, Kronimus, Schagen, and Schuermann (2002). Naturally, downgrade and default probabilities are higher in low states than in high states.

In order to calculate the N-period transition matrix necessary to calculate portfolio losses N years ahead (assuming a yearly time step), CPV starts by simulating many realizations of the default rate for the N periods as described above. For each path and each year, the 1-year transition matrix is taken to be M_h if the default rate is below its unconditional mean and M_l if it is above.

Then, assuming that transition matrices are Markovian and denoting as DR^* the historical average default rate, the multiperiod transition matrix is calculated as

$$M_N = \prod_{t=1}^{N} M(DR_t) \qquad (6\text{-}11)$$

where the function $M(.)$ is such that $M(DR_t) = M_l$ if $DR_t > DR^*$ and $M(DR_t) = M_h$ if $DR_t < DR^*$.

When we simulate a large number of replications of Equation (6-11) we can approximate the distribution of default rates for any rating class as well as the distribution of migration probabilities from any initial to any terminal rating. Combining cumulative default rates with an assumption about LGD (not specified within the model) as well as each exposure characteristic, CPV can approximate portfolio loss distributions.

The main advantage of CPV is that it relies on inputs that are relatively easy to obtain. Its main weakness is that it models aggregate default rates and not obligor-specific default probability.

CreditRisk+

CreditRisk+ is one of the rare examples of an analytical commercial model. It is a modified version of a proprietary model developed by Credit Suisse Financial Products (CSFP) to set its loan loss provisions. A complete description of the model is available in Credit Suisse Financial Products (1997).

CreditRisk+ follows an actuarial approach to credit risk and only captures default events. Changes in prices, spreads, and migrations are ignored. This model is therefore more appropriate for investors choosing buy-and-hold strategies.

The issue is not whether specific securities in the portfolio default, but rather what proportion of obligors will default in a sector and will default at the portfolio level. Facilities are grouped in homogeneous buckets with identical loss given default. The default rate in a given sector is assumed to be stochastic.

Inputs
The required inputs are

+ Individual credit exposure profiles
+ Yearly default rates per industry or category of assets
+ Default rate volatilities
+ An estimate of recovery rates (assumed constant in this model)

The Main Steps
Assuming that probabilities of default are small and time-homogeneous, the probability of default in a given sector can be approximated by a Poisson distribution with mean μ such that the probability of n defaults is

$$P(n \text{ defaults}) = \frac{e^{-\mu}\mu^n}{n!} \qquad (6\text{-}12)$$

CreditRisk+ assumes that the mean default rate μ is itself stochastic and gamma-distributed. Introducing the probability generating function (PGF), it is possible to express the PGF of the default losses in each bucket and to aggregate them into the probability generating function of portfolio losses.

An algorithm then allows us to derive the distribution of portfolio losses from the PGF, thereby providing a fast analytical solution to the calculation of economic capital and other risk measures.

Factor correlations are not modeled in CreditRisk+. In that model the factors are the default rates in the buckets, which are assumed to be independent. CSFP argues that there is not enough data to estimate default correlations with reasonable accuracy and that the CreditRisk+ model captures fat tails in loss distributions (similar to those generated using correlated factors) through their assumption of stochastic default rates.

For a detailed description of the model, see Appendix 6D.

Strengths and Weaknesses of Commercial Models

We have discussed the features of five of the most well-known commercial models of credit portfolio risk. This section focuses on comparing the relative merits of competing approaches. For brevity, we will use the following acronyms: CM (CreditMetrics), PRT (Portfolio Risk Tracker), CPV (CreditPortfolioView), PM (Portfolio Manager), and CR+ (CreditRisk+).

The first four models are simulation-based and therefore much more time-consuming than CR+ for large portfolios. This is the main advantage of CR+ over its competitors. Unfortunately it comes at the cost of several disadvantages.

First CR+ is a default-only model, as is PM. This means that portfolio losses due to migrations are ignored. For a portfolio of investment-grade bonds, default risk itself is quite limited, and a substantial share of portfolio losses is due to downgrades. Ignoring this substantially underestimates the total credit risk. Similarly, spread risk is not taken into account by any product but PRT.

CR+ assumes constant LGDs and does not specifically account for correlations (second-order effects are incorporated in CR+ via the randomness of default rates). Other models use beta-distributed LGDs and incorporate correlations of assets, factors, or macroeconomic variables. Table 6-3 summarizes some strengths and weaknesses of the main commercial models.

A criticism often directed toward some off-the-shelf products is their lack of transparency. This lack of transparency, along with a lack of flexibility, has led first-tier banks to develop their own internal models over which they have total control. Some of these models are similar to those presented above, while others rely on alternative approaches, to which we now turn.

ALTERNATIVE APPROACHES

In this section we review two recent alternatives to standard portfolio models. Their primary goals are to achieve fast computation of portfolio losses while providing more flexibility than CreditRisk+. The first approach relies on saddle point methods, while the second one combines fast Fourier transforms and Monte Carlo.

Saddle Point Methods[7]

We have stressed above that on the one hand there are "exact" and fast models of portfolio credit risk that enable us to calculate portfolio losses instantly but at the cost of stringent assumptions about the distribution of

TABLE 6-3

Strengths and Weaknesses of Main Models

	CreditMetrics	CreditPortfolio View	Portfolio Risk Tracker	Portfolio Manager	CreditRisk+
Type of credit risk covered	Defaults and transitions	Defaults and transitions	Defaults and transitions	Defaults	Defaults
Interaction of market & credit risks	None	None	Included via interest and exchange rates and equity prices	None	None
Correlation of default events	Has to rely on accuracy of mapping between factor and default correlations		Explicit via risk factors and idiosyncratic term		Not explicit
Recovery rates	Beta distribution Not correlated with PD	Beta distribution Not correlated with PD	Beta distribution Correlated with PD	Beta distribution Not correlated with PD	Constant
Numerical approach	Can be slow for large number of simulations				Fast

factors, and on the other hand there are simulated approaches that can accommodate more complex distributions but must rely on time-consuming simulations. Saddle point methods are an alternative way to approximate the true distribution without the use of simulations. They are very fast and particularly accurate in the tails of the distributions, which are of specific interest to risk managers.

Saddle point methods are based on the observation that although some combinations of distribution functions may be impossible to calculate analytically, their moment generating function or cumulant generating function (CGF) may remain tractable. For example, assume that we have a portfolio of two assets whose returns are both distributed according to some distribution. The portfolio returns thus correspond to a weighted sum of this distribution, which may not be easy to calculate. However, the CGF may be much easier to calculate.

An approximate but fairly accurate mapping of the CGF to the distribution function is then performed. It allows the risk manager to obtain fast approximations of the tail of its portfolio loss distributions. A detailed description of the approach is provided in Appendix 6D.

Combining Fast Fourier Transforms and Monte Carlo

In a recent paper Merino and Nyfeler (2002) propose a new technique combining fast Fourier transforms and Monte Carlo simulations that is both fast and accurate over the entire portfolio loss distribution. The algorithm is applied to the class of conditionally independent models introduced in Chapter 5 and relies on several results already used in the derivation of CreditRisk+. This approach is described in Appendix 6E.

CALCULATING RISK-ADJUSTED PERFORMANCE MEASURES (RAPM)

So far we have dealt with the estimation of portfolio loss distributions. We now consider the most commonly used indicators of portfolio risk. We then explain the two usual ways to split economic capital between facilities in a portfolio. Finally we review risk-adjusted return on capital (RAROC).

The output of a risk model is generally a distribution of losses, i.e., the levels of possible losses with their associated probabilities. This distribution captures all the information about the losses that can be incurred on a specific portfolio at a specific horizon. In order to make decisions, we need to transform the distribution into some synthetic measures of risk which enable the risk manager to communicate with the board of the bank or with external counterparts such as clients or regulators. Some of the most widely used measures of risk are expected and unexpected losses, value at risk, economic capital, and expected shortfall.

Common Measures of Portfolio Risk

Expected Loss

The first indicator of risk that a bank considers is expected loss. It is the level of loss that the bank is exposed to on average.

The expected loss on a security i is defined as

$$EL_i = EAD_i \times PD_i \times LGD_i \tag{6-13}$$

where EL is the expected loss and EAD is the exposure at default (the amount of investment outstanding in security i).

The expected loss of a portfolio of N assets is the sum of the expected losses on the constituents of the portfolio:

$$EL_p \equiv E(L_p)$$

$$= \sum_{i=1}^{N} EL_i \tag{6-14}$$

where L_p denotes the random loss on the portfolio.

The expected loss contribution of a specific asset i to a portfolio is thus easy to determine. It carries information about the mean loss on the portfolio at a given horizon. This expected loss is normally assumed to be covered by the interest rates the bank charges to its clients. It does not bring any information about the potential extreme losses the bank faces because of a stock market crash or a wave of defaults, for example.

Unexpected Loss

The unexpected loss UL_p is defined as the standard deviation of portfolio losses:

$$UL_p = \sqrt{E\{[L_p - E(L_p)]^2\}} \tag{6-15}$$

If portfolio losses were normally distributed, expected and unexpected loss would completely characterize the loss distribution. The normal distribution is indeed specified by its first two moments.

Unfortunately, portfolio losses are far from being normal (Figure 6-1), and EL_p and UL_p are very partial measures of riskiness. In particular, unexpected loss ignores the asymmetric nature of returns (upside versus downside potential). Unexpected loss also fails to qualify as a coherent[8] measure of risk as defined by Artzner, Delbaen, Eber, and Heath (1999). It is indeed possible to find two portfolios where $UL_p > UL_{p^*}$, although all $L_p \leq L_{p^*}$. Note that in the Basel II framework, UL corresponds to value at risk, rather than to the standard deviation of portfolio losses.

Value at Risk

Value at risk is by far the most widely adopted measure of risk, in particular for market risk. It is also frequently used in credit risk although it is arguably less appropriate for reasons we explain below.

Value at risk addresses the issue of tail risk, i.e., the risk of large losses. The value at risk at the confidence level α (e.g., 95 percent) at a given horizon (usually 10 days for market risk and 1 year for credit risk) is the level of losses on the portfolio that will only be exceeded $1 - \alpha$ percent of the time on average over that horizon. More formally,

$$\text{VaR}(\alpha) = \min \{ j \mid P(L_p > j) \leq 1 - \alpha \} \qquad (6\text{-}16)$$

It is important to bear in mind that a VaR measure is only meaningful if we know both the chosen horizon and the confidence level. Expected loss and value at risk are illustrated graphically in Figure 6-9.

Several criticisms are commonly directed at value at risk. First, the value at risk at the α confidence level says nothing about the size of losses beyond that point. It is easy to create examples where the values at risk of two portfolios are identical but their level of extreme tail risk is very different. For example, Figure 6-10 shows two loss distributions that have the same 95 percent VaR. However, one of the loss distributions (solid line) has a much thinner right tail than the other one. The likelihood of a very large loss is much smaller with this distribution than with the other (dotted line).

VaR has the added drawback that it is not a coherent measure of risk (Artzner et al., 1999). In particular, it is not subadditive. In financial terms, it means that the value at risk of a portfolio may exceed the sum of the VaRs of the constituents of the portfolio.

Finally, VaR tends to be very unstable at high confidence levels. For levels above, say, 99 percent confidence, changing the level of α by a small

FIGURE 6-9

Portfolio Loss Distribution

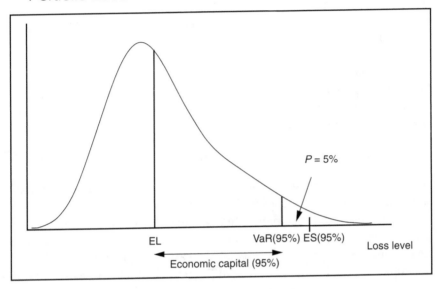

FIGURE 6-10

Two Loss Distributions with Indentical VaR(95%)

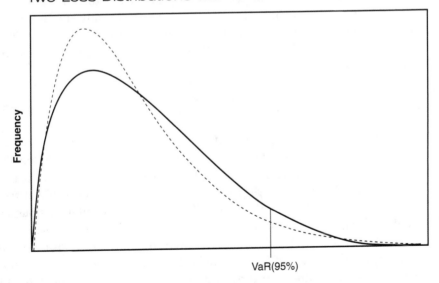

amount may lead to large swings in the calculated value at risk. In many instances, the plot of VaR(α) against α would look similar to Figure 6-11, computed for economic capital (EC). This is a matter of concern for banks, as they typically report their values at risk at confidence levels ranging from 99 to 99.99 percent.

Economic Capital

Economic capital is one of the key indicators for bank portfolio managers. Most of the time it is calculated at a 1-year horizon. The common market practice is to estimate the economic capital as

$$EC_p(\alpha) = VaR(\alpha) - EL_p \qquad (6\text{-}17)$$

where EL_p is the expected loss and VaR(α) is the value at risk at the confidence level α—for example, 99.9 percent.

Economic capital is interpreted as the amount of capital buffer that a bank needs to put aside to avoid being insolvent with α confidence level. Banks targeting a specific rating, say AA, will often consider it appropriate to hold a level of capital $EC_p(\alpha)$ such that $1 - \alpha$ corresponds to the probability of default of an AA-rated entity. This reasoning is flawed in general, as the rating agency analyst will consider many factors (business risk, for example) that are not reflected in economic capital (for more details see Chapter 7).

Another problem with economic capital that is directly inherited from the properties of value at risk is that it is very sensitive to the choice of the confidence level α and can be very unstable at high confidence levels. Figure 6-11 is a plot of the sensitivity of economic capital to the chosen confidence level:

$$\frac{\partial EC_p(\alpha)}{\partial \alpha} = \frac{\partial VaR(\alpha)}{\partial \alpha} \qquad (6\text{-}18)$$

The results are those of a Monte Carlo experiment, described in Chapter 5, where we simulated a very granular portfolio of 10,000 facilities with identical probability of default and pairwise correlation. Clearly at confidence levels above 99 percent, economic capital and value at risk become highly unstable. This implies that the level of capital on a bank's book may change dramatically for only minor changes in the chosen level of confidence. Given that there is no theoretical reason for choosing one α over another, it is a significant drawback of both economic capital and value-at-risk measures. This observation shows that practitioners do not

FIGURE 6-11

Derivative of EC(α)

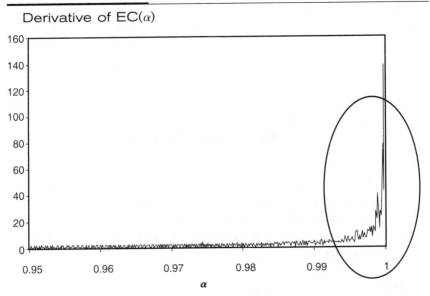

have a precise measurement of their risk far at the tail, i.e., corresponding to very improbable events. In order to compensate for such uncertainties, extreme value theory (EVT) models have been introduced in financial applications. This type of approach is devised to fit the tail of the distribution despite the scarcity of the data. EVT models stimulated a lot of interest among practitioners in the late nineties, but applications of these models to credit risk remain rare.

Other approaches are being developed to tackle the problem of tail instability. In particular, economic capital can be made a function of VaRs over a continuum of confidence levels. This average is weighted by a function reflecting the bank's risk aversion (utility function). The averaging provides a much more stable measure of risk and capital (see Chapter 7).

Expected Shortfall

Expected shortfall (ES) is an alternative risk measure that focuses on the tail of the loss distribution. It is the average loss conditional on the loss being above the VaR(α) level and is thus similar to an insurance premium:

$$ES(\alpha) = E[L_p \mid L_p > VaR(\alpha)] \qquad (6\text{-}19)$$

Expected shortfall is a coherent measure of risk and is progressively becoming a very popular complement of VaR. Combining VaR and ES indeed provides the risk manager with both a measure of the amount of risk at a given confidence level and also an estimate of the (mean) size of losses once that amount is breached. ES is also shown on Figure 6-9.

Splitting Economic Capital between Facilities in a Portfolio

The previous section has shown how risk managers calculate the overall risk of their portfolios, in particular unexpected loss and value at risk. In this section, we explain how these two measures can be split into individual risk contributions at the facility level. This will be important in order to allocate capital appropriately to the various facilities (which we focus on in a later section).

Incremental and Marginal VaR

In order to determine what facilities contribute most to the total risk of the portfolio, it is customary to use incremental or marginal VaR. The key academic reference on this topic is Gouriéroux, Laurent, and Scaillet (2000).

The incremental VaR of a facility i (IVaR_i) is a measure defined as the difference between the value at risk of the entire portfolio (VaR_p) minus the VaR of the portfolio without facility i (VaR_{p-i}):

$$\text{IVaR}_i(\alpha) = \text{VaR}_p(\alpha) - \text{VaR}_{p-i}(\alpha) \tag{6-20}$$

The main drawback of this measure is that incremental VaRs do not add up to the total value at risk of the portfolio. Therefore they are not appropriate for allocating economic capital, as

$$\text{EC}_p(\alpha) \neq \sum_{i=1}^{N} \text{IVaR}_i(\alpha) - \sum_{i=1}^{N} \text{EL}_i \tag{6-21}$$

unless IVaRs are specifically rescaled to satisfy the equation.

Another way to allocate economic capital to facilities is to consider marginal VaRs (MVaRs, also called delta VaRs). MVaRs are similar to IVaRs but are based on partial derivatives:

$$\text{MVaR}_i(\alpha) = \frac{\partial \text{VaR}_p(\alpha)}{\partial A_i} A_i \tag{6-22}$$

where A_i is the number of units of asset i held in the portfolio. MVaRs satisfy the additivity condition (the sum of marginal VaRs is the portfolio VaR):

$$\text{VaR}_p(\alpha) = \sum_{i=1}^{N} \text{MVaR}_i(\alpha) \qquad (6\text{-}23)$$

which immediately leads to a rule for splitting economic capital among facilities:

$$\text{EC}_{p;i}(\alpha) = \text{MVaR}_i(\alpha) - \text{EL}_i \qquad (6\text{-}24)$$

Note that we write $\text{EC}_{p;i}(\alpha)$ and not $\text{EC}_i(\alpha)$. This is to emphasize that the economic capital allocated to facility i depends on the constitution of the portfolio and is not the economic capital corresponding to a portfolio of facility i only.

Individual Contributions to Unexpected Loss

Recall that unexpected loss is simply the standard deviation of portfolio losses [Equation (6-15)]. The variance (square of the standard deviation) of portfolio losses is the sum of the covariances of the losses of individual facilities. Therefore

$$\text{UL}_p = \sqrt{\sum_{i=1}^{N} \sum_{j=1}^{N} \text{UL}_i \times \text{UL}_j \times \rho_{ij}} \qquad (6\text{-}25)$$

where ρ_{ij} denotes the correlation of losses on facilities i and j.

The individual risk contribution RC of facility i to the unexpected loss of the portfolio is given by

$$\text{RC}_i = \frac{\partial \text{UL}_p}{\partial \text{UL}_i} \, \text{UL}_i \qquad (6\text{-}26)$$

The risk contribution is thus the sensitivity of the portfolio's unexpected loss to changes in the unexpected loss of facility i times the size of RC_i.

Differentiating Equation (6-25) and using (6-26), we can calculate the risk contributions explicitly:

$$\text{RC}_i = \frac{2\text{UL}_i + 2\sum_{j \neq i} \text{UL}_j \times \rho_{ij}}{2\text{UL}_p} \, \text{UL}_i$$

$$= \frac{\sum_{j=1}^{N} \text{UL}_i \times \text{UL}_j \times \rho_{ij}}{\text{UL}_p} \qquad (6\text{-}27)$$

Risk contributions calculated as above are the sum of covariances of asset i with all other assets scaled by the volatility (standard deviation) of portfolio losses. They satisfy

$$\sum_{i=1}^{N} RC_i = UL_p \qquad (6\text{-}28)$$

which is a desirable property for a risk measure. It means that the total risk of the portfolio is the sum of the individual risks of its constituents. It also leads to a formula for economic capital allocation at the portfolio level.

Assume that the risk manager has calculated the bank's economic capital and unexpected loss such that

$$EC_p(\alpha) = m_\alpha \times UL_p \qquad (6\text{-}29)$$

where m_α is the multiplier, which typically ranges from 5 to 15 in practice. This multiplier calculated from Equation (6-29) can then be applied to calculate economic capital at the facility level.

The economic capital $EC_{P,i}$ allocated for a loan i in the portfolio is calculated with the following formula:

$$EC_{P,i}(\alpha) = m_\alpha \times RC_i \qquad (6\text{-}30)$$

This rule is easy to implement in practice and widely used. We should bear in mind that it implies that risk is accurately measured by variances and covariances. While this is an appropriate assumption if losses are normally distributed, it is not correct in the case of credit losses.

To show this, it suffices to calculate the individual risk contributions RC_i using Equation (6-27) and individual economic capital using Equation (6-24). Then it is possible to calculate the multiplier m_α from Equation (6-30). If unexpected loss contribution were a good measure of marginal risk, we would find a multiplier that is similar across assets. In practice m_α exhibits very large variations from one facility to the next, which indicates that covariances only partly capture joint risk among the facilities in the portfolio.

Risk-Adjusted Performance Measures

Now that we have an assessment of the individual contribution of a facility to the total risk of a portfolio, the next logical step is to balance this risk against the return offered by individual assets.

Traditional Risk-Return Measures

Traditional performance measures in the finance literature can generally be written as

$$\text{Return}/\text{risk} \qquad (6\text{-}31)$$

For example, the Sharpe ratio is calculated as the expected excess return (over the riskless rate r_f) on facility i divided by the volatility of the returns on asset i, σ_i:

$$\text{SR}_i = \frac{E[R_i] - r_f}{\sigma_i} \qquad (6\text{-}32)$$

The Treynor ratio replaces the total risk (volatility) by a measure of undiversifiable risk—the β of the capital asset pricing model (see, e.g., Alexander, Bailey, and Sharpe, 1999):

$$\text{TR}_i = \frac{E[R_i] - r_f}{\beta_i} \qquad (6\text{-}33)$$

Both these measures and many others devised for portfolio selection treat assets as stand-alone facilities and do not consider diversification/concentration in the bank's portfolio.

RAPMs

Unlike Equations (6-32) and (6-33), risk-adjusted performance measures enable bank managers to select projects as trade-offs between expected returns and cost in terms of economic capital [EC enters Equation (6-31) as the risk term]. We have seen that economic capital does integrate dependences across facilities, and the asset selection thus becomes specific to the bank's existing portfolio.

Many RAPMs have been proposed, depending on the definition of the risk, revenue R_i, and cost c_i variables: RAROC, RORAC, RARORAC, and so on. It is easy to get lost in the numerous acronyms. Common practice is to use the generic term RAROC[9] defined as

$$\text{RAROC} = \frac{R_i - c_i - \text{EL}_i}{\text{Risk contribution of } i} \qquad (6\text{-}34)$$

The denominator may be chosen to be the risk contribution calculated in Equation (6-27) or the marginal value at risk in Equation (6-22), or a version of the marginal economic capital [Equation (6-24) or (6-30)].

As mentioned above, the great novelty of RAROC compared with traditional risk-return trade-offs is the use of a risk measure that is specific to a bank's existing holdings and incorporates dependences.

The simple formula (6-34) is intuitive and appealing but unfortunately not very easy to implement in practice for many instruments. In particular, the allocation of costs is not obvious. Costs include fixed operating costs as well as interest costs for funding the facility. Should these costs be split equally across assets?

Looking now at the traditional organization of a bank, many questions remain difficult to solve from a practical standpoint:

♦ Banks often calculate their RAPM measures at the facility level rather than at the counterparty level. Should RAPM measures aggregate all the exposures vis-à-vis a client across all products, or should they be transaction-based? A client measure should clearly be preferred, given bankers' appetite for cross-selling. From a practical standpoint it can be very difficult to implement, and it explains why many banks look primarily at transaction RAROC.

♦ Allocating economic capital to existing customers ex post is a difficult task. At the origination level (ex ante) it is even more difficult to determine what the impact of a new facility will be on the whole portfolio of the bank without running the portfolio model. No bank, however, could afford to run a simulation-based model, including more than 50,000 credit lines, several times each day. Apart from making the assumption that the contribution of any new facility to the economic capital of the bank is marginal (which will often be a heroic assumption), the only alternative is to use quick analytic methods based, for example, on saddle point approximation.

Introducing Risk Aversion

Once RAROC or another performance measure has been chosen and implemented, it enables the bank to rank its facilities from the best performing (highest risk-return ratio) to the worst.

However, this is insufficient for deciding whether an investment is worthwhile. For that purpose the bank needs to determine what the minimum acceptable level of risk-adjusted performance is for each of its business units. This corresponds to spelling out its risk aversion.

The critical level or risk-adjusted performance above which investments will be considered justified is called the hurdle rate. We can thus introduce an excess RAPM measure:

$$RAPM^* = RAPM - \text{hurdle rate} \qquad (6\text{-}35)$$

Note that RAPM* does not change the ranking of projects. It only makes more explicit the risk premium corresponding to the bank's risk aversion. The hurdle rate is specified by the bank's management and corresponds to the minimum return acceptable in a given business unit. The definition of an appropriate hurdle rate is very important. The process allowing us to define the hurdle rate is described in Chapter 7.

RAROC for More Complex Instruments

A fundamental assumption we have made up to this point is that the exposure at default is known in advance. This implicit assumption is made in Equation (6-13) and indirectly in all the following ones. While determining the EAD_i for a standard loan is easy, it is much less straightforward for derivative products such as swaps and options. Assume that we have bought a call from a bank and that the bank defaults before the maturity of our option. At the maturity, if the call expires out of the money (worthless), our exposure at default is zero and default is harmless. However, if the call ends up deep in the money, the exposure at default will be substantial. The same is true for a swap contract where the counterparts are positively or negatively exposed to default risk depending on whether they are on the receiving or paying side of the contract (i.e., if interest rates change in their favor or not).

The "proper" way to deal with such complexity is to use a full model for the underlying stock price or interest rate to determine the distribution of the exposure at default. The risk measures described above can be computed by Monte Carlo simulations. The process can prove time-consuming, and it is often not easy to determine the joint distribution of the default events and the price of the underlying asset of the option.

In order to simplify this process, banks rely on a fairly crude approach of "loan equivalence." The loan equivalent of a complex instrument is an average of the positive exposure during the life of the contract. Once this average is computed, it is plugged into Equation (6-13) and onward, and it is assumed that the loss on the derivative instrument is similar to the loss on a loan with this average exposure at default.

Summary

RAROC is a useful tool for measuring performance and is widely used by banks. In the survey by Brannan, Mengle, Smithson, and Zmiewski (2002), the authors report that 78 percent of the banks explicitly using a performance measure for their credit portfolio use RAROC. There seem to be as many definitions of RAROC as there are financial institutions, but they all have in common the calculation of a risk-return trade-off that takes into account portfolio diversification. The chosen RAROC measure will only be as good (or as bad) as its constituents, namely the net return measure (numerator) and the risk component (denominator). We have seen that many commonly used risk measures (in particular those based on unexpected loss) suffer from severe deficiencies linked to the fact that credit portfolios are skewed and fat-tailed.

As a final word of caution, we would like to stress that the usual RAROC is calculated ex ante, i.e., in order to select the best assets for the future. The effect of an additional facility (a new investment) is assumed to have a marginal impact on the portfolio and on the economic capital of the bank. This may be a fair assumption if the new facility is small, but ex ante RAROC may differ substantially from ex post RAROC for large positions. The usefulness of RAROC for dynamic capital allocation may therefore be very limited, as we will see in the next chapter.

STRESS-TESTING PORTFOLIO LOSS CALCULATIONS

In this section we want to briefly highlight the impact of the business cycle on portfolio loss distributions. By doing so, we will show how important it is to carry out careful stress tests on the various inputs of the model, in particular on probabilities of default and correlations.

We perform a simulation experiment on a portfolio of 100 non-investment-grade bonds with unit exposure, identical probabilities of default, and pairwise default correlations. We consider three scenarios:

1. *Growth scenario.* The default probability for all bonds is equal to the average probability of default of a NIG bond in a year of expansion[10] (4.32 percent), and the correlation is set equal to its average value in expansion (0.7 percent).

2. *Recession scenario.* The default probability for all bonds is equal to the average probability of default of a NIG bond in a year of recession (8.88 percent), and the correlation is set equal to its average value in recession (1.5 percent).

3. *Hybrid scenario.* Default probability = recession value, and correlation = expansion value.

For all scenarios the recovery associated with each default is drawn from a beta distribution with mean 0.507 and standard deviation 0.358.[11]

Portfolio losses are then calculated as the sum of losses on individual positions. The smoothed distributions of losses are plotted on Figure 6-12. When moving from the growth scenario to either the hybrid or the recession scenario, we can observe a shift in the mean of the loss distribution. This shift is due to the significant increase in probabilities of default in recessions. Comparing the tail of the loss distribution in the hybrid scenario with that in the recession case (both cases have the same mean default rate), we can see that the recession scenario has a fatter tail. This is purely attributable to increases in correlations.

Figure 6-13 focuses specifically on the tail of the distributions. More precisely, it compares the credit VaR in the three scenarios for various confidence levels. The gap between the growth VaR and the hybrid VaR is due exclusively to the increase in PDs during recessions, whereas the gap between the hybrid and the recession cases is the correlation contribution.

Figure 6-14 displays the same information but in relative terms. It shows the percentage of the increase in portfolio credit VaR that can be attributed to the increase in correlation or to the increase in probabilities of default in a recession year. At very high confidence levels, the correlation becomes the dominant contributor.

FIGURE 6-12

Correlation and the Business Cycle

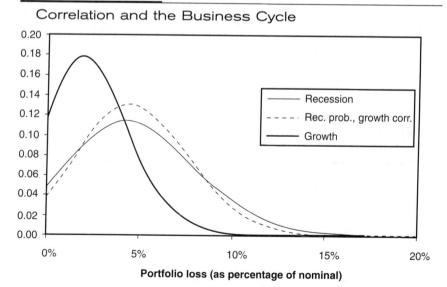

Portfolio loss (as percentage of nominal)

FIGURE 6-13

Credit VaR in Growth and Recession

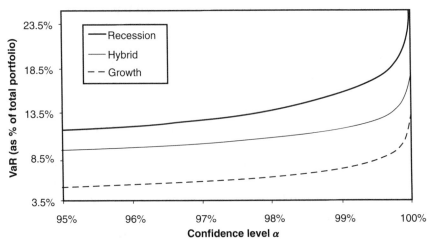

FIGURE 6-14

Relative Contributions of Correlation and PDs to VaRs

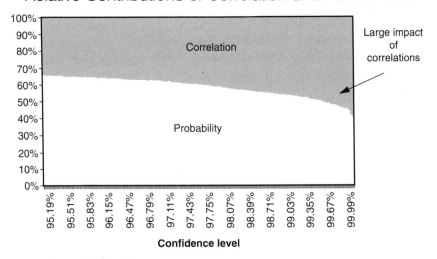

The implication for banks is that they should perform careful stress tests not only on their PD assumptions but also on their correlation assumptions. When reporting VaR at very high confidence levels, a substantial part of the information conveyed by the figures relates to correlations. We have seen in Chapter 5 that default correlations were estimated with a lot of uncertainty and that different sources of data (equity versus realized defaults, for example) could lead to very different results. It is therefore advisable to triangulate the approaches to correlations and to treat correlation inputs in credit portfolio models conservatively.

CONCLUSION

Portfolio models have received considerable attention in the past years. Some canonical methodologies have been developed, including the rating-based approach and the actuarial models. Calculation speed has then become a major area of focus with the introduction of semianalytical methods such as fast Fourier transform, saddle point, and related techniques.

With the wider use of more complex financial products like ABSs, CDOs, and credit default swaps, the current challenge is to integrate these new tools in portfolio management tools in a relevant manner. Another outstanding issue is the precise measurement of the benefits of portfolio diversification under changing economic conditions.

For the future, we anticipate a trend aimed at reuniting pricing and risk measurement. Portfolio tools used by banks indeed provide marked-to-model information. Shifting to marked-to-market is, in our view, the next frontier.

A P P E N D I X   6 A

Simulating Random Variables

DRAWING RANDOM VARIABLES FROM AN ARBITRARY DISTRIBUTION

Many computer packages include built-in functions to generate random variables in specific standard distributions such as the normal, gamma, χ^2, etc.

A general procedure to draw random variables from an arbitrary but known distribution is the following:

1. Draw random variables (R.V.) from a uniform [0,1] distribution. This is always available in standard computer packages.
2. Invert the cumulative distribution function to obtain random variables with the chosen distribution.

Example: Drawing Exponentially Distributed R.V. with Parameter λ

The cumulative distribution function is $F(x) = 1 - \exp(-\lambda x)$. The first step consists of drawing n uniform [0,1]-distributed random variables U_i, for $i = 1...n$. Then by inverting the distribution function, we can obtain $Y_i = F^{-1}(U_i) = -1/\lambda \log(1 - U_i)$, which follows the appropriate exponential distribution.

For many distributions, such as the normal or the beta used to simulate factors or recovery rates in credit models, there is no closed form for the inverse function $F^{-1}(x)$. A numerical inversion can, however, be performed.

Figure 6A-1 summarizes the procedure for the normal distribution and the t-distribution with 3 degrees of freedom. Drawing a random number x from the uniform distribution and inverting the normal distribution and t-distribution, we can obtain two different random numbers from the chosen distributions.

GENERATING CORRELATED NORMAL ASSET REALIZATIONS

Factors used in credit risk portfolio models are frequently correlated and have to be simulated jointly. Assume, for instance, that we want to draw

F I G U R E 6A-1

Drawing Normal and *t*-Distributed Random Variables

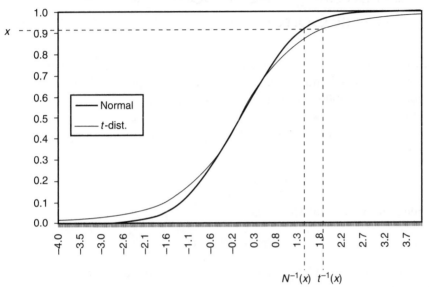

$N^{-1}(x)\ \ t^{-1}(x)$

N realizations of a matrix of M correlated standard normal variables (as in CreditMetrics, for example, where factors follow a multivariate normal distribution). We will thus draw an $N \times M$ matrix A with random elements.

We use Ω to denote the $M \times M$ factor covariance matrix and proceed in three steps:

- Draw an $N \times M$ matrix of uncorrelated *uniform* random variables.
- Invert the cumulative standard normal distribution function as explained above to obtain an $N \times M$ matrix B of uncorrelated standard normal variables.
- Impose the correlation structure by multiplying B by the Choleski decomposition of the covariance matrix Ω [chol(Ω)].

Then $C = \text{chol}(\Omega) \times B$ is an $N \times M$ matrix of normally distributed R.V. with the desired correlations.

APPENDIX 6B

Calculating Asset Correlation and Default Correlation

In this appendix we want to calculate the default correlation between Vivendi Universal and General Motors. Vivendi Universal is a company involved in mobile telecommunications (T) and leisure (L). General Motors is the world's largest car manufacturer (industry C).

The analyst considers that the exposure of Vivendi is the following[12]:

$$A_{Viv} = 0.4T + 0.2L + \varepsilon_{Viv}$$

while that for General Motors is

$$A_{GM} = 0.9C + \varepsilon_{GM}$$

The factor correlation matrix, estimated from equity indices, is the following:

Sectors	T	L	C
T	1.0	0.3	0.1
L	0.3	1.0	0.1
C	0.1	0.1	1.0

We can immediately calculate the two firms' asset correlation[13]:

$$\text{Corr}(A_{Viv}, A_{GM}) = \text{cov}(A_{Viv}, A_{GM})$$

$$= 0.4 \times 0.9 \times \text{cov}(T,C) + 0.2 \times 0.9 \times \text{cov}(L, C)$$

$$= 0.4 \times 0.9 \times 0.1 + 0.2 \times 0.9 \times 0.1$$

$$= 5.4\%$$

The variances of the idiosyncratic term can be calculated using the constraint that the asset returns have unit variance:

$$\sigma^2_{Viv} = 1 - 0.4^2 - 0.2^2 - 2 \times 0.4 \times 0.2 = 0.64$$

$$\sigma^2_{GM} = 1 - 0.9^2 = 0.19$$

At the end of 2002, Vivendi and GM were rated BB and BBB, respectively, by S&P. Looking up the 1-year average default rates for issuers in BB and BBB categories, we find 1.53 percent and 0.39 percent.

We can now immediately calculate the joint probability of default JPD for Vivendi and GM at the 1-year horizon (see Chapter 5):

$$JPD = N_2(p_{Viv}, p_{GM}, 5.4\%)$$

$$= N_2[N^{-1}(1.53\%), N^{-1}(0.39\%), 5.4\%]$$

$$= 0.00008777$$

Finally, the default correlation is obtained as

$$DC = \frac{JPD - p_{Viv}p_{GM}}{\sqrt{p_{Viv}(1 - p_{Viv})p_{GM}(1 - p_{Viv})}}$$

$$= 0.37\%$$

APPENDIX 6C

A Description of Credit Risk+

In this appendix we provide a more extensive derivation of the loss distribution and finally review implementation issues and extensions. We have already dealt with the inputs for the model and the general setup in the main body of the chapter.

FULL DERIVATION OF THE MODEL

In this section we derive the main results of the CreditRisk+ model. We start by introducing the simple case where the portfolio consists of only one asset with constant probability of default, and we introduce the concept of the probability generating function. We then extend the setup to the case of multiple assets and finally allow for the grouping of assets in homogeneous groups and for probabilities of default to be stochastic.

One Risky Asset with Constant Probability of Default

The model considers two states of the world for each issuer:

- Default with probability p_A
- No default with probability $(1 - p_A)$

The probability of default for a given issuer is assumed to be constant through time. We can then calculate the probability distribution of a portfolio of N independent facilities.

The probability generating function (PGF) F_x for a random variable x is defined as

$$F_x(s) = E(s^x) \tag{6C-1}$$

where s in an auxiliary variable.

In the case of a binomial random variable such as A above, we find

$$F_A(s) = p_A\, s^1 + (1 - p_A)\, s^0$$

$$= 1 + p_A(s - 1) \tag{6C-2}$$

Multiple Risky Assets with Constant Probability of Default

The PGF $F(s)$ of a sum of N independent random variables is the product of the individual PGF:

$$F(s) = \prod_{A=1}^{N} F_A(s) \tag{6C-3}$$

Taking logarithms, we get

$$\log F(s) = \log \left(\prod_{A=1}^{N} F_A(s) \right) \tag{6C-4}$$

$$= \sum_{A=1}^{N} \log [F_A(s)] \tag{6C-5}$$

$$= \sum_{A=1}^{N} \log [1 + p_A(s - 1)] \tag{6C-6}$$

Recall that for Z small, $\log(1 + Z) \approx Z$. Using this approximation, we find

$$F(s) \approx \exp\left(\sum_{A=1}^{N} p_A(s - 1) \right) \qquad (6C\text{-}7)$$

$$\equiv \exp[\mu(s - 1)] \qquad (6C\text{-}8)$$

where $\mu = \sum_{A=1}^{N} p_A$ is the mean number of defaults.

Expanding the exponential in (6C-8) and comparing with (6C-1), we find

$$F(s) \approx \exp[\mu(s - 1)] \qquad (6C\text{-}9)$$

$$= E_\mu(s^i) \qquad (6C\text{-}10)$$

where $E_\mu(.)$ denotes the expectation of a Poisson distribution with parameter μ.

This shows that, providing that the approximation in (6C-7) is acceptable (small probabilities of default), the distribution of a portfolio of independent binomial variables (default/no default) follows a Poisson distribution.

Grouping Exposures in Homogeneous Buckets

CreditRisk+ then groups exposures in m homogeneous buckets. Each bucket is characterized by having exposures of the same size $v_j L$ and with identical expected loss $\varepsilon_j L$ for $j = 1...m$. L is the size of a unit loss (e.g., $100,000). The smaller L, the more precise the buckets, but also the more numerous. Exposures in one group are assumed to be independent of exposures in other groups.

In each bucket the expected number of defaults is μ_j, which is assumed to be known. For each individual bucket we are therefore in a similar situation as in (6C-10):

$$\mu_j = \sum_{v_A = v_j} p_A \qquad (6C\text{-}11)[14]$$

Dividing the mean loss by the size of the individual losses, we have the mean number of losses:

$$\frac{\varepsilon_j}{v_j} = \mu_j = \sum_{v_A=v_j} \frac{\varepsilon_A}{v_A} \tag{6C-12}$$

We can now compute the PGF of the entire portfolio $G(Z)$ by aggregating the losses arising from all independent groups:

$$G(s) = E(s^n)$$

$$= \sum_{n=0}^{\infty} p(\text{total \# losses} = n)s^n \tag{6C-13}$$

Using the independence assumption, we get

$$G(s) = \prod_{j=1}^{m} G_j(s)$$

$$= \prod_{j=1}^{m} \left(\sum_{k=0}^{\infty} p(\text{\# losses in group } j = k)s^{kv_j} \right)$$

$$\approx \prod_{j=1}^{m} \exp\left(-\mu_j + \mu_j s^{v_j}\right) \tag{6C-14}$$

using the same approximation as in (6C-7).

Continuing the calculations, we get

$$G(s) = \exp\left(\sum_{j=1}^{m} \mu_j(s^{v_j} - 1) \right)$$

$$\equiv \exp\left[\mu(P(s) - 1) \right] \tag{6C-15}$$

with

$$\mu = \sum_{j=1}^{m} \mu_j \tag{6C-16}$$

and

$$P(s) = \frac{1}{\mu} \sum_{j=1}^{m} \mu_j s^{v_j} \tag{6C-17}$$

We have just obtained a closed-form expression for the probability generating function of the loss of the portfolio.

In order to obtain the actual distribution of losses from the PGF, we use the following relationship:

$$A_n \equiv P(\text{total \# losses} = n) = \frac{1}{n!} \left.\frac{d^n G(s)}{ds^n}\right|_{s=0} \qquad (6C\text{-}18)$$

This can be calculated recursively using the following algorithm proposed by CreditRisk+:

$$A_n = \sum_{j/v_j \le n} \frac{\varepsilon_j}{n} A_{n-v_j} \qquad (6C\text{-}19)$$

$$A_0 = e^{-\mu} \qquad (6C\text{-}20)$$

Multiple Risky Assets with Random Probability of Default

We now consider the case where probabilities of default are random. Facilities remain independent, but the randomness in probability of default will help generate fat tails in the portfolio loss distribution. The portfolio still comprises N facilities grouped in n sectors. An individual borrower A has probability of default X_A, which has mean p_A and standard deviation σ_A.

The default rate X_k in a specific sector k is assumed to follow a gamma distribution with mean $\mu_k = \Sigma p_A$ and standard deviation $\sigma_k = \Sigma \sigma_A$ for $k = 1\ldots n$. The probability density function for the gamma distribution is

$$f_k(x) = \frac{1}{\beta_k^{\alpha_k}\, \Gamma(\alpha_k)}\, e^{-\frac{x}{\beta_k}} x^{\alpha_k - 1} dx \qquad (6C\text{-}21)$$

with

$$\Gamma(\alpha_k) = \int_0^\infty e^{-u} u^{\alpha_k - 1} du \qquad (6C\text{-}22)$$

We again introduce the probability generating function $F(s)$ of portfolio losses in terms of sector loss PGF $F_k(s)$:

$$F(s) = \sum_{i=0}^\infty P(i\text{ defaults})s^i$$

$$= \prod_{k=1}^n F_k(s) \qquad (6C\text{-}23)$$

using the independence assumption.

The PGF for sector losses is less straightforward than in previous cases because the mean loss rate is itself random. However, conditional on a specific realization of the mean loss rate $X_k = x$, we can treat X_k as a constant, and we are back to the case described in Equation (6C-37) and onward:

$$F_k(s) \mid \{X_k = x\} = e^{x(s-1)} \tag{6C-24}$$

The probability generating function for the loss in a given sector k can be expressed as the sum (integral) of the probability generating function conditional on realizations of the factors:

$$F_k(s) = \int_0^\infty e^{x(s-1)} f_k(x)\, dx \tag{6C-25}$$

Plugging (6C-21) and (6C-22) into (6C-25) and simplifying, we obtain

$$F_k(s) = \left(\frac{1 - p_k}{1 - p_k s} \right)^{\alpha_k} \tag{6C-26}$$

where

$$p_k = \frac{\beta_k}{1 + \beta_k} \tag{6C-27}$$

Developing (6C-27), we get a nice formula for the PGF in a given sector:

$$F_k(s) = \sum_{n=0}^{\infty} C_{n+\alpha_k-1}^n p_k^n (1 - p_k)^{\alpha_k} s^n \tag{6C-28}$$

We recognize the expectation of s^n using the binomial law, from which we conclude using (6C-1):

$$P(n \text{ defaults}) = C_{n+\alpha_k-1}^n p_k^n (1 - p_k)^{\alpha_k} \tag{6C-29}$$

Grouping Exposures in Homogeneous Buckets

In the same way that (6C-15) extends (6C-10) when homogeneous buckets are created, (6C-23) to (6C-29) extend to

$$G(s) = \prod_{k=1}^{n} G_k(s) = \prod_{k=1}^{n} \left(\frac{1 - p_k}{1 - p_k P_k(s)} \right)^{\alpha_k} \tag{6C-30}$$

where

$$P_k(s) = \frac{1}{\mu_k} \sum_A \frac{\varepsilon_A}{v_A} s^{v_A} \qquad (6C\text{-}31)$$

The probability generating function can be written as a power series expansion:

$$G(s) = \sum_{n=0}^{\infty} A_n s^n \qquad (6C\text{-}32)$$

where the A_n terms can be calculated using a recurrence rule.

NUMERICAL IMPLEMENTATION OF CREDITRISK+

The recurrence rule proposed in CreditRisk+ is easy to implement. It is based on the widely used Panjer (1981) algorithm. Unfortunately it suffers from numerical problems. For example, for very large portfolios, μ [in Equation (6C-20)] may be very large. At some point the computer will round off $e^{-\mu}$ to 0, and the algorithm will stall. Another caveat comes from the fact that the recurrence algorithm accumulates rounding errors. After several iterations, the calculated values may differ significantly from the true output of the algorithm because of rounding by the computer.

Gordy (2002) proposes to apply saddle point methods (see Appendix 6D) to benchmark the standard algorithm. While the output of saddle points does not outperform the standard algorithm in all regions of the distribution and for all values of the input parameters, it appears to be accurate in the cases where the Panjer algorithm leads to numerical difficulties.

Giese (2003) offers yet another alternative. Unlike saddle point approximations, it is exact but relies on a faster and more stable algorithm that does not break down when the portfolio size or the number of factors is large. The author also suggests a way to incorporate correlations between factors.

APPENDIX 6D

A Description of the Saddle Point Method

In this appendix we start by introducing moment and cumulant generating functions and then describe the saddle point methodology and give an example to illustrate its accuracy.

MOMENT AND CUMULANT GENERATING FUNCTIONS

In some cases where the distribution of portfolio losses f_X is very complex, there may be a tractable expression for the moment generating function (MGF) M_X.

The MGF of the random loss X is defined in terms of an auxiliary variable s:

$$M_X(s) = E[e^{sX}] = \int e^{st} f_X(t)\, dt \qquad (6D\text{-}1)$$

Conversely we can obtain the density from the MGF through

$$f_X(t) = \left(\frac{1}{2\pi i}\right) \int_{-i\infty}^{+i\infty} M_X(s) e^{-st}\, ds \qquad (6D\text{-}2)$$

Assume, for example, that the random variable X defines a risky bond that may default with probability p. If it does default, then the loss is h (h can be seen as loss given default times exposure at default); if not, the loss is zero.

We can simply calculate $M_X(s)$ as

$$M_X(s) = E[e^{sX}]$$

$$= pe^{sh} + (1-p)e^0$$

$$= 1 - p + pe^{sh} \qquad (6D\text{-}3)$$

Cumulant generating functions have the nice property that they are multiplicative for independent random variables X_i, for $i = 1 \ldots n$. Alternatively, their logarithms [the cumulant generating functions $K_X(s)$] are additive.

Define

$$\overline{X} = \sum_{i=1}^{n} X_i$$

Then

$$K_{\overline{X}}(s) = \sum_{i=1}^{n} K_{X_i}(s)$$

For a portfolio of independent bonds, we obtain[15]:

$$M_{\bar{X}}(s) = \prod_{i=1}^{n} (1 - p_i + p_i e^{sh_i}) \qquad (6D\text{-}4)$$

and

$$K_{\bar{X}}(s) = \sum_{i=1}^{n} \log (1 - p_i + p_i e^{sh_i}) \qquad (6D\text{-}5)$$

Naturally the various lines in a portfolio are not independent. However, in the usual framework of conditionally independent defaults correspon-ding to most factor models, we can extend this approach.

Consider the case of a one-factor model (already introduced in Chapter 5). The firms' asset returns follow:

$$A_i = \rho_i C + \sqrt{1 - \rho_i^2}\ \varepsilon_i \quad \text{for } i = 1...n \qquad (6D\text{-}6)$$

such that $\text{var}(A_i) = 1$, $\text{cov}(A_i, A_j) = \rho_i \rho_j$ for $i \neq j$, $\text{cov}(\varepsilon_i, \varepsilon_j) = 0$ for $i \neq j$ and $\text{cov}(C, \varepsilon_i) = 0$ for all i.

Denote $a_i(c) = A_i \mid C = c$, i.e., the firm value return conditional on a specific realization of the systemic factor. Then we have $\text{cov}[a_i(c), a_j(c)] = 0$ for $i \neq j$. Therefore firm values (and resulting defaults) are *conditionally independent*.

Let us now go back to our portfolio example. Our individual asset loss can be written as $X_i = h_i\ I\{A_i < T_i\}$, where $I\{A_i < T_i\}$ is an indicator func-tion taking the value 1 if $A_i < T_i$ and 0 otherwise. T_i is the default thresh-old such that the firm enters default if $A_i < T_i$.

The conditional individual asset loss then is

$$x_i(c) = h_i\ I\{a_i(c) < T_i\} \qquad (6D\text{-}7)$$

We have seen that the $a_i(c)$ are independent and therefore so are the $x_i(c)$. Thus the conditional moment generating function for the portfolio is

$$M_{\bar{x}(c)}(s) = \prod_{i=1}^{n} [1 - p_i(c) + p_i(c)e^{sh_i}] \qquad (6D\text{-}8)$$

where $p_i(c)$ denotes the probability of default of obligor i, conditional on $C = c$.

We can then integrate the conditional MGF with respect to the dis-tribution of the systemic factor C [with density $g(c)$] to obtain the uncon-ditional MGF:

$$M_{\bar{X}}(s) = \int_{-\infty}^{+\infty} M_{\bar{x}(c)}(s)g(c)\ dc$$

$$= \int_{-\infty}^{+\infty} \left[\prod_{i=1}^{n} [1 - p_i(c) + p_i(c)e^{sh_i}] \right] g(c)\, dc \qquad (6D\text{-}9)$$

We also have

$$K_{\bar{X}}(s) = \log \left(\int_{-\infty}^{+\infty} \left[\prod_{i=1}^{n} [1 - p_i(c) + p_i(c)e^{sh_i}] \right] g(c)\, dc \right) \qquad (6D\text{-}10)$$

In the usual case of Gaussian factor models, $g(c)$ is the normal density.

SADDLE POINTS

Saddle point approximations rely on cumulant generating functions. Equation (6D-2) above can be rewritten in terms of CGF:

$$f_X(t) = \frac{1}{2\pi i} \int_{-i\infty}^{+i\infty} \exp\,[K_X(s) - st]\, ds \qquad (6D\text{-}11)$$

For a specific loss level t, the saddle point is the point $s = \hat{t}$ at which

$$\left. \frac{\partial K_X(s)}{\partial s} \right|_{s=\hat{t}} = t$$

Using Equation (6D-1) and the fact that $K_X(s) = \log M_X(s)$, we can write the Taylor expansion of the CGF at the saddle point:

$$K_X(\hat{t}) = Q_1[X]\,\hat{t} + \frac{1}{2}\,Q_2[X]\hat{t}^2 + \frac{1}{3!}\,Q_3[X]\hat{t}^3 + \ldots + \frac{1}{n!}\,Q_n[X]\hat{t}^n + \ldots$$

$$\approx Q_1[X]\hat{t} + \frac{1}{2}\,Q_2[X]\hat{t}^2$$

$$= E[X]\hat{t} + \frac{1}{2}\,\mathrm{Var}[X]\hat{t}^2 \qquad (6D\text{-}12)$$

This is the approximation: We truncate the Taylor expansion after the second order and neglect higher-order cumulants Q_n, for $n > 2$.

The main result is the following. The right-tail probability of loss (for values above the mean) is approximated by

$$f_X(t) \approx \frac{\exp\left[K_X(\hat{t}) - \hat{t}\hat{t}\right]}{\sqrt{2\pi \left.\dfrac{\partial^2 K_{\overline{X}}(s)}{\partial s^2}\right|_{s=\hat{t}}}} \qquad (6D\text{-}13)$$

and

$$P(\overline{X} > t) \approx \exp\left(K_{\overline{X}}(\hat{t}) - \hat{t}\hat{t} + \frac{1}{2}\hat{t}^2 \left.\frac{\partial^2 K_{\overline{X}}(s)}{\partial s^2}\right|_{s=\hat{t}}\right) N\left(-\sqrt{\hat{t}^2 \left.\frac{\partial^2 K_{\overline{X}}(s)}{\partial s^2}\right|_{s=\hat{t}}}\right)$$

$$(6D\text{-}14)$$

where $N(.)$ denotes the cumulative standard normal distribution.

Therefore, if we are able to calculate the CGF and its first two derivatives, we can approximate the tail of the loss distribution easily and thereby calculate VaR. This approach also enables us to calculate risk contributions such as the sensitivities of VaRs to the constitution of the portfolio (see Browne, Martin, and Thomson, 2001b).

Gordy (2002) relies on this approach to approximate the portfolio loss distribution in CreditRisk+ without relying on the recurrence rule algorithm mentioned above. Haff and Tashe (2002) extend his contribution to the calculation of VaR and expected shortfall contributions in the CreditRisk+ framework.

GAMMA-DISTRIBUTED LOSSES

We now provide a simple example of a distribution that we will approximate using the saddle point method described above.

Assume that the portfolio loss distribution is gamma(α,β). The probability density function is

$$f_{\overline{X}}(s) = \frac{1}{\beta^{\alpha}\Gamma(\alpha)}\, e^{-s/\beta}s^{\alpha-1}$$

The cumulant generating function for that distribution is

$$K_{\overline{X}}(s) = -\alpha \log\left(1 - \beta s\right) \qquad (6D\text{-}15)$$

We find the saddle point $s = \hat{t}$ such that

$$t = \left. \frac{\partial K_X(s)}{\partial s} \right|_{s=\hat{t}}$$

Solving, we get

$$\hat{t} = \frac{1}{\beta} - \frac{\alpha}{t}$$

Then we can calculate the building blocks for Equations (6D-13) and (6D-14):

$$K_X(s) = -\alpha \log \left(\frac{\alpha\beta}{t} \right) \quad \text{and} \quad \left. \frac{\partial^2 K_X(s)}{\partial s^2} \right|_{s=\hat{t}} = \frac{t^2}{\alpha}$$

Plug the terms in (6D-13) and (6D-14).

Example: Gamma-Distributed Losses

Figures 6D-1 and 6D-2 illustrate the performance of the saddle point method in approximating the gamma distribution. The fit in the tail is remarkable, as shown in particular in Figure 6D-2

FIGURE 6D-1

Performance of Saddle Point Approximation

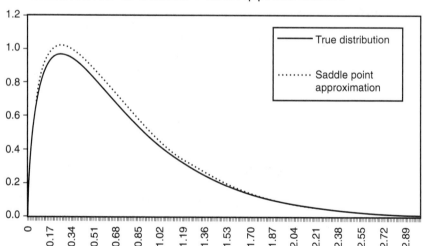

FIGURE   6D-2

Performance in the Tails

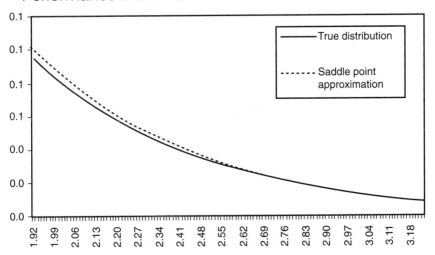

APPENDIX   6E

The Use of Fast Fourier Transforms

We will explain this approach in the simple context of a one-factor model, but it encompasses a much broader class of model. We assume that the portfolio consists of N facilities with unit exposures and that the random factor is W, with probability distribution function $F(w)$.

L is the random loss on the portfolio. It is the sum of individual losses on constituents:

$$L = \sum_{i=1}^{N} l_i = \sum_{i=1}^{N} Y_i \mathrm{LGD}_i \tag{6E-1}$$

where Y_i is the indicator function taking the value of 1 if facility i defaults and zero otherwise.

Using the property of conditionally independent models, the probability of default can be written in terms of conditional probability. Conditional on the factor realization $W = w$, the defaults on individual facilities are independent. The conditional distribution of the portfolio loss can then be obtained as the convolution of the distributions of individual losses:

$$P^L_{W=w} = \overset{N}{\underset{i=1}{\otimes}} \; P^{l_i}_{W=w} \tag{6E-2}$$

where $\otimes$ denotes the convolution of discrete densities.

The unconditional distribution is the sum of the conditional distribution over the factor

$$P^L = \int_{\mathfrak{R}} P^L_{W=w} \, dF(w) = \int_{\mathfrak{R}} \left(\overset{N}{\underset{i=1}{\otimes}} \; P^{l_i}_{W=w} \right) dF(w) \tag{6E-3}$$

The three main steps of the algorithm of Merino and Nyfeler (2002) are thus to reduce the dimensionality of the problem [at the moment Equation (6E-3) involves the convolution of N distributions, with N often $> 10{,}000$] and then to calculate the convolution (6E-2) and the integral (6E-3).

REDUCING THE DIMENSIONALITY OF THE PROBLEM

Before calculating the convolution, it is convenient to use two assumptions already made in CreditRisk+:

1. The binomial distribution for all individual exposures can be approximated by a Poisson distribution (this is acceptable for small probabilities of default).

2. Exposures are grouped in v homogeneous buckets B_j of facilities with identical loss given default $\overline{\text{LGD}}_j$.

Using assumption 2, the conditional loss in a bucket is therefore

$$L_j \mid \{W = w\} = \overline{\text{LGD}}_j \sum_{i \in B_j} Y_i \mid \{W = w\} \tag{6E-4}$$

Given assumption 1 and the fact that the sum of independent Poisson variables is also Poisson, we can replace (6E-2) by

$$P^L_{W=w} = \overset{v}{\underset{j=1}{\otimes}} \; P^{L_j}_{W=w} \tag{6E-5}$$

The bucketing has thus enabled us to reduce the problem to a v-fold convolution, which is a much more manageable problem than calculating an N-fold convolution, as $v \ll N$.

CALCULATING THE CONDITIONAL DISTRIBUTION OF PORTFOLIO LOSSES

The Fourier transform[16] of the convolution of two distributions x and y is the product of their Fourier transforms:

$$F(x \otimes y) = F(x) \odot F(y) \qquad \text{(6E-6)}$$

where $\odot$ denotes the term-by-term product. The Poisson distribution is available in closed form, which makes the computation of the convolution much easier. It can be efficiently calculated using fast Fourier transforms.

CALCULATING THE UNCONDITIONAL DISTRIBUTION OF PORTFOLIO LOSSES

The first two steps involved the reduction of dimensionality and the calculation of the distribution conditional on a realization of the factor $W = w$. The final step deals with the calculation of the unconditional probability of portfolio losses. Merino and Nyfeler (2002) propose to calculate (6E-3) numerically by numerical integration:

$$P^L \approx \frac{1}{K} \sum_{k=1}^{K} P^L_{W=w^k} \qquad \text{(6E-7)}$$

where w^k, for $k = 1...K$, is a large number of independent draws from the distribution of the factor W.

CHAPTER 7

Credit Risk Management and Strategic Capital Allocation

$\mathbf{A}$s we have seen in preceding chapters, risk management has recently become an area of major focus within banks partly because of regulatory reforms. This move has led banks to undertake simultaneously extensive data collection and an internal cultural revolution. In this respect RAROC measures have become common knowledge in the banking community.

At some stage, senior executives of banks, and in particular senior risk managers, have thought of this process as the way to reach the Holy Grail of optimal dynamic capital management. Accordingly, various external consultants have promoted methodologies for a dynamic bottom-up[1] piloting of banks. Most of the time, however, top management teams have remained quite cautious and critical vis-à-vis these approaches, and in particular, few have used the results of such models for their communication with investors.[2]

With some more experience, practitioners now better understand the limits of those new tools. The recent financial crisis has shown how the perception of the performance of a bank by shareholders may differ from that of the bank's management. Top-down approaches have gained some credibility because of their ability to provide what is lacking with bottom-up schemes: the ability to assign customized return objectives to the various business units of the bank. This exercise is often denominated as strategic capital allocation.

The literature on this topic is limited and is often produced by practitioners. From a practical standpoint, strategic capital allocation is an exercise that many banks talk about but that few have actually implemented using quantitative tools. The first characteristic of this type of approach is that it looks at encompassing both the risk that is embedded in the balance sheet of the bank and the risk that is intrinsic to the businesses in which the bank operates. The second characteristic is that it is not dealing only with information coming from the risk department of the bank, but also with a much wider set of information such as financial markets input, data related to the cost structure of the bank and to its rigidity, and input on the assumed growth rates for the various business units of the bank.

Several authors[3] have insisted on the importance of aggregating credit risk, market risk, and operational risk in order to obtain a comprehensive estimate of economic capital. This is perfectly correct. However, we want to take a slightly different angle in this chapter. Instead of considering a split of economic capital by type of risks, we are more interested in splitting the capital in relation with the different functions of the banking firm: liquidity intermediation, risk intermediation, and information intermediation. As a consequence, we emphasize here the impact of liquidity and information issues on economic capital.

In this chapter we first focus on bank capital and rating agencies—in particular on whether rating agencies explicitly constrain the behavior of banks that target a specific rating. Next we define what capital stands for. We then focus on the various static capital allocation methodologies, and finally we describe some principles of dynamic management. Figure 7-1 illustrates top-down versus bottom-up approaches to risk management.

DO RATING AGENCIES HAVE A POINT OF VIEW ON STRATEGIC CAPITAL ALLOCATION?

Rating agencies are often involved in the way many banks perform their capital measurement, although unwillingly. As noted in Chapter 6, it is common practice for banks to define economic capital as the value at risk at a confidence level α of the loss distribution of the bank portfolio minus the expected loss: $EC = VaR_\alpha - EL$.

α is often determined as the default rate corresponding to the target rating of the bank (e.g., 99.97 percent for an AA objective). In previous chapters we have discussed the shortcomings of this approach.

Looking at rating agencies criteria, it appears clearly that a bank's rating is the result of the integrated analysis of many factors. As shown in Table 7-1, it is going far beyond the mere calculation of economic capital using quantitative techniques. In addition, the view of rating agencies about capital can be different from what regulators and the banks themselves are interested in. Their objectives are different:

FIGURE 7-1

Top-Down versus Bottom-Up Approaches

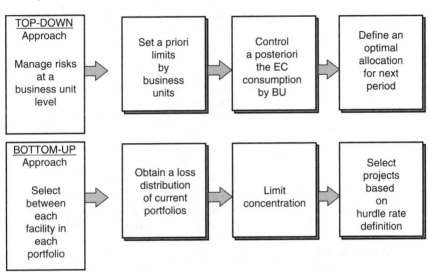

In general, however, regulators aim to protect bank depositors, while Standard and Poor's is looking to timely repayment of principal and interest for debtholders and counterparties. Thus, while it is important that a bank meet the capital requirements of its domestic regulators, Standard & Poor's looks at a bank's capital in a broader context and does not include in its capital adequacy computations certain instruments that can only absorb losses in a reorganization or liquidation scenario (Standard & Poor's, 1999, p. 27)

In short, rating agencies do not tend to focus exclusively on economic capital as the sole indicator of bank risk. Obviously, the more capital, the better, but banks are seen both in relation to the economic environment in which they operate (the robustness of the business of the bank) and from an internal management point of view—a good capital buffer is not in itself a guarantee of a good rating.[4]

WHAT IS BANK CAPITAL MEANT FOR?

Does the Top Management Have Its Say on the Appropriate Amount of Capital for a Bank?

In Chapter 3 we saw that when a bank builds its own internal rating system, based on a scoring methodology, it needs to address a crucial question: Where should the cutoff point between good (nondefaulting) and

TABLE 7-1

Rating Analysis Methodology Profile

	A Summary of the Core Content
1 Economic risk	Performance of the economy in which the bank operates
2 Industry risk	Quality of the banking system and trends
3 Market position	Competitive advantages/weaknesses
4 Diversification	Business lines/geography/products
5 Management and strategy	Reputation and credibility of the management/ internal organization
6 Credit risk	Granularity of exposures/low credits/problem loans/ distressed loans
7 Market risk	ALM/trading book/trading strategies
8 Funding and liquidity	Diversity of funding sources/liquidity strategy
9 Capitalization	Capital composition/ability to tap external sources
10 Earnings	Interest income/non-interest income/extraordinary gains/tax issues
11 Risk management	Approval process/monitoring/watch list process/ market risk technology/audit functions
12 Financial flexibility	Funding/value of business units on their own/ governmental support

Source: Extracted from "Financial Institutions Criteria," Standard & Poor's (1999).

bad (defaulting) companies be set? Should a company with a 1-year probability of default of 6 percent be considered as defaulting, or should the cutoff point be set at the level of 14 percent? The choice of 6 percent shows much higher risk aversion than the choice of 14 percent. There is no absolute truth in this activity, and two banks dealing with the same population may decide to choose different cutoff points, although they may be using very similar models.

Surprisingly banks calculate economic capital without incorporating the impact of any strategic choice. All is based on the loss distribution of their portfolio and the confidence level they should retain to be in accordance with their rating objective. There seems to be no room left for risk aversion and the utility function of the managers of the bank as well as that of their shareholders. From a practical standpoint, should the department of a bank that is specialized in selling protection against highly unlikely catastrophic events be treated in the same way as another department of the same bank, focused on retail where quite frequent, low-size losses are the rule? In the first case, an extreme confidence level for VaR is required, but not in the second case.

The portfolio loss distribution of a bank is generally skewed and fat-tailed. This means that there exists a nonnegligible probability of observing high losses. The further we go in the tail, the higher the potential loss but (in most cases) the lower the probability of occurrence. A lot of strategic decisions are then possible: hedging risk very far in the tail in order to avoid the most damaging risks or alternatively minimizing risks that may not trigger the bank's insolvency but may be sufficient to tarnish its reputation or lead to a rating downgrade. These kinds of decisions typically depend on the choice of senior executives and managers across the bank. Figure 7-2, extracted from Hall (2002), superimposes the portfolio loss distribution and the potential level of distress. In the figure the convexity of the financial distress cost curve reflects the sensitivity of the bank's management to the different levels of distress. It is different for different banks, as they display varying degrees of risk aversion.

We saw in Chapter 6 that VaR may be less appropriate than expected shortfall as a measure of risk because of coherence issues. Both these indicators are "neutral" in the sense that they report a factual risk measurement without incorporating the risk aversion of the bank. Some literature exists on incorporating utility functions in risk measures (see, e.g., Acerbi, 2002; Bezard, 2002; or Kusuoka, 2001). These papers show that there are risk aversion measures that are coherent and that allow us to factor in the risk aversion profile defined by the top management of banks.[5]

We believe that banks will increasingly have to devise such customized measures, not only at a holding level but also at a business unit level, in order to better translate the impact of internal decision policies on the dynamics of risks of the bank.

Can RAROC Provide an Answer to Optimal Capital Allocation?

In this book we generally omit market risk and operational risk. These can be integrated in economic capital in a similar way as for credit risk. Table 7-2, however, shows an example of a bottom-up approach to splitting capital by type of risk and by business unit, taking into account diversification effects.

In the previous chapters, we have gone through the extensive steps involved in data collection and data aggregation a bank has to perform in

FIGURE 7-2

Loss Distribution and Financial Distress Costs

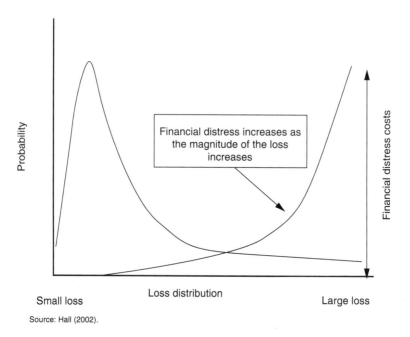

Source: Hall (2002).

order to measure credit portfolio loss distributions. Based on this, economic capital can be calculated at the bank level, on its current portfolio
and subsequently split between all its assets, in order to provide a risk-
adjusted performance measurement. In addition, some stress testing and
back testing can offer interesting results on the sensitivity of such a split,
depending on crisis scenarios that may not have properly been covered
by traditional Monte Carlo simulations.

Although this approach seems very compelling, it is not fully adequate
as a basis for strategic capital allocation. Let us consider several examples.

♦ An equity broker will have no credit risk, virtually no market
risk, and little operational risk. Does it mean that this business
requires very little capital? The recent downturn in the economy
has led to a significant turmoil in the equity markets. Brokers
have been and are still highly impacted by this crisis. Those that
are not sufficiently capitalized may be very close to insolvency.
In this case, allocating capital on the basis of a bottom-up
approach would have failed to protect many brokers.

TABLE 7-2

A Bottom-Up Capital Allocation Process

Bank	Credit Risk	Market Risk	Operational Risk	Total of Risks	Diversification Effect	Capital Requirement
Corporate banking	65%	4%	3%	72%	–5%	67%
Fixed income	6%	9%	9%	24%	–4%	20%
Equity	2%	6%	3%	11%	–4%	7%
Asset and liability management	1%	10%	2%	13%	–2%	11%
Total business units	74%	29%	17%	120%	–20%	105%
Diversification effect	–4%	–2%	–3%	–9%		–5%
Capital requirement	70%	27%	14%	111%	–11%	100%

♦ A financial start-up providing e-services in the area of savings management will typically again sustain very little credit, market, and operational risks. Most of these firms have, however, probably collapsed over the past years. The risk they have been facing is the risk of an entrepreneur who has unsuccessfully bet on a quick change in the behavior of potential customers.

♦ An advisory department within a bank normally faces very little credit, market, or operational risk. The recent slowdown of M&A markets worldwide has, however, had a very significant impact on the risk profile of many banks.

All these examples lead us to distinguish between production risk and business risk. From a production standpoint, credit, market, and operational risks are very important. They have to be kept under tight control in order to avoid production disorders. What the twentieth century taught us, compared with the nineteenth century, is that production performance is not, however, sufficient to run a successful business.

Let us consider another example: High-speed trains are technically very efficient and safe. They are used in Japan and in Europe but not in the United States. Furthermore, demand has existed for them in Japan and in Europe but not in the United States. Companies that have failed to sell such trains in the United States have faced business risk rather than production issues. The information required in order to assess the level of business risk incurred by the related train companies was not internal technical data, but rather external market data to be observed in the outside world.

Bottom-up approaches provide very sensible results on how the bank is run as a "production unit," based on some monitoring of internal indicators. They are, however, not very informative about how the bank as a "business" is performing, subject to external constraints. Because strategy is not a production issue, strategic tools will have to be found elsewhere.

What Is the Adequate Horizon to Determine the Amount of Economic Capital Required by the Portfolio of a Bank?

Most models consider the 1-year horizon as the most obvious one, in order to calculate bottom-up economic capital.[6] This short-term horizon implies that most models do not consider liquidity as a determinant for the appropriate level of economic capital. The 1-year horizon is convenient from an accounting perspective, but it does not take into consideration the average maturity of commercial bank portfolios that traditionally stands between 2 and 5 years, with very illiquid lines. We saw in Chapter 5 that default correlation increases substantially with the horizon.[7] As a result, it is hazardous to extrapolate 1-year results to longer holding periods. The choice of an adequate horizon is therefore very important.

It is sensible to consider economic capital at a horizon that corresponds to the average duration of the portfolio or to the required time to access financial markets for additional equity funding in a situation of distress. In addition, looking beyond the average maturity of the portfolio and monitoring the loss distribution at various time horizons is another requirement. In this respect a review of the commitments exhibiting high-risk exposures in the long term is particularly sensible.

What Is the Contribution of Microeconomics to the Determination of Optimal Capital?

There is a large academic literature on the rationale for bank capital. Bank capital is often described as corresponding both to the funding of the business and to a cushion devised to absorb the risk of the business. Merton and Perold (1993) distinguish between cash capital and risk capital.[8] In addition, from a regulatory perspective, minimum capital allocation can provide insurance against bank runs. Insurance capital offers an alternative or a complement to deposit insurance. Therefore, increasing the level of required regulatory capital could help to minimize systemic risk in the economy and compensate for increasingly higher risks related to funding trends (see Figure 7-3).

Cash Capital and Liquidity

Several authors have suggested that the level of capital held by a bank is closely linked to the liquidity intermediation service it provides to the economy. In particular, Diamond and Rajan (2000) find an inverse relationship between the size of bank capital and the creation of liquidity. To explain why too much capital can penalize the bank, the authors note that in addition to leading to a higher interest rate requirement, a high level of capital will cause the bank to be less reactive, i.e., less cautious in bargaining, extracting repayments, and monitoring the customers.[9]

From a historical point of view, Berger, Herring, and Szego (1995) display the evidence that the capital-asset ratio has steadily declined in the United States from an average of 55 percent in 1840 to around 10 percent today. This tends to confirm the idea that in order to keep offering liq-

FIGURE 7-3

Funding Trends: Loans/Deposits for the 50 Largest
U.S. Banks

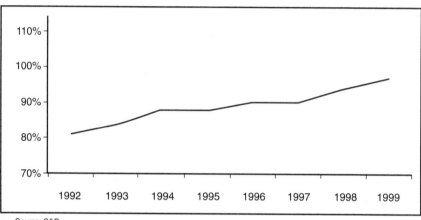

Source: S&P.

uidity intermediation services in an efficient way in an economy where
liquidity is increasing, banks have to decrease the proportion of capital
they hold. Such a behavior enables banks to reduce their competitiveness
gap with markets and to boost profits.

Risk Capital

From a different perspective, Froot and Stein (1998) suggest that a tight
level of capital increases significantly the risk aversion of the bank. The
reason is that any shocks that deplete the bank's capital will be costly, as
there may not exist a quick way to refinance on equity markets at reasonable conditions. The absence of frictionless efficient markets makes the
Modigliani and Miller (1958) framework inadequate and justifies, therefore, the recourse to modern risk-based capital management of banks. In
the model of Froot and Stein (1998), capital limitation and risk aversion
are linked in a monotonic way. As a result, increasing the level of capital
held by a bank can, up to a certain level, contribute to its business momentum and therefore to its performance. In this respect the capital requirement will typically depend on the risk aversion of the bank and not just
on the constituents of its balance sheet. From a practical standpoint, this
may lead banks to decide not to allocate all their capital between activities
or loans but keep a capital reserve corresponding to the strategic level of
risk aversion targeted by the bank as a whole.

In the wake of Froot and Stein (1998), Froot (2001) suggests the necessity of a split between the warehoused business[10] and the non-warehoused business. In banking regulation, most capital requirement calculation tends to focus on the warehoused part of the activity. Froot and Stein (1998) suggest that banks focus on holding primarily non-hedgeable risks and on offloading hedgeable ones. Froot (2001) observes that since many banks now do offload a significant part of their transactions, their balance sheet may not reflect fully the breadth of their business. As a consequence, beyond the observable portfolio of the bank, there is non-balance-sheet risk linked, for instance, with origination and distribution. This being the case, no more will the risk held only on the balance sheet be representative of the risk of the business.

In other words, business risk will correspond to on-balance-sheet risk as well as to value-of-goodwill risk. From an even broader perspective, business risk will typically be linked with deviations of the value of the business from its expected level. The main outcome of this is that capital should not be associated with the existing portfolio of the bank only, but also with the nature of the businesses the bank is running as well as the volatility of their earnings.

Capital, Balance Sheet, and P&L

With a marked-to-market approach of the balance sheet of banks, as promoted by the new international accounting standard, capital and asset and liability management will become intimately linked. The whole balance sheet of a bank will have to be actively managed, not just the liability side of it. As a consequence, the perception of how much capital a bank detains is bound to become much more imprecise and volatile. Balance sheet capital may, therefore, lose some of its importance as the only reference for risk measurement.

In addition, balance sheet capital may not be the sole relevant criterion when looking at the strength of a bank in the long run. In this respect, Koopman, Lucas, and Klaassen (2002) show that net interest margin[11] plays a key role in the formation of a capital buffer. This is intuitive: Over a long period, the cash flow of a performing business contributes to the amount of capital available to the bank. As a result, looking at the balance sheet of the bank, without paying sufficient attention to its P&L, may lead to a shortsighted bias. This observation coincides with the idea that capital requirement should be linked to business risk and not just to portfolio risk.

Should Banks Diversify Their Activities?

Following the seminal book of Markowitz (1959), modern portfolio theory has been increasingly used for asset and fund management. More recently the theory has been applied to debt instruments. The main difficulty is that debt returns are not normally distributed and the traditional mean-variance setup is no more appropriate for risk-return measurement. A substantial effort has been made over the past 20 years to overcome these problems and measure in a robust way the benefit of diversification. The first six chapters of this book described the most significant achievements in this field, as well as the areas that remain uncertain.

We noted in Chapter 5 that a much larger number of lines is needed in a credit portfolio compared with an equity portfolio in order to obtain the full benefits of diversification. Because the level of correlation is generally low and quite volatile through time, it is difficult to measure precisely. It is, therefore, also difficult to measure accurately the actual diversification effect at the bank level. A high level of diversification is nonetheless usually thought to be desirable for a bank. From a microeconomics perspective, several authors such as Diamond (1984) and Boyd and Prescott (1986) have advocated bank diversification.

In the industrial sector, on the contrary, "pure players," i.e., well-established firms focused on their core business, have recently become fashionable again, with market participants that show some reluctance vis-à-vis diversified holding companies. The main drivers of activity focus have been the increase of management's expertise and the reduction of agency problems. Several authors have favored specialization in a few related sectors, such as Jensen (1986), Berger and Ofek (1996), and more recently Acharya, Hasan, and Saunders (2002). In this respect Stoughton and Zechner (1999, 2000) try to estimate the impact of agency issues and of asymmetric information on the performance of the bank. They suggest adjusted risk-return measures in order to compensate for such imperfections.

Among the various reasons supporting diversification, efficient information intermediation and transparency stand as central issues:

♦ In particular, the monitoring of customers becomes more cost effective when the range of services provided increases, because the larger the amount of services, the smaller the monitoring cost contribution allocated to each service.

♦ In addition, the lending business is characterized by its asymmetry, because it bears more downside than upside. As a result, banks have tried to expand in activities that mitigate the downside risk, such as advisory services where there is more upside than down-side, trading where upside and downside are better balanced.

♦ Though bank diversification has become a standard, there seems to be a cost attached to it that is not yet fully measured. It is linked to opacity. Morgan (1997) illustrates this opacity using the example of bank assessments by rating agencies. He shows that major rating agencies tend to disagree more in the banking sector than in the corporate sector. Froot (2001) also focuses on transparency, observing that a securitized pool exhibits far greater both static and dynamic transparency than a bank. Therefore, the more a bank is diversified, the more financial markets may perceive it as opaque, unless the level of communi-cation it provides is sufficient to offset this effect. In the Basel II framework, market transparency is considered a very critical element, being one of the three pillars of risk monitoring (Pillar 3). It is, however, still one of the less developed aspects of the new regulation.

♦ This issue about transparency is utterly critical for one additional reason mentioned in Leland (1997). The bank's loss distribution risk measure is asymmetric and skewed, but shareholders typical-ly use performance tools based on a normal distribution assump-tion such as the CAPM betas. This phenomenon entails a myopia on the part of the shareholders, who will not be able to evaluate, with the same level of accuracy, the performance of banks in com-parison with that of industrial companies. Such uncertainty may lead investors to a higher degree of risk aversion vis-à-vis banks that would typically be reflected in lower price-earnings ratios.[12]

Looking at the most significant examples of banks' distress, it appears that both diversified (Credit Lyonnais in France and many Japanese banks) and specialized institutions (saving and loans, the Bank of New England, or Continental Illinois) have encountered serious difficulties.

THE VARIOUS STATIC METHODOLOGIES TO ALLOCATE EQUITY CAPITAL AMONG BUSINESS UNITS

As we have seen earlier in this chapter, it may be sensible not to allocate all the available capital among business units. In particular some of it may be used as a buffer to reduce the risk aversion of a bank or as a way to mitigate its strategic risk. In what follows, however, we look at procedures that fully allocate capital among business units, as this approach is the most widespread.

Review of Alternative Methodologies

In this section we review six different methods that can be used by banks in order to allocate economic capital among their various business units (BUs). Table 7-3 provides a synthetic view of the various methods. Most of the methods correspond to a top-down rather than a bottom-up approach. The rationale for such preference is that a bottom-up approach tends not to capture the changing nature of the individual business units, but to focus on their static pool at a given time.

Let us consider, for example, a trading desk that has just been hired from a competitor. Although in the first few months of activity of the desk, the size of the portfolio may remain very small, the value of the desk may already be substantial because of the expertise and reputation that the traders have obtained in the past. What is incorporated in the value of the desk is its ability to generate future cash flows. This shows that a static picture of the bank portfolio at a given time may tell little about the true level of risk-return of the underlying activities.

The top-down approach, on the other hand, tries to capture information about the value or the risk of the business on an ongoing basis. The only problem with such an approach is that there is no real consensus about an objective way to measure this information. It can alternatively be based on market data, on fair value pricing, on a past history track record, or on assumptions about the dependence on macroeconomic factors.

In Table 7-3 we therefore mention the source of the data used for each method. Obviously, the exclusive recourse to external market-based information or to internal data provides an indication on the potential limitation of the related approach. Conversely, methods blending the two types of sources will deserve a higher level of attention.

Notation Definitions[13]
Let $EC(t)$ be the economic capital of the bank at time t and $EC_j^A(t)$ be the amount of economic capital allocated to the business unit j, for $j = 1,...,n$. There will be a split of the global economic capital of the bank, so that

$$EC_j^A(t) = w_j(t)EC(t)$$

TABLE 7-3

A Summary of Various Methods Used to Split
Economic Capital among Business Units

	Method 1 Stand-Alone	Method 2 Scaling	Method 3 Internal Betas	Method 4 Marginal Capital	Method 5 APT	Method 6 Fair Value
Top-down approach	Value-based		BU return-based	BU value-based	BU value-based	BU return-based
Bottom-up approach		RAROC-based				
Use of internal risk data (*I*)/use of external market data (*E*)	*E*	*I*	*I* + *E*	*I*	*E*	*I* + *E*

where $w_j(t)$ is the corresponding weight with

$$\sum_{j=1}^{n} w_j(t) = 1$$

and

$$EC(t) = \sum_{j=1}^{n} EC_j^A(t)$$

We describe below different methods to extract the weights $w_j(t)$.

Method 1: Stand-Alone Market-Based Allocation Rule

Kimball (1998) mentions this top-down approach. What is required is to split the bank in various business units and to compare these BUs and their capital structures to "pure-play" competitors.

For each pure player i, a size-based value ratio is determined:

$$R_i = \frac{V_i}{\text{revenue}_i}$$

where V_i is the market value. Then the average ratio $R = \underset{i}{\text{mean}}(R_i)$ is calculated. This ratio is used to allocate capital to the business unit in the bank: $EC_j^M(t) = \text{revenue}_j \times R$.

Because

$$EC^M(t) = \sum_{j=1}^{n} EC_j^M(t)$$

may not be equal to $EC(t)$, some proportional scaling is applied with a constant multiplier

$$v(t) = \frac{EC(t)}{EC^M(t)}$$

used for all business units, so that

$$EC_j^A(t) = v(t) EC_j^M(t) \quad \text{and} \quad EC(t) = \sum_{j=1}^{n} EC_j^A(t)$$

The problem is that such an allocation methodology does not take into consideration the different levels of creditworthiness of the various business units unless this is defined as an additional requirement. Also this type of approach neglects diversification effects among all the business units.

Price-earnings ratios (R_i) estimated by various equity brokers exhibit some wide variations, depending on the broker. This casts some doubt on the precision of the measurement of economic capital using that

TABLE 7-4

Investment Bank Capital Allocation Using a Stand-Alone Market-Based Allocation Rule*

Corporate Banking	Average Value Ratio (Figures for Illustration Only)	Revenues in % of Total Bank Revenues	Economic Capital on a Market Base	Economic Capital Allocated to the Business Units
Project finance	1.5	3%	5%	3%
Structured finance	1	11%	11%	8%
Trade finance	0.7	15%	11%	8%
Corporates	1.3	15%	20%	14%
Advisory	2	8%	15%	11%
Total aggregated		52%	61%	
Fixed Income				
Government bonds	1	7%	7%	5%
Credit	1	8%	8%	6%
Forex	1	8%	8%	6%
Credit derivatives	2	12%	24%	18%
Equity derivatives	2	7%	14%	10%
Interest rate derivatives	2	8%	15%	11%
Total aggregated		48%	74%	
Total activities		100%	135%	100%
Calculation of the multiplier			74%	

*Economic capital is allocated to each BU according to the value ratio in column 1, which is extracted from market information. Column 3 = (column 1 × column 2), and column 4 = (column 3 multiplier).

287

method. Table 7-4 offers an example to illustrate the allocation of capital using a market-based allocation rule.

Method 2: RAROC-Based Proportional Scaling Rule

This type of method usually corresponds to the result of a bottom-up process where economic capital is calculated for homogeneous portfolios correspon-ding to the business units. The sum of stand-alone capital allocated to the dif-ferent business units typically exceeds the total amount of economic capital obtained for the bank as a whole, given the benefit of diversification.

We first calculate the economic capital resulting from the sum of the economic capital for the stand-alone business units:

$$EC^{SA}(t) = \sum_{j=1}^{n} EC_j^{SA}(t)$$

This is typically done using the bottom-up methods described in Chapter 6, through some VaR calculation for each of the business units.

A multiplier $a(t)$ is defined as $a(t) = EC(t)/EC^{SA}(t)$, where typically $a(t) \le 1$.

An allocation rule would be to consider the multiplier as a stable fac-tor to split the global economic capital among units:

$$EC_j^A(t) = a(t)EC_j^{SA}(t) \quad \text{and} \quad EC(t) = \sum_{j=1}^{n} EC_j^A(t)$$

The assumption of a stable multiplier for all business units does not correspond to reality. This approach also assumes implicitly that the level of risk correlation between businesses is stable over time and at any confi-dence level chosen to calculate economic capital. This assumption can prove risky given the changes in correlations observed empirically. Table 7-5 illustrates this approach using an example. In addition, this type of approach would lead to allocating very little economic capital to business units where the main risk is business risk.

Method 3: Internal Betas Rule

This type of method is usually used in a top-down context, where the issue is to allocate the benefits of diversification to various business units.

Let us consider $V_j(t)$ to be the current value[14] of the jth business and define its return as R_j. Then $V_j(t + 1) = V_j(t)R_j$, and the global value of the bank at time $t + 1$ is

$$V(t + 1) = \sum_{j=1}^{n} V_j(t)R_j$$

and its variance is

TABLE 7-5

Investment Bank Capital Allocation Using a Scaling Rule*

	Economic Capital on a Stand-Alone Basis (Credit)	Economic Capital Allocated to the Business Units (Credit)
Corporate Banking		
Project finance	11%	9%
Structured finance	28%	23%
Trade finance	24%	19%
Corporates	40%	32%
Advisory	0%	0%
Total aggregated	*103%*	
Subportfolio effect (1)	−16%	
Total after diversification effect (1)	*87%*	
Fixed Income		
Government bonds	2%	1%
Credit	2%	1%
Forex	2%	1%
Credit derivatives	9%	8%
Equity derivatives	3%	3%
Interest rate derivatives	5%	4%
Total aggregated	*22%*	
Subportfolio effect (2)	−3%	
Total after diversification effect (2)	*19%*	
Total activities	**106%**	
Global portfolio effect (3)	−6%	
Total investment banking	**100%**	**100%**
Calculation of the multiplier	*80%*	

*Stand-alone economic capital is computed for each of the BUs, as well as for the whole bank. A multiplier is then calculated and used to obtain an economic capital allocated to each of the BUs.

$$\text{Var}[V(t+1)] = \sum_{j=1}^{n} V_j(t) \sum_{k=1}^{n} \sigma_{j,k} V_k(t)$$

where $\sigma_{j,k} = \text{cov}(R_j, R_k)$.

The weights are then defined as

$$w_j(t) = V_j(t) \sum_{k=1}^{n} \frac{\sigma_{j,k} V_k(t)}{\text{var}[V(t+1)]} = \frac{\text{cov}[V_j(t+1), V(t+1)]}{\text{var}[V(t+1)]} = \beta_j(t)$$

A beta is allocated to each business unit. This beta corresponds to the covariance between the returns on the business unit and the return on the bank as a whole divided by the variance of bank returns.

Thanks to this beta, the economic capital can be allocated to business unit j: $EC_j^A(t) = \beta_j(t)EC(t)$.

Therefore the higher the correlation, the larger the risk contribution and subsequent equity capital required.

This approach supposes that the business is already well established and stable. It would not be very efficient in particular for a new business unit. It also assumes that all the returns on the business unit are normally distributed and that the economic capital is proportional to the second moment of the distribution. It is a strong assumption given the type of skewed distribution that is typically observed for the lending activity. Table 7-6 provides an example capital allocation using an internal beta rule.

Method 4: Incremental Capital Allocation Rule

This method again usually employs a top-down approach. Incremental capital is calculated as the difference between the economic capital required for a bank with all its business units and that required for the same bank where one of the business units is omitted.

Let us consider $IC_j(t) = EC(t) - EC_{-j}(t)$, where $IC_j(t)$ is the marginal contribution, or incremental capital, of business unit j and $EC_{-j}(t)$ is the economic capital for the bank, the business unit j being excluded.

An aggregate marginal capital can be defined:

$$IC(t) = \sum_{j=1}^{n} IC_j(t)$$

The weights $w_j(t)$ are then defined by $w_j(t) = IC_j(t)/IC(t)$.

Merton and Perold (1993) have shown that the sum of marginal capital allocations may be less than the total economic capital required for the bank: $IC(t) < EC(t)$. Rescaling may, therefore, have to be applied. For an example of this approach, see Table 7-7.

Method 5: A Rule Based on Arbitrage Pricing Theory[15]

Baud et al. (2000) suggest that factor analysis be applied to economic capital calculation. Banks are assumed to have standard business units (the factors) and an indiosyncratic term. The return is

TABLE 7-6

Investment Bank Capital Allocation Using an Internal Beta Rule[*]

	Internal Betas (Figures for Illustration Only)	Economic Capital in %
Corporate Banking		
Project finance	2%	2%
Structured finance	10%	10%
Trade finance	5%	5%
Corporates	28%	28%
Advisory	2%	2%
Total aggregated		*47%*
Fixed Income		
Government bonds	3%	3%
Credit	7%	7%
Forex	8%	8%
Credit derivatives	11%	11%
Equity derivatives	15%	15%
Interest rate derivatives	9%	9%
Total aggregated		*53%*
Total activities	**100%**	100%

[*]The economic capital allocated to each of the BUs will be the product of the beta calculated for each BU times the economic capital computed for the whole bank.

$$R^i(t) = \sum_{j=1}^{n} a_j^i(t) R_j(t) + u_t^i \quad \text{where} \quad \sum_{j=1}^{n} a_j^i(t) = 1$$

The authors then estimate the factor loadings $a_j^i(t)$ on a panel of banks assuming some correlation between the banks.[16]

Knowing the economic capital corresponding to bank i, that is, $EC^i(t)$, the economic capital allocated to the business unit j in bank i at time t therefore is $EC_j^i(t) = a_j^i(t)EC^i(t)$. It takes into account the benefit of diversification specific to each bank.

This approach supposes a high level of availability of external data related to the behavior of business units within financial institutions. In reality such information is very scarce. As a result, Baud et al. (2000) have

TABLE 7-7

Investment Bank Capital Allocation Using an
Incremental Capital Allocation Rule[*]

	Global Economic Capital without Business (Figures for Illustration)	Marginal	Allocated Economic Capital
Corporate Banking			
Project finance business	92	8	8
Structured finance business	86	14	15
Trade finance business	93	7	7
Corporate business	79	21	22
Advisory business	97	3	3
Fixed Income			
Government bonds business	95	5	5
Credit business	97	3	3
Forex business	92	8	8
Credit derivatives business	89	11	12
Equity derivatives business	91	9	9
Interest rate derivatives business	94	6	6
Total		95	100
Multiplier		105%	

[*]The incremental capital allocation rule does not sum to the economic capital of the bank. Rescaling has to be applied.

had to limit their investigation to eight business units only. Table 7-8 presents an example of the arbitrage pricing theory (APT) approach.

Method 6: A Fair Value Allocation Rule

Henrotte and Hyafil (2002) suggest a different approach to capital allocation among business units. They propose to evaluate the net asset value, $NAV_j(t)$, for each business unit j. Net asset value can be estimated in different ways, for example on the basis of the value of the business unit perceived by the bank, given its utility function. It can also be estimated through discounted cash flow methodologies.[17]

TABLE 7-8

Investment Bank Capital Allocation Using an APT Allocation Rule[*]

	Average Return for Each Business (Figures for Illustration)	Bank Factor (Figures for Illustration)	Allocated Economic Capital
Corporate Banking			
Project finance business	5%	7%	7
Structured finance business	8%	6%	6
Trade finance business	2%	11%	11
Corporates business	3%	17%	17
Advisory business	11%	6%	6
Fixed Income			
Government bonds business	6%	1%	1
Credit business	6%	3%	3
Forex business	7%	7%	8
Credit derivatives business	15%	10%	10
Equity derivatives business	18%	15%	15
Interest rate derivatives business	9%	16%	16
Total		100%	100

[*]Factor loadings determine the split of the economic capital of the bank among BUs.

The net asset value of the bank is equal to the net asset value of its constituents:

$$\text{NAV}(t) = \sum_{j=1}^{n} \text{NAV}_j(t)$$

The economic capital for each business unit is extracted from the volatility of the future net asset value at a given horizon T (see Figure 7-4). It corresponds to the amount that should be considered such that the risk of the change in NAV [$\Delta\text{NAV}_j(T)$] going beyond a given distress threshold has a probability of occurrence that is smaller than $1 - \alpha$ percent. The economic capital of business unit j corresponds to the value at

FIGURE 7-4

NAV-Simulated Distribution (10,000 Trials)

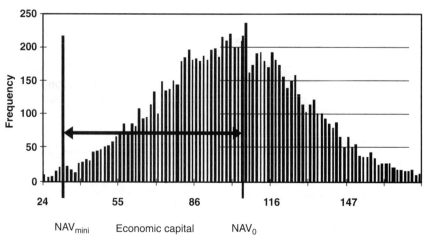

Source: Henrotte and Hyafil (2002).

risk $EC_j(\alpha,T) = VaR_\alpha[\Delta NAV_j(T)]$ of the $NAV_j(T)$ distribution (Figure 7-4). The impact of correlations among the various business units on the $\Delta NAV_j(t)$ distribution is mentioned without precise indications of how to evaluate them.[18]

As a result, the economic capital for the bank is the sum of the economic capitals calculated for each business unit:

$$EC(\alpha,T) = \sum_{j=1}^{n} EC_j(\alpha,T)$$

Table 7-9 illustrates the fair value allocation rule.

Which Method Should Be Selected?

♦ The first two methods (stand-alone and scaling) are crude approaches that were used in the 1990s and that are mentioned here mainly for completeness.

♦ Incremental VaR can prove quick and interesting but is tainted by the problem of non-subadditivity of value at risk.

♦ The APT approach does not seem very tractable at first sight, given the need to assume that any bank is made of a few standardized business units.

♦ Internal betas and fair value can be used but may prove a little bit challenging to implement in practice.

TABLE 7-9

Investment Bank Capital Allocation Using a
Fair Value Allocation Rule[*]

	Value at Risk at the 99.5% Confidence Level NAV Distribution, Horizon: 3 Years (Figures for Illustration Only)
Corporate Banking	
Project finance business	10
Structured finance business	25
Trade finance business	12
Corporates business	17
Advisory business	19
Fixed Income	
Government bonds	2
Credit business	8
Forex business	7
Credit derivatives business	15
Equity derivatives business	19
Interest rate derivatives	16
Bank global economic	*150*

[*]The economic capital is determined through net asset value volatility.

Integrating Liquidity and Information Issues in Strategic Capital Allocation

Integrating the Cost of Illiquidity by Setting a Nonallocated Capital Buffer Dedicated to Reducing Risk Aversion

Froot and Stein (1998) suggest that banks should first offload liquid risks from the balance sheet of the bank, on fair market terms—i.e., at market prices that are attractive for the bank—and then focus on the remaining traditional warehoused activity of illiquid assets. Once tradable risks are hedged, their underlying assets incur no capital charge.

In addition, the risk aversion of the bank is a decreasing function of the amount of equity capital it holds, as mentioned earlier in the chapter in the section on the contribution of microeconomics. Therefore, reducing the size of the portfolio of the bank without modifying its capital will have a positive impact, as it is equivalent to increasing the amount of capital while keeping the same portfolio. As a consequence, the risk aversion of the bank decreases.

Another important idea is that at the optimum it will make economic sense not to allocate all the economic capital of the bank among the business units in order to keep some specifically dedicated to reducing further the risk aversion of the bank.

Froot (2001) stresses that non-balance-sheet business risk should in particular be factored in, requiring some economic capital to be set aside in addition to the capital that is directly allocated to transactions.

From a practical point of view, capital allocation using the Froot and Stein (1998) approach is possible.[19] First, since the capital allocation depends on the wealth of the shareholder, this wealth has to be translated into a risk aversion function for the bank. This risk aversion measure is then applied to the definition of the hurdle rate of each business unit of the bank. Ultimately an economic capital calculation based on method 3 (internal betas rule) can be implemented.

Integrating the Existence of Asymmetric Information within the Bank as a Capital Cost

Stoughton and Zechner (1999) study the impact of asymmetric information between the headquarters of the bank and its divisional managers on optimal capital allocation. The initial condition they mention is that the economic capital of the bank exceeds its value at risk, so that it corresponds to a buffer against potential risk[20]: $EC(t) \geq VaR_\alpha(t)$.

The economic capital allocated to each division is called incremental value at risk:

$$EC_j(t) = IVaR_{\alpha,j}(t) \quad \text{and} \quad EC(t) = \sum_{j=1}^{n} EC_j(t) = \sum_{j=1}^{n} IVaR_{\alpha,j}(t)$$

Under the assumption of complete information, $IVaR_{\alpha,j}(t) = \lambda_j \sigma_j + v_j$, where σ_j is the standard deviation of cash flows of business unit j, λ_j is a factor depending on the marginal contribution of the business unit to the bank risk, and v_j is a function that depends on the risk taken by other divisions.

Under the assumption of asymmetric information and decentralized management within the bank, the bank capital allocation is changed. The bank allocates more capital for a given increase in volatility than with complete information. $\overline{\text{IVaR}}_{\alpha,j}(t) = \overline{\lambda}_j\sigma_j + \overline{v}_j$, $\overline{\lambda}_j$ and $\overline{v}_j$ are modified terms that integrate private information. In particular $\overline{\lambda}_j \geq \lambda_j$.

This contribution is very important in that it shows that asymmetric information within the bank should impact the split of the economic capital of the bank among the various business units. Practically, this means that business units where the risks of the business are not fully understood by the management should be penalized in the economic capital allocation process.

From a capital allocation standpoint, whatever the rule chosen, correcting weights should be considered for each business unit in order to factor in the effect of asymmetric information.

Allowing for Internal Bargaining for Capital Allocation as a Way to Set Priorities and Favor Information Revelation

This approach is proposed by Denault (2001). The purpose of the approach is to split the economic capital of the bank among its constituents using a coherent measure of risk.[21]

Coherent measures ensure that there is always a diversification effect when increasing the number of business units within the bank. The main problem, however, is that there does not exist a fair way to allocate this benefit of diversification among business units (see Appendix 7A). Business unit managers therefore face two issues. On the one hand they benefit from belonging to a single firm, as it brings them capital relief due to diversification. On the other hand they have to bargain internally (claiming unfair treatment) in order to keep the capital consumption they are charged as low as possible, compared with peers.

Denault (2001) suggests a fair way to allocate the benefit of diversification. He assumes that business unit managers can coordinate among one another in order to increase their bargaining power. He then uses game theory to provide a contribution that is an average contribution given various possible priority orders. He acknowledges, however, that this method is not really tractable when the number of business units within a bank exceeds 10.

From a practical standpoint, this approach demonstrates that economic capital allocation will remain an art rather than a science. It also shows that internal bargaining among the various business units is part of the process. Bargaining has a positive effect, as it induces business unit managers to reveal information and thus reduces the risk associated with asymmetric information.

PERFORMANCE MEASUREMENT, THE COST OF CAPITAL, AND DYNAMIC EQUITY CAPITAL ALLOCATION

The many approaches we have briefly described so far focus on splitting economic capital among business units at a given time t. This outcome is certainly a great achievement for a bank but does not help in optimally driving the bank in the future. In this section, we consider optimal *dynamic* capital allocation, performance measurement, and decision tools at the bank level, at the business unit level, and at the transaction level. The main question we address is the definition of the choice of the appropriate hurdle rate in each business unit of a bank.

Method 1: Linking RAROC and EVA

The traditional approach to dynamic capital optimization is to revert to shareholder value, using concepts like EVA (economic value added). EVA is defined as

$$\text{EVA} = \text{adjusted earnings} - k \times K$$

where K is the equity allocated to the business unit and k is the opportunity cost of this equity.[22]

As RAROC can be defined as adjusted earnings divided by economic capital (EC), the temptation is to set EC $= K$ and thus EVA $= (\text{RAROC} - k) \times K$ or EVA $= (\text{RAROC} - k) \times \text{EC}$. As a consequence, the performance objective required by shareholders, k, should correspond to the hurdle rate required by the management of the bank on all its business units.

At first sight this approach seems very appealing and straightforward, but in fact it is flawed for several reasons:

1. We have seen that bottom-up approaches can lead to biases regarding the allocation of economic capital between business units and ultimately between facilities (recall the above example of the advisory department of a bank).

2. Shareholders tend to look at EVA based on market information, whereas RAROC is based on accounting and at best on marked-to-model information.

3. Because they focus on businesses, shareholders include a goodwill component in their value assessment. It is not the case for RAROC[23] approaches that focus on the current deal flow rather

than on the business profile. As a result, K and EC will correspond to different concepts.

4. Selecting a unique cost of equity for all business units does not make a lot of sense. Using the RAROC framework, advisory services would support virtually no constraint,[24] whereas SME lending may find it difficult to pass the hurdle. Does this mean that all banks should focus primarily on advisory services? In periods of economic downturn, such advisory services tend to almost dry up, which is not the case for SME lending.

RAROC measures with a fixed hurdle rate over time lead banks to adopt a procyclical behavior:

♦ RAROC measures are not independent of risk since they do adjust for systematic risk. RAROC measures are performance measures based on economic capital. If a crisis happens, the bottom-up requirement for economic capital increases substantially both because of a weaker level of creditworthiness of the assets in the portfolio and because of an increase in correlation, i.e., an increase in systematic risk.

♦ In a downturn, when systematic risk is rising, RAROC measures tend to stand at a lower level. As a result, many new projects will be rejected, and existing ones will drop below the fixed hurdle rate. Conversely, when systematic risk is falling, RAROC measures tend to rise automatically and many risky projects may be accepted although they would fall below the hurdle threshold during recession periods (see Figure 7-5).

Therefore, RAROC measures should not be used in conjunction with fixed hurdle rates set at a specific point in time if the bank as a whole wants to obtain a stable average level of hurdle rate "through the cycle."

As internal prices must compensate for the level of systematic risk exposure, the hurdle rate retained for each position has to be specific and flexible. For its calculation at a facility level, Froot (2001) identifies three separate contributions:

♦ The covariance between the specific position and the market (market risk premium)

♦ The covariance between the specific position and the portfolio risk of the bank (bank-level risk premium)

♦ The covariance between the specific position and the business unit portfolio risk (business unit risk premium)

FIGURE 7-5

Risk-Return Relationship

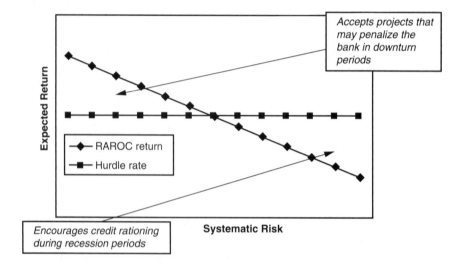

A hurdle rate is calculated for each asset in the portfolio that integrates these three components. In addition, it shows that banks have to cover more than just market requirement. They also have to compensate for bankwide and business unit risks.

We have shown here that the link between RAROC and EVA is far from being direct and obvious. The EVA measure corresponds to a top-down process, whereas the RAROC process corresponds to a bottom-up one. Our suggestion is to use top-down approaches to go from the bank level to the business unit level and to reconcile bottom-up and top-down approaches at the BU level, through an adequate choice of hurdle rates provided by the top-down exercise.

Method 2: Applying Traditional Portfolio Allocation Techniques to Top-Down Dynamic Capital Allocation

Baud et al. (2000) suggest a dynamic approach based on the definition of an efficient frontier. For them, dynamic capital allocation is the result of an optimization process under constraints. The optimization objective is to obtain the best performance in a traditional risk–expected return framework. Their proxy for risk-return corresponds to the traditional mean-variance approach. Their decision tool is very similar to Sharpe ratio techniques.

The constraints they consider are

+ Regulatory requirement
+ Strategic issues
+ Technical constraints due to the inertia regarding the adjustment of the size of any business unit, given the low level of liquidity of its assets.

The main drawbacks with this approach are threefold:

+ First, their approach is assuming a Gaussian environment. This assumption about normality is weak when dealing with lending activities that display very asymmetric and skewed returns.
+ Second, strategic issues should never be considered a constraint. By nature, strategy is a driver of business development integrating a planning horizon that is beyond that of short-term optimization.
+ Third, the approach relies on a detailed level of balance sheet information at a BU level which is not publicly available.

Method 3: Internal Debt Capital Allocation Process

Henrotte and Hyafil (2002) propose an alternative way to derive dynamic capital allocation using a top-down framework. They first build a balance sheet for each business unit. The asset side of the balance sheet corresponds to the net asset value (discussed previously). The liability side corresponds to debt and economic capital. Economic capital is calculated as shown earlier in the chapter.

This process enables us to allocate debt to each business unit as the difference between the NAV and the economic capital of each business unit. In case the difference is positive, then the business unit shows a (virtual) debt capacity. If the difference is negative, it shows that the business unit requires a (virtual) cash collateral[25] (Figure 7-6).

An aggregation of balance sheets among all business units is then performed in order to obtain a consolidated view of the bank (Figure 7-7). It is then compared with the true balance sheet liabilities of the bank holding.

If the equity capital (the market capitalization) is higher than the sum of economic capitals, then the bank is outperforming expectations. If not, the bank is underperforming, and some steps should be taken to

FIGURE 7-6

Debt Capacity and Collateral

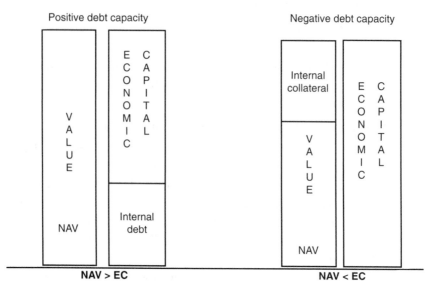

Source: Henrotte and Hyafil (2002).

FIGURE 7-7

Balance Sheet Consolidation

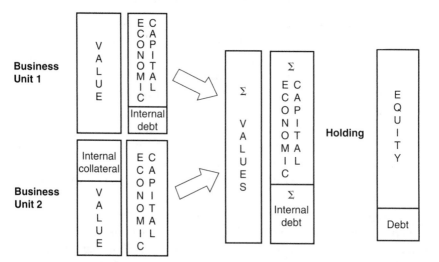

Source: Henrotte and Hyafil (2002).

improve its performance. A review over time of the stability of this difference may lead to specific actions by the senior management of the bank.

For each of the business units a cost of capital (CoC) is supposed to be determined by the market. As the cost of debt R is related to the rating of the bank, the cost of economic capital k_{BU} is calculated as

$$k_{BU} = CoC + (internal\ debt/economic\ capital) \times (CoC - R)$$

♦ *Consequence for the definition of RAROC-based internal hurdle rates at the business-unit level.* k_{BU} corresponds to a hurdle rate extracted from market information. Such a hurdle rate constitutes the basis for the definition of a required hurdle rate associated with bottom-up RAPM measures.[26]

$$k_{BU}^{RAROC} = k_{BU} \times \left(\frac{EC_{top\text{-}down}^{BU}}{\sum\limits_{BU} EC_{top\text{-}down}^{BU}} \times \frac{\sum\limits_{BU} EC_{bottom\text{-}up}^{BU}}{EC_{bottom\text{-}up}^{BU}} \right)$$

where:

k_{BU}^{RAROC} is the level of hurdle rate required when using a bottom-up approach

$EC_{bottom\text{-}up}$ is the level of economic capital obtained through a bottom-up exercise

$EC_{top\text{-}down}$ corresponds to the economic capital calculated in this section

Let us now assume that a certain level of risk aversion applies to the bank. This is based, for instance, on the fact that the total level of economic capital effectively detained by the bank constantly exceeds the sum of top-down economic capital contributions allocated to each of the business units, according to the Froot and Stein (1998) framework. This will impact the new bottom-up hurdle rate[27]:

$$\overline{k_{BU}^{RAROC}} = k_{BU} \times \left(\frac{EC_{top\text{-}down}^{BU} + \Delta^{BU}EC_{risk\ aversion}}{EC_{bank}} \times \frac{\sum\limits_{BU} EC_{bottom\text{-}up}^{BU}}{EC_{bottom\text{-}up}^{BU}} \right)$$

♦ *Linking EVA to RAROC.* In order to link *EVA* to *RAROC,* the definition of *RAROC* has to be based on economic terms; that is,
RAROC = (*ΔNAV* – *R* × *D*)/*EC,* where *D* is the corresponding
amount of debt and *EC* is the top-down economic capital.
Bottom-up *RAROC* does not fit with *EVA,* as mentioned earlier.

   In terms of creation of value, the performance measure that
enables us to evaluate the contribution of each business unit is
(*RAROC* – k_{BU}) × *EC* = *ΔNAV* – *CoC* × NAV_0.

   This approach provides an interesting framework for
dynamic capital allocation. *ΔNAV* measures can nevertheless
prove difficult to estimate, taking into account correlation issues.
Instead, internal betas could be used as an alternative.

The dynamic process of capital management is split in two parts:

1. A detailed business plan for each business unit is elaborated.
   An internal valuation of business units and some sensitivity
   analysis are then performed (by Monte Carlo simulation). This
   provides a measure of economic capital that enables the computation of performance measure and a hurdle rate for each business unit (Figure 7-8).

2. Active decision making follows at a senior executive level (Figure
   7-9). If the internal view of the aggregated balance sheet of the

FIGURE 7-8

Defining a Hurdle Rate for Each BU

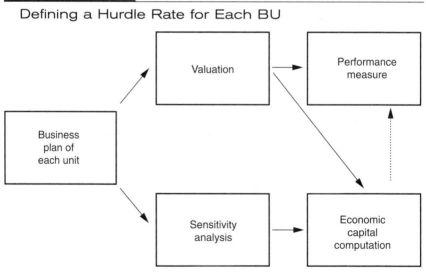

Source: Henrotte and Hyafil (2002).

FIGURE 7-9

Decision Making by Senior Management

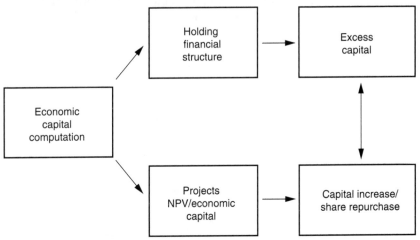

Source: Henrotte and Hyafil (2002).

bank differs persistently from the perception of the market, then the managers of the bank have to consider actions such as shares repurchase or capital increase. These decisions will depend on the degree of risk aversion of senior executives. Some of them will feel comfortable with stable excess capital[28]; others will not.

CONCLUSION

This chapter emphasizes the complexity of strategic capital allocation and dynamic management. To be properly implemented, these concepts need to incorporate several important factors:

◆ Liquidity, risk, and information issues as highlighted in micro-economic theory
◆ Risk aversion that is central to modern finance

In addition we believe that instead of being the ultimate outcome of a bottom-up approach (as traditionally considered), strategic capital allocation and dynamic management have to come *first* through an initial top-down analysis of the bank.

In other words strategy has to be defined first. The defined strategy helps to set hurdle rates for all business units and enables us to define a risk aversion measure for the bank. The traditional bottom-up exercise can then be performed in a second step, using the former two pieces of information (strategy and risk aversion) as inputs in order to make relevant decisions at an individual transaction level.

APPENDIX 7A

This appendix shows that when trying to allocate capital to business units, the level of capital charged to each unit will depend on the way the bank constructs or deconstructs its portfolio of activities. As a consequence, there is room for internal bargaining among business unit managers, as any capital allocation is "path-dependent."

Let us suppose that bank B acquires two new business units BU_1 and BU_2. If the business unit BU_1 is acquired first, then the economic capital allocated to this new business unit will be $EC_{BU_1} = EC_{B \cup BU_1} - EC_B$, where EC_B is the initial economic capital of the bank. The business unit BU_2 being subsequently acquired, its economic capital will be $EC_{BU_2} = EC_{B \cup BU_1 \cup BU_2} - EC_{B \cup BU_1}$.

Let us now consider the opposite case where the business unit BU_2 is acquired first. The economic capital allocated to this new business unit will be $\overline{EC}_{BU_2} = \overline{EC}_{B \cup BU_2} - EC_B$. The business unit BU_1 is subsequently acquired, and its economic capital will be $\overline{EC}_{BU_1} = EC_{B \cup BU_1 \cup BU_2} - \overline{EC}_{B \cup BU_1}$.

What we will observe is that $\overline{EC}_{BU_2} \neq EC_{BU_2}$ and $\overline{EC}_{BU_1} \neq EC_{BU_1}$, though EC_B and $EC_{B \cup BU_1 \cup BU_2}$ are equal in the two cases. Should therefore a bank consider its business units according to the order of acquisition, to the order of importance for the bank, or to any other order? Whatever the choice, there will be an impact on economic capital allocation.

Yield Spreads

We have so far focused on risk measurement and tried to estimate the key determinants of credit risk such as the probability of default and the recovery rate. We now turn to the important question of how credit risk is reflected in the prices of securities or in their yields.

The yield to maturity (YTM) is the annualized rate of return promised to an investor who buys a bond at the current market prices, holds the security until maturity, and reinvests the interim coupons at a rate equal to the YTM. YTMs are more intuitive than bond prices, as they enable investors to compare the rates of returns on instruments with differing maturities.

Yield spreads are the most widely used indicators of credit quality in the markets. A spread is defined as the difference between two yields. Sovereign spreads, for example, are obtained by taking the yield on a bond issued by a given country, say Germany, and subtracting it from the yield on a bond with the same maturity issued by another sovereign, for example Italy. Convergence trades based on sovereign spreads were particularly popular strategies among hedge funds in the late 1990s. They involved speculating on the narrowing of the spreads between the yields of southern European countries (Italy and Spain) and core members of the European Union such as Germany or France in the run-up to monetary union.

Being able to measure and model spreads accurately is important on several counts. First, a model for spreads and for riskless yields immediately provides a model for corporate bonds. Second, as we will see in

Chapter 9, credit derivatives are becoming increasingly important financial instruments. Among this class of products, credit spread options are
contingent claims whose payoffs depend on the value and behavior of
spreads in the market. A spread model is therefore crucial for pricing these
instruments. Third, from a risk management perspective, spreads are a
key input of a ratings-based model of credit risk such as CreditMetrics
(see Chapter 6). Finally, forward spreads serve to determine the possible
future values of the various lines in a credit portfolio and therefore to calculate credit VaR.

Most of our discussion will focus on corporate spreads, which can
be calculated as the difference between the yield on a risky corporate bond
and the yield of an "equivalent" riskless Treasury bond. By "equivalent," we
mean a bond with the same maturity but also the same embedded options
such as calls and puts and, ideally, the same coupon rate.

In this chapter we explain how to construct spreads from corporate
and Treasury bond data. We then focus on the dynamics of U.S. credit
spreads and discuss possible specifications for a stochastic model of spreads.
The appropriateness of spreads as a proxy for credit risk relies on the ability
to extract default probability and recovery rate from spreads. The study by
Delianedis and Geske (2001), among others, has shown that only a small
portion of investment-grade spreads (5 to 22 percent) can be attributed to
default risk and has therefore raised doubts on the suitability of spreads
to serve that purpose. We review what other factors can impact on yield
spreads and how these factors can be proxied in empirical work. Finally
we focus on the ability of models based on the value of the firm (structural
models) to account for the observed dynamics and levels of spreads.

CORPORATE SPREADS

Corporate spreads are the difference between the yield on a corporate
bond $Y(t,T)$ and the yield on an identical but (default) riskless security
$R(t,T)$. T denotes the maturity date, and t stands for the current date.

The spread is therefore $S(t,T) = Y(t,T) - R(t,T)$. Recall that the price
$P(t,T)$ at time t of a risky zero-coupon bond maturing at T can be obtained
by

$$P(t,T) = \exp\left[- Y(t,T) \times (T - t)\right] \qquad (8\text{-}1)^1$$

Similarly, for the riskless bond $B(t,T)$:

$$B(t,T) = \exp \left[-R(t,T) \times (T - t)\right] \qquad (8\text{-}2)$$

Therefore

$$S(t,T) = 1/(T - t) \log \left[B(t,T)/P(t,T)\right] \qquad (8\text{-}3)$$

Thus, all else being equal, the spread widens when the risky bond price falls.

For the sake of simplicity, assume for now that investors are risk-neutral. In a risk-neutral world, an investor is indifferent between receiving $1 for sure and receiving $1 in expectation.

Thus, we must have $B(t,T) = P(t,T)/(1 - pL)$, where L is the expected loss in default (1 minus the recovery rate) and p the probability of default. Therefore, using Equation (8-3), we get $S(t,T) = - 1/(T - t) \log (1 - pL)$.

The risk-neutral spread reflects both the probability of default and the recovery risk. In reality, of course, investors exhibit risk aversion, which will also be translated into spreads. We will review in some detail below the determinants of corporate spreads, but before we turn to the explanation of the dynamics and levels of spreads, we first focus on the calculation of spreads from the data.

Calculating Spreads

In theory calculating spreads is very straightforward. One just has to compute the risky and riskless yields and take the difference. Unfortunately, in most cases, there will not exist a riskless bond with identical features to the corporate bond.

On many occasions a corporate bond will be associated with an underlying Treasury security with approximately the same maturity.[2] Market practitioners would then calculate the spread as the difference between the two yields.

We will now present a way to calculate spreads on an entire cross-section of bonds (say, on a portfolio of U.S. straight corporate securities[3]) without assuming the knowledge of the specific underlying Treasuries.

Assume that:

♦ We have a portfolio of N corporate bonds with maturity T_i, annual coupon rate C_i, for $i = 1,...,N$, and principal $100.

♦ We have a sample of n Treasury bills and bonds with maturities θ_j, annual coupon rate c_j, for $j = 1,...,n$, and principal $100.

♦ $\min_j \theta_j \le \min_i T_i$ and $\max_j \theta_j \ge \max_i T_i$.

We start by stripping the Treasury curve,[4] i.e., by calculating the yields of riskless zero-coupon bonds from the prices of coupon-bearing bonds. We then obtain n' zero-coupon bond yields $R(t, \theta_k)$[5] with maturities spanning $[\min_j \theta_j, \max_j \theta_j]$.

As mentioned earlier, there will typically be a mismatch between the maturities of corporate and Treasury bonds in the sample. For the sake of accuracy we need to be able to interpolate the riskless yields in order to have a continuum of maturities and to calculate spreads for all T_i.

Many interpolation methods have been proposed in the literature,[6] and an exhaustive review is beyond the scope of this book. One popular choice is the Nelson-Siegel procedure (Nelson and Siegel, 1987) described in Appendix 8A.

Once the entire yield curve is fitted, we can calculate riskless bond prices and yields with exactly the same maturity and coupon rate as the corporate bonds in our portfolio.

Recall that the price $B^c(t,\theta)$ of a coupon bond with annual coupon rate c (paid semiannually), maturity θ, and principal \$100 can be obtained from the prices of zero-coupon bonds $B(.,.)$ using

$$B^c(t,\theta) = \sum_{i=1}^{2g} \frac{100c}{2} B\left(t, \frac{i}{2}\right) + 100\, B(t,\theta) \qquad (8\text{-}4)$$

where g is the number of periods (half years) between t and θ.

From the entire set of "synthetic" riskless bonds generated above, we can then calculate the yields and finally the desired corporate spreads.

Dynamics of Credit Spreads

In this section we review the dynamics of credit spread series in the United States. The data consist of 4177 daily observations of Aaa and Baa average spread indices from the beginning of 1986 to the end of 2001. Spread indices are calculated by subtracting the 10-year constant-maturity Treasury yield from Moody's average yield on U.S. long-term (> 10 years) Aaa and Baa bonds: $S_t^{Aaa} = Y_t^{Aaa} - Y_t^T$, and $S_t^{Baa} = Y_t^{Baa} - Y_t^T$. All series are available on the Federal Reserve's web site,[7] and bonds in this sample do not contain option features.

Aaa is the best rating in Moody's classification with a historical default frequency over 10 years of 0.64 percent, while Baa is at the bottom of the investment-grade category and has historically suffered a 4.41 percent default rate over 10 years (see Keenan, Shtogrin, and Sobehart, 1999). Both minima were reached in 1989 after 2 years of very low default experience. At the end of our sample, spreads were at their historical maximum, only matched by 1986 for the Aaa series. 2001 was branded by rating agencies the worst year ever in terms of the amount of defaulted debt. Summary statistics of the series are provided in Table 8-1.

Figure 8-1 depicts the history of spreads in the Aaa and Baa classes, and Figure 8-2 is a scatter plot of daily changes in Baa spreads as a function

TABLE 8-1

Summary Statistics for Spreads Data

	S_t^{Aaa}	S_t^{Baa}
Average	1.16%	2.04%
Standard dev.	0.40%	0.50%
Min	0.31%	1.16%
Max	2.67%	3.53%
Skew	0.872	0.711
Kurt	3.566	2.701

FIGURE 8-1

U.S. Baa and Aaa Spreads—1986 to 2001

FIGURE 8-2

Daily Changes in U.S. Baa Spread Indices

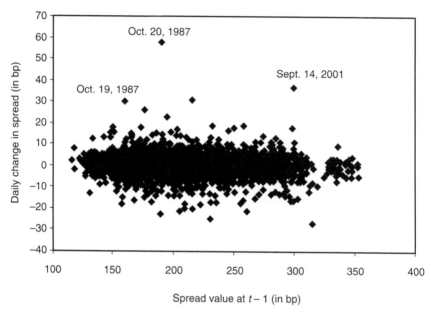

of their level. The Aaa series oscillates around a mean of about 1.2 percent, while the term mean of the Baa series appears to be around 2 percent.

Several noticeable events have affected spread indices over the past 20 years. The first major incident occurred during the famous stock market crash of October 1987. This event is remembered as an equity market debacle, but corporate bonds were equally affected, with Baa spreads soaring by 90 basis points over 2 days, the biggest rise ever (see Figures 8-1 and 8-2).

The 1991 Gulf War is also clearly visible on Figure 8-1. On the run-up to the war, Baa spreads rose by nearly 100 basis points. They started to tighten immediately after the start of the conflict, and by the end of the war, they had narrowed back to their initial level. Aaa spreads were little affected by the event.

Finally, let us mention the spectacular and sudden rises that occurred after the Russian default of August 1998 and after September 11, 2001.[8]

Explaining the Baa–Aaa Spread

As we noted earlier, some events such as the Gulf War did substantially impact on Baa spreads while Aaa spreads were little affected. It is therefore interesting to focus on the relative spread between Baa and Aaa yields. Figure 8-3 is a plot of this differential, showing a clear downward trend

FIGURE 8-3

Spread between Baa and Aaa Yields

between 1986 and 1998, only interrupted by the Gulf War. This contraction in relative spreads was due mainly to the improvement in liquidity of the market for lower-rated bonds.

We can observe three spikes in the relative spread (Baa–Aaa): 1991, 1998, and 2001. These are all linked to increases in market volatility, and the peaks can be explained in the light of a structural model of credit risk.

Recall that in a Merton-type model, a risky bond can be seen as a riskless bond minus a put on the value of the firm. The put's exercise price is linked to the leverage of the issuing firm (in the simple case where the firm's debt only consists of one issue of a zero-coupon bond, the strike price of the put is the principal of the debt). Obviously the values of Baa firms are closer to their "strike price" (higher risk) than those of Aaa firms. Therefore Baa firms have higher vega than Aaa issuers.[9] As a result, as volatility increases, Baa spreads increase more than Aaa spreads.

What Model for Spreads?

In the pricing of credit derivatives such as credit spread options, it is important to be able to model the dynamics of spreads accurately. We also believe that dynamic models of credit spreads will be very important in the next generation of credit portfolio models (extensions of the CreditMetrics approach).

The main approach to spread modeling (see Lando, 1998, and Duffie and Singleton, 1999) consists of describing the default event as the unpredictable outcome of a jump process.[10] Default occurs when a Poisson process with intensity λ_t jumps for the first time. $\lambda_t\,dt$ is the instantaneous probability of default. Under some assumptions, Duffie and Singleton (1999) establish that default-risky bonds can be priced in the usual martingale framework[11] used for pricing Treasury bonds. Hence the price of a credit-risky zero-coupon bond is

$$P(t,T) = E_t^Q\left[e^{-\int_t^T A_s ds}\right]$$

where $A_s = r_s + \lambda_s L_s$.

L_s is the loss in default, and the second term therefore takes the interpretation of an expected loss (probability of default times loss given default). It can also be seen as an instantaneous spread, the extra return above the riskless rate. This approach is very versatile, as it allows us to price bonds and also credit-risky securities as discounted expectation under Q but with a modified discount rate. However. the instantaneous spread above does not translate into an explicit process for the spread of a given maturity, say 10 years, which is the variable of interest for some pricing purposes.

Another approach consists of a direct modeling of the spread process. It may be more appropriate if the focus is on the spread itself, for example in the pricing of spread options. Longstaff and Schwartz (1995b) choose a simple specification and implement it on real data. The main stylized fact incorporated in their model is the mean-reverting behavior of spreads: The logarithm of the spread is assumed to follow an Ornstein-Uhlenbeck process under the risk-neutral measure Q:

$$ds_t = \kappa(\theta - s_t)\,dt + \sigma\,dW_t$$

where the log of the spread is s_t with long-term mean θ and volatility σ. The speed of mean reversion is κ.

Mean reversion is an important feature in credit spreads and has been found in Longstaff and Schwartz (1995b) and Prigent, Renault, and Scaillet (PRS, 2001). Interestingly the speed of mean reversion is not the same for Baa and Aaa spreads, for example. PRS provide a detailed parametric and nonparametric analysis of the credit spread indices described above and find that higher-rated spreads tend to revert much faster to their long-term mean than lower-rated spreads. A similar finding is reported on a different sample by Longstaff and Schwartz (1995b).

Another property of spreads is that their volatility tends to be increasing in their level. This is not captured by the model above. To tackle this, Das and Tufano (1996) suggest an alternative specification, similar to the Cox-Ingersoll-Ross (1985) specification for interest rates:[12]

$$ds_t = \kappa(\theta - s_t)\, dt + \sigma \sqrt{s_t}\, dW_t$$

PRS keep a constant volatility but argue that spreads exhibit jumps, which is supported by observation of Figure 8-1. They therefore extend the model of Longstaff and Schwartz (1995b) in a different direction and incorporate binomial jumps[13]:

$$ds_t = \kappa(\theta - s_t)\, dt + \sigma\, dW_t + dN_t$$

where N_t is a compound Poisson process whose jumps take either the value $+a$ or $-a$ (given that the specification is in logarithm, they are percentage jumps).

Jumps are found to be significant in both series (Aaa and Baa), and a likelihood ratio test of the jump process versus its diffusion counterpart strongly rejects the assumption of no jumps at the 5 percent level. Note that the size of percentage jumps in Baa spreads is about half that of jumps in Aaa spreads. In *absolute* terms however, average jumps in both series are approximately the same size because the level of Aaa spreads is about half that of Baa spreads.

Determinants of Spreads

We have seen earlier in this chapter that spreads should at least reflect the probability of default and the recovery rate. In a careful analysis of the components of corporate spreads in the context of a structural model, Delianedis and Geske (2001) report that only 5 percent of AAA spreads and 22 percent of BBB spreads can be attributed to default risk. We now turn in greater details to the possible components of an explanatory model for spreads.

Recovery

The *expected recovery rate* for a bond of given seniority in a given industry is a natural candidate for inclusion in a spread model. Recoveries were discussed at length in Chapter 4; recall that they tend to fluctuate with the economic cycle. So ideally a measure of expected recovery conditional on the state of the economy would be a more appropriate choice.

Probability of Default

Spreads should also reflect default probability. The most readily available measure of creditworthiness for large corporates is undoubtedly *ratings*, and they are easy to include in a spread model. Figure 8-4 is a plot of U.S. industrial and Treasury bond yields. Spreads are clearly increasing as credit rating deteriorates. The model by Fons (1994) provides an explicit link between default rates per rating class and the level of risk-neutral spreads. The main difficulty, as described in Appendix 8D, is to model the risk premium associated with the volatility in the default rate as market spreads incorporate investors risk aversion.

A similar but dynamic perspective on the relationship between ratings and spreads is provided in Figure 8-5. We again observe what appears to be a structural break in the dynamics of spreads in August 1998. The post-1998 period is characterized by much higher mean spreads and volatilities for all risk classes. While the event triggering the change is well identified (Russian default followed by flight to quality and liquidity), analysts disagree on the reasons for the persistence of high spreads in the markets. Some argue that investors' risk aversion has durably changed and that each extra "unit" of credit risk is priced more expensively in terms of risk premium. Others put forward the fact that asset volatility is still very high and that default rates have increased steadily over the period. Keeping

FIGURE 8-4

U.S. Industrial Bond Yield Curves (March 11, 2002)

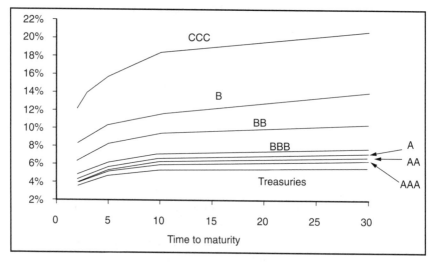

Source: Riskmetrics.

FIGURE 8-5

10-Year Spreads per Rating

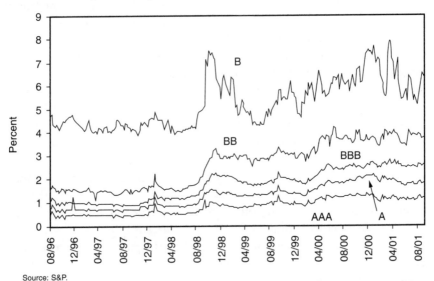

Source: S&P.

unchanged the perception of risk by investors, spreads merely reflect higher real credit risk.

An alternative explanation lies in the fact that the change coincided with the increasing impact of the equity market on corporate bond prices. The reasons for this are twofold: the recent popularity of equity–corporate bond trades among market participants and the common use of equity-driven credit risk models such as those described in Chapter 3.

Probability of Default Extracted from Structural Models

In many empirical studies of spreads, *equity volatility* often turns out to be one of the most powerful explanatory variables. This is consistent with the structural approach to credit risk where default is triggered when the value of the firm falls below its liabilities. The higher the volatility, the more likely the firm will reach the default boundary and the higher the spreads should be. Several choices are possible: historical versus implied volatility, aggregate versus individual, etc. Implied volatility has the advantage of being forward-looking (the trader's view on future volatility) and is arguably a better choice. It is, however, only available for firms with traded stock options. At the aggregate level, the VIX index, released by the Chicago Board Options Exchange, is often chosen as a measure of implied volatility. It is a weighted average of the implied volatilities of eight options with 30 days to maturity.

The second crucial factor of default probability in a structural approach is the *leverage* of a firm. This measures the level of indebtedness of the firm scaled by the total value of its assets. Leverage is commonly measured in empirical work as the book value of debt divided by the market value of equity plus the book value of debt. The reason for the choice of book value in the case of debt is purely a matter of data availability. A large share of the debt of a firm will not be traded, and it is therefore impossible in many cases to obtain its market value. This problem does not arise with the equity of public companies. If no information about the level of indebtedness is available or if the model aims at estimating aggregate spreads, then equity returns (individual or at the market level) can be used as a rough proxy for leverage. The underlying assumption is that book values of debt outstanding are likely to be substantially less volatile than the market value of the firms' equity. Hence, on average, a positive stock return should be associated with a decrease in leverage and in spreads.

At the macroeconomic level, the *yield curve* is often used as an indicator of the market's view of future growth. In particular a steep yield curve is frequently associated with an expectation of growth, while an inverted or flat yield curve is often observed in periods of recessions.

FIGURE 8-6

Default Rates and Economic Growth

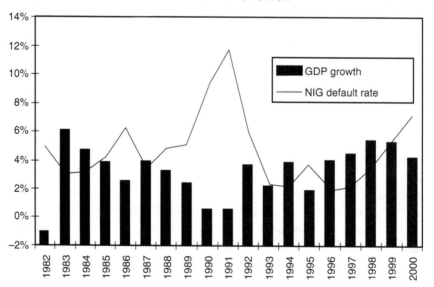

Source: S&P and Federal Reserve.

Naturally default rates are much higher in recessions (see Figure 8-6). Therefore the slope of the yield curve can be used as a predictor of future default rates, and we can expect yield spreads to be inversely related to the slope of the term structure.

Riskless Interest Rate

There has been much debate in the academic literature on the interaction between *riskless interest rates* and spreads. Most papers (e.g., Duffee, 1998) report a negative correlation, implying that when interest rates increase (or decrease), risky yields do not reflect the full impact of the rise (or fall). Morris, Neal, and Rolph (1998) make a distinction between the negative short-term impact and the positive long-term impact of changes in risk-free rates on corporate spreads. One possible explanation for this finding is that risky yields adjust slowly to changes in the Treasury rate (short-term impact) but that in the long run an increase in interest rates is likely to be associated with a slowdown in growth and therefore an increase in default frequency and spreads.

Risk Premium

The credit spread measures the excess return on a bond granted to investors as a compensation for credit risk. Measuring credit risk as the probability of default and the recovery is insufficient. Investors' risk aversion also needs to be factored in.

If the purpose of the exercise is to determine the level of spreads for a sample of bonds, we can extract some information about the "market price of credit risk" from credit spread indices. Assuming that the risk differential between highly rated bonds and speculative bonds remains constant through time (which is a strong assumption), changes in the difference between two credit spread indices such as those studied earlier in the chapter should be the result of changes in the risk premium.

Is a Systemic Factor at Play?

Many of the variables identified above are instrumental in explaining the levels and changes in corporate yield spreads. A similar analysis could be performed to determine the drivers of sovereign spreads such as that of Italy versus Germany or Mexico versus the United States. The fundamentals in these markets are, however, very different, and we could argue that trading or investment strategies in these various markets should be uncorrelated. This intuition would appear valid in most cases, but spreads tend to exhibit periods of extreme co-movement at times of crises.

To illustrate this, let us consider the Russian and LTCM crises in 1998. We have seen that the Russian default in August did push up corporate spreads dramatically. This was, however, not an isolated phenomenon. Figure 8-7 jointly depicts the spread of the 10-year Italian government bond yield over the 10-year Bund (German benchmark) on the right-hand scale and the spread of the Mexican Brady[14] discount bond versus the 30-year U.S. Treasury on the left-hand scale.

Figure 8-7 is instructive on several counts. First it shows that financial instruments in apparently segmented markets can react simultaneously to the same event. In this case it would appear that the Russian default in August 1998 was the critical event.[15]

Second it explains partly why hedging, diversification, and risk management strategies failed so badly over the period from August 1998 through February 1999. Typical risk management tools, including value at risk, use fixed correlations among assets in order to calculate the required amount of capital to set aside. In our case the correlation between the two spreads from January to July 1998 was −11 percent. Then suddenly, although the markets are not tied by economic fundamentals and although the crisis occurred in a third market apparently unrelated, cor-

FIGURE 8-7

Mexican Brady and ITL/DEM Spreads

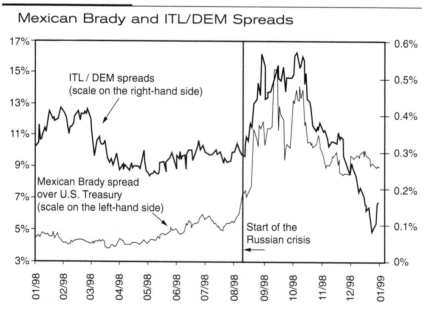

Source: Anderson and Renault (1999).

relations all turned positive and very significantly so. In this example the correlation over the rest of 1998 increased to 62 percent.

Some may argue that the Russian default may just have increased default risk globally or that market participants expected spillover effects in all bond markets. Another explanation lies in the flight to liquidity and flight to safety observed over that period: Investors massively turned to the most liquid and safest products, which were U.S. Treasuries and German Bunds. Many products bearing credit risk did not seem to find any buyer at any price in the immediate aftermath of the crisis.

From a risk management perspective, it is sensible to consider that a global factor (possibly investors' risk aversion) impacts across all bond markets and may lead to substantial losses in periods of turmoil.

Liquidity

Finally, and perhaps most importantly, yield spreads reflect the relative *liquidity* of corporate and Treasury securities. Liquidity is one of the main explanations for the existence of corporate yield spreads. This has been recognized early (see, e.g., Fisher, 1959) and can be justified by the fact that government bonds are typically very actively traded large issues, whereas the corporate bond market is an over-the-counter market whose volumes and trade frequencies are much smaller. Investors require some compensation (in terms of added yield) for holding less liquid securities.

In the case of investment-grade bonds, where credit risk is not as important as in the speculative class, liquidity is arguably the main factor in spreads. Liquidity is, however, a very nebulous concept, and there does not exist any clear-cut definition for it. It can encompass the rapid availability of funds for a corporate to finance unexpected outflows, or it can mean the marketability of the debt on the secondary market. We will focus on the latter definition. More specifically we perceive liquidity as the ability to close out a position quickly on the market without substantially affecting the price. Liquidity can therefore be seen as an option to unwind a position.

Longstaff (1995) follows this approach and provides upper bounds on the liquidity discounts on securities with trading restrictions. If a security cannot be bought or sold for, say, 7 days, it will trade at a discount compared with an identical security for which trading is available continuously. This discount represents the opportunity cost of not being able to trade during the restricted period. It should therefore be bounded by the value of selling[16] the position at the best (highest) price during the restricted period. The value of liquidity is thus capped by the price of a lookback put option.

Little research has been performed on the liquidity of non-Treasury bonds. Kempf and Uhrig (1997) propose a direct modeling of liquidity spreads—the share of yield spreads attributable to the liquidity differential between government and corporate bonds. They assume that liquidity spreads follow a mean-reverting process and estimate it on German government bond data. Longstaff (1994) considers the liquidity of municipal and other credit-risky bonds in Japan. Ericsson and Renault (2001) model the behavior of a bondholder who may be forced to sell her position due to an external shock (immediate need for cash). Liquidity spreads arise because a forced sale may coincide with a lack of demand in the market (liquidity crisis). Their theoretical model based on a Merton (1974) default risk framework generates a downward-sloping term structure of liquidity spreads like those reported in Kempf and Uhrig (1997) and also in Longstaff (1994). They also find that liquidity spreads should be increasing in credit risk: If liquidity is the option to liquidate a position, then this option is more valuable in the presence of credit risk, as the inability to unwind a position for a long period may force the bondholder to keep a bond entering default and to face bankruptcy costs. On a sample of more than 500 U.S. corporate bonds, they find support for the negative slope of the term structure of liquidity premiums and for the positive correlation between credit risk and liquidity spreads.

On the empirical side, the liquidity of equity markets (and to a lesser extent also of Treasury bond markets) has been extensively studied, but very little has yet been done to measure liquidity premiums in default-risky securities. Several variables can be used as proxy for liquidity. The natural candidates are the number of trades and the volume of trading on the market. The OTC nature of the corporate bond market makes the data difficult to obtain. As second best, the issue amount outstanding can also serve as a proxy for liquidity. The underlying implicit assumption is that larger issues are traded more actively than smaller ones.

A stylized fact about bonds is that they are more liquid immediately after issuance and rapidly lose their marketability as a larger share of the issues becomes locked into portfolios. (See, for example, Chapter 10 in Fabozzi and Fabozzi, 1995). The age of an issue could therefore stand for liquidity in an explanatory model for yield spreads. In the same spirit, the on-the-run/off-the-run spread (the difference between the yields of seasoned and newly issued bonds with the same residual time to maturity) is frequently used as an indicator of liquidity. During the Russian crisis of 1998, which was associated with a substantial liquidity crunch, the U.S. long bond (30-year benchmark) was trading at a premium of 35 basis points versus the second longest bond with just a few months less to maturity, while the historical differential was only 7 to 8 basis points (Poole, 1998).

Taxes

In order to conclude this nonexhaustive list of factors influencing spreads, we should mention taxes. In some jurisdictions (such as the United States), corporate and Treasury bonds do not receive the same tax treatment (see Elton, Gruber, Agrawal, and Mann, 2001). For example, in the United States, Treasury securities are exempt from some taxes while corporate bonds are not. Investors will, of course, demand a higher return on instruments on which they are taxed more.

We have reported that many factors impact on yield spreads and that spreads cannot be seen as purely due to credit. We will now focus more specifically on the ability of structural models to explain the dynamics and level of spreads.

Spreads and Structural Models of Credit Risk

In this section we describe how models based on the value of the firm (Merton-type structural models) can account for the level and dynamics of spreads.

There are four major difficulties in the implementation of structural models[17] on real data. The first two sources of difficulty are not specific to firm-value-based models. They arise from the nature of the available data and from the very definition of yield spreads. As noted above, yield spreads are not pure credit spreads and will typically include many contractual features of the debt (options, sinking provisions, collateral, etc.), as well as a liquidity premium and, in some countries, a tax differential between private and public debt. As all these components are blended into the yield spread, it is very hard to extract the pure credit component. By construction, most structural models will tend to price only credit risk and to ignore the other factors. This explains the severe mispricing of early models (see below), particularly on investment-grade bonds where only a small portion of spreads is attributable to credit.

The second problem in testing corporate bond pricing models is the lack of corporate bond data. All empirical implementations have been performed on a limited number of databases, suffering either from low frequency or from a small number of bonds.

The two other main difficulties are specific to the structural approach. The first one originates from the estimation of the parameters of the firm value process and, in particular, the volatility (a key parameter in the model). Several approaches have been suggested to estimate this parameter, such as the use of the historical volatility of asset value changes. This is, however, not robust, as balance sheet data are available with low frequency and we have to estimate a variance with as little as 10 data points. As an alternative, we can use the implied volatility, which prices the equity of the firm perfectly.[18] This relies on the underlying assumption that the equity pricing model is perfectly specified: In practice, all model misspecifications for the equity component will be reflected in the implied volatility. A third possibility is to calculate the volatility, which minimizes the quadratic error between observed prices and model prices over a given period. This typically leads to unrealistic values for the volatility.

Another source of problems for the structural model derives from the complexity of the capital structures of most firms. Structural models can at most cope with a simple capital structure with senior and junior debt and equity. A realistic capital structure may include five bond issues, some bank debt, trade credit, convertibles, preferred shares, etc. It therefore becomes necessary to aggregate the various instruments into a limited number of claims such as long-term and short-term debt and equity. These approximations no doubt impact on the accuracy of the pricing model. They can also be costly in terms of processing time.

Early Attempts to Implement Structural Models

Jones, Mason, and Rosenfeld (JMR, 1984, 1985) led the first studies into the empirical performance of structural models. These articles remained almost the only references for about 15 years and served to the detractors of structural models as proof of the failure of the contingent claim approach to corporate bond pricing.

JMR's results were indeed very disappointing. The authors report, for example, an average pricing error of 6 percent, which led Fisher Black (1985) to comment: "I am surprised that JMR could create a model with such a large error. Surely an investment banker can price a new bond more accurately than that." Note, however, that the significance of the empirical analysis of JMR has to be tempered by the small size of their sample (15 issuers and a total of 163 prices), by the complex capital structures implemented in their model (in particular, the number of covenants in the bonds), and by their choice of the simple Merton (1974) assumptions for the underlying default model. JMR's test is therefore a joint test of the contingent claims approach and of their pricing model for the options embedded in the debt contracts.

A more optimistic contribution for firm-value-based models can be found in Sarig and Warga (1989), who study the U.S. term structures of credit spreads. They find a strong resemblance between observed term

structures and those predicted by a Merton-type model for highly leveraged firms.

Recent Results

The following 10 years did not bring any major contributions in the
empirical testing of structural models,[19] but there has been renewed interest in this area over the past few years. An interesting contribution is that
of Anderson and Sundaresan (2000), who estimate several structural models
(including a strategic model[20]) on aggregate U.S. Aaa and Baa yield indices
over the period 1970–1996. They obtain mixed results: A structural model
seems able to explain large parts of the variation in yield spreads over
some periods (1970–1979, for example), but spreads look completely disconnected to the fundamentals over other periods (e.g., 1980–1983).

The GS-spread model of Goldman Sachs is in a similar spirit (see
Bevan and Garzarelli, 2000). Bevan and Garzarelli use a model inspired by
Merton (1974) and estimate a "fair value" model for long-term Baa spreads
using proxies for the corporate leverage and volatility at the macro level.

Both models above are estimated on aggregate, low-frequency data.
Ericsson and Reneby (2001) estimate a firm-value-based model on *individual*
bond data. They assume that the total debt of the firm can be modeled as
a perpetual debt issue paying a continuous coupon. Their results are quite
encouraging. In particular, they report no systematic bias (while most previous studies including JMR reported a systematic underestimation of
spreads), much smaller pricing errors, and a satisfactory out-of-sample
explanatory power. Among the observations made by Ericsson and Reneby
(2001), there is the difficulty of pricing short-term debt accurately using a
structural model. Their model indeed generates much larger residuals for
short-dated bonds. Similar results have been reported by Bakshi, Madan,
and Zhang (2001) in the context of a reduced-form model of credit risk.
These results are compatible with a decreasing term structure of liquidity
spreads as suggested by Ericsson and Renault (2001), but an alternative
explanation lies in the impossibility of a diffusion model reaching a dis-
tant boundary in a short time interval.

The CreditGrades model of Riskmetrics is also based on the contingent claims approach and relies on further assumptions about the default
boundary/recovery level to generate higher short-term credit spreads and
tackle the criticism mentioned above. To do so, the bankruptcy barrier
itself is assumed to be stochastic (following a lognormal distribution). A
firm may therefore default at any time even if its asset value follows a
standard diffusion process (a geometric Brownian motion with zero drift).

The model can then be used to calculate default probabilities, credit spreads, or default swap rates.

CONCLUSION

We have shown that spreads include valuable information about the creditworthiness of corporates. Unfortunately, credit quality is far from being the only driver of spreads, and liquidity is sometimes more important, particularly in the investment-grade bracket. This leads to questioning the approach often adopted by banks to value loan prices on the basis of creditworthiness only. It might fail to track marked-to-market price dynamics. Commercial banks have indeed shown a tendency to price some facilities close to their actuarially fair value, without taking into account a liquidity premium or a level of risk aversion similar to those observed in the markets.

APPENDIX 8A

The Nelson-Siegel Procedure for Fitting the Yield Curve

The procedure proposed by Nelson and Siegel (1987) consists of fitting the following nonlinear form through the observed yields $R(.,.)$:

$$R(t,T) = \alpha + (\beta + \gamma) \frac{1 - \exp\left[-(T-t)/\delta\right]}{(T-t)/\delta} - \gamma \exp\left[-(T-t)/\delta\right] \tag{8A-1}$$

The parameter α takes the interpretation of the infinite maturity yield $\alpha = R(t,\infty)$, while the instantaneous maturity yield is

$$\lim_{(T-t)\to 0} R(t,T) = \alpha + \beta$$

Equation (8A-1) can also be written in terms of forward rates or bond prices. The set of parameters $\Omega = (\alpha,\beta,\gamma,\delta)$ is estimated by minimizing the sum of the squared differences between observed yields and model yields. More formally, the estimate $\hat{\Omega}$ of Ω is obtained as

$$\hat{\Omega} = \arg\min_{\Omega} \left(\sum_k \left[\overline{R(t,\theta_k)} - R(t,\theta_k, \Omega) \right]^2 \right)$$

The Nelson-Siegel procedure is therefore easy to implement and parsimonious (only four parameters to estimate). It enables us to fit increasing, decreasing, and hump-shaped yield curves. Svensson (1994) has proposed an extension to the specification (8A-1), enabling the capture of term structures with two humps.

APPENDIX 8B

Fundamental Theorems of Asset Pricing and Risk-Neutral Measure

In many places in this book we encounter the concept of risk-neutral measure and of pricing by discounted expectation. We will now summarize briefly the key results in this area. A more detailed and rigorous exposition can be found, for example, in Duffie (1996).

Intuitively, the price of a security should be related to its possible payoffs, to the likelihood of such payoffs, and to discount factors reflecting both the time value of money and investors' risk aversion.

Standard pricing models, such as the dividend discount models, use this approach to determine the value of stocks. For derivatives, or securities with complex payoffs in general, there are two fundamental difficulties with this approach:

1. Determining the actual probability of a given payoff
2. Calculating the appropriate discount factor

The seminal papers of Harrison and Kreps (1979) and Harrison and Pliska (1981) have provided ways to circumvent these difficulties and have led to the so-called fundamental theorems of asset pricing (FTAP).

> *First FTAP.* Markets are arbitrage-free if and only if there exists a measure Q equivalent[21] to the historical measure P under which asset prices discounted at the riskless rate are martingales.[22]
>
> *Second FTAP.* This measure Q is unique if and only if markets are complete.

A complete market is a market in which all assets are replicable. This means that you can fully hedge a position in any asset by creating a portfolio of other traded assets.

The first fundamental theorem provides a generic option pricing formula that does not rely either on a risk-adjusted discount factor or on the necessity of finding out the actual probability of future payoffs. Assume that we want to price a security at time t whose random payoff $g(T)$ is paid at $T > t$. By no arbitrage, we know that at maturity the price of the security should be equal to the payoff $P_T = g(T)$. By the first FTAP we immediately get the price:

$$P_t = E_t^Q\left[e^{-r(T-t)}P_T\right] = E_t^Q\left[e^{-r(T-t)}g(T)\right]$$

The probability Q can typically be inferred from traded securities. It is called the risk-neutral measure or the martingale measure.

The second theorem says that the measure Q (and therefore also security prices calculated as above) will be unique if and only if markets are complete. This is a very strong assumption, particularly in credit markets, which are often illiquid.

APPENDIX 8C

An Introduction to Reduced-Form Models[23]

REDUCED-FORM MODELS

In this chapter we have already discussed structural models of credit risk, i.e., models in which the default event is explicitly related to the value of the issuing firm. One of the difficulties with this approach lies in the estimation of the parameters of the asset value process and the default boundary. For complex capital structures or securities with nonstandard payoffs such as credit derivatives, firm-value-based models are also cumbersome to deal with. Reduced-form models aim at making the pricing of these instruments easier by ignoring what the default mechanism is. In this approach, default is unpredictable and driven by a jump process: When no jump occurs, the firm remains solvent, but as soon as there is a jump, default is triggered.

In this appendix we first review the usual processes used in the pricing literature to describe default, namely Poisson and Cox processes. Once their main properties have been recalled, we give pricing formulas for default-risky bonds and explain some key results derived using the reduced-form approach. Finally we build on the continuous-time transition matrices reviewed in Appendix 2A of Chapter 2 to cover rating-based pricing models for bonds and credit derivatives.

The concepts recalled in this appendix are useful for understanding this chapter and are also useful for understanding credit derivatives in Chapter 9 and loss given default in Chapter 4.

POISSON AND COX PROCESSES

Let N_t be a *standard Poisson process*. It is initialized at 0 ($N_0 = 0$) and increases by 1 unit at random times $T_1, T_2, T_3, \ldots$. Durations betweens jump times $T_i - T_{i-1}$ are exponentially distributed.

The traditional way to approach Poisson processes is to consider discrete time intervals and to take the limit to continuous time. Consider a process whose probability of jumping over a small time period Δt is proportional to time: $P[N_{t+\Delta t} - N_t = 1] \approx \lambda \Delta t$ and[24] $P[N_{t+\Delta t} - N_t = 0] \approx 1 - \lambda \Delta t$. The constant λ is called the *intensity* or *hazard rate* of the Poisson process.

Breaking down the time interval $[t,s]$ into n subintervals of length Δt and letting $n \to \infty$ and $\Delta t \to dt$, we obtain the probability of the process not jumping:

$$P[N_s - N_t = 0] = \exp\left[-\lambda(s - t)\right]$$

and the probability of observing exactly m jumps is

$$P[N_s - N_t = m] = \frac{1}{m!}(s - t)^m \lambda^m \exp\left[-\lambda(s - t)\right]$$

Finally, the intensity is such that $E[dN] = \lambda\, dt$. These properties characterize a Poisson process with intensity λ.

An *inhomogeneous Poisson process* is built in a similar way as the standard Poisson process and shares most of its properties. The difference is that the intensity is no longer a constant but a deterministic function of time $\lambda(t)$. Jump probabilities are slightly modified accordingly:

$$P[N_s - N_t = 0] = \exp\left[-\int_t^s \lambda(u)\, du\right] \tag{8C-1}$$

and

$$P[N_s - N_t = m] = \frac{1}{m!}\left[\int_t^s \lambda(u)\, du\right]^m \exp\left[-\int_t^s \lambda(u)\, du\right] \tag{8C-2}$$

Cox processes, or "doubly stochastic" Poisson processes, go one step further and let the intensity itself be random. Therefore, not only is the time of jump stochastic (as in all Poisson processes), but so is the conditional probability of observing a jump over a given time interval. Equations (8C-1) and (8C-2) remain valid but in expectation; they are replaced with

$$P[N_s - N_t = 0] = E\left[\exp\left(-\int_t^s \lambda_u\, du\right)\right] \tag{8C-3}$$

and

$$P[N_s - N_t = m] = E\left[\frac{1}{m!}\left(\int_t^s \lambda_u\, du\right)^m \exp\left(-\int_t^s \lambda_u\, du\right)\right] \tag{8C-4}$$

where λ_u is a positive-valued stochastic process.

DEFAULT-ONLY REDUCED-FORM MODELS

We will now study the pricing of defaultable bonds in a hazard rate setting by assuming that the default process is a Poisson process with intensity λ. The case of Cox processes is studied afterward. We further assume that multiple defaults are possible and that each default incurs a fractional loss of a constant percentage L of the principal. This means that in case of default, the bond is exchanged for an identical maturity security with lower face value.

Let $P(t,T)$ be the price at time t of a defaultable zero-coupon bond with maturity T. Using Ito's lemma, we derive the dynamics of the risky bond price:

$$dP = \frac{\partial P}{\partial t}dt + \frac{\partial P}{\partial r}dr + \frac{1}{2}\frac{\partial^2 P}{\partial r^2}(dr)^2 - LP\,dN \qquad (8\text{C-}5)$$

The first three terms in the equation above correspond to the dependence of the bond price on calendar time and on the riskless interest rate. The last term translates the fact that when there is a jump ($dN = 1$), the price drops by a fraction L.

Under the risk-neutral measure Q (see Appendix 8B), we must have $E^Q[dP] = rP\,dt$ and thus, assuming that the riskless rate follows

$$dr = \mu_r\,dt + \sigma_r\,dW_1$$

under Q, we obtain

$$0 = \frac{\partial P}{\partial t} + \frac{\partial P}{\partial r}\mu_r + \frac{1}{2}\sigma_r^2\frac{\partial^2 P}{\partial r^2} - (r + L\lambda)P \qquad (8\text{C-}6)^{25}$$

Comparing this partial differential equation with that satisfied by a default-free bond $B(t,T)$:

$$0 = \frac{\partial B}{\partial t} + \frac{\partial B}{\partial r}\mu_r + \frac{1}{2}\sigma_r^2\frac{\partial^2 B}{\partial r^2} - rB \qquad (8\text{C-}7)$$

we can easily see that the only difference is in the last term and that if we can solve (8C-7) for $B(t,T)$, the solution for the risky bond is immediately obtained as $P(t,T) = B(t,T)e^{-L\lambda(T-t)}$. The spread is therefore $L\lambda$, which is the risk-neutral expected loss.

The example above is simplistic in many ways. The probability of default over an interval of given length is always constant because the intensity of the process is constant. This also implies that default risk and interest rates are not correlated.

A more versatile specification lets the hazard rate be stochastic with intensity λ_t, such that under the risk-neutral measure[26]:

$$dr = \mu_r \, dt + \sigma_r \, dW_1$$

$$d\lambda = \mu_\lambda \, dt + \sigma_\lambda \, dW_2$$

and the instantaneous correlation between the two Brownian motions W_1 and W_2 is ρ.

The derivation closely follows that described above in the case of a Poisson intensity. We start by applying Ito's lemma to the dynamics of the bond price:

$$dP = \frac{\partial P}{\partial t} dt + \frac{\partial P}{\partial r} dr + \frac{\partial P}{\partial \lambda} d\lambda$$

$$+ \frac{1}{2} \left(\sigma_r^2 \frac{\partial^2 P}{\partial r^2} + \sigma_\lambda^2 \frac{\partial^2 P}{\partial \lambda^2} + 2\rho\sigma_r\sigma_\lambda \frac{\partial^2 P}{\partial r \partial \lambda} \right) dt - LP \, dN \quad (8C\text{-}8)$$

We then impose the no-arbitrage condition: $E^Q[dP] = rP \, dt$, which leads to the partial differential equation:

$$0 = \frac{\partial P}{\partial t} + \frac{\partial P}{\partial r} \mu_r + \frac{\partial P}{\partial \lambda} \mu_\lambda$$

$$+ \frac{1}{2} \left(\sigma_r^2 \frac{\partial^2 P}{\partial r^2} + \sigma_\lambda^2 \frac{\partial^2 P}{\partial \lambda^2} + 2\rho\sigma_r\sigma_\lambda \frac{\partial^2 P}{\partial r \partial \lambda} \right) - (r + L\lambda)P \quad (8C\text{-}9)$$

The solution of this equation of course depends on the specification of the interest rate and intensity processes, but again we can observe that the spread is likely to be related to $L\lambda$.

Rather than solving Equation (8C-9) directly subject to appropriate boundary conditions, it is possible to derive the solution using martingale methods. It is the approach chosen by Duffie and Singleton (1999).

From the FTAP (see Appendix 8B), we know that the riskless and risky bond prices must, respectively, satisfy

$$B(t,T) = E_t^Q \left[1 \times \exp \left(-\int_t^T r_s \, ds \right) \right] \quad (8C\text{-}10)$$

and

$$P(t,T) = E_t^Q \left[(1 - L)^{N_T} \times \exp \left(-\int_t^T r_s \, ds \right) \right] \quad (8C\text{-}11)$$

Equation (8C-11) expresses the fact that the payoff at maturity is no longer always \$1, as in the case of the riskless security, but is reduced by a percentage L each time the process has jumped over the period $[0,T]$. N_T is the total number of jumps before maturity, and the payoff is therefore $(1 - L)^{N_T} \leq 1$.

Using the properties of Cox processes, we can simplify Equation (8C-11)[27] to obtain

$$P(t,T) = E_t^Q \left[\exp \left(-\int_t^T (r_s + L\lambda_s) \, ds \right) \right]$$

$$\equiv E_t^Q \left[\exp \left(-\int_t^T A_s \, ds \right) \right] \qquad (8C\text{-}12)$$

Equation (8C-12) is extremely useful, as it signifies that we can use the familiar Treasury bond pricing tools to price defaultable bonds as well. We just have to substitute the risk-adjusted rate $A_t \equiv r_t + L\lambda_t$ for the riskless rate, and all the usual formulas remain valid. Similar formulas can be derived for defaultable securities with more general payoffs.

RATING-BASED MODELS

The seminal article in the rating-based class is Jarrow, Lando, and Turnbull (JLT, 1997). We review their continuous-time pricing approach and then mention two other articles that have removed some of the original assumptions from the JLT model.

Key Assumptions and Basic Structure

The model by Jarrow, Lando, and Turnbull (1997) considers a progressive drift in credit quality toward default and no longer a single jump to bankruptcy, as in many intensity-based models. Recovery rates are assumed to be constant, and default is an absorbing state.

JLT assume the availability of riskless and risky zero-coupon bonds for all maturities and the existence of a martingale measure Q equivalent to the historical measure P. In the remainder of the appendix we work directly under Q.

Appendix 2A in Chapter 2 describes in detail how to calculate a continuous-time transition matrix, which is the main tool in the JLT model. We will not recall that here. JLT assume that the transition process under the historical measure is a time-homogeneous Markov chain with K nondefault states (1 being the best rating and K the worst) and one absorbing default state $(K + 1)$.

The risk-neutral transition matrix over a given horizon h is

$$Q(h) = \begin{bmatrix} q_h^{1,1} & q_h^{1,2} & \cdots & q_h^{1,K+1} \\ \cdots & \cdots & & \cdots \\ q_h^{K,1} & q_h^{K,2} & \cdots & q_h^{K,K+1} \\ 0 & 0 & \cdots & 1 \end{bmatrix} \qquad \text{(8C-13)}$$

where, for example, $q_h^{1,2}$ denotes the risk-neutral probability of migrating from rating 1 to rating 2 over the time period h.

Transition matrices for all horizons h can be obtained from the generator[28] matrix Λ:

$$\Lambda = \begin{bmatrix} \lambda_1 & \lambda_{12} & \cdots & \\ \lambda_{21} & \lambda_2 & & \\ \vdots & & \ddots & \lambda_{K,K+1} \\ 0 & 0 & & 0 \end{bmatrix} \qquad \text{(8C-14)}$$

via the relationship $Q(h) = \exp(h\Lambda)$. Over an infinitesimal period dt, $Q(dt) = I + \Lambda\, dt$, where I is the $(K+1) \times (K+1)$ identity matrix.

Pricing Zero-Coupon Bonds

Let $B(t,T)$ be the price of a riskless zero-coupon bond paying \$1 at maturity T, with $t \leq T$. It is such that

$$B(t,T) = E_t^Q \left[\exp\left(-\int_t^T r_s\, ds \right) \right]$$

$P^i(t,T)$ is the value at time t of a defaultable zero-coupon bond with rating i due to pay \$1 at T. In case of default (assumed to be absorbing in the JLT model), the recovery rate is constant and equal to $\delta < 1$. The default process is assumed to be independent from interest rates, and the time of default is denoted as τ. Finally, let $G(t) = 1\dots K$ be the rating of the obligor at time t.

The price of the risky bond therefore is

$$P^i(t,T) = E_t^Q \left[\exp\left(-\int_t^T r_s\, ds \right) \left(\delta 1_{(\tau \leq T)} + 1_{(\tau > T)} \right) \middle| G(t) = i \right] \qquad \text{(8C-15)}$$

Given that the default process is independent from interest rates, we can split the expectations into two components:

$$P^i(t,T) = E_t^Q\left[\exp\left(-\int_t^T r_s\,ds\right)\right] E_t^Q\left[\delta 1_{(\tau\leq T)} + 1_{(\tau>T)}\Big|G(t) = i\right]$$

$$= B(t,T)E_t^Q\left[1 - (1 - \delta)1_{(\tau\leq T)}\Big|G(t) = i\right] \qquad\text{(8C-16)}$$

$$= B(t,T)\left[1 - (1 - \delta)q_{T-t}^{i,K+1}\right]$$

where $q_{T-t}^{i,K+1} = E_t^Q[1_{(\tau\leq T)}|G(t) = i]$ is the probability of default before maturity T for an i-rated bond.

Looking at the formula for yield spread [Equation (8-3) in the main part of this chapter], we can observe that the term structure of spreads is fully determined by the changes in probability of default as T changes. We return to spreads further below.

Pricing Other Credit-Risky Instruments

The main comparative advantage of a rating-based model does not reside in the pricing of zero-coupon bonds for which the only relevant information is whether or not default will occur before maturity. JLT-type models are particularly convenient for the pricing of securities whose payoffs depend on the rating of the issuer. Some credit derivatives are written on the rating of specific firms, for example derivatives compensating for downgrades.[29] More commonly, step-up bonds whose coupon is a function of the rating of the issuer can also be priced using rating-based models.

We will consider a simple example of a European-style credit derivative based on the terminal rating $G(T)$ of a company. We assume that its initial rating is $G(t) = i$ and that the derivative pays nothing in default. The payoff of the derivative is $\Phi[G(T)]$, and its values are known conditional on the realization of a terminal rating $G(T)$.

From the FTAP, the price of the derivative is

$$C^i(t,T) = E_t^Q\left[\exp\left(-\int_t^T r_s\,ds\right)\Phi[G(T)]\Big|G(t) = i\right] \qquad\text{(8C-17)}$$

Given that the rating process is independent from the interest rate, we can write

$$C^i(t,T) = E_t^Q\left[\exp\left(-\int_t^T r_s\,ds\right)\right]E_t^Q\left\{\Phi[G(T)]\,|\,G(t) = i\right\}$$

$$= B(t,T)\sum_{j=1}^K q_{T-t}^{ij}\Phi(j) \qquad\text{(8C-18)}$$

Deriving Spreads in the JLT Model

Let

$$f(t,T) = -\frac{\partial \log B(t,T)}{\partial T}$$

be the riskless forward rate agreed at date t for borrowing and lending over an instantaneous period of time at time T. It is such that $f(t,t) = r_t$.

The risky forward rate for rating class i is [from Equation (8C-16)]:

$$f^i(t,T) = -\frac{\partial \log P^i(t,T)}{\partial T} = -\frac{\partial \log (B(t,T)[1 - (1 - \delta)q_{T-t}^{i,K+1}]}{\partial T}$$

Hence

$$f^i(t,T) = f(t,T) + 1_{\tau>t}\left[\frac{(1 - \delta)\frac{\partial q_{T-t}^{i,K+1}}{\partial T}}{1 - (1 - \delta)q_{T-t}^{i,K+1}}\right] \tag{8C-19}$$

The credit spread in rating class i for maturity T is defined as $f^i(t,T) - f(t,T)$. From Equation (8C-19) we can indeed observe that spread variations reflect changes in the probability of default and changes in the steepness of the curve relating the probability of default to time T.

In order to obtain the risky short rate, we take the limit as $T \to t$ and $f(t,T) \to r_t$:

$$r_t^i = r_t + 1_{\tau>T}(1 - \delta)\lambda_{i,K+1}$$

which immediately yields the spot instantaneous spread as $r_t^i - r_t$.

SOME EXTENSIONS TO THE JARROW, LANDO, AND TURNBULL MODEL

Das and Tufano

The specificity of the model by Das and Tufano (1996) is to allow for stochastic recovery rates correlated to the riskless interest rate. A wider variety of spreads can be generated due to this flexibility. In particular, the model includes these features:

- Credit spreads can change although ratings are unchanged. In the JLT model, a given rating class is associated with a unique term structure of spreads, and all bonds with the same maturity and rating are identical.

+ Spreads are correlated with interest rates.
+ Spreads are "firm-specific" and not just "rating class–specific."
+ The pricing of credit derivatives is facilitated.

While the JLT model assumed that recovery in default was paid at the maturity of the claim,[30] Das and Tufano (1996) assume that recovery is a random fraction of par paid at the default time τ. We discussed the various recovery assumptions in Chapter 3.

Arvanitis, Gregory, and Laurent

Arvanitis, Gregory, and Laurent (1999) extend the JLT model by considering nonconstant transition matrices. Their model is "pseudo non-Markovian" in the sense that past rating changes impact on future transition probabilities. This conditioning enables the authors to replicate much more closely the observed term structure of spreads.

In particular, their class of models allows for correlations between default probabilities and interest rate changes, correlation of spreads across credit classes, and spread differences within a given rating class for bonds that have been upgraded or downgraded.

APPENDIX 8D

Fons's Credit Spread Model

The model by Fons (1994) is an early attempt to model credit spreads using a reduced-form approach. Assuming risk neutrality, the author uses historical default and recovery rates published by Moody's to derive fair value spreads per class of rating.

In this appendix we review the original specification of the model and suggest ways to incorporate risk aversion. We also update Fons's empirical results using Standard & Poor's CreditPro database.

BUILDING BLOCKS

We have seen earlier in the chapter that the two determinants of spreads in a frictionless and risk-neutral world are the probability of default and the recovery rate. As described in Chapter 4, the recovery rate depends on many factors such as the state of the economy and the seniority of the facility. We will now focus on probabilities of default at various horizons per rating class. The first step is to derive *marginal* default probabilities for all rating classes. For all bonds in the rated universe, we record their rating at the beginning of each year $t = 1,2,\ldots$. Then we observe whether the bond defaults in the first year after t or in the second, third, and so on until the end of the period covered by our sample.

Marginal probabilities for a given year are computed in a similar way as in Appendix 2A in Chapter 2. For example, the sample-weighted marginal default rate in rating i at horizon h is[31]

$$p_h^{i,K+1} = \frac{\displaystyle\sum_{t=1}^{k} D_t^i(h)}{\displaystyle\sum_{t=1}^{k} n_t^i} \quad \text{for } i = 1,\ldots,K \tag{8D-1}$$

Repeating the calculations for all rating classes and all horizons provides a series of term structures of marginal default probabilities.

The survival rate, i.e., the probability of not defaulting before time h, for bonds in rating i can be calculated as

$$S_h^i = \prod_{t=1}^{h}(1 - p_t^{i,K+1})$$

$$\equiv 1 - D_k^i \tag{8D-2}$$

where D is the cumulative default rate. The probability of defaulting exactly in year h (and not before) is thus $S_{h-1}^i p_h^{i,K+1}$, which is the probability of not defaulting before year h times the probability of defaulting in year h. This probability is instrumental in the bond pricing formula to which we now turn.

RISKY BOND PRICES AND SPREADS

Equation (8D-3) below is the price at time 0 of an i-rated risky bond with principal \$1 paid at time θ. The security also pays an annual coupon c_i if the bond is not in default. In case of default at time h, the recovery rate is δ_h.

$$P_i^c(0,\theta) = \sum_{h=1}^{\theta} \frac{c_i S_h^i}{[1 + R(0,h)]^h} + \sum_{h=1}^{\theta} \frac{S_{h-1}^i p_h^{i,K+1} \delta_h}{[1 + R(0,h)]^h} + \frac{(1 + c_i) S_\theta^i}{[1 + R(0,\theta)]^\theta} \tag{8D-3}$$

with $R(0,h)$ denoting the yield on a riskless bond with maturity h.

The interpretation of Equation (8D-3) is straightforward. The first term is the sum of the discounted interim cash flows, i.e., coupons weighted by their probabilities of occurrence. The probability of a given coupon being paid at time h is the survival probability until h. The second term is the discounted value of recoveries in default multiplied by the probabilities of default occurring in each specific year. The third and final term is the discounted value of the last cash flow (coupon and principal) times the probability of not defaulting until maturity θ.

The credit spread for maturity θ in rating class i can then be calculated as $S_i(0,\theta) = Y_i(0,\theta) - R(0,\theta)$, where $Y_i(0,\theta)$ is the yield on the risky bond. Assuming that the risky bond is priced at par implies that the coupon rate is equal to the yield and that the spread takes the simpler form:

$$S_i(0,\theta) = c_i - R(0,\theta) \qquad (8D\text{-}4)$$

The required inputs for the model therefore are

- Marginal default rates for all maturities and all rating classes
- A riskless term structure of interest rate
- Average recovery rates for all rating categories

Figures 8D-1 and 8D-2 are plots of credit spreads calculated with the above methodology using the CreditPro database with data covering the period 1981–2001. The average recovery rate is assumed to be 50 percent.

FIGURE 8D-1

U.S. Actuarial Spreads (BB, B, CCC)

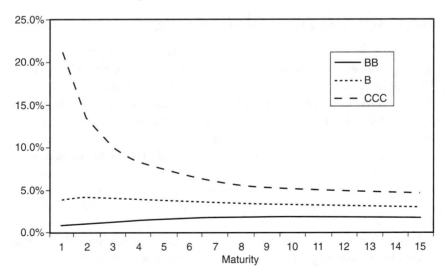

F I G U R E   8D-2

U.S. Actuarial Spreads (AA, A, BBB)

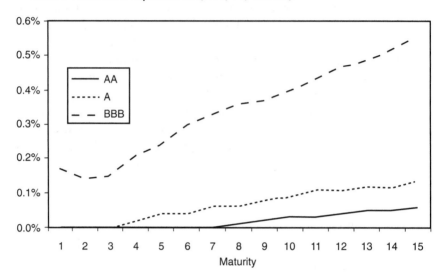

Actuarial spreads for high-quality bonds with short maturities are zero because the probability of default is also zero. The shape of the CCC spread curve is particularly striking. It is a convex curve reflecting the fact that marginal probabilities of default at short horizons are very high and quickly decrease. This shape is consistent with the Merton (1974) model for firms with very high leverage.

INCORPORATING RISK AVERSION

The main drawback with Fons's specification is that the investor is assumed to be risk-neutral. Spreads therefore tend to be much lower than those observed in practice. Banks may nonetheless want to use this approach to mark their positions to market by approximating a term structure of spreads for industries with too few issuers per maturity bracket. We thus need a methodology to extract the risk aversion parameter.

If investors are not risk-neutral, Equation (8D-1) must be replaced with

$$P_i^c(0,\theta) = \sum_{h=1}^{\theta} \frac{c_i s_h^i}{[1 + R(0,\theta)]^h} + \sum_{h=1}^{\theta} \frac{s_{h-1}^i q_h^{i,K+1} \delta_h}{[1 + R(0,\theta)]^h} + \frac{(1 + c_i) s_\theta^i}{[1 + R(0,\theta)]^\theta} \qquad (8D\text{-}5)$$

where s is the *risk-neutral* survival probability and q is the risk-neutral marginal probability of default. We can assume that $q_h^{i,K+1} = \alpha_h^i p_h^{i,K+1}$,

FIGURE 8D-3

Process to Calculate Fair Value Spreads

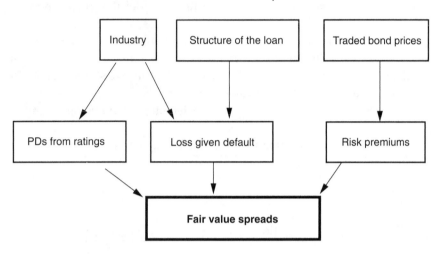

where α_h^i is constant (and > 1 because of risk aversion), or impose some more restrictions, such as $\alpha_h^i = \alpha_h$, $\forall i$ (constant risk adjustment for all rating categories) or $\alpha_h^i = \alpha^i$, $\forall h$ (constant risk adjustment for all periods in a given rating class).

Then it is possible to extract the α parameters from a cross-industry sample using an average recovery rate (δ) and to extrapolate industry-specific spread curves by selecting an industry-specific recovery rate and assuming that investor's risk aversion is the same across industries.

The entire process for calculating "fair value" spreads is summarized in Figure 8D-3.

APPENDIX 8E

Calculating Spreads from Historical Probabilities of Default

In this book we have mainly focused on historical probabilities of default, i.e., probabilities estimated on objective data. However, for pricing purposes (for the calculation of spreads), we need to estimate risk-neutral probabilities. In this appendix we show a customary way to obtain spreads from historical probabilities: A similar calculation is used by KMV and many banks (see, e.g., McNulty and Levin, 2000).

Recall that the cumulative default probability (historical probability) for a firm i (HP_t^i) is defined as the probability of default at the horizon t under the historical measure P. In the KMV model this corresponds to their EDF.

We now introduce the risk-neutral probability RNP_t^i, which is the equivalent probability under the risk-neutral measure (see Appendix 8B). Under Q, all assets drift at the risk-free rate, and thus we should substitute r for μ_i in the dynamics of the value of the firm.[32]

The formulas for the two cumulative default probabilities are therefore

$$HP_t^i = N\left(-\frac{[\log(A_0^i) - \log(X_i) + (\mu_i - \sigma_i^2/2)t]}{\sigma_i\sqrt{t}}\right)$$

and

$$RNP_t^i = N\left(-\frac{[\log(A_0^i) - \log(X_i) + (r - \sigma_i^2/2)t]}{\sigma_i\sqrt{t}}\right)$$

where:

$N(.)$ = the cumulative standard normal distribution
A_0^i = the firm's asset value at time 0
X_i = the default point (value of liabilities)
σ_i = the volatility of asset values
μ_i = the expected return (growth rate) on asset values
r = the riskless rate

The expected return on asset includes a risk premium, and we must therefore have $\mu_i \geq r$ and thus

$$RNP_t^i \geq HP_t^i$$

Writing the risk-neutral probability of default as a function of HP_t^i, we obtain

$$RNP_t^i = N\left(-\frac{[\log(A_0^i) - \log(X_i) + (\mu_i - \sigma_i^2/2)t - (\mu_i - r)t]}{\sigma_i\sqrt{t}}\right)$$

$$= N\left(N^{-1}(HP_t^i) + \left(\frac{\mu_i - r}{\sigma_i}\right)\sqrt{t}\right)$$

According to the capital asset pricing model (CAPM—see, e.g., Sharpe, Alexander, and Bailey, 1999), the risk premium on an asset should depend only on its systematic risk measured as the covariance of its returns with the returns on the market index.

More precisely, for a given firm i with expected asset return μ_i, we have

$$\mu_i = r + \beta_i[E(r_m) - r]$$

$$\equiv r + \beta_i \, \pi_t$$

where $E(r_m)$ is the expected return on the market index and π_t is the market risk premium. $\beta_i = \sigma_{im}/\sigma_m^2 = \rho_{im}\,\sigma_i/\sigma_m$ is the measure of systemic risk of the firm's assets, where σ_m, σ_{im}, and ρ_{im} are, respectively, the volatility of the market and the covariance and correlation of asset returns with the market.

Using these notations, the quasi probability becomes

$$RNP_t^i = N\left(N^{-1}(HP_t^i) + \rho_{im}\left(\frac{\pi_t}{\sigma_m}\right)\sqrt{t}\right)$$

We now want to calculate spreads in terms of risk-neutral probabilities of default. Let $P^C(t,T)$ be the value at time t of a T-maturity risky coupon bond paying a coupon C (there are n coupon dates spaced by Δt years). We assume that the principal of the bond is 1 and that the value recovered in case of default is constant and equal to R.

We have[33]

$$P^C(t,T) = \sum_{k=1}^{n} B(t,t + k\,\Delta t)[C \times (1 - RNP_{t+k\Delta t})$$

$$+ R \times (RNP_{t+k\Delta t} - RNP_{t+(k-1)\Delta t})] + B(t,T) \times (1 - RNP_T)$$

Spreads can then be calculated as shown earlier in the chapter by comparing the price of the risky coupon bond to that of a riskless bond as given by Equation (8-4), for example.

Structured Products and Credit Derivatives

This chapter presents financial products that have been developed to transfer and repackage credit risk: credit derivatives and securitization[1] instruments such as collateralized debt obligations (CDOs).

Credit derivatives are increasingly popular products. Figure 9-1 shows the dramatic growth in the volume outstanding of credit derivatives. These have started from zero in the early 1990s to exceed $2000 billion in 2002. Credit derivatives are instruments whose payoffs depend on a credit event such as a default, a downgrade, or a spread change. These products have been designed to isolate the credit risk component of an asset and to enable their users (buyers or sellers) to hedge or to take positions in pure credit risk.

CDOs were created in the late 1980s and have grown dramatically since the mid-1990s. The issuance of CDOs has been supported by regulatory arbitrage opportunities and also by the possibility to realize positive spreads on similarly rated instruments. They are also useful in tailoring the risk profiles of the issues to the risk aversion of investors. All these issues are discussed later in the chapter.

In this chapter we introduce the main types of credit derivatives. We show how they can be used for managing credit risk and explain their structure. We then take an overall view of credit derivatives and discuss their benefits and their risks for banks, corporates, and the economic system as a whole.

FIGURE 9-1

Notional Amount Outstanding of Credit Derivatives

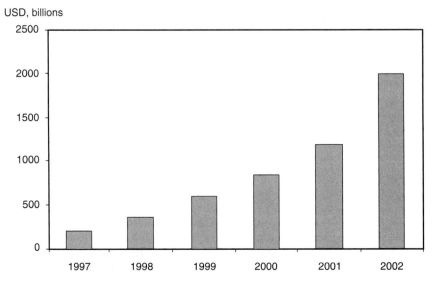

USD, billions

Source: British Bankers Association (excludes asset swaps).

CREDIT DERIVATIVES

As mentioned above, credit derivatives are relatively new products. They started in the early 1990s and now constitute a key component of credit markets. They were identified as a specific derivative class at an ISDA[2] conference in 1992. A credit derivative is a bilateral financial contract that enables investors to trade the risk associated with the creditworthiness of a debtor. This contract is usually over the counter, and its payoff is contingent on credit events on the underlying reference entity. Some credit derivatives are cash-settled (the payoff is delivered in cash), while others are physically settled (payment is made by delivering the underlying financial instrument).

Six of the most actively traded types of credit derivatives are introduced in the section that follows. The subsequent section discusses the benefits and risks of credit derivatives for various players in the credit markets.

Figure 9-2 shows the holdings of the main types of institutions involved in the credit derivatives business. Banks are, unsurprisingly, by far the dominant players. They appear to be net buyers of protection,

FIGURE 9-2

Buyers and Sellers of CDS Protection

% of total notional market value

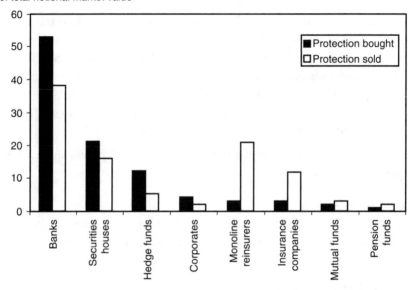

Source: State Street, Global, 2002.

while reinsurance companies buy little protection but sell a lot. They are the most exposed to drops in the credit quality of issuers. This has implications for the riskiness of reinsurers as well as for the volatility of credit and equity markets, as will be shown below.

Main Types of Products

As mentioned previously, credit derivatives are largely over-the-counter products. Each deal can therefore be considered as different from all previous ones, and frequently new characteristics are added to a given class of products. Here we will explain the stylized features of six of the main credit derivatives products:

1. Historically, credit derivatives started with *asset swaps*, which still represent a significant share of the market.

2. *Credit default swaps* (CDSs) are now the dominant product in the credit derivatives market. They are very popular because they are

liquid and because they reflect in a transparent way the market's view on the default likelihood of a specific counterpart.

3. *Credit-linked notes* (CLNs) are similar to CDSs but are packaged with a specific debt issue.

4. *Total return swaps* (TRSs) are contracts by which two parties exchange the returns on two assets.

5. *Credit spread options* (CSOs) are derivatives whose payoff depends on the value of the yield spread of an issue.

6. And finally *basket instruments* are products that integrate correlation effects among various obligors in addition to individual obligor credit risk.

The breakdown of the credit derivatives market by instrument type is reported in Figure 9-3.

Asset Swaps

Asset swaps were the first type of credit derivatives. They can be seen as a standard interest rate swap on credit-risky products (Figure 9-4). An

FIGURE 9-3

Amount Outstanding by Asset Type

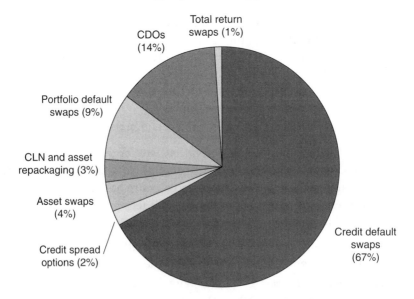

Source: Based on a survey by Patel (2002). Data as of 2001.

FIGURE 9-4

Asset Swap

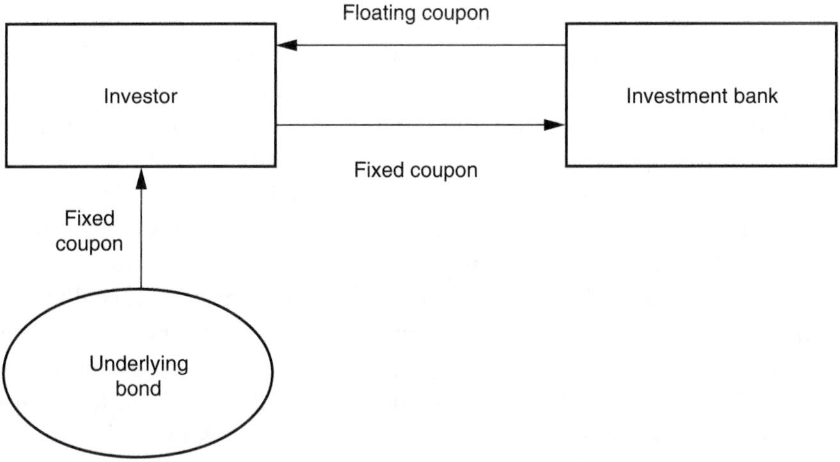

investor who has a position in a fixed-coupon bond swaps the interest payment with a counterpart (usually an investment bank) for a floating stream of coupons.

The main motivation for asset swap investors is to isolate interest rate from credit risk. They want to obtain a spread without being exposed to the risk of rising riskless interest rates. Most corporate bonds are issued with fixed coupons, and asset swaps enable investors to exchange the bonds' coupons for Libor plus a predetermined spread.

One very substantial drawback of asset swaps is that the swap agreement is not terminated if the underlying bond defaults. The investor remains liable for the payment of fixed coupons and still receives the floating payments. After default the investor thus becomes exposed to the interest rate risk that he tried to avoid originally.

Credit Default Swaps

Credit default swaps are probably the simplest type of credit derivatives. They can be seen as insurance against the default of an obligor (Figure 9-5). The protection buyer pays a regular fee (as a percentage of the nominal amount of the contract) against the promise of a fixed amount (the par of the underlying asset) paid by the protection seller in case of default on the underlying asset. The main difference with a traditional insurance contract is that the amount paid in default is predetermined and does not depend on the severity of the loss on the underlying asset.

Unlike asset swaps, most CDSs are standardized and often liquid contracts. They can be marked to market, and their price reflects very closely the market's view on the probability of default of the underlying obligor. When the PD changes, the price of the CDS will change, and so will the spread on the underlying bond. CDSs can therefore be used as hedges against spread changes and not just against default.

The attractiveness of this product for portfolio managers is obvious: When they feel that they are overexposed to a specific counterpart, they may reduce their credit exposure while keeping the asset in their portfolios. This is particularly useful when the underlying asset is very illiquid, such as a bank loan, as the bank may not be able to sell the position on the secondary market. For protection sellers (an insurance company, for example) the appeal of CDS comes from the fact that they can take pure credit risk bets without having to incur interest rate risk (as in the case of a standard purchase of corporate bonds).

The pricing of a CDS is relatively straightforward. It consists of determining at time t the annual fee that the buyer has to pay the seller for default protection between times t and T. This price is then expressed as an annual percentage fee. Risk-neutral probabilities of default used in

FIGURE 9-5

Credit Default Swap

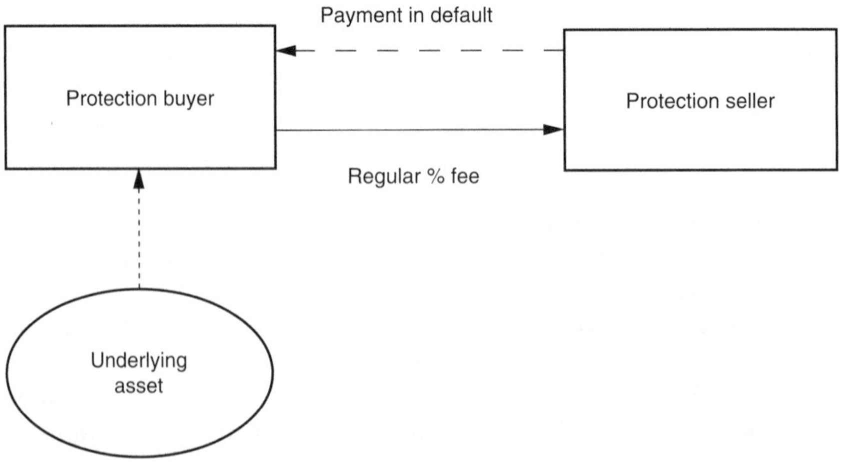

the pricing of CDSs can be extracted from the prices of traded bonds. A simple introduction to the pricing of CDSs can be found in Hull (2002).

Conversely, when one can observe a CDS price, one can infer immediately the market assessment of the default probability of the issuer. For some obligors, the CDS market is more liquid than that of the underlying bonds, and CDS spreads are frequently used in lieu of yield spreads.

Figure 9-5 assumes implicitly that the protection seller is itself not subject to default. Otherwise, the protection would become worthless in case of default of the protection seller. This is why protection sellers are generally AA- or AAA-rated and chosen to have low default correlation with the underlying issuer. Some puzzling CDS contracts are, however, available on the market. For example, it is not rare to see a bank offering default protection against its own sovereign. It is, though, unlikely that the bank would be in a position to meet its obligation, should the country it is based in default.

Credit-Linked Notes

Credit-linked notes are debt obligations with contingent coupon and redemption value. They use the CDS technology explained above in a debt package. The issuer of a CLN sells the notes to investors and receives the proceeds (Figure 9-6). At the same time, the isssuer sells a CDS contract on another obligor to an investment bank. The investment bank therefore pays a regular fee to the issuer which is transferred in part to the CLN investors in the form of an enhanced coupon. In case of default of the other obligor, the issuer has to pay the investment bank, and the CLN investor loses parts (or all) of the principal.

CLNs enable investors to combine a standard bond of a well-known and usually well-rated issuer with a credit derivative that provides enhanced yield. Many types of institutions that cannot invest in off-balance-sheet credit derivatives can invest in CLNs because they remain on the balance sheet of the investor. Banks are also interested in the CLN business because they are protection buyers on counterparts that are often linked to loans on their books.

Total Return Swaps

A total return swap is a simple product that allows an investor to exchange the payment of a stream of floating coupons (usually specified as Libor or a similar interest rate plus a spread) for the return on a bond, a loan, a portfolio, or an index (or any other asset). It therefore enables her to take an exposure in the underlying asset without having to own the

FIGURE 9-6

Credit-Linked Notes

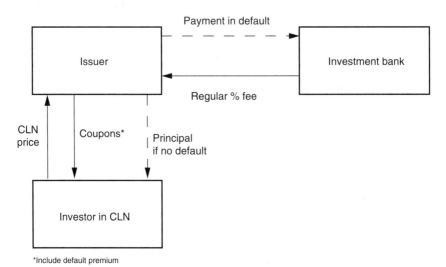

*Include default premium

asset. Figure 9-7 illustrates the stylized structure of this product. The types of underlying assets include specific bonds, portfolios, indexes, etc. The term "total return" refers to the fact that the investor receives not only the interest payments or dividend but also the changes (positive or negative) in the market value of the underlying instruments.

There are many advantages of investing in total return swaps rather than in the cash market. Leverage is an obvious one: The investor does not need to raise the necessary funds to buy the portfolio in the cash market. Transaction costs are also avoided; this is particularly true when the TRS is based on the return of a broad corporate bond index. TRSs also enable some investors to short some credits although they may be prevented from doing so directly in the cash market for regulatory reasons.

Credit Spread Options

Credit spread options are derivatives whose underlying is the yield spread on a bond. Many CSOs are actually forward contracts and not really options, the buyer of such product being exposed to adverse moves in the credit spread. "True" credit spread options exhibit an asymmetric payoff structure, with the downside limited to the option premium.[3]

They can be American- or European-style options.[4] They can also include a trigger barrier. For example, an "up-and-out" option is designed

FIGURE 9-7

Total Return Swaps

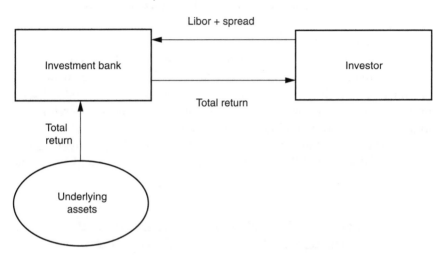

such that if the spread increases above, say, 200 basis points, the option becomes worthless.

Credit spread options have not had the success one could have expected when they were first launched in the early nineties. Trading and new issuance of these options is still relatively low. This may seem surprising as they can offer a very valuable protection for portfolio managers who are significantly affected by changes in the level of spreads. Several reasons may help explain this fact. First, they are more complex instruments to price and hedge than standard products (CDS contracts, for example).

Second, most corporate bond issues are quite illiquid, and it is therefore possible to manipulate their spread. When trading is thin, a large order may affect the spread on an issue and drive credit spread option prices to abnormal levels. This problem could be avoided by writing options on spread indices rather than on specific names. However, there is no market standard for corporate bond indices similar to the S&P 500 for equities, for example. A multitude of indexes are available, but no consensus has yet emerged on the most reliable or trustworthy. Furthermore, most indexes are calculated by investment banks, and their competitors may doubt their impartiality and may not be willing to trade options based on them.

Third, and most importantly, the popularity of CDSs may explain the limited success of CSOs. It is possible to hedge a substantial part of credit spread movements by taking positions in CDSs. CDSs are cheaper (tighter bid-ask spreads) than CSOs, and although the hedge provided by CDSs may be imperfect, they are often preferred by investors for cost reasons.

Basket Instruments

CDSs are increasingly becoming a well-established and standardized industry. Investment banks have moved on to develop more customized products such as basket instruments. The idea is to trade credit risk on multiple issuers with one contract. Default correlations are therefore key to the hedging and valuation of these products. A popular type of basket credit derivative is the *nth-to-default option*, which pays the buyer a given amount if at least n obligors default (out of a specified pool) during the life of the option.

Benefits, Drawbacks, and Economic Implications of Credit Derivatives

Credit derivatives are a new asset class, and it is worthwhile discussing their economic implications as well as their advantages and risks for users. Many of the benefits for individual products have already been discussed in the chapter. In this section we focus primarily on general considerations regarding this class of asset and not on specific characteristics of products.

Benefits

The main benefit of credit derivatives is to isolate the credit component of commonly traded instruments such as bonds and loans. By doing so they enable users to fine-tune their exposure to various counterparts. For example, they can help a bank expand its lending to one of its clients while avoiding overconcentration on a specific name. They are therefore very efficient tools for hedging and managing credit risk in order to optimize portfolio diversification.

In addition, credit derivatives bring more liquidity to debt markets. Some companies do not issue public debt but borrow money from banks. Thanks to credit derivatives, investors obtain access to counterparties or markets that were not publicly available previously. More generally, they contribute to building complete markets,[5] implicitly providing prices for an increasing number of debt instruments at various maturities.

In addition, credit derivatives enable investors to enhance their yields. In the current period where interest rates are low, many investors are looking for alternatives in order to increase their performance. Insurers and hedge funds have therefore become significant sellers of credit protection. Asset managers are increasingly considering entering such markets.

These indisputable advantages have to be balanced with a series of drawbacks, some affecting the investors, some the sellers of credit derivatives, and some the global financial system.

Legal Issues

Like most derivative instruments, credit derivatives can be used to increase the leverage of a bank and thus have important implications in terms of risk management and regulation. A distinguishing feature of credit derivatives is the complexity of the legal documentation involved to support the products. Credit derivatives have been tainted by several high-profile legal disputes due to the complexity of the contingent payments involved.

For example, in 1998 Russia defaulted on its domestic debt while maintaining normal payment of coupon and principal on its external debt. At the time, many credit derivatives were written on Russia in fairly vague terms. The question at that time was to determine whether the moratorium on domestic debt should be considered as a credit event for all credit derivatives on Russia. Protection buyers and sellers naturally had very different views on the matter.

Another example of legal problems arising in credit derivatives is the dispute between UBS and Deutsche Bank (DB) about a credit default swap contract on Armstrong World Industries (AWI) in 2001. UBS was seeking default protection from DB on AWI, which was facing major asbestos claim liabilities. Between the time the swap was agreed and the time it was confirmed in writing by DB, a new holding company (Armstrong Holding) was formed such that AWI became a subsidiary, but the holding did not assume the liabilities of AWI. The contract received by UBS was a credit default swap on the holding and not on AWI and was therefore not offering protection against a default (which eventually occurred) related to asbestos claims.

In order to clarify legal issues and help standardize and expand the market for credit derivatives, ISDA put forward, in July 1999, some standardized documentation that is widely accepted by market participants. This ISDA framework reports six credit events that can trigger payment on a credit default swap: bankruptcy, failure to pay, obligation default, obligation acceleration, repudiation/moratorium, and restructuring.

A lot of debate has surrounded this ISDA documentation, in particular about the criteria to define precisely a payment trigger.[6] Market participants have recently attempted to further narrow the list of events that could trigger payouts by eliminating what is often called "soft" credit events. Such events correspond indeed to credit deterioration rather than to default. In addition, different interpretation of the occurrence of such events has frequently led to litigation. In April 2002, European market participants abandoned two such soft credit events—obligation acceleration and repudiation/moratorium. They were following the initiative already taken by U.S. dealers. Despite these changes, uncertainty remains over the issue of debt restructuring, on which there has been ongoing disagreement among traders. This has led to the trading of credit default swaps both with and without restructuring clauses. European banks, for instance, have often offered contracts with ISDA's 1999 terminology, while since May 2001 U.S. dealers have been switching to contracts with a narrower definition of restructuring. This debate on the restructuring clauses is now also related to regulatory issues. The Basel Committee is currently reviewing whether dropping them should impact capital relief associated with credit derivatives.

Regulatory Issues

The explosion of credit derivatives has been directly linked to regulatory arbitrage. Under the Basel I framework, banks have been allowed to pour large parts of their banking book in their trading book, thanks to credit derivatives.

Practically speaking, a loan on the banking book of bank A would receive a capital charge of 8 percent. By buying a protection complying with regulatory requirements, bank A would offload its risk and obtain full capital relief. The credit derivative transaction between bank A and bank B will be a transaction between two OECD banks for the same exposure. The new capital charge will therefore be limited to 1.6 percent for bank B.

With Basel II new rules, such arbitrage opportunities will be partially reduced, as the treatment of regulatory capital charges for transactions between banks will depend on their creditworthiness and no longer on their domicile (OECD or not).[7]

Increased Complexity of Bank Exposures

Credit derivatives are complex in their structure and often involve shifting risk off balance sheet. They are therefore treated by regulators with a lot of caution. Transparency is of paramount importance to gain the confidence of investors, and off-balance-sheet deals make it difficult for analysts to determine the actual exposure of a bank to various credits.

Another problem linked to the multiplicity of positions in a given name is that of "overcrowding" a credit. A bank may have a commercial unit dealing with a specific corporate and have at the same time an investment banking arm selling protection on the same name. If credit limits are set at the group level, the commercial bank may not be able to expand its exposure to the corporate. The credit is crowded out, and a genuine corporate financing need is ruled out because of credit derivatives activity.

Impact of Credit Derivatives on Market Volatility

The increased volatility reported in the credit (in particular in the spreads of corporate bonds) and equity markets has been blamed on the growing importance of credit derivatives. Credit derivatives allow us to sell credit short, which was not possible a few years ago. Therefore speculation on negative as well as positive credit events leads to larger swings in credit positions.

In order to understand the statement about the increased volatility in the *equity* markets, it is useful to recall that equity-based models of credit risk are being adopted by a large proportion of market participants. Equity volatility therefore spills over to credit markets. The reverse is also true because of hedging strategies undertaken by default protection sellers.

Figure 9-8, taken from Keppler and Williams (2003), illustrates how risk is passed along the financial systems and how the various players hedge their positions. It starts with an airline company borrowing from a regional bank. The bank grants the loan and enters simultaneously in a CDS contract with a larger institution (money center bank). The regional bank therefore receives interest from the airline company and pays a fee to the money center bank in exchange for protection against default by the airline. The money center bank then passes the risk to a reinsurance company, which is the natural buyer for this risk (see Figure 9-2). The reinsurance company will frequently hedge its exposure by shorting the equity of the airline company: If the airline goes into difficulties, the likelihood of paying the default value increases but the equity price drops, thereby protecting the insurance company. The last step shows one of the perverse effects of the transfer of risk via CDSs. The risk does not disappear but is reinjected into the economy via higher equity volatility. This equity volatility affects all agents, from the corporate itself to the banks and on to the reinsurance companies.

FIGURE 9-8

Risk Transfer in the Financial System

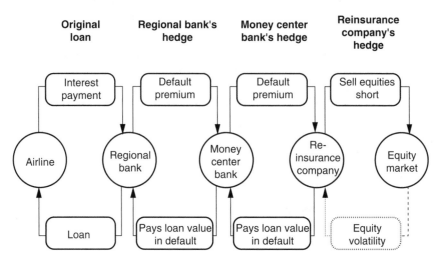

Source: Financial Insights.

COLLATERALIZED DEBT OBLIGATIONS

Introduction

In this section we study structured products called collateralized debt obligations that were introduced in the late eighties following the development of the high-yield bond market and the long experience of mortgage bonds.

"CDO" is a generic term for a vast class of securitization[8] products, in which a portfolio of debt instruments is used as collateral to back the issuance of new debt issues. The portfolio is often transferred from a bank's balance sheet to a bankruptcy-remote company (a special-purpose vehicle, or SPV). The SPV then issues bonds of various seniorities backed by the pool of assets (Figure 9-9).

The senior notes (usually well rated) are repaid first using either the sale of assets in the SPV or the cash flows generated by these assets. Once the senior notes have been repaid in full, the SPV repays the subordinated (mezzanine) notes, and finally the equity (the first loss tranche) gets all the upside, after repayments of the other notes.

Tranching is the process of creating notes of various seniorities and risk profiles backed by the same pool of assets. This process enables the

FIGURE 9-9

Simple CDO Structure

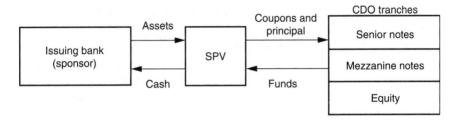

FIGURE 9-10

Example of a Tranching of a CDO

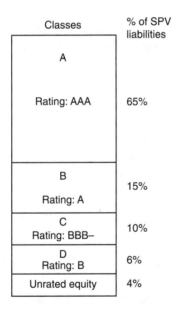

issuer to target investors with different risk aversions or trading restrictions. The top tranche is the senior class, which is designed to obtain an AAA rating (see Figure 9-10). The remainder of the liabilities of the SPV is subordinated to this class and obtains lower ratings. The bottom tranche is called equity.

The repayment of notes follows the priority order and is often compared to a waterfall. Cash flows are used to repay the most senior tranche first. Once the senior note is repaid in full, additional cash flows are used to service the mezzanine and subordinated notes, and, finally, all the cash left over goes to equity holders.

When the pool consists of loans or bonds only, the structure is called, respectively, collateralized loan obligation (CLO) or collateralized bond obligation (CBO). CDOs encompass CLOs, CBOs, and securitizations backed by a portfolio comprising both loans and bonds.

Some types of assets commonly used in CDOs are listed in Table 9-1. In fact, any type of debt can be securitized, and the table represents only a small sample of the categories of assets that can back these structures.

Types of Structures

The taxonomy of CDOs is generally performed according to three main criteria:

1. *The nature and the source of repayment of the collateral pool.* Using the *cash flows* generated by the ongoing receipts on the physical assets in the pool or the cash flows generated by the *synthetic* pool[9] or the *market value*, i.e., the proceeds from the sale of those assets

2. *The stability of the collateral pool.* Either a *static pool* or an actively *managed pool* by means of reinvestment and/or substitution

3. *The motivation behind securitization. Balance sheet* management or *arbitrage,* either regulatory arbitrage or arbitrage stemming from capital market dislocations

The Nature and the Source of Repayment of the Collateral Pool

Cash Flow CDOs   A simple cash flow CDO structure is described in Figure 9-11. The issuer (special-purpose vehicle) purchases a pool of collateral (bonds, loans, etc.) that will generate a stream of future cash flows (coupon or other interest payment and repayment of principal). Standard cash flow CDOs involve the physical transfer of the assets.[10]

This purchase is funded through the issuance of a variety of notes with different levels of seniority. The collateral is managed by an external party (the collateral manager) who deals with the purchases of assets in the pool and the redemption of the notes. The manager also takes care of the collection of the cash flows and of their transfer to the note holders via the issuer. The risk of a cash flow CDO stems primarily from the number of defaults in the pool. The more frequently and the more quickly oblig-

TABLE 9-1

Main Types of Underlying Collateral

Debt Securities	Corporate Loans	Extended Applications Repackage
High-yield and investment-grade bonds	High-yield and investment-grade bonds	Asset-backed securities
Distressed/nonperforming bonds	Distressed/nonperforming loans	CBOs/CDOs/EMCBOs*
Emerging market (sovereign/private sector)	Revolving loans	Commercial mortgage-backed securities/residential mortgage-backed securities
Structured finance	Secured and unsecured	
Project finance	Bilateral loans	Private equity
Synthetic securities	Term loans	Hedge funds
Municipal finance	Unfunded commitments to lend	

* CBOs with obligors in multiple jurisdictions.

FIGURE 9-11

Structure of a Cash Flow CDO

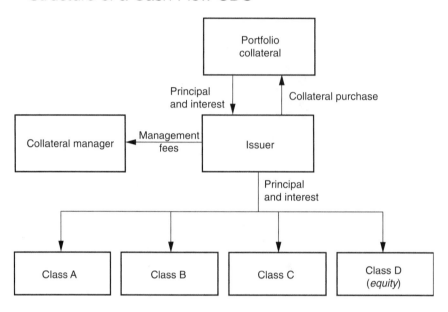

ors default, the thinner the stream of cash flows available to pay interest and principal on the notes. The cash flows generated by the assets are used to pay back investors in sequential order from senior investors (class A) to equity investors that bear the first-loss risk (class D). The par value of the securities at maturity is used to pay the notional amounts of CDO notes.

Synthetic CDOs   An alternative to the actual transfer of assets to the SPV is provided by synthetic CDOs (see Figure 9-12).[11] These structures benefit from advances in credit derivatives and transfer the credit risk associated with a pool of assets to the SPV while keeping the assets on the balance sheet of the bank. The SPV sells credit protection to the bank via credit default swaps.

Although synthetic CDOs are sometimes classified as balance sheet securitizations, the capital relief associated with them is often lower than for structures involving the actual sale of assets. The motivation for avoiding a true sale of the assets may be to preserve client relationships (a corporate may perceive as a sign of mistrust the sale of its loans to an SPV)

FIGURE 9-12

Structure of a Synthetic CDO

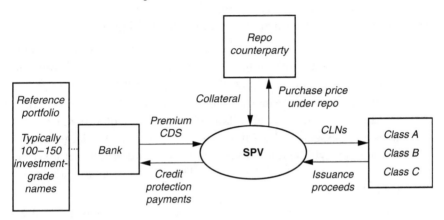

or to maintain secrecy about the composition of the bank's balance sheet. Some loans may also not be eligible for resale for contractual reasons but may still be securitized through a synthetic structure.

Synthetic deals may be fully funded, through recourse to CLN (credit-linked notes), or partially funded in order to cover the risk on the AAA tranche only. Some CDOs can be a mix of cash flow and synthetic transactions when the collateral pool includes both physical and synthetic assets.

Market Value CDOs   A market value CDO differs from a cash flow CDO in that the underlying pool is marked to market on a periodic basis. If the aggregate value of the collateral pool goes beyond a defined threshold, then the collateral manager has to sell collateral and pay down CDO notes in order to restore an acceptable level. The collateral manager plays a much more active role and has a lot of flexibility in the allocation of the pool of collateral. In particular, the manager can increase or decrease the leverage of the structure to boost returns or mitigate risk.

The Stability of the Collateral Pool

Traditional CDOs, such as cash flow CDOs, generally rely on a static pool, although it is not always the case. In contrast, market value CDOs and synthetic CDOs rely on revolving pools based on active management and trading by the collateral manager during the reinvestment period.

The Motivation behind Securitization

In principle, cash flow, synthetic, and market value transactions correspond to either balance sheet or arbitrage motivations, explained below. The various types of transactions are presented in Figure 9-13

> *Balance sheet* deals are structured in order to obtain regulatory capital relief. Assets consuming too much capital are removed from the bank's balance sheet and are used to back the issuance of the notes.

> *Arbitrage* CDOs are primarily seeking to exploit the difference in yield between the pool of collateral (often constituted of speculative-grade assets) and the notes issued by the CDO. A large share of the notes will be rated investment grade and will therefore command low spreads over Treasuries. The difference in spreads is considered an arbitrage.

> We will return to the distinction between balance sheet and arbitrage deals in the next section on issuer motivations.

Motivations for Issuers and Investors

Issuers' Motivations

As mentioned above, there are, broadly speaking, two types of motivations for issuers: arbitrage and balance sheet management.

FIGURE 9-13

Global CDO Sector Rated by S&P in 2001

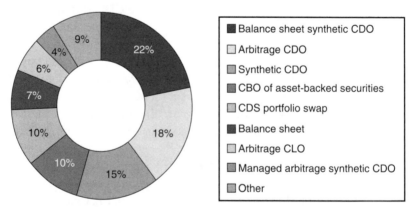

Excludes market value deals—US$130 billions, 242 deals.

Source: Standard & Poor's.

Arbitrage denotes the search for yield or revenue. It can take several forms:

♦ Issuers may seek to realize a positive spread between the high-yield assets in the pool and the lower yield on the notes.

♦ A bank offloading parts of its balance sheet via a CDO can free up some credit lines and increase its assets under management. This helps generate stable management fees.

♦ Most issuers keep parts of equity tranche and can therefore benefit from all the upside after repayment of the other notes.

Balance sheet management was historically the primary reason for CDO issuance. The idea is to move assets off balance sheet in order to benefit from capital relief.

In order to illustrate the benefits of CDOs in reducing regulatory capital requirements, let us go back to the CDO example noted earlier (Figure 9-10). Assume that a bank has $1 billion of commercial loans on its balance sheet on which it earns an average interest rate of Libor + 150 basis points. The bank funds the loans at Libor and therefore earns a net spread of 150 basis points.

The current Basel rules (see Chapter 10) imply that the bank must keep at least 8 percent of this nominal amount as regulatory capital. The return on regulatory capital is therefore: $15 million/$80 million = 18.75 percent.

If the bank decides to securitize its loan portfolio using the CDO structure shown above, it will still earn Libor + 150 basis points from the loans. However, it will have to pay an average of Libor + 67 basis points on the various tranches of the CDO (the assumed rates are shown in Figure 9-14). The $40 million (4 percent of $1 billion) equity tranche is retained on the balance sheet and must be covered by $40 million in capital. All other loans are transferred to an SPV and therefore are no longer subject to capital allocation. Hence the return on regulatory capital becomes ($15 million − $6.7 million)/$40 million = 20.75 percent.

Given the very substantial sums involved, 2 percent extra return represents a significant amount. Naturally the savings depend on market conditions (how much return can be obtained from the loans and the interest rates to be paid on the CDO tranches), but the current regulatory regime tends to encourage regulatory arbitrage. Forthcoming changes in the regulatory capital charges will dampen this incentive, at least for good-quality loans on the balance sheet. These will indeed benefit from

FIGURE 9-14

CDO Tranches and Associated Interest Rates

Classes	Percent of SPV liabilities	Interest rate
A Rating: AAA	65%	Libor + 40 bp
B Rating: A	15%	Libor + 80 bp
C Rating: BBB–	10%	Libor + 140 bp
D Rating: B	6%	Libor + 250 bp
Unrated equity	4%	Libor (retained on balance sheet)

lower capital charges, and it may no longer be worthwhile for banks to securitize them.

Obviously the risk of the bank is affected by the transaction. It has sold (via an SPV) the safer tranches of the CDO but retains the very speculative equity. One can therefore argue that in the scenario detailed above, the bank is now more risky than when it held the loan on its balance sheet. In essence, it has increased its leverage.

CDO securitization, of course, does not systematically entail a higher level of risk. For instance, there is true risk mitigation when part or all of the first loss tranche is sold.

Investors' Motivations

CDO notes have proved popular with investors for many reasons:

- ◆ CDO tranches tend to offer a yield premium on bonds with identical ratings and are therefore attractive for their rate of interest.

- They also enable investors unwilling or unable (for example, for regulatory reasons) to invest in speculative securities to take an exposure to that market. By investing in an investment-grade tranche of a high-yield CDO, the investor has a safe investment and yet is linked to the performance of the high-yield market.
- A CDO tranche can be seen as a stake in a diversified portfolio. It is therefore a way to benefit from some diversification while investing in one security only.[12]

While some of the objectives of issuers in the various tranches are common, their interests are divergent as far as the investment policy and the management of the SPV collateral are concerned. Investors in the equity tranche benefit from high volatility in the collateral pool.[13] In the case of cash flow CDOs, equity tranche holders would prefer a large proportion of high-coupon very speculative debt as the pool. Their bet would be to have the principal of the debt repaid quickly using the high-coupon payments before a large number of defaults puts an end to their interest payments.

Investors in AAA tranches, on the other hand, favor lower coupons from stable and well-rated issues. Their upside potential is capped by the principal of the debt, and volatility therefore damages the value of their investment.

Investors in subordinated notes occupy a middle ground. They do not share the unlimited upside of equity holders but require sufficient cash flow to recover their investment.

The conflicting interests of investors highlight the difficulty of the work of the collateral manager. His job is to manage the pool of assets to satisfy the diverse needs of investors. A too-prudent investment policy would in many cases lead to the equity tranche expiring worthless. A management policy favoring return over prudence would jeopardize the investment of the highest tranches. The collateral manager is involved in a multiperiod game in which he has to reconcile the interests of both types of investors in order to attract them to forthcoming structures he will manage.

Rating Approaches to CDOs

In this section we deal with the rating of CDO tranches. We present an overview of the analytical tools used by Standard & Poor's and Moody's.

While these tools are actually used by rating agencies and by structurers of CDOs targeting a specific rating breakdown for their notes, they constitute only a small part of the credit assessment and rating allocation process. Within S&P, it actually corresponds to one step out of nine, as reported in Table 9-2. In particular there are several important due diligence elements that have to be mentioned such as:

- A careful analysis of the assets of the pool (step 1)
- A detailed review and monitoring of the collateral manager (step 3)
- A review of the guarantees and interest rate/currency hedges of the structure (step 5)
- The analysis of coverage ratios (step 6)

S&P's CDO Evaluator

S&P's main tool for assessing the risk of CDO tranches is a Monte Carlo engine called CDO Evaluator. It is easy to use and straightforward. Its architecture is similar to several of the factor-based models described in Chapter 6.

The inputs of the model are the list of exposures, their amounts, the industry of the issuers, and their ratings. The engine simulates correlated binary random variables that represent default (1) or nondefault (0) and are calibrated on the probability of default induced by the rating.

In order to be rated AAA, the senior tranche must have a probability of default equivalent to that of a AAA corporate. CDO Evaluator calculates the maximum proportion X of defaults in the asset pool that would be compatible with a full payment of coupon and principal by the tranche. The tranche can then be rated AAA if the probability of observing a proportion of default $x > X$ during the life of the CDO is less than or equal to the probability of an AAA corporate defaulting during the same period of time.

Figure 9-15 illustrates the output of the model.[14] It shows two possible realizations for the loss distributions in the underlying CDO pool. The x-axis corresponds to the proportion of default in the pool. Assuming that an AAA corporate bond with the same maturity as that of the CDO has on average a 1 percent probability of default, we are looking at the 1 percent threshold in the CDO loss distribution. It is similar to looking for a VaR threshold at the 99 percent confidence level.

In the first case, defaults are assumed to be uncorrelated, and the AAA threshold is situated at about 26 percent defaults in the pool. This figure means that there is only a 1 percent chance that more than 26 per-

TABLE 9-2

The Steps for the CDO Rating Process

Steps	Insight
1. Reviewing the structural basics and legal structure	As each transaction is unique, a specific due diligence is required including eligibility criteria for assets. Includes conditions on asset additions or changes, coverage tests, and the retained definition of default
2. Sizing the default frequency of the proposed asset pool	Consists of rating the components of the pool and tranching using CDO Evaluator and CDO Monitor
3. Reviewing the collateral manager	A detailed review of the quality of the asset manager is performed
4. Sizing the loss severity	Corresponds to a detailed analysis of recovery expectation and time to recovery in case of default of collateral assets
5. Reviewing the transaction's collateral and structural features	Corresponds to a measure of the impact of the payment structure, of the waterfall structure, etc.
6. Establishing the required level of credit support for each related tranche	Implies cash flow modeling coverage tests and stress tests (generally not for synthetic transactions)
7. Convening a ratings committee to assess preliminary ratings	
8. Reviewing final documentation and legal opinions	
9. Issuing the rating(s) of the transaction	

Source: Derived from S&P Global Cash Flow and Synthetic CDO Criteria (March 21, 2002).

cent of the securities in the pool will default during the life of the CDO. Therefore, if the tranche can withstand at least 26 percent of defaults in the pool without itself defaulting, it can be rated AAA.

When correlations are introduced (30 percent intra-industry asset correlation, 0 percent interindustry asset correlation in this example), the AAA threshold shifts to a 49 percent default rate in the pool. Correlations swell the likelihood of extreme bad events, and it is therefore natural that the threshold should increase.

It is important to emphasize again that the model in itself does not guarantee a specific rating. It is just provided as a guide for CDO structurers and is used by S&P to obtain a first impression on the deal. The model's output is indeed complemented by additional stress-testing adjustments and of course by all the steps briefly described in Table 9-2.

In particular, for cash flow CDOs, a review of the performance of the collateral pool based on some predetermined stressed default patterns is key to ensure that the stream of expected cash flows is compatible with the tranching defined using CDO Evaluator. The objective is to ensure that the underlying notes will pay timely interest and ultimate principal

FIGURE 9-15

Effect of Correlation on Portfolio Defaults
and Rating Threshold

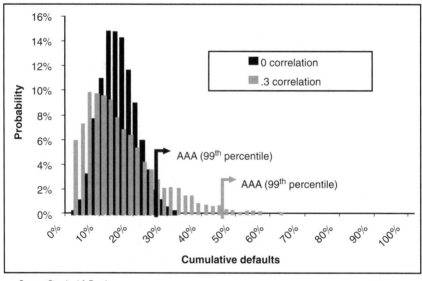

Source: Standard & Poor's.

at a given default rate. For instance, if CDO Evaluator determines that the AAA tranche is bounded by a maximum 49 percent default rate, the cash flow model will have to exhibit a higher maximum default rate (the break-even rate), for example 52 percent.

Moody's Binomial Expansion Technique

Instead of simulating the actual distribution of losses in the pool, Moody's relies on an approximate analytical shortcut mapping the actual portfolio of correlated assets to a homogeneous pool of uncorrelated assets using a *diversity score*.

The idealized pool is such that each asset has the same probability of default and same exposure size and that all assets are uncorrelated. Calculating the loss distribution of such a simplified portfolio is easy, as will be shown below.

Ignoring LGD,[15] two inputs are necessary for the calculation of the loss distribution: the probability of default p and "decorrelation" adjustment (diversity score) for all assets in the idealized pool. Using these two inputs, we can calculate the default loss distribution using the binomial law.

We proceed in three steps:

♦ *Calculating the average probability of default in the pool.* Let us assume that there are N assets in the pool. Each of them has a "real" probability of default[16] p_i, for $i = 1...N$, during the life of the CDO. The idealized probability of default $\bar{p}$ is calculated as the weighted average of PDs:

$$\bar{p} = \frac{\displaystyle\sum_{i=1}^{N} A_i \times p_i}{\displaystyle\sum_{i=1}^{N} A_i}$$

where A_i denotes the par value of asset i.

♦ *Incorporating concentration risk.* As recalled earlier, the main idea is to replace a complex portfolio of N correlated assets with a simpler pool of $D \leq N$ homogeneous uncorrelated facilities. Ignoring correlation leads to an underestimation of tail risk (see Figure 9-15, for example), and the idealized portfolio must be adjusted to compensate for this downward bias. The diversity score measures how concentrated the pool of assets is, in terms of industrial sectors. Moody's has a list of about 30 sectors and counts the number of assets that are classified in each sector. Sectors with large concentrations of assets are penalized with a large weight. The weights used by Moody's as a function of the number of firms in a given sector are provided in Table 9-3. Appendix 9A shows how one can relate the determination of a diversity score to the problem of matching the mean and variance of the real and idealized loss distributions.

An example will help clarify the procedure leading to the calculation of the number of firms D in the idealized portfolio. Assume that we have a portfolio of $N = 100$ correlated assets. These assets are grouped in the various sectors, and the number of assets in each sector is counted. Assume that in our example we find that, in a given sector, there are either 0, 1, 2, 3, 4, or 5 assets (Table 9-4). For example, there are 11 sectors with 3 assets and 5 sectors with 5 assets, etc.[17]

Each sector concentration is weighted by a diversity score (row B) extracted from Table 9-3. Row D reports this weighted number of firms. It is calculated as the product of B and C. The sum of the elements of the last row is the portfolio diversity score (D). In this example $D = 61$. It means that a portfolio of 61 independent firms is assumed to mimic the true portfolio of 100 correlated firms accurately.

TABLE 9-3

Diversity Score for CDO Risk Evaluation

Number of Firms in Same Industry	Diversity Score
1	1.00
2	1.50
3	2.00
4	2.33
5	2.67
6	3.00
7	3.25
8	3.50
9	3.75
10	4.00
>10	On a case-by-case basis

Source: Moody's.

TABLE 9-4

Example of a Diversity Score Calculation

A	Number of firms in sector	1	2	3	4	5
B	Diversity score	1	1.5	2	2.33	2.67
C	Number of cases	2	4	11	8	5
D	(B) × (C)	2	6	22	18.64	13.35

♦ *Calculating the loss distribution.* Given that the constituents of the idealized portfolio are by construction uncorrelated and have the same probability of default, we can immediately obtain the probability of observing $j \leq D$ defaults using the binomial distribution:

$$\Pr(j \text{ defaults}) = \frac{D!}{j!(D-j)!} \, \bar{p}^{\,j}(1-\bar{p})^{D-j}$$

The rating can then be assigned based on the probability of observing a given amount of loss, as in the simulation method proposed by S&P.

Pricing and Assessing the Risk of CDO Tranches

Pricing and assessing the risk of CDO notes are complex procedures. CDOs are often cumbersome structures with embedded options, guarantees, prepayment covenants, a variety of collateral types, etc.

Closed-form solutions for CDOs therefore come at the cost of heroic simplifying assumptions or are available only for the simplest structures. Duffie and Garleanu (2001) analyze the risk and valuation of CDOs in an intensity model where the issuers' hazard rates are assumed to follow a jump diffusion process. A model by Pykhtin and Dev (2002) for calculating capital for CDO tranches is described in Appendix 9B.

A numerical methodology is adopted in the S&P Risk Solutions' Portfolio Risk Tracker model (see Chapter 6). It consists of simulating realizations of the value of the collateral pool and calculating the price of the CDO tranches by a technique similar to least-square Monte Carlo proposed by Longstaff and Schwartz (2001). The algorithm starts by calculating the payoff of each tranche at the maturity of the CDO and rolls backward until the issuance of the notes by estimating the payoff of each tranche conditional on the performance of the pool of assets at each time step.

CONCLUSION

Credit derivatives and CDOs have become very popular products for managing credit risk. They allow for a better tailoring of the risk-return profile associated with credit instruments and for more effective management of balance sheet structures. Financial innovation in the area of structured credit products is still ongoing. CDOs of CDOs (where the pool of underlying bonds itself comprises CDO tranches) are becoming more widespread. Credit derivatives are increasing in liquidity and coverage.

Innovations often come at the cost of more uncertainty. Structured credit products are still recent and are not understood by all market players. Regulators are struggling to cope with the recent development in credit derivatives and securitizations, and some investors have learned the hard way that these instruments are, like any other, not offering extra yield without involving more risk.

These teething problems will probably disappear once the market is more mature. They are likely to become standard products as familiar as interest rate swaps are today.

APPENDIX 9A

Calculating the Diversity Score

The idea behind the diversity score is that one looks for a simple portfolio of homogeneous (same exposure size, same PD) uncorrelated assets that will replicate the mean and variance of the loss distribution of the true pool of assets. (The other moments of the distribution will not be matched.) The real portfolio consists of N assets with pairwise default correlation ρ_{ij}, individual default probability p_i and exposure size A_i. The sum of individual exposures is denoted as A. The replicating portfolio has D facilities with identical probability of default $\bar{p}$ and face value F.

The steps below illustrate how to derive the diversity score D:

1. *Calculating the exposure size.* The total portfolio size must equal the real portfolio size. Therefore the face value of idealized exposures is just the mean exposure size:

$$F = \frac{\sum_{i=1}^{N} A_i}{D} = \frac{A}{D}$$

2. *Calculating the probability of default.* The mean loss on the idealized portfolio must equal that of the true portfolio. Therefore:

$$\sum_{i=1}^{N} p_i A_i = D\,\bar{p}F$$
$$= A\bar{p}$$

which leads to

$$\bar{p} = \frac{\sum_{i=1}^{N} p_i A_i}{A}$$

The idealized probability of default is just the face value–weighted average of default probabilities.

3. *Computing the diversity score D.* The diversity score is finally obtained by matching the variance of the losses of the true and idealized portfolios.

The variance of the true portfolio is the sum of the covariances of the individual assets:

$$\text{Var}\left(\sum_{i=1}^{N} A_i 1_i\right) = \sum_{i=1}^{N} \sum_{j=1}^{N} \text{cov}\,(A_i 1_i, A_j 1_j)$$

where 1_i is the indicator function taking value 1 if asset i defaults and 0 otherwise. Recalling that the variance of a binomial distribution with probability p_i is $p_i(1 - p_i)$, we get

$$\text{Var} \left(\Sigma_{i=1}^N A_i 1_i \right) = \Sigma_{i=1}^N \Sigma_{j=1}^N A_i A_j \rho_{ij} \sqrt{p_i(1 - p_i)p_j(1 - p_j)}$$

The variance of the loss in the idealized portfolio is

$$\text{Var} \left(\Sigma_{i=1}^D F 1_i \right) = DF^2 \bar{p} (1 - \bar{p})$$

Matching the variances of the two portfolios gives us

$$\Sigma_{i=1}^N \Sigma_{j=1}^N A_i A_j \rho_{ij} \sqrt{p_i(1 - p_i)p_j(1 - p_j)} = DF^2 \bar{p} (1 - \bar{p})$$

$$= D \frac{A^2}{D^2} \frac{\Sigma_{i=1}^N p_i A_i}{A} \left(\frac{A - \Sigma_{i=1}^N p_i A_i}{A} \right)$$

and finally

$$D = \frac{(\Sigma_{i=1}^N p_i A_i)[\Sigma_{i=1}^N (1 - p_i)A_i]}{\Sigma_{i=1}^N \Sigma_{j=1}^N A_i A_j \rho_{ij} \sqrt{p_i(1 - p_i)p_j(1 - p_j)}}$$

Once D and $\bar{p}$ are determined as above, they can be inserted into the binomial probability equation in order to obtain the idealized loss distribution.

APPENDIX 9B

Pykhtin and Dev CDO Model

Pykhtin and Dev (2002) propose a simple factor-based model[18] for the evaluation of CDO risk. Their model is based on several key assumptions:

1. The portfolio of loans underlying the securitization tranche is asymptotically fine-grained (a very diversified pool of collateral with no large proportion accounted for by any asset).
2. This portfolio of loans is driven by *one* systematic risk factor.
3. The investor's portfolio where the CDO tranche is held is also asymptotically fine-grained.

4. The investor's portfolio is driven also by *one* (different) systematic risk factor.
5. The investor's exposure to the CDO tranche is small compared with the size of her portfolio.

UNDERLYING POOL OF ASSETS

The CDO is based on a portfolio of bonds with a loss rate probability distribution function $F(l) = 1 - G(l)$. Thus $G(l)$ is the probability that the loss rate L on the collateral portfolio is above the level l.

The portfolio consists of M identical loans with probability of default p and with normally distributed LGD with mean μ. Each issuer is characterized by asset returns that follow a simple Gaussian one-factor model identical to those described in Chapters 5 and 6:

$$X_i = \sqrt{\rho_A}\, Y + \sqrt{1 - \rho_A}\, \xi_i \quad \text{for } i = 1 \ldots M$$

ξ_i is the idiosyncratic factor for issuer i, and Y is the common factor. The default threshold is identical for all loans and is obtained as $N^{-1}(p)$.

We can thus apply the formula of Vasicek (1991) in order to calculate the distribution of the loss rate in the portfolio:

$$G(l) = \begin{cases} N\left(\dfrac{N^{-1}(p) - \sqrt{1-\rho_A}\, N^{-1}(l/\mu)}{\sqrt{\rho_A}}\right) & \text{if } l < \mu \\[2em] 0 & \text{otherwise} \end{cases}$$

THE CDO TRANCHE

Let us consider a securitization tranche with lower bound T_1 and upper bound T_2. Investors in this stand-alone tranche face the loss profile depicted in Figure 9B-1.

The expected loss on this tranche is

$$U(T_1, T_2) = \frac{1}{T_2 - T_1} \int_{T_1}^{T_2} G(l)\, dl$$

The formula above also corresponds to the expected loss on an infinite portfolio of infinitesimally small loans with probabilities of default $G(l)$ and LGD = 100 percent.

FIGURE 9B-1

Loss in the Pool versus Loss in the CDO Tranche

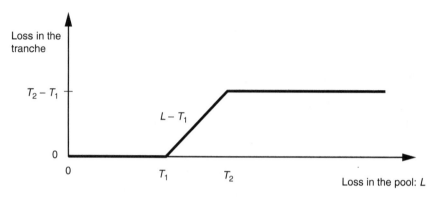

ASSESSING THE RISK OF THE TRANCHE IN A PORTFOLIO

The analogy of the CDO tranche with a portfolio of loans allows us to calculate the risk associated with the tranche as the sum of the risks of the "infinitesimally small loans."

In order to calculate (regulatory) capital for the CDO tranche, Pykhtin and Dev assume that the tranche is held in a very diversified portfolio and that its relative size compared with that of the portfolio is negligible. The losses on the portfolio are driven by another normally distributed random variable, correlated to the common factor Y. The authors assume that the two factors satisfy

$$Y = \sqrt{\rho_Y} Z + \sqrt{1 - \rho_Y} \; \varepsilon$$

where ε is another idiosyncratic term.

The capital is the amount that would withstand losses on the portfolio with $1 - q$ percent probability (where q, for example, is equal to 1 percent). It is obtained by assuming that the realization of the risk factor Z is equal to it\s $1-q$ percentile: z_{1-q}, and calculating the probability of default of infinitely small loans conditional on the risk factor:

$$K(T_1, T_2) = \frac{1}{T_2 - T_1} \int_{T_1}^{T_2} G(l \mid Z = z_{1-q})(l) \, dl$$

Pykhtin and Dev (2002) obtain a closed-form solution for this equation, only involving the bivariate normal distribution.

In a separate paper, Pykhtin and Dev (2003) lift assumption 1 above, which is frequently violated (the pool of assets will in many cases comprise only 30 to 50 issuers).

CHAPTER 10

Regulation

Over the past 5 years, a considerable amount of work has been undertaken by the Basel Committee, by practitioners, and by academics in order to design a new master regulatory framework for banks. The task is proving a real challenge because the banking industry has undergone substantial transformations as a consequence of the deregulation of financial markets. At the same time, risk management and risk transfer have gained in sophistication. Regulators, therefore, have to cope with two different issues simultaneously. First and foremost, they want to provide an accurate insolvency frontier applicable to banks, in order to avoid macroeconomic and microeconomic shocks. In addition they aim at educating banks in order to set common risk practices among the financial community.

The current regulatory framework (Basel I) was initiated in 1988. The regulatory constraint expressed by the 1988 "Cooke ratio" (discussed later in the section on banking regulation) has quickly been bypassed by banks thanks to innovation and arbitrage. Based on this experience, the main concern with the new accord currently under development (Basel II) is related to its potential flexibility in order to cope with the ongoing developments of financial markets. Another source of concern is the risk that the new accord may hinder a sufficient level of diversity across the banking industry.

In this chapter we first review regulation from a historical point of view and focus on the microeconomics of regulation. We then describe the main limitations of the first Basel Accord, and we review the main components of the Basel II Accord. Finally, we discuss the strengths and weaknesses of the proposed new framework.

A BRIEF HISTORY OF BANKING REGULATION

In this section we focus primarily on U.S. history but also report on some recent European developments. Banking regulation has been intimately linked with the transformation of the banking industry over the twentieth century. The title of a paper by Berger, Kashyap, and Scalise (1995) summarizes well the financial revolution: "The transformation of the US banking Industry: What a long, strange trip it's been." We could extrapolate, saying: The transformation of the banking regulation: what a long strange trip it has been.

In the United States, the history of banking regulation is clearly tied to the decreasing level of capital detained by banks. In 1840 for instance, banks' accounting value of equity represented 55 percent of loans. Since then this level has steadily decayed until the enforcement of the first Basel Accord.

The Federal Reserve System was created in 1914 and has helped to reduce bank failures by providing liquidity through central bank refinancing. The Federal Deposit Insurance Corporation (FDIC) was founded in 1933 and since then has offered an unconditional guarantee to most creditors of American banks. It has also restricted the level of interest rate that could be offered by banks on deposits.

Since the 1929–1939 crisis and before the first Basel Accord, a standard level of capital was required from banks. This level was defined independently from the risk borne by banks, either on balance sheet or off balance sheet. This situation did not lead to real difficulties as long as the business scope of banks was tightly controlled (in the United States, the Glass-Steagall Act of 1933 separated commercial banking and investment banking, and the McFadden Act of 1927 prevented banks from establishing branches in multiple states).

In the 1980s, following the end of the Bretton Woods international monetary system in 1973, banks have expanded internationally. This evolution occurred in a period of increased level of inflation, massive development of new financial products, and ongoing deregulation. It has led to significant banking crises, such as the partial collapse of the savings and loans industry at the beginning of the 1990s in the United States. Banks had become more aggressive and expanded to new markets in which they had no experience. They also increased their exposure vis-à-vis emerging markets and sometimes adopted pricing policies that did not fully reflect the effective level of risk of their investments. In addition, most international banks did not increase their level of equity accordingly. At the same time disintermediation of the highest-quality credits (in particular through commercial paper issuance) has tilted the balance sheet of some banks toward more speculative investments. These radical changes left the banks in an open and competitive environment where the role of financial markets was ever increasing.

The last major change in the U.S. banking landscape has arisen from the Financial Services Act of 1999 that repealed the major provisions of the Glass-Steagall Act and has allowed banks to expand significantly their range of financial services in any type of business, including brokerage and insurance. All these evolutions have translated into radical changes in the financial industry: Banks have been involved in an increasing wave of mergers.

In parallel, the Basel Committee on Banking and Supervision was created in 1974 by the governors of the Group of Ten[1] (G10) central banks. Its necessity was felt after several crises on forex markets as well as after bank failures such as the Herstatt Bank crisis in 1974. The committee does not possess any formal supranational supervisory authority, and its conclusions do not have legal force. Rather it formulates broad supervisory standards and guidelines and recommends statements of best practice in the expectation that individual authorities (local regulators) will take steps to implement them through detailed arrangements that are best suited to their own national systems.

At the end of the eighties and at the beginning of the nineties, regulators focused on reducing the level of bank insolvency. Capital has received a particular emphasis in this respect, as it has been considered altogether as a cushion in order to absorb potential losses, as an instrument to reduce moral hazard linked with the deposit insurance safety net, and as a way to protect depositors and insurers. The first Basel Accord of 1988 became applicable by 1992. It has been an important step in banking regulation. The objective was to strengthen and stabilize the whole international banking system, first of all by setting some standardized criteria for capital levels, but also by promoting a single homogeneous framework that would lead to fair competition among international banks. The main breakthrough of this regulatory scheme was to introduce a risk-based definition of capital.

National regulators have cooperated to implement the Basel rules and to provide a common and consistent regulatory platform. The first

Basel Accord was translated as an American mandatory requirement in 1991 (Federal Deposit Insurance Improvement Act) and in Europe in 1993 (directive on the solvability ratio). The adaptation of the banking industry to this new regulation in the 1990s has shown its limits. As a result, in 1996 an amendment regarding market risk was adopted. It allows banks to use their own internal models on their trading books. This amendment has, however, created a split between the trading book and the banking book of banks. A high level of arbitrage between the two books has therefore emerged since then. In addition, regulators themselves have been able to identify some structural weaknesses: "While examination assessments of capital adequacy normally attempt to adjust reported capital ratios for shortfalls in loan loss reserves relative to expected future charge-offs, examiners' tools are limited in their ability to deal effectively with credit risk—measured as uncertainty of future credit losses around their expected levels" (Federal Reserve, 1998).

The central criticism about the first Basel Accord is probably focused on its inability to evolve in accordance with financial practice, as Alan Greenspan pointed out in 1998 in the B.I.S. Review: "While no one is in favor of regulatory complexity, we should be aware that capital regulation will necessarily evolve over time as the banking and financial sectors themselves evolve." From a practical standpoint, we can distinguish two periods in the history of regulation. The period until the mid-1990s was characterized by a rather rigid and standardized regulatory approach. Since the mid-1990s, market discipline and the recourse to internal models have been constantly progressing. The new Basel II Accord that should be applicable in 2006–2007 corresponds to an intermediary step in regulation. It pushes toward individualized solutions and focuses on self-discipline but falls short of allowing internal portfolio models as drivers for the calculation of regulatory capital.

Time will tell whether this new regulatory framework contains sufficient flexibility and adaptation potential to cope with the ongoing trend of innovation in the financial arena.

THE PRINCIPLES OF BANKING REGULATION

Borio (2003) suggests a distinction between "macro-prudential" and "micro-prudential" perspectives. In the former the focus is on safeguarding global financial stability by avoiding systemwide distress. In the latter the objective is to limit distress risk in each financial institution and thereby protect consumers and investors. The equivalence of the two approaches is often assumed, but it is not clear whether individual failures always entail systemic risk. This is particularly unclear when the trigger for a failure lies in idiosyncratic factors. This open question represents a fundamental issue regarding the justification of the heavy regulation procedures currently being developed for Basel II.

In what follows, we review the microeconomics of banking regulation and try to identify when systemic risk is at stake or not. Practically, we are going to review major contributions from the academic literature that have attempted to answer the following questions: Why regulate? Is regulation biasing the banking system? How should the regulator intervene? And how should rules be defined?

Why Regulate?

There is no real consensus on the intrinsic value of regulation. For Fama (1985) there should not be any difference regarding the treatment of a bank and an industrial firm. As a consequence there will be little rationale for a specific regulation that may bring noise to market equilibrium and generate misallocation of resources and lost growth opportunities. Regulation may, however, be considered acceptable if it enables us to minimize market imperfections such as imperfect information and monopolistic situations or to protect public good.

Four main motivations are generally mentioned to justify the existence of banking regulation[2]:

* *To protect banks' depositors from a loss in case of bankruptcy.* Depositors are small atomized creditors. They do not have access to sufficient information in order to monitor their bank properly (Dewatripont and Tirole, 1994).
* *To ensure the reliability of a public good, i.e., money.* Money corresponds not only to the currency but also to the distribution, payment, and settlement systems (Hoenig, 1997).
* *To avoid systemic risk arising from domino effects (Kaufman, 1994).* This type of effect typically comes from a shock on a given financial institution that impacts gradually all the other financial institutions because of business links or reputation effect. The precise mechanism entails three steps: (1) contagion, and then (2) amplification, leading ultimately to (3) a macroeconomic cost that impacts the gross domestic product. In this respect the action of the Federal Reserve to protect the banking system

against the adverse consequences of the collapse of the hedge fund LTCM characterizes such a preventive action. In contrast, the bankruptcies of the banks BCCI and Drexel Burnham Lambert show that when there is no real perceived contagion risk, the intervention of regulators may not be required.

♦ *To maintain a high level of financial efficiency in the economy.* The distress or insolvency of a major financial institution could have an impact on the industry and services in a region. In this respect Petersen and Rajan (1994) consider that the collapse of a bank could lead to a downturn in the industrial investment in a region. Other banks may not be in a position to quickly provide a substitute offer, given their lack of information on the firms impacted by the fall of their competitor.

Deposit Insurance and Moral Hazard

In the United States, depositors are protected by the Federal Deposit Insurance Corporation. Most banks subscribe to it. Merton (1978) very early mentioned moral hazard issues linked with deposit insurance. Deposit insurance can indeed generate costly instability because it may provide incentive for banks to increase their risks. In case of insolvency, banks know they will not face major consequences vis-à-vis depositors. There have been several contributions about the cost of the insurance premium. Kane (1989) suggests that it should reflect the true risk of each bank. Merton and Bodie (1992) suggest several measures to minimize these effects, such as linking the value of the insurance premium to the risk level of the assets, setting a reserve requirement that should be transferred to the central bank; requiring an appropriate equity level, limiting the recourse to the lender of last resort, or restricting too large diversification. Chan, Greenbaum, and Thakor (1992) show that if the premium is calculated in an optimal way, moral hazard is then reduced.

Deposit insurance also carries another weakness. Given the safety net it provides, it suppresses the natural incentive for depositors to monitor their bank. Calomiris and Kahn (1991) and Peters (1994) show that depositors will withdraw their deposits when they receive signals that the bank has a risky behavior. This approach is very much linked with the topic of bank runs due to the diffusion of information. Peters (1994) suggests that a limited coverage of risk through deposit insurance is optimal because it still leaves room for monitoring by depositors.

The "Too-Big-to-Fail" Doctrine

When liquidity is offered by a lender of last resort to an insolvent bank without any specific requirement, the service provided is not different from deposit insurance (Bhattacharya, Boot, and Thakor, 1998). Rochet and Tirole (1996) indicate that governments behave like lenders of last resort when they provide liquidity to banks that are in difficulty or when they nationalize them. This intervention by states is inefficient, as it reduces the incentive for banks to monitor one another on the interbank market. The intervention is based on the too-big-to-fail doctrine. This means that when a financial institution is large, the risk of contagion may be so important that it leads a government to react and prevent such an event. In the wake of Bagehot (1873), Rochet and Tirole (1996) suggest that governments should intervene if and only if the distressed bank remains intrinsically viable though facing a sudden crisis. Acharya and Dreyfus (1989), Fries, Mella-Barral, and Perraudin (1997), and Mailath and Mester (1994) have tried to define criteria in order to decide whether a bank should be closed or saved.

Consequences for Capital Regulation

Prudential rules focused on minimum capital requirements have been criticized. For Kahane (1977) they are inaccurate, and for Koehn and Santomero (1980) they lead to more risky behaviors. For Besanko and Kanatas (1993) and Besanko and Thakor (1993), initial shareholders become less important, and their incentive to manage the bank properly is reduced. According to this theory, the cost of capital for the bank implies an increase in interest rates charged to its clients and therefore a reduction in lending activity.

Is There an Optimal Regulation?

Regulation entails two specific actions: setting prudential rules and monitoring banks adequately. Optimal regulation has recently been defined as a choice—a menu—of different alternatives offered to banks. Whatever the choice made by banks, regulation aims at inducing them to reveal early private information about their risks and about the way they are managed. This increased transparency enables regulators and banks to anticipate crisis situations.

In order to discriminate among banks, three directions have been suggested:

+ *Customizing the premium of the deposit insurance, based on risk.* Chan, Greenbaum, and Thakor (1992) suggest that the premium of the deposit insurance should be calculated in order to factor in the risk held by banks without having to proceed to costly verification. Their suggestion is to play both on the deposit insurance premium cost and on a minimum capital requirement. They show that banks holding substantial risk would be ready to pay a high premium provided that the level of capital required remains low. Conversely, risk-averse banks will typically opt for a low premium cost and a high capital level.[3]

+ *Focusing on discriminating senior executives.* Rochet (1992) focuses on the identification of the efficient or inefficient senior management of banks. He shows that the composition of the portfolio of a bank can reveal insight into how to categorize management with regard to efficiency.

+ *Relying on the precommitment approach.* Kupiec and O'Brien (1995a, 1995b, 1997) have centered their analysis on the level of trustworthiness that internal models for risk management can bring to regulators. Credibility stands at the center of their "precommitment approach." According to this approach, banks should declare, using their own tools, what their maximum level of loss over 10 working days can be in the next 6 months. This underpins the definition by banks of a level of required capital. If banks go beyond this threshold, they are then penalized through fines, the release of information to markets, etc.

Prescott (1997) distinguishes between what he considers to be the three ages of banking regulation:

+ A standardized approach corresponding to the Cooke ratio and its extensions.

+ An approach based on internal models to define the capital at risk.

+ An approach where the banks themselves choose the rules they are going to be judged on. This corresponds more or less to the precommitment approach. This approach does not mean a weak level of control. It has to be seen as a customized trade-off between obligations and penalties.

Regulation and Economic Cycles

It is widely accepted that risk increases during growth periods and bank failures tend to materialize during recessions. Two main reasons account for this. First, growth periods may lead to the underestimation of risk and to more lenient lending criteria, as described by Honohan (1997). Second, as we saw in Chapter 2, defaults tend to increase during downturn periods, thereby increasing the likelihood of bank failures.

In this respect, tracking systematic risk and providing incentive to diversify risk at a bank level is a sound reaction. It typically corresponds to the microprudential focus of the regulation described in Borio (2003). Understanding the sensitivity of the whole banking system to economic cycles remains, however, an element to be investigated in greater detail. The capability of any regulation framework to account and adjust for these cycles is currently under discussion, with an increasing literature on the potential procyclical effects of regulation. This shows that the macroprudential aspect of current bank regulation may not yet be fully dealt with.

Perspectives

The approach currently followed by regulators assumes that common methodologies will lead to a common understanding of risk and reduce major insolvency issues. In other words the new Basel II regulatory framework can be seen as the definition of an insolvency frontier that prevents any failure of banks at a microeconomic level. The underlying assumption is that microeconomic security will automatically generate macroeconomic stability.

There is, however, growing concern among the financial community that the criteria that define the conditions for macroeconomic stability may not yet be fully understood and included in the Basel II Accord. In particular, several concepts have recently emerged that have not yet found fully satisfactory answers, such as:

- "Procyclicality" risk, as discussed above
- "Liquidity" risk linked with the banking portfolio[4]
- "Time horizon" for the evaluation of risk which may go beyond 1 year[5]
- "Earning management" by banks and its related risk[6]
- "Growing consolidation" among financial institutions by mergers, along with their impact on macrofinancial stability

The main pending issue related to the previous discussion is that the cost-benefit structure of the current regulatory scheme may be found acceptable, looking from a microprudential standpoint, as it may indeed provide a robust insolvency frontier for each bank. It is still criticized, though, from a macroprudential standpoint since it may not provide sufficient specific remedy to the effect of macroeconomic instability on the financial system.

A RETROSPECTIVE LOOK AT THE 1988 BASEL ACCORD

The cornerstone of the first Basel Accord is the Cooke ratio. This ratio is defined as the amount of capital divided by risk-weighted assets. This ratio has to exceed 8 percent. In the 1988 Basel Accord, there are only four risk buckets:

- OECD sovereigns: 0 percent risk weight
- OECD banks and non-OECD sovereigns: 20 percent risk weight
- Mortgage loans: 50 percent risk weight
- Corporates and non-OECD banks: 100 percent risk weight

Risk-weighted assets are simply the amount lent multiplied by the risk weight. For instance, at least 8 percent of risk-weighted corporate assets must be held as capital by the bank. Let us consider $100 lent to a corporate. It has to be backed up by at least 8 percent × 100 percent × $100 = $8 of capital, while the same loan to an OECD bank only requires 8 percent × 20 percent × $100 = $1.6.

The accord was amended, later on, in order to integrate market risk. The great novelty with the 1996 amendment is that it has allowed banks to use their own internal model in order to measure market risk.[7] In addition, this amendment has enabled banks to integrate off-balance sheet instruments such as securitization.

The accord has been praised for ensuring an internationally accepted minimum capital standard. Many shortcomings of the simple rule described above have, however, also been recognized. In particular:

- There has not been any clear motivation for setting the level of capital requirement at 8 percent.
- The definition of the risk buckets does not reflect sufficiently the true level of risk of obligors (for example, all corporates are in the same bucket).

- The Cooke ratio may not be very informative about the effective level of insolvency risk of banks, given its static bias and its unsophisticated distinction among risks (no impact of seniority, no maturity effect, etc.).
- The effect of diversification is not factored in.
- Arbitrage between the banking and the trading books has increased extensively (with, for example, the dramatic development of credit derivatives).

This regulatory framework has also had an impact on accounting practices within banks, as it has provided some incentive to develop new financial instruments dedicated to regulatory purposes only.

CORE ELEMENTS OF THE SECOND BASEL ACCORD

One of the main motivations for Basel II was to escape from the "one-size-fits-all" setting of Basel I. Initially, the Basel Committee was considering a menu of three types of approaches to deal with credit risk (Santos, 2000):

- *The IRBA (internal ratings-based approach).* In each bank a rating is allocated to any counterparty, and for each rating there is a corresponding probability of default.
- *The FMA (full models approach).* Internal models developed by banks to measure credit risk are accepted following some due diligence by regulators.
- *The PCA (precommitment approach).* Each bank provides ex ante its maximum loss at a given time horizon. A penalty is applied ex post if the effective loss exceeds the ex ante declaration.

There are shortcomings associated with each of these three approaches. For example, the IRBA will not account properly for diversification, as it will be accounted for in a stylized way only. The FMA would suppose that the portfolio methodologies used by banks have been tested over a significant period of time in order to demonstrate a sufficient level of reliability. The PCA may show some limitations if the risk of bankruptcy deters the regulator from penalizing noncredible banks appropriately.

In its January 2001 proposals, the Basel Committee stepped back and narrowed its focus to a simplified scheme. The main rationale for this move was probably that the degree of sophistication of banks was quite unequal, with an understanding of credit risk that was not sufficiently homogeneous.

It has, however, kept the idea of a menu with three options[8] (see Figure 10-1):

♦ A (revised) standardized approach derived from the 1988 Basel Accord. The main difference is that unlike in the first accord, the weight allocated to each facility depends on the creditworthiness of the obligor via external ratings.

♦ An internal ratings-based (IRB) foundation approach where the bank calculates PDs using its internal rating system, but other inputs such as loss given default are obtained from external sources (the regulator).

♦ An IRB advanced approach where the banks' own estimates of input data are used exclusively (probabilities of default, loss given default, maturities).

Credit mitigation as well as asset securitization techniques are incorporated in all three approaches. A lot of emphasis has been put on the regulator to define precisely the treatment of collateral, credit derivatives,

FIGURE 10-1

Credit Risk Assessment in the Three Approaches to Basel II

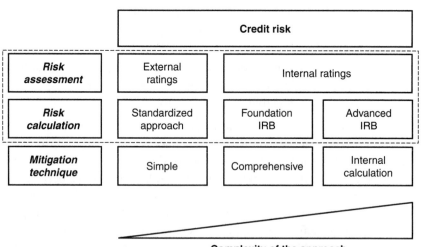

Complexity of the approach

Source: Standard & Poor's.

netting, and securitization. The application of these mitigation techniques sometimes is nonspecific to the rating approach selected.

The Key Principles of the New Regulation

Like the 1988 Basel Accord, the Basel II framework is, above all, targeting internationally active banks. It has to be applied on a consolidated basis, including all banking entities controlled by the group as well securities firms, other financial subsidiaries,[9] and the holding companies within the banking group perimeter.

The Basel Committee recognizes that its main challenge is to deal with the complexity of the new risk-based rules. As a result, the clarification and simplification of the structure of the accord has been one of its core objectives. This effort is tangible when looking at the difference in the presentation of the IRB approach between the initial version dated January 2001 and the QIS 3 version as per late 2002 and the CP3 consultative paper in 2003. In order to minimize the effect of the complexity in the rules, the committee has tried to work in a cooperative manner with the industry to develop practical solutions to difficult issues and to draw ideas from leading industry practice.

The ultimate goals of the Basel Committee are precisely defined and announced:

- Providing security and stability to the international financial system by keeping an appropriate level of capital within banks
- Providing incentive for fair competition among banks
- Developing a wider approach to measure risks
- Measuring in a better way the true level of risk within financial institutions
- Focusing on international banks

Practical Conditions of the Implementation of the New Regulation

The Basel Committee has defined in a precise way the conditions under which the accord should work.

First, the Basel Committee has provided a lot of documentation about the methodologies applying to the collection and use of quantitative data.

In addition, its objective has been to complement the internal calculation of regulatory capital by two external monitoring actions: regulatory supervision and market discipline. In order to emphasize that these last two components are as important as the first one, the committee has described capital calculation, regulatory supervision, and market discipline as the three pillars of a sound regulation (see Figure 10-2).

- ♦ *Pillar 1—minimum capital requirements*. The objective is to determine the amount of capital required, given the level of credit risk in the bank portfolio.

- ♦ *Pillar 2—supervisory review*. The supervisory review enables early action from regulators and deters banks from using unreliable data. Regulators should also deal with issues such as procyclicality that may arise as a consequence of a higher risk sensitivity of capital measurement.

- ♦ *Pillar 3—market discipline*. The disclosure of a bank vis-à-vis its competitors and financial markets is devised to enable external monitoring and a better identification of its risk profile by the financial community.

Minimum Capital Requirements[10]

In what follows, we focus exclusively on credit risk, but the Basel Accord also incorporates market and operational risks. The general framework is described on Figure 10-3.

The Standardized Approach

Under the standardized approach, the calculation of the risk-weighted assets defined in Figure 10-3 is split between the determination of risk weights and the size of the exposure.[11] We detail first how risk weights depend on the creditworthiness of the underlying assets. We then focus on the calculation of the exposure, given the mitigation brought by various types of collateral and hedging tools.

Risk Weights and Probabilities of Default   With this approach, a bank determines the probability of default of a counterparty based on accepted rating agencies' ratings[12] or export agencies' scores when available. A standard weight applies to counterparties without any external creditworthiness reference.

FIGURE 10-2

The Three Pillars of Basel II

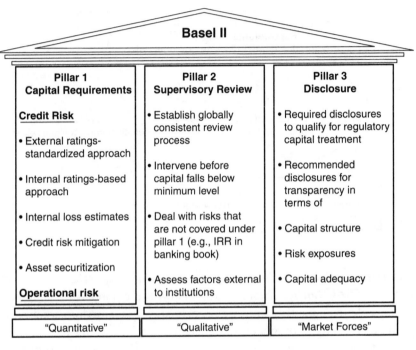

Pillar 1 Capital Requirements	Pillar 2 Supervisory Review	Pillar 3 Disclosure
Credit Risk • External ratings- standardized approach • Internal ratings-based approach • Internal loss estimates • Credit risk mitigation • Asset securitization **Operational risk**	• Establish globally consistent review process • Intervene before capital falls below minimum level • Deal with risks that are not covered under pillar 1 (e.g., IRR in banking book) • Assess factors external to institutions	• Required disclosures to qualify for regulatory capital treatment • Recommended disclosures for transparency in terms of • Capital structure • Risk exposures • Capital adequacy
"Quantitative"	"Qualitative"	"Market Forces"

Source: S&P documentation.

The standard risk weight for assets is normally 100 percent. Some adjustment coefficients are, however, determined in order to reflect the true level of credit risk associated with each counterparty. Table 10-1 gives a comprehensive description of the risk weights, based on Standard & Poor's rating scale.[13]

This revised approach entails significant differences with the Cooke ratio of Basel I. The former approach considered in particular the difference between OECD and non-OECD countries as critical for sovereign and bank risk weights. With the new approach references to the OECD have been replaced with the rating of the institution, as shown in Tables 10-2 and 10-3 (recall that Greece and Poland are OECD members, while Chile, Kuwait, and Singapore are not).

FIGURE 10-3

General Capital Adequacy Calculation

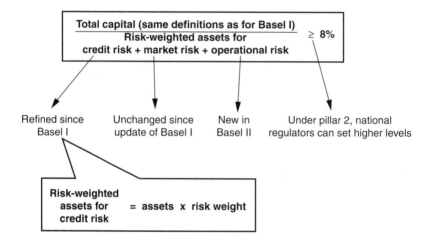

Determination of the Exposure Taking into Account
Credit Risk Mitigation
Banks following the standardized approach will be able to adjust the exposure of each asset by taking into account the positive role played by guarantees, collateral, and hedging tools such as credit derivatives. The Basel II framework provides guidance to mitigate the negative impact of the volatility of the collateral due to price or exchange rate changes by offering precise and adequate haircut rules. The principles of credit risk mitigation (CRM) are summarized in Table 10-4.

From a practical standpoint, there are two types of approaches to account for CRM—the simple approach and the comprehensive one:

♦ Under the simple approach, one defines rules for changes in the risk weights, given the quality of the collateral, while leaving the exposure unchanged.

♦ Under the comprehensive approach, the risk weights remain unchanged, but the exposures are adjusted to account for the benefit of the collateral. The exposure adjustment supposes the definition of haircuts to adjust for the volatility generated by market movements on the value of both the asset and the collateral. Banks have the choice between a standard haircut and their own estimated haircut. Under both cases, the framework is similar; i.e., the exposure after mitigation is equal to the current value of the

TABLE 10-1

Risk Weights under the Standardized Approach[*]

Counterparty		Assessment from ECAIs						
		AAA to AA−	A+ to A−	BBB+ to BBB−	BB+ to BB−	B+ to B−	Below B−	Unrated
Sovereigns		0%	20%	50%	100%	100%	150%	100%
Banks: Option 1		20%	50%	100%	100%	100%	150%	100%
Option 2		20%	50%	50%	100%	100%	150%	50%
Option 2 (short term)		20%	20%	20%	50%	50%	150%	20%
Corporates		20%	50%	100%	100%	150%	150%	100%
Retail	75%							
Secured loans/residential mortgage	40%							
Secured loans/commercial real estate	100%							
Securitization		20%	50%	100%	350%	Deduction	Deduction	Deduction
Other assets (with exceptions)	100%							

Source: QIS 3 October 2002.

[*]For the treatment of banks, the choice of option 1 or 2 depends on national supervisors.

TABLE 10-2

New Sovereign Risk Weights

	Current Weighting	New Weightings
Greece Rating A–	0%	20%
Chile Rating A–	100%	20%

TABLE 10-3

New Bank Risk Weights

	Current Weighting	New Weighting Option 1	New Weighting Option 2
Kuwait—Bank Rating BB–	100%	100%	100%
Singapore—Bank Rating AAA	100%	20%	20%
Poland—Bank Rating BBB+	20%	100%	50%

exposure augmented by a haircut, minus the value of the collateral, which is reduced by two haircuts—one related to its volatility and the second linked with currency risk when it exists.

The Internal Ratings-Based Approach

Once a bank adopts an IRB approach, the bank is expected to apply that approach across the entire banking group. A phased rollout is, however, accepted in principle and has to be agreed upon by supervisors.

The appeal of the IRB approach for banks is that it may allow them to obtain a lower level of capital requirement than when using the standardized approach. This result will, though, be conditional on the quality of the assets embedded in their portfolio. In addition, the benefit of using the IRB approach is limited to 90 percent of the capital requirement of the previous year during the first year of implementation of the approach and to 80 percent in the second year.

The IRB approach exhibits a different treatment for each major asset class.[14] The framework remains, however, quite standard. It is described below.

TABLE 10-4

Treatment of Credit Risk Mitigants[*]

Collateral	• Cash on deposit
	• Gold
	• Debt securities rated by ECAIs with a minimum rating
	• Debt securities unrated by ECAIs under sever conditions
	• Equities in a main index or listed on recognized exchange
	• UCITS/mutual funds under certain conditions
	• Miscellaneous
On-balance sheet netting	• Provided a legal basis exists for it in the country where the bank operates
	• The bank is able to determine at any time the components of the netting agreement
	• Miscellaneous
Guarantees and credit derivatives	• Very precise conditions such as representing a direct, explicit, and irrevocable claim
	• Additional conditions related to the structure of the instrument
	• Mismatch issues
	• High creditworthiness of the guarantor/credit protection provider
	• Miscellaneous

[*] In case of maturity mismatches between the exposure and the related hedge, a methodology to define the adjusted impact is provided.

Calculation of Risk Weights Using Probabilities of Default, Loss Given Default, Exposure at Default, and Maturity
Risk-weighted assets are given as RW = $K \times 12.50 \times$ EAD, where K corresponds to the capital requirement. Exposures at default, EAD, are precisely defined in the accord. Unlike in the standardized approach, collateral is not deducted from EAD.

The capital requirement K is determined as the product of three constituents:

$$K = \underbrace{\text{LGD}}_{P1} \times \underbrace{\text{PD}^*}_{P2} \times \underbrace{f(M,b)}_{P3}.$$

We will examine these three constituents, in turn, below.

P1: The Loss Given Default[15]

The LGD factor has a considerable impact on the capital requirement K, as they are linearly related, as shown in Figure 10-4. Thus an increase in LGD raises capital requirements by a similar factor irrespective of the initial level of LGD.

- In the foundation IRB approach, LGD levels are predetermined. For example, senior claims on corporates, sovereigns, and banks will be assigned a 45 percent LGD, whereas subordinated claims will be assigned a 75 percent LGD. In addition, some collateral types, such as financial collateral or commercial and residential real estate, are eligible in order to reduce LGD levels.
- In the advanced IRB approach, banks will use their own internal estimates of LGD.

P2: The Probability of Default

In the capital requirement equation (above), PD* corresponds to a function that integrates the effect of correlation. PD* can be seen as a stressed probability of default taking into account the specific correlation factor of the asset class.

Unlike for LGD, the function mapping the probability of default to the capital requirement is concave.[16] As a consequence, at high levels of PDs (e.g., non-investment grade), the relative impact on capital requirements of an increase in the LGD term is stronger than for the PD term (see Figure 10-5).

Basel II uses a simple one-factor portfolio model like those described in Chapters 5 and 6. Asset returns A are assumed to be normally distributed [$A \sim N(0,1)$] and driven by a systematic factor C and an idiosyncratic factor ε, both also standard normally distributed:

FIGURE 10-4

LGD Factor in Basel II Calculation K

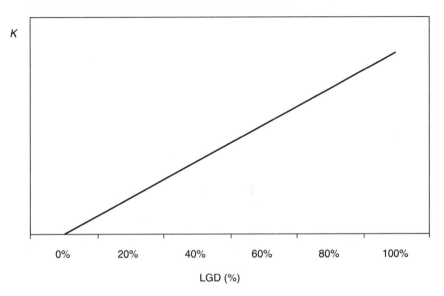

$$A = R C + \sqrt{1 - R^2}\ \varepsilon$$

where R is the factor loading.

The probability of default corresponds to the probability that the asset return falls below some threshold K:

$$PD = P(A < K)$$

Under an average scenario ($C = 0$), we can calculate

$$PD = P\left(\varepsilon < \underbrace{\frac{K}{\sqrt{1 - R^2}}}_{-DD} \right) = N(-DD)$$

where DD is the distance to default.

Basel considers a stressed scenario corresponding to the worst realization of the systematic factor at the 99.9 percent level. Under the standard normal distribution, this scenario corresponds to 3 standard deviations, i.e., $C = -3$. The stressed probability is

FIGURE 10-5

PD Factor in Basel II Capital Calculation K

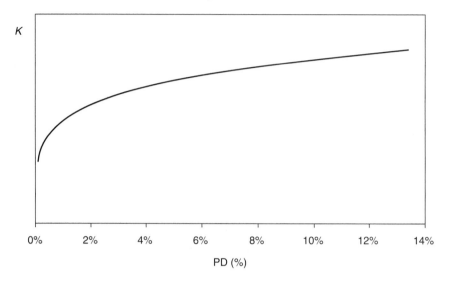

$$PD^* = P(-3R + \sqrt{1 - R^2}\ \varepsilon < K)$$

$$PD^* = P\left(\varepsilon < \underbrace{\frac{K}{\sqrt{1 - R^2}}}_{-DD} + 3\ \underbrace{\frac{R}{\sqrt{1 - R^2}}}_{\rho} \right)$$

Using the normal distribution, $PD^* = N[-DD + 3\rho]$, where $N(.)$ is the cumulative distribution function for a standard normal random variable and $\rho = [R/(1 - R^2)^{1/2}]$.

For various asset classes, the systematic factor loading R is adjusted. Figure 10-6 shows the different rules for R. The Basel II Accord determines different correlation levels for the various asset classes as a function of the PD of the obligor.

P3: Maturity Adjustment

In the capital requirement equation (above), $f(.)$ is a function of M, the maturity of the loan, and b is a maturity adjustment factor depending on the probability of default. In the foundation IRB approach, the effective maturity of the facility is assumed to be 2.5 years. In the advanced IRB approach, the capital requirement formula is adjusted for the effective

FIGURE 10-6

Proposed Correlations (R) for Various Asset Functions

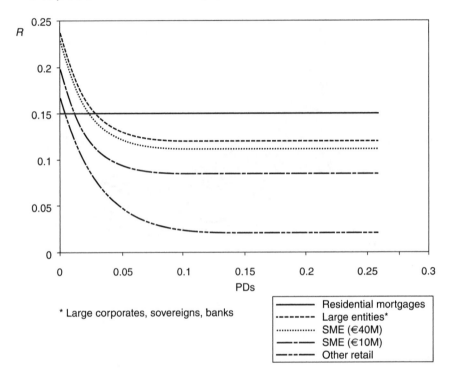

* Large corporates, sovereigns, banks

	Residential mortgages
	Large entities*
	SME (€40M)
	SME (€10M)
	Other retail

maturity of each instrument, depending on the level of PD.[17] The impact of maturity is described in Figures 10-7 and 10-8.

Figure 10-7 shows that high-quality (investment-grade) facilities are more penalized by the maturity adjustment than low-quality ones. It implies that some of the relief granted in Basel II to the best credits is offset by the maturity adjustment.

Securitization

There is a large development in the Basel II package regarding the treatment of securitization. Risk transfer through securitization is recognized as a risk mitigation tool both in the standardized and in the IRB approaches.

The Basel Committee distinguishes between traditional and synthetic securitization.[18] The general criteria necessary to define when securitization enables capital relief are:

FIGURE 10-7

Maturity Adjustment as a Function of the PD

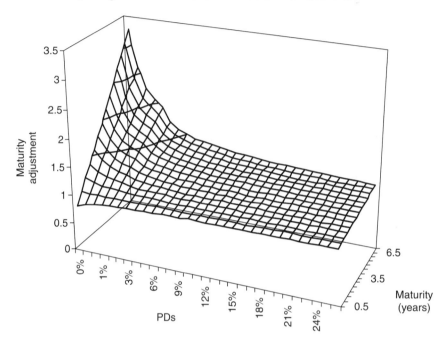

- ◆ *In the case of traditional securitization.* The assets located in the vehicle are isolated from the bank transferring credit risk.
- ◆ *In the case of synthetic securitization.* The underlying credit derivatives are complying with the requirements expressed previously in the Basel II package in Table 10-4.

When banks are choosing the standardized approach, the various weights are incorporated as shown earlier in Table 10-1. The ratings provided by external agencies still play a major role, for both the standardized and the IRB approaches. In the IRB approach, the K_{IRB}, which is the amount of required capital,[19] becomes the central concept. Practically, there are two ways to calculate the amount of required economic capital: the ratings-based approach (RBA) and the supervisory formula approach. The former uses predetermined risk weights associated with the ratings of each tranche, and the latter is based on a parametric formula determined by the Basel Committee.

FIGURE 10-8

Risk Weights for Large Entities for Various Maturities

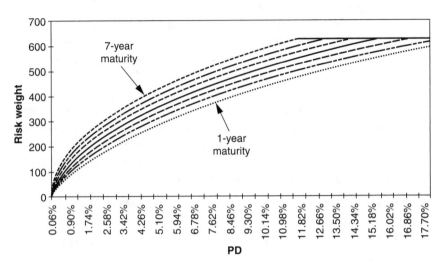

In addition to credit risk, the Basel II Accord focuses on operational risk. We have, however, deliberately chosen not to detail associated requirements, as they go beyond credit risk.

THE NEW BASEL REGULATION—ITS STRENGTHS AND SHORTCOMINGS

In the first part of his testimony to a congressional subcommittee on why a capital standard is necessary, Roger W. Ferguson, Jr., (2003) vice chairman of the Board of Governors of the U.S. Federal Reserve System, recognized that a change in the banking regulation was highly necessary. In this respect, the Basel II Accord corresponds to a clear improvement, compared with the Basel I framework. Ferguson testified:

> Basel II presents an opportunity for supervisors to encourage these banks[20] to push their management frontier forward. Of course, change is always difficult, and these new mechanisms are expensive. But a more risk-sensitive regulatory and capital system would provide stronger incentives to adopt best practice internal risk management.
>
> Let me be clear. If we do not apply more risk-sensitive capital requirements to these very large institutions, the usefulness of capi-

tal adequacy regulation in constraining excessive risk-taking at these entities will continue to erode. Such an erosion would present U.S. bank supervisors with a highly undesirable choice. Either we would have to accept the increased risk instability in the banking system or we would be forced to adopt alternative—and more intrusive—approaches to the supervision and regulation of these institutions. (Ferguson, 2003)

Although there is a universal recognition that banking regulation should change rapidly, the consensus about what type of improvement is the most appropriate does not seem to be very strong yet.

Here we review five categories of criticisms that are commonly discussed regarding the new regulatory scheme:

1. The already growing gap between industry best practices and Pillar 1
2. The capability of Basel II to offer equal treatment to banks that operate in a competitive but diversified environment
3. The capability of Basel II to provide fair regulation that is not uniform, leading to gregarious behaviors of banks
4. The difference between regulatory constraint and risk management
5. The coherence between the new regulatory framework and the new accounting rules

Dealing with Potential Gaps between Industry Best Practices and Pillar 1

The Basel II framework corresponds, as we have shown in the previous sections, to a significant technical improvement compared with Basel I. It reflects the evolution of the state-of-the-art practices in risk management over the past 10 years. If there is a broad acceptance that the present Basel II package reflects current best practices, there is still some concern for the future. Considering the current research in credit risk management, it is likely that the proposed framework will need to be updated in at least five directions in the next few years:

♦ The inclusion of diversification and concentration in regulatory capital calculation in a customized manner and a more refined approach of dependencies

- The refinement and replacement of the loan equivalent measure for the calculation of the exposure at default of contingent products
- The replacement of VaR by coherent measures
- The measurement of liquidity risk
- The value of linking the definition of an adequate time horizon for the calculation of the economic capital and the average maturity of the underlying portfolio of each bank.

Let us consider an example of a shortcoming of the current regulatory framework:

Although correlation is included in Basel II, there is no real benefit associated with diversification under the IRB approach.[21] Let us assume a portfolio composed of a single facility corresponding to a large corporate with an exposure of $100, an LGD of 45 percent, a maturity of 2.5 years, and a 1-year PD of 1 percent. It will receive the same regulatory capital, whatever the regulatory approach used, as a very diversified portfolio containing 100 facilities for various large corporates, each having a $1 exposure, an LGD of 45 percent, a maturity of 2.5 years, and a 1 percent PD.[22]

Moreover the general treatment of correlations in Basel II will probably have to be under review. For example, the Basel Committee has been openly challenged by some European governments regarding the treatment of SMEs, and as a result, the SME correlations were changed. We have seen in Chapter 5 that the link between PDs and correlations for large corporates is unclear. Equity-based models and empirical default correlations tend to exhibit correlations that increase in the level of PDs, but some intensity-based models report the opposite. For SMEs, empirical evidence is even more scarce. We therefore expect the Basel Committee to revise its correlation assumptions in a few years when more research is available on the topic.

Beyond this example, the challenge for the Basel Committee and for regulators will be to modify the technical framework corresponding to Pillar 1, subsequent to any substantial change in industry best practice. The good news is that this point is already widely discussed and accepted by regulators. In particular, Roger W. Ferguson, Jr., who was quoted earlier, notes: "Just as the methods of determining the inputs [EAD, PD, and LGD] can change as the state of the art changes, the formulas that translate the inputs into capital requirements can be modified as well by the regulators. Basel II can improve as knowledge improves" (Ferguson, 2003).

The Ability of Basel II to Offer Equal Treatment to Banks That Operate in a Competitive Environment

The proposed new regulatory framework ensures a common approach to risk and to required regulatory capital. There remains, however, some fear that this apparently very scientific and unbiased approach leads to unequal treatment among banks, for many different reasons:

- *Different perimeter.* In the United States, Basel II treatment[23] may eventually be applied to the 10 largest banks only, whereas in Europe the current consideration is rather for a much larger scope.

- *Competitive bias I.* The behavior of retail customers in each country can vary significantly, with some countries where individuals have a net positive savings position and others where there is a net negative one on average. Because of this, the retail business may not correspond to the same level of risk in each country, though its regulatory treatment will remain equal across countries.

- *Competitive bias II.* Regarding residential and commercial real estate, the situation is identical in some countries where the effect of cycles is more pronounced than in others.

- *Diversification.* In some countries the integration of the banking activity with the insurance business is much more widespread than in others. Arbitrage between banking and insurance regulation may provide an advantage to the more integrated financial groups.

- *Regulatory bias.* Within the context of the Basel II rules, each regulator is entitled, under Pillar 2, to ask for an additional cushion on top of the level of capital defined by the calculation of Pillar 1. There is a concern that regulators may not behave in the same manner in all countries, expressing different levels of systemic risk aversion. In particular, regulators may decide to be more conservative in countries where liquidity is constrained because of weak financial markets.[24]

Time will tell whether such fears are justified or not. Being able to be flexible enough to adapt the regulation, on a global basis, in order to cope with potential issues such as these will represent a real challenge for the Basel Committee.

The Ability of Basel II to Provide Fair Regulation That Promotes Diversity in Risk Systems

This section illustrates the debate between those who favor the definition of a unique regulatory framework and those who think that regulation is more a matter of individual precommitment. The former, who think that there is no alternative but the definition of objective and precise regulatory guidelines for banks, will find what follows irrelevant. In particular, they will say that regulators have nothing to do with the strategy of each bank. The latter, who think that a one-size-fits-all view of any banking regulation can prove dangerous, will consider this section very important.

We will not enter this debate here but want to explain the main issue. We have seen in Chapters 6 and 7 that senior executives of banks have to manage both technical risk[25] and business risk.[26] Basel II typically focuses on technical risk only and ignores business risk that is linked with value creation. In particular, given the profile, the perception, and the expectations of the shareholders of a specific bank, the senior executives of that bank may decide to adopt a certain risk aversion profile. For instance, the shareholders of a regional, nondiversified bank will not have the same type of expectations as those of a geographically diversified universal bank. As a consequence, the senior executives of each of these banks will tend to set different hurdle rates for their business units and will also provide different guidelines regarding diversification requirements. In other words, for them technical risk management rules should arguably depend on business risk management principles. There is a natural trend to adjust risk management rules to the characteristics of the business.

By isolating technical risk management from business risk management, pro-precommitment supporters believe that regulators incur the risk of providing a strong incentive for gregarious behaviors. The experience of the nineties in the area of market risk has shown that the recourse to tools that adjust for risk in a similar way during crisis periods may lead to market overreaction and increased macroeconomic risk.

Regulatory Constraint and Optimal Risk Management

Should the new regulatory framework be considered the tool for internal risk management? With Basel I, banks have learned to separate regulatory requirements from internal risk management. The main difference between Basel I and Basel II is about costs. The cost of implementation of the new accord within each bank is indeed much larger than previously. As a result, senior executives of banks often would like to be able to merge the two risk approaches by using the Basel II scheme as their only monitoring tool for risk management.

Looking at the facts, the answer is, however, mixed. The positive aspect is that the vast data collection effort that is required by Basel II corresponds to a clear necessity for any type of bottom-up risk management approach. As the cost associated with Basel II is largely the consequence of data collection, there is no duplication of cost at stake in this respect. Regarding the modeling part of the Basel Accord, the perspective of the regulator and that of banks differ. The former tries to set a robust insolvency frontier, whereas the latter looks for tools that provide dynamic capital allocation and management rules. It thus does not seem very appropriate to rely on the Basel II framework only. The previous chapters of this book and the other sections of this chapter have constantly underscored these differences. The good news, however, is that the cost of adopting an alternative bottom-up methodology is not that large compared with the cost of data acquisition.

The Difference between the Regulatory Framework and the New Accounting Rules

In 1998 Arthur Levitt, former chairman of the SEC, gave what is now known as "The Numbers Game" speech. He criticized the practice of manipulating accounting principles in order to meet analysts' expectations. Eighteen months after, his comment was that "the zeal to project smoother earnings from year to year cast a pall over the quality of the underlying numbers . . . ." Since then, the failure of Enron, Worldcom, and others has shed a vivid light on this issue. Galai, Sulganik, and Wiener (2002) show how earnings smoothing and management can also be applicable to banks.

In order to reduce accounting bias, the International Accounting Standards Committee (IASC) has been working on a revision of its principles. In particular, IAS 39, "Financial Instruments: Recognition and Measurement," was issued in early 1999. It is heading toward a wider use of fair values for financial instruments. As of today, only the trading book is measured on the basis of marked-to-market prices. The banking book is currently measured using historical prices, including related amortization. With IAS 39, there will be a strong incentive to shift the banking book to fair value measurement.[27]

IAS and Basel II will be applicable to banks roughly at the same time. There is concern that the uncoordinated implementation of the new accounting scheme and of the Basel II Accord will lead to a good deal of confusion. Advocates of Basel II claim that fair value pricing will introduce a lot of volatility in the balance sheet of the bank and at the same time duplicate the effort in terms of transparency. People who favor IAS claim to have solved risk management issues in an easy way, without having to use the complex Basel II framework. The debate is far from over.

In our view the IAS approach tries to tackle what the Basel II Accord has carefully avoided up to now: measuring liquidity risk. In principle, bringing liquidity risk to the debate is fine. From a practical perspective, it may, however, still be quite difficult to evaluate it in a homogeneous way. For instance, two banks holding the same asset may come with two different fair values, because of their own evaluation of the related liquidity premium or because of different trading experiences.

CONCLUSION

In our view the Basel II Accord should be seen as a starting point. Banks will have to move ahead, and this new framework is a clear incentive for them to make progress in the area of risk management.

The main question remains, however: Will the financial system be better protected against systemic risk?

Basel II acknowledges that relying only on models and regulators is insufficient. Pillar 3 (about transparency) is aimed at promoting self-regulation. Banks are still perceived as very opaque entities (much more so than corporate companies), and the development of off-balance-sheet instruments has further increased opacity. Up to now many banks have tried to minimize the cost of opacity by building a strong reputation. The recent difficulties that large U.S. banks have experienced related to internal conflicts of interest show that reputation may not be a sufficient answer to sustain high shareholder value. Market disclosure and transparency may soon become the most important pillar of Basel II if financial markets are sufficiently efficient at discriminating among banks based on their release of accurate information.

Credit risk is undoubtedly the new frontier in finance, just as interest rate risk and asset and liability management were 15 years ago.

Providing a comprehensive treatment of credit risk is proving increasingly difficult every day, given the volume of ongoing research being carried out globally on this topic. In addition, not all the techniques currently being developed will result in significant breakthroughs. For instance, extreme value theory was very fashionable a few years ago, but its contribution to credit risk management is proving much more limited than initially expected.

In this book we therefore have had to make some hypotheses about what is likely to become central to credit risk management, and we have minimized the focus on what we think may not be as important. Thus there is some subjectivity in our presentation, just as in all other surveys. Overall, however, we have tried to provide a clear idea of the state of the art and to report major developments.

Credit risk is not a discipline arising from a void. It draws from microeconomics, banking theory, and finance theory. Progress is this field is, however, hampered by the lack of data, and many recent credit risk models would have been impossible to test until recently.

The increased level of transparency brought by the collection of data by banks in recent years has boosted the development of a wide range of risk management products such as credit derivatives and CDOs, as banks become better able to measure their impact as well as their interest.

The development of this new set of skills does not mean that bank risk management is now fully mastered. Available tools indeed tend to display robust results under normal macroeconomic conditions. Their performance under stressed environments can prove more critical, in particular when the benefit of portfolio diversification vanishes when it matters most. In this respect the volatility of the credit risk (and of the related performance) of a business over time and through crises remains difficult to assess. There is therefore still a need for more work in this respect, and the recent focus on risk attached to procyclicality has provided strong incentive for banks and academics alike to embark on research in that direction.

The speed at which regulatory requirements have been developed is also remarkable. Although there is room for criticism about what is currently being promoted, the reactivity of regulators is quite impressive. The progress toward Basel II has led to the dissemination of a new credit risk culture among banks in less than 5 years. As a consequence, banks tend to lead insurance companies and asset managers in the credit field.

The major drawback of the Basel II initiative is that it is often associated with high costs rather than improved competitiveness. Although it is true that the banking business is becoming ever more like a heavy industry, the new set of credit risk measurement and management tools provides significant flexibility in order to improve bank performance.

Banks have recently learned that an appropriate management of their customer basis, as well as the development of a wide product distribution network, is key to obtaining a high performance level. What the new credit risk techniques mean to them is that investing in the acquisition and the development of large databases, advanced tools, and methodologies will be critical to maintain their advantage. We anticipate that in the coming years the level of techniques within the lending activity of banks will become a major criterion to assess the critical mass and rationale for mergers.

Ultimately we have observed over the past years a significant trend toward tying credit risk measurement to market pricing. We believe that such linkage makes a lot sense and will help to increase market depth and stability. There is, however, one key function fulfilled by banks that needs to be assessed in conjunction with this trend: the intermediation of liquidity. Banks indeed offer a very valuable service in providing liquidity where financial markets do not exist or have dried up. This service is possible as long as banks do not react like financial markets. Such duality between market focus and an appropriate service to the economy is difficult to handle. Based on the limited knowledge of the financial community regarding liquidity behavior, we think that there is room for research there in order to work out a solution that protects the stability of the international financial system.

NOTES

CHAPTER 1

1. As described by Arrow and Debreu (1954).
2. A complete market is a market for everything. For instance, a market for which, for each company, there does not exist a series of loans offering all types of contracts at all maturities cannot be a complete market.
3. Pareto optimal: One cannot increase the utility of one agent in the economy without simultaneously reducing the utility of another. A Walrasian market fulfilling Pareto optimality is:

   - *Perfect*. That is, agent atomicity, free movement of production factors, no restriction to free trade, product homogeneity, and information transparency.
   - *Efficient*. All available information is immediately incorporated in prices.
   - *Complete*. Markets exists for all goods, all possible states of the world, and all maturities.

4. Various important authors dealing with banking microeconomics have illustrated this approach: Douglas Diamond, Raghuran Rajan, Franklin Allen, Douglas Gale, etc. See the references at the end of the book.
5. See surveys in books from Freixas and Rochet (1997) and de Servigny and Zelenko (1999) and in articles from Bhattacharya and Thakor (1993) and Allen and Santomero (1999).

6. For further details on this way to split banking microeconomics, see de Servigny and Zelenko (1999).

7. The terms "moral hazard" and "adverse selection" are defined later.

8. The initial article on owner/manager issues is Berle and Means (1932).

9. Instrumental consideration.

10. The market value of a firm is independent from its financial structure and is obtained through expected future cash flows discounted at a rate that corresponds to the risk category of the firm. Modigliani and Miller (1958) assume that markets are perfect: no taxes, no transaction costs, no bankruptcy costs, etc. Another important assumption is that the asset side of a firm balance sheet does not change as leverage changes. This rules out moral hazard inside the firm. Asymmetric information pertains to the investor/firm relationship.

11. See Aghion and Bolton (1992).

12. We think specifically of models by Aghion and Bolton (1992) and Dewatripont and Tirole (1994) in a situation of incomplete contracts.

13. A popular example in the literature is about "lemons" (used cars); see Akerlof (1970).

14. This should translate into the entrepreneur's utility function.

15. See Blazenko (1987) and Poitevin (1989).

16. For example, projects with positive net present value.

17. The notion has been introduced by Myers (1984) and Myers and Majluf (1984).

18. See seminal articles from Holmström (1979), Grossman and Hart (1982), Tirole (1988), Fudenberg and Tirole (1991), and Salanié (1997).

19. See Jensen (1986). The manager overinvests to legitimize his role.

20. A standard debt contract (SDC) is an optimal incentive-compatible contract (Gale and Hellwig, 1985; Townsend, 1979). An incentive-compatible contract is a contract in which the entrepreneur is always encouraged to declare the true return of a project. Such a contract supposes direct disclosure—that is:

    ◆ The debtor pays the creditor on the basis of a report written by the debtor on the performance of the project.

    ◆ An audit rule specifies how the report can be controlled. Such a control will be at the expense of the creditor (costly state of verification).

    ◆ A penalty is defined when there is a difference between the report and the audit.

21. See Dionne and Viala (1992, 1994). In a model including asymmetric information both on the return of a project and on the entrepreneur's involvement, they show that an optimal loan contract contains a bonus contract based on an observable criterion of effort intensity.

22. Banking theory includes a dynamic perspective between the monitor and the debtor. As soon as we operate in a dynamic environment, the appropriate framework becomes incomplete contracts.

23. Entrepreneur, debtor, or creditor or shareholder, etc.

24. This approach to incomplete contracts and contingent allocation of control rights has been developed by Grossman and Hart (1982), Holmström and Tirole (1989), Aghion and Bolton (1992), Dewatripont and Tirole (1994), and Hart and Moore (1998).

25. Aghion and Bolton (1992) observe that debt is not the only channel to reallocate control rights. If, for example, it is efficient to give control to the entrepreneur despite low first-period returns and to the investors though first-period returns are stronger than expected, then the ideal type of contract would be debt convertible to equity.

26. They mainly focused on bank runs.

27. The liquidation cost is assumed to be zero.

28. For instance, a cost linked with providing incentive to the top management.

29. See Chapter 9.

30. These very significant categories have been introduced by Niehans (1978).

31. Santomero (1995) mentions three other incentives for reducing profit volatility: benefits for the managers, tax issues, and deterrent costs linked with bankruptcy.

32. Froot and Stein (1998) explain that risk management should focus on pricing policy particularly for illiquid assets, as a bank should always try to bring back liquid ones to the market.

33. Chang (1990) finds Diamond's results in an intertemporal scenario.

34. The case of short-term debt with repeated renegotiation has been covered by Boot, Thakor, and Udell (1987) and Boot and Thakor (1991). Rajan (1992) shows that when a loan includes renegotiation, the bank is able to extract additional economic surplus.

35. Mookherjee and P'ng (1989) have shown that when the entrepreneur was risk-averse and the bank risk-neutral, then optimal monitoring consisted of random audits.

36. In Stiglitz and Weiss (1981) credit rationing can occur when banks do not coordinate themselves. For an example of credit rationing, see Appendix 1A.

37. The topic of annuities has been developed in Sharpe (1990). Ex ante, banks tend to have low prices in order to attract new customers and then increase prices sharply when the customer is secured. Von Thadden (1990) shows that when debtors can anticipate such a move, they tend to focus primarily on short-term lending to reduce their dependency on the bank. Such an approach can be damaging for the whole economy, as it tends to set a preference for short-term projects over long-term ones. Rajan (1996) believes that universal banks tend to avoid extracting surplus from their customers too quickly in order to secure their reputation with their customers and therefore sell them their whole range of financial products.

38. Many academic authors tend to acknowledge this point, such as Allen and Santomero (1999) and Diamond and Rajan (1999).

39. As these types of large firms typically have a relationship with several banks/lenders, the argument of efficiency from bank monitoring vis-à-vis multiple lenders presented in Diamond (1984) can be used in the same way in considering a rating agency vis-à-vis a large number of banks.

40. Boot and Thakor (1991) try to identify the best split between bank and market roles. They find that markets are more efficient in dealing with adverse selection than banks, especially when industries require a high level of expertise. But banks are better at reducing moral hazard through monitoring. Their model does not reflect the impact of reputation.

41. See Kaplan and Stromberg (2000).

CHAPTER 2

1. We use the more common term "rating agencies," rather than "rating organizations," bearing in mind, however, that they are not linked with any government administration.

2. The presentation of the rating process is based on Standard & Poor's corporate rating criteria, 2000.

3. A notching down may be applied to junior debt, given relatively worse recovery prospects. Notching up is also possible.

4. Quantitative, qualitative, and legal.

5. This table is for illustrative purposes and may not reflect the actual weights and factors used by one agency or another.

6. For some industries, observed long-term default rates can differ from the average figures. This type of change can be explained by major business changes—for example, regulatory changes within the industry. Statistical effects such as a too limited and nonrepresentative sample can also bias results.

7. Mainly the United States, but also including Europe and Japan.

8. Obligor-specific, senior unsecured ratings data from Moody's. Changes in the rated universe are to be mentioned:

   ◆ 1970: 98 percent U.S. firms (utilities, 27.8 percent; industries, 57.9 percent; banks, very low).
   ◆ 1997: 66 percent U.S. firms (utilities, 9.1 percent; industries, 59.5 percent; banks, 15.8 percent).

9. When working on the same time period, the two transition matrices obtained were similar.

10. This dependence has been incorporated in the credit portfolio view model (see Chapter 6).

11. A Markov chain is defined by the fact that information known in $(t - 1)$, used in the chain, is sufficient to determine the value at (t). In other words, it is not necessary to know all the past path in order to obtain the value at (t).

12. Monotonicity rule: Probabilities are decreasing when the distance to the diagonal of the matrix increases. This property is a characteristic derived from the trajectory concept: Migrations occur through regular downgrades or upgrades rather than through a big shift.

13. See Chapter 6 for a review of this model.

14. "Rating Migration and Credit Quality Correlation 1920–1996," a study largely based on the U.S. universe.

15. For this reason, several authors have tried to define "good or generally accepted rating principles" (see, for example, Krahnen and Weber, 2001).

16. Portfolio models that are based on internal ratings as inputs, but that rely on external information (often based on information from rating agencies) to determine ratings volatility, tend to bias significantly their results.

17. The two graphs represent the concentration or dispersion of probabilities across transition matrices.

18. And where it is difficult to define criteria because of the limited size of the sample within the bank.

19. A large sample with a sufficient number of defaults is necessary to reach reasonable accuracy. When the number of rating classes increases, the number of necessary observations increases too.

20. The fact that for AAA the number of years is lower only reflects a very limited and unrepresentative sample.

21. Basel II requires 5 years of history, but a lot of banks have less data.

22. See, for example, Allen and Saunders (2002), Borio, Furfine, and Lowe (2002), Chassang and de Servigny (2002), Danielsson et al. (2001), and Strodel (2002).

23. For very good ratings, a longer observation period is required, given the scarcity of defaults.

24. EL (expected loss) = EAD (exposure at default) × PD (probability of default) × LGD (loss given default)

25. Von Thadden (1990).

26. Continuous/discrete.

27. Rating agencies have also complemented their rating-scale choice with dynamic information such as "outlooks."

28. Note that a generator does not always exist. Israel, Rosenthal, and Wie (2001) identify the conditions for the existence of a generator. They also show how to obtain an approximate generator when a "true" one does not exist.

29. This property means that the current rating is sufficient to determine the probability of terminating in a given rating class at a given horizon. Previous ratings or other past information is irrelevant.

30. Kijima (1998) provides technical conditions for transition matrices to capture the rating momentum and other stylized desirable properties such as monotonicities.

31. BBB_u, BBB_s, and BBB_d denote BBB-rated firms that were upgraded (to BBB), had a stable rating, or were downgraded over the previous period.

32. In terms of mean default rate.

CHAPTER 3

1. A geometric Brownian motion is a stochastic process with lognormal distribution. μ is the growth rate, while σ_v is the volatility of the

process. Z is a standard Brownian motion whose increments dZ have mean zero and variance equal to time. The term $\mu V\, dt$ is the deterministic drift of the process, and the other term $\sigma_v V\, dZ$ is the random volatility component. See Hull (2002) for a simple introduction to geometric Brownian motion.

2. We drop the time subscripts to simplify notations.

3. Recent articles and papers focus on the stochastic behavior of this default threshold. See, for example, Hull and White (2000) and Avellaneda and Zhu (2001).

4. This is the probability under the historical measure. The risk-neutral probability is $N(-k) = 1 - N(k)$, as described in the equity pricing formula noted earlier.

5. For businesses with gross sales of less than $5 million and loan face values up to $250,000.

6. Loans under $100,000.

7. Front-end users are salespeople who look for a fast and robust model that performs well for new customers. These new customers may have slightly different characteristics from those customers already in the database that was used to calibrate the model.

8. The linear discrimination analysis supposes the assumption of an ellipsoidal distribution of factors. Practically, however, experience shows that linear discriminant analysis is doing well without any distributional assumptions.

9. For variables selection, see Appendix 3B.

10. Logistic analysis is also optimal if multivariate normal distribution is assumed. However, linear discriminant analysis is more efficient than linear regression if the distributions are really ellipsoidal (e.g., multivariate normal), and logistic regression is less biased if they are not.

11. ROC and other classification performance measures are explained later.

12. In this case, x_i has to be positive.

13. The k-nearest neighbor (kNN) methodology can also be seen as a particular kernel approach. The appeal of kNN is that the equivalent kernel width varies according to the local density.

14. Class-conditional distributions and a priori distributions are identified.

15. For a more detailed analysis of these techniques, we recommend Webb (2002) and references therein.

16. The key point about support vector machines is that they find the best separating hyperplane in a space of very high dimensionality obtained by transforming and combining the raw predictor variables. Methods using the best separating hyperplane have been around since the late 1950s. (See, e.g., the literature on perceptrons, including the book by Minsky and Papert, 1988.)

17. In our example there are only two variables (ROA and leverage). Therefore the hyperplane boils down to a line.

18. $\| w \|$ denotes the norm of vector w.

19. For example, Blochwitz, Liebig, and Nyberg (2000).

20. Compared with the area corresponding to a "perfect model."

21. To give an example of unequal misclassification costs, let us consider someone who is sorting mushrooms. Classifying a poisonous mushroom in the edible category is far worse than throwing away an edible mushroom.

22. The ROC convex hull (ROCCH) decouples classifier performance from specific class and cost distribution by determining an efficient frontier curve corresponding to minimum error rate, whatever the class distribution is (see Provost and Fawcett, 2000).

23. Hand (1994, 1997) has focused on reliability. He called it imprecision. His observation is that knowing that $p(\omega_i \mid x)$ is the greatest is not sufficient. Being able to compare the true posterior probability $p(\omega_i \mid x)$ with the estimated one $\hat{p}(\omega_i \mid x)$ is also very significant in order to evaluate the precision of the model. Hand (1997) suggests a statistical measure of imprecision, for a given sample:

$$R = \sum_{j=1}^{C} \frac{1}{n} \sum_{i=1}^{n} [\phi_i(x_i)[z_{ji} - \hat{p}(\omega_j \mid x_i)]\,]$$

where $z_{ji} = 1$ if $x_i \in \omega_j$ and 0 otherwise. ϕ_j is a function that determines the test statistic, for example $\phi_j(x_i) = [1 - \hat{p}(\omega_j \mid x_i)]^2$.

24. See D'Agostino and Stephens (1986).

25.
$$\frac{N_i - Np_i}{\sqrt{Np_i}}$$

converges to $N(0, \sqrt{1 - p_i})$, as N tends to ∞ with

$$\sum_{i=1}^{K} N_i - Np_i = 0$$

and therefore

$$D_N = \sum_{i=1}^{K} \frac{(N_i - Np_i)^2}{Np_i}$$

converges toward a χ^2_{K-1}.

26. A utility function $U(W)$ is a function that maps an agent's wealth W to the satisfaction (utility) she can derive from it. It is a way to rank payoffs of various actions or investment strategies. Utilities are chosen to be increasing (so that more wealth is associated with more utility) and concave (the utility of one extra dollar when the agent is poor is higher than when she is rich).

27. Variables with subscripts such as p_y, O_y, or b_y are the scalar constituents of vectors p, O, and b.

28. These can be derived analytically in some cases but depend on q (the vector of q_y).

29. The relative performance measure becomes the logarithm of the likelihood ratio for two models.

30. Calibration describes how predicted PDs correspond to effective outcomes.

31. The standard deviation of the rating distributions over several years shows a peak in the subinvestment-grade part (see Figure 3-17b).

32. Galindo and Tamayo (2000) show that for a fixed-size training sample, the speed of convergence of out-of-sample error can define a criterion.

33. One thing to bear in mind is that the error estimate of a classifier, being a function of the training and testing sets, is a random variable.

34. Vapnik (1998) says that the optimal prediction for a given model is achieved when the in-sample error is close to the out-of-sample error.

35. The apparent error rate is the error rate obtained by using the design set.

36. This is particularly interesting when the underlying sample is limited.

37. The problem with this type of solution is that in the end it is very easy to remove defaulting companies, considered as outliers.

38. As obtaining a clear and stable definition of misclassification costs can prove difficult, a way to compensate for this is to maximize the performance of the classifier. The ROC convex hull decouples classifier performance from specific class and cost distribution by determining

an efficient frontier curve corresponding to the minimum error rate, whatever the class distribution is. (See Provost and Fawcett, 2000.)

CHAPTER 4

1. See for example Jensen (1991).
2. Manove, Padilla, and Pagano (2001).
3. Jackson (1986), Berglof et al. (1999), Hart (1995), Hart and Moore (1998a), and Welch (1997).
4. Franks and Sussman (2002).
5. Elsas and Krahnen (2002).
6. In this respect we recommend access to the document "A Review of Company Rescue and Business Reconstruction Mechanisms—Report by the Review Group" from the Department of Trade and Industry and HM Treasury, May 2000.
7. Such as U.S. Chapter 11.
8. This type of measurement can be performed even if information on all the underlying collateral is not precisely known. It can be estimated.
9. Default is defined as interest or principal past due.
10. Before moving on to reviewing what we think are the key drivers of recovery rates, we want to stress that all the recovery rates considered here do not include the cost of running a bank's distress unit. Statistics shown in this chapter and in most other studies therefore tend to underestimate the real cost of a default for a bank.
11. Debt cushion—how much debt is below a particular instrument in the balance sheet.
12. $H = \sum s_i^2$, where s_i corresponds to the market share of firm i.
13. The negative link is, however, captured in the Merton's (1974) firm value–based model. When the value of the firm decreases, the probability of default increases and the expected recovery rate falls.
14. A similar graph can be found in Frye (2000b).
15. To go into more detail, collateral types include cash, equipment, intellectual property, intercompany debt, inventories, receivables, marketable securities, oil and gas reserves, real estate, etc.
16. The model Portfolio Risk Tracker presented in Chapter 6 allows for a dependence of the value of collateral on systematic factors. This is a significant step toward linking PDs and LGDs.
17. By Gilson (1990), Gilson, John, and Lang (1990), and Franks and Torous (1993, 1994).

18. Get hold of the equity.

19. In Spain, for example, the bankruptcy rate is 0.5 percent in the SME sector. This is abnormally low and suggests that most defaults lead to private settlements.

20. Portfolio losses are measured by credit value at risk. See Chapter 6 on portfolio models for an introduction to this concept.

21. PD and LGD are assumed uncorrelated.

22. The recovery rate in CreditRisk+ is, however, assumed to be constant.

23. There does not exist any algebraic solution of the maximum-likelihood equations, but several approximations have been proposed in the literature (see, e.g., Balakrishnan, Johnson, and Kotz, 1995).

24. This is not only a theoretical exercise. Asarnow and Edwards (1995), for example, report a bimodal distribution for the recovery rates on defaulted bank loans.

25. Beta kernels have been introduced by Chen (1999) in the statistics literature.

26. The experiment is carried out as follows: We draw 10,000 independent random variables from the "true" bimodal distribution, which is a mixture of two beta distributions, and we apply the beta kernel estimator.

27. Their optimization criterion is based on an "excess wealth growth rate" performance measure, close to maximum likelihood. It is described in Chapter 2.

28. The 1993–2003 Japanese crisis of the banking system stands as a good example for such risk of correlation between default rates and real estate–based recovery rates.

29. In the Basel II framework, loan-to-value requirements are specified.

30. Based on 37,259 defaulted lease contracts.

31. Data from 12 leasing companies.

CHAPTER 5

1. Correlation is directly related to the covariance of two variables.

2. Correlation here refers to factor correlation. The graph in Figure 5-1 was created using a factor model of credit risk and assuming that there are 100 bonds in the portfolio and that the probability of default of all bonds is 5 percent. More details on the formula used to calculate the probabilities of default in the portfolio are provided in Appendix 5A.

3. Embrecht et al. (1999a,1999b) give a very clear treatment of the limitations of correlations.

4. X and Y are comonotonic if we can write $Y = G(X)$ where $G(.)$ is an increasing function. They are countermonotonic if $G(.)$ is a decreasing function.

5. An in-depth analysis of copulas can be found in Nelsen (1999).

6. Rather than considering the correlation of default events, Li (2000) introduced the notion of correlation of times-until-default for two assets A and B:

$$\rho_{AB} = \frac{\text{cov}(T_A, T_B)}{\sqrt{\text{Var}(T_A)\,\text{Var}(T_B)}}$$

where T_A, T_B correspond to the survival times of assets A and B. Survival-time correlation offers significant empirical perspectives regarding default and also rating migration events.

7. A 1-year default correlation involving AAA issuers cannot be calculated as there has never been any AAA-rated company defaulting within a year.

8. Appendix 5A provides more details on factor models of credit risk. Commercial models of portfolio credit risk are reviewed in Chapter 6.

9. Recall from the earlier section on copulas that we could choose other bivariate distributions while keeping Gaussian marginals.

10. The AAA curve cannot be computed as there has never been an AAA default within a year.

11. This is also consistent with the empirical findings presented in the following paragraph.

12. In distributions with little tail dependency (e.g., the normal distribution), correlations are concentrated in the middle of the distribution. Thus correlations decrease very steeply as one considers higher exceedance levels. In general, the flatter the exceedance correlation line, the higher the tail dependency.

CHAPTER 6

1. Some of those are provided on a regular basis by Riskmetrics.

2. CreditMetrics relies on equity index correlations as proxies for factor correlations. The correlation matrix is supplied by RiskMetrics on a regular basis.

3. A database from Standard & Poor's Risk Solutions.

4. Unlike CreditMetrics, Portfolio Manager does not consider equity index correlation but tries to capture asset correlation.

5. All these factors are diagonalized in order to reduce the dimensionality of the problem.

6. In the Asset Manager's version of the product.

7. Useful references on this topic are Rogers and Zane (1999) and Browne et al. (2001a, 2001b).

8. A risk measure ρ is said to be coherent according to Artzner et al. (1999) if it satisfies four properties:

   ♦ *Subadditivity*, for all bounded random variables X and Y: $\rho(X + Y) \leq \rho(X) + \rho(Y)$.

   ♦ *Monotonicity*, for all bounded variables X and Y, such that $X \leq Y$: $\rho(X) \geq \rho(Y)$.

   ♦ *Positive homogeneity*, for all $\lambda \geq 0$ and for all bounded variables X: $\rho(\lambda X) = \lambda\rho(X)$.

   ♦ *Translation invariance*, for all $\alpha \in (-\infty; +\infty)$ and for all bounded variables X: $\rho(X + \alpha r_f) = \rho(X) - \alpha$, where r_f, corresponds to a riskless discount factor.

9. RAROC was introduced by Bankers Trust in the late 1970s and adopted in one form or another by the entire financial community.

10. As defined by the NBER.

11. These figures correspond to the mean and standard deviation of the loss rate for senior unsecured bonds reported in Keisman and Van de Castle (1999).

12. In this example we are ignoring country effects. Country factors could also be incorporated in the same way.

13. Recall that asset returns are scaled to have unit variance.

14. $\nu_A = \nu_j$ in the summation means that we are summing over all exposures having size $\nu_j L$—that is, all exposures in bucket j.

15. Subscripts i now denote specific bonds in the portfolio.

16. For a thorough discussion of Fourier transforms, see, for example, Brigham (1988).

CHAPTER 7

1. From the facility level to the bank level (see Figure 7-1).

2. Within banks the most current usage of such bottom-up techniques has rather been focused on sensitivity analyses, linked to back testing and stress testing.

3. See, for example, Crouhy, Galai, and Mark (2001).

4. Such an exclusive focus on the confidence level for the calculation of economic capital may reduce the incentive for the bank to integrate in its internal system the monitoring of what is precisely followed by rating agencies.

5. The converse proposition is also true.

6. De Servigny (2001, p. 122) lists 10 different horizons that could alternatively be retained for various reasons.

7. More than what equity-driven correlation models would suggest.

8. Capital, and in particular equity, is a buffer against shocks, but capital is also the fuel for the core activity of the bank: lending money.

9. "In summary, the optimal capital structure for a bank trades off three effects of capital—more capital increases the rent absorbed by the banker, increases the buffer against shocks, and changes the amount that can be extracted from borrowers. . . . financial fragility is essential for banks to create liquidity" (Diamond and Rajan, 2000).

10. Business that is kept on the book of the bank.

11. Coupon minus funding costs, minus expected loss.

12. Leland (1997) shows how an adjusted beta should be calculated when asset returns are not normally distributed.

13. In what follows, we use Turnbull (2002) notations.

14. A clear definition of what is considered the current value has to be defined. Several options are possible—it could be a market value, a fair value, an accounting value, etc.

15. See Ross (1976).

16. There is correlation between banks, but not between business units. Returns of business units are taken as independent correlation factors. Surprisingly, the level of correlation seems to be time-independent.

17. This assumes that the cost of capital for each of the business units of the bank is observed.

18. An idea could be to have the NAV distribution for each business partially depend on exogenous macrofactors in the context of a multifactor model.

19. From a theoretical standpoint it is sensible, but there are strong technical constraints associated with the rigidity of costs within the bank.

20. They do not consider the impact of expected loss.

21. See Note 8 in Chapter 6.

22. Corresponding to the requirement of the shareholders.

23. Such a measure looks at a facility level only, with the myopic bias of considering a static balance sheet, and not at a business level where the balance sheet is dynamic.

24. Based on the fact that the amount of economic capital that should be allocated to such business units is typically very low, as no credit risk, market risk, or operational risk is incurred.

25. This case can happen if, for example, the presence of a business unit within a bank damages the whole value of this bank. Practically, let us consider a large retail bank that owns a small investment bank business unit. The investment bank division is not profitable. Because of the uncertainty generated by this business unit, the price-earnings ratio of the bank is significantly lower than that of its peers.

26. Or alternatively

$$k_{BU}^{RAROC} = k_{BU} \times \frac{EC_{top\text{-}down}}{EC_{bottom\text{-}up}}$$

27. Or alternatively

$$\bar{k}_{BU}^{RAROC} = k_{BU} \times \frac{EC_{top\text{-}down} + \Delta EC_{risk\ aversion}}{EC_{bottom\text{-}up}}$$

28. See Froot and Stein (1998).

CHAPTER 8

1. If time to maturity $(T - t)$ corresponds to n years and a discrete interest rate compounding is adopted, we could use $P(t,T) = 1/[1 + y(t,T)]^n$, where y is the discretely compounded yield.

2. For example, the German firm Daimler may have issued a bond with maturity 3/20/2010, which would be associated with a Bund maturing 3/31/2010.

3. Some further adjustments would have to be made to incorporate option features.

4. See, for example, Sundaresan (1997).

5. And therefore also bond prices using Equation (8-2).

6. See, e.g., Garbade (1996).

7. http://www.federalreserve.gov.

8. September 14 was the first trading day after the tragedy.

9. The vega (or kappa) of an option is the sensitivity of the option price to changes in the volatility of the underlying. The vega is higher for options near the money, i.e., when the price of the underlying is close to the exercise price of the option (see, for example, Hull, 2002).

10. Appendix 8C provides a summary of intensity-based models of credit risk.

11. See Appendix 8B for a brief introduction to this concept.

12. Their specification is actually in discrete time. This stochastic differential equation is the equivalent specification in continuous time.

13. Models estimated by PRS are under the historical measure and cannot be directly compared with the risk-neutral processes discussed earlier.

14. Brady bonds are securities issued by developing countries as part of a negotiated restructuring of their external debt. They were named after U.S. Treasury Secretary Nicholas Brady, whose plan aimed at permanently restructuring outstanding sovereign loans and arrears into liquid debt instruments. Brady bonds have a maturity of between 10 and 30 years, and some of their interest payments are guaranteed by a collateral of high-grade instruments (typically the first three coupons are secured by a rolling guarantee). They are among the most liquid instruments in emerging markets.

15. A more thorough investigation of this case can be found in Anderson and Renault (1999).

16. We assume the investor has a long position in the security.

17. We will use interchangeably the terms "structural model," "firm value–based model," or "equity-based model."

18. A structural model will enable one to price debt and equity. If equity data are available and if the focus is on bond pricing, then one can use the volatility that fits the equity price perfectly into the bond pricing formulas.

19. We can nonetheless mention Wei and Guo (1997), who compare the performance of the Longstaff and Schwartz (LS, 1995a) and Merton (1974) models on Eurodollar bond data. Although more flexible, the LS model does not seem to enable a better calibration of the term structure of spreads than Merton's model.

20. Strategic models are a subclass of structural models in which debt and equity holders are engaged in strategic bargaining. In the presence of bankruptcy costs, equity holders may force bondholders to accept a debt service lower than the contractual flow of coupons and

principal. If the firm value deteriorates, it may indeed be more valuable for the debt holders to accept a lower coupon rather than force
the firm into liquidation and have to pay bankruptcy costs. For an
example of strategic models, see Anderson and Sundaresan (1996).

21. Two measures are said to be equivalent when they share the same
null sets, i.e., when all events with zero probability under one measure
have also zero probability under the other.

22. A martingale is a driftless process, i.e., a process whose expected
future value conditional on its current value is the current value.
More formally: $X_t = E[X_s \mid X_t]$ for $s \geq t$.

23. This appendix is inspired by the excellent survey by Schönbucher (2000).

24. For Δt sufficiently small, the probability of multiple jumps is negligible.

25. Given that $E^Q[dN] = \lambda \, dt$ and $E^Q[dr] = \mu_r \, dt$.

26. We drop the time subscripts in r_t and λ_t to simplify notations.

27. See Schönbucher (2000) for details of the steps.

28. Loosely speaking, the matrix of intensities.

29. See Moraux and Navatte (2001) for pricing formulas for this type of
option.

30. Or identically that recovery occurs at the time of default but is a fraction δ of a T-maturity riskless bond.

31. i, h, $D_t^i(h)$, and n_t^i denote, respectively, the rating, the horizon, the
number of bonds rated i in year t that defaulted h years after t, and
the number of bonds in rating i at the beginning of the period t. The
rating system has $K + 1$ categories, with 1 being the best quality and
$K + 1$ the default class.

32. That is, we have $dA_t = rA_t dt + \sigma A_t \, dW_t$ under Q and $dA_t = \mu A_t \, dt + \sigma A_t \, dW_t^*$ under P.

33. We drop the superscript i in the probabilities for notational convenience.

CHAPTER 9

1. Securitization is the process by which a pool of assets is gathered to
back up the issuance of bonds. These bonds are called asset-backed
securities. The supporting assets can be anything from mortgages to
credit card loans, bonds, or any other type of debt.

2. International Swaps and Derivatives Association.

3. For the buyer.

4. An American option can be exercised at any time between the inception of the contract and maturity, whereas a European option can only be exercised at maturity. The terms "American" and "European" do not refer to where these options are traded or issued.

5. See Chapter 1 for a definition of complete markets.

6. For more details, see *BIS Quarterly Review*, May 27, 2002, Chapter 4.

7. See Chapter 10 for more details.

8. Securitization is the process of converting a pool of assets into securities (bonds) secured by those assets.

9. Within synthetic transactions, there are *funded* and *unfunded* structures.

10. Loan terms vary. The lack of uniformity in the manner in which rights and obligations are transferred results in a lack of standardized documentation for these transactions.

11. The typical maturity for a synthetic CDO is 5 years.

12. This is similar to the rationale for investing in a fund.

13. See Chapter 1 for similar results in the context of corporate securities.

14. Corresponding to a highly diversified pool of 50 corporate bonds with a 10-year maturity and the same principal balance.

15. In practice, LGD is incorporated based on the seniority and security of the asset (see Chapter 4).

16. This PD is determined by the rating of the asset, using average cumulative default rates in that specific rating class.

17. We can check that the sum of $A \times C$ is indeed equal to $N = 100$.

18. See Chapters 5 and 6 for an introduction to factor models of credit risk.

CHAPTER 10

1. There are now 13 countries that are members of the committee: the United States, Canada, France, Germany, United Kingdom, Italy, Belgium, the Netherlands, Luxembourg, Japan, Sweden, Switzerland, and Spain.

2. See Bhattacharya, Boot, and Thakor (1998), Rochet (1992), and Rajan (1998).

3. This result is interesting from a theoretical standpoint. It is, however, doubtful that in a very competitive banking environment such analysis can offer much discriminating power.

4. That is, the fact that the degree of liquidity in the banking book may be very different for various institutions. The ability of banks to refinance quickly will vary accordingly.

5. In Basel II, regulatory capital is calculated at a 1-year horizon only.

6. Smoothing earnings is very easy for banks, based on their use of provisioning and of latent profit and losses. This leads to greater opacity.

7. The capital measurement corresponded to the 10-day VaR at a 99 percent confidence level.

8. Article 42 of the third consultative paper (Basel Committee, 2003) should be mentioned. It allows regulators to accept that banks with a regional coverage keep the risk treatment corresponding to the Basel I Accord.

9. The capital invested in insurance entities will be deducted from the consolidated balance sheet of the bank and will be placed out of the banking regulatory perimeter.

10. For the most up-to-date version of the capital requirements, the reader can visit the BIS web site: http://www.bis.org.

11. The concept of risk-weighted assets existed before Basel II; in fact it was already a Basel I concept.

12. These agencies are called ECAIs—external credit assessment institutions. The assessment they provide has to rely on a review of quantitative and qualitative information.

13. The choice of option 1 or option 2 for bank exposures depends on each regulator.

14. Corporate exposures, specialized lending, sovereign exposures, bank exposures, retail exposures, and equity exposures.

15. One minus the recovery rate.

16. The fact that correlation depends on PD contributes to this concavity.

17. In some cases such as for corporates, banks, and sovereigns.

18. For further details, see Chapter 9.

19. Defined as the ratio of the IRB capital requirement for the underlying exposures in the pool to the notional or loan equivalent amount of exposures in the pool.

20. "A small number of very large banks operating across a wide range of product and geographic markets."

21. We thank Dr. Dirk Tasche for a fruitful discussion on this topic.

22. The different treatment for SMEs can be seen as a way to take into account, at least partially, this granularity effect.

23. The IRB approach.

24. The rationale to account for such conservatism is that, in some countries, the 1-year horizon may not be sufficient for the calculation of economic capital, given the absence of straightforward refinancing strategy in the context of bank distress.

25. Technical risk: the risk that credit risk, market risk, or operational risk exceeds the level of capital retained by the bank.

26. Business risk: the risk that the value of the bank collapses.

27. Indeed, the determinant to use fair value instead of the historical basis will be whether the facilities in the banking book can potentially be traded or held to maturity only.

REFERENCES

Acerbi, C. (2002), "Spectral measures of risk: A coherent representation of subjective risk aversion," *Journal of Banking and Finance*, 26, 1505–1518.

Acharya, S., and J. Dreyfus (1989), "Optimal bank reorganization policies and the pricing of federal deposit insurance," *Journal of Finance*, 44, 1313–1333.

Acharya, V., I. Hasan, and A. Saunders (2002), "Should banks be diversified? Evidence from individual bank loan portfolios," working paper, BIS.

Aghion, P., and P. Bolton (1992), "An incomplete contracts approach to financial contracting," *Review of Economic Studies*, 59, 473–494.

Akaike, H. (1974), "A new look at the statistical model identification," *IEEE Transactions on Automatic Control*, 19, 717–723.

Akerlof, G. (1970), "The market for 'lemons': Quality uncertainty and the market mechanism," *Quarterly Journal of Economics*, 84, 488–500.

Alexander, G., J. Bailey, and W. Sharpe (1999), *Investments*, 6th ed., Prentice Hall.

Allen, F., and D. Gale (1994), *Financial Innovation and Risk Sharing*, MIT Press.

Allen, F., and D. Gale (1997), "Financial markets, financial intermediaries and intertemporal smoothing," *Journal of Political Economy*, 105, 523–546.

Allen, F., and A. Santomero (1999), "What do financial intermediaries do?" working paper, Wharton.

Allen, J. (1995, February 23), "A promise of approvals in minutes, not hours," *American Banker*, 23

Allen, L., and A. Saunders (2002), "A survey of cyclical effects in credit risk measurement models," working paper, NYU.

Altman, E. (1968), "Financial ratios, discriminant analysis and the prediction of corporate bankruptcy," *Journal of Finance*, 23, 589–609.

Altman, E., and V. Kishore (1996, November–December), "Almost everything you wanted to know about recoveries on defaulted bonds," *Financial Analysts Journal*, 57–64.

Altman, E., A. Resti, and A. Sironi (2001), "Analyzing and explaining default recovery rates," research report, ISDA.

Amihud, Y., and H. Mendelson (1991), "Liquidity, maturity and the yields on U.S. Treasury securities," *Journal of Finance*, 46, 1411–1425.

Ammer, J., and F. Packer (2000), "How consistent are credit ratings? A geographic and sectoral analysis of default risk," *International Finance Discussion Papers*, Board of Governors of the Federal reserve System.

Anderson, R., and O. Renault (1999, December), "Systemic factors in international bond markets," *IRES Quarterly Review*, 75–91.

Anderson, R., and S. Sundaresan (1996), "Design and valuation of debt contracts," *Review of Financial Studies*, 9, 37–68.

Anderson, R., and S. Sundaresan (2000), "A comparative study of structural models of corporate bond yields: An exploratory investigation," *Journal of Banking and Finance*, 24, 255–269.

Arrow, K., and G. Debreu (1954), "Existence of equilibrium for competitive economy," *Econometrica*, 22, 265–290.

Artzner, P., F. Delbaen, J-M. Eber, and D. Heath (1999), "Coherent measures of risk," *Mathematical Finance*, 9, 1487–1503.

Arvanitis, A., C. Browne, J. Gregory, and R. Martin (1998, December), "A credit risk toolbox," *Risk*, 50–55.

Arvanitis, A., J. Gregory, and J-P. Laurent (1999, Spring), "Building models for credit spreads," *Journal of Derivatives*, 27–43.

Asarnow, E., and D. Edwards (1995), "Measuring loss on defaulted bank loans: A 24-year study," *Journal of Commercial Lending*, 77, 11–23.

Avellaneda, M., and J. Zhu (2001), "Modeling the distance-to-default process of a firm," working paper, Courant Institute.

Bagehot, W. (1873), *Lombard Street. A Description of the Money Market*, Scribner, Armstrong & Co.

Bahar, R., and L. Brand (1998), "Recoveries on defaulted bonds tied to seniority rankings," Special Report, Standard & Poor's.

Bahar, R., and K. Nagpal (2000, March), "Modeling the dynamics of rating transitions," *Credit*, 57–63.

Bahar, R., and K. Nagpal (2001, March), "Measuring default correlation," *Risk*, 129–132.

Bakshi, G., D. Madan, and F. Zhang (2000), "What drives default risk?" working paper, University of Maryland.

Bakshi, G., D. Madan, and F. Zhang (2001), "Understanding the role of recovery in default risk models: Empirical comparisons and implied recovery rates," working paper, University of Maryland.

Balakrishnan, N., N. Johnson, and S. Kotz (1995), *Continuous Univariate Distributions*, Wiley.

Bangia, A., F. Diebold, A. Kronimus, C. Schagen, and T. Schuermann (2002), "Ratings migration and the business cycle, with application to credit portfolio stress testing," *Journal of Banking and Finance*, 26, 445–474.

Barron, M., A. Clare, and S. Thomas (1997), "The effect of bond rating changes and new ratings on UK stock returns," *Journal of Business, Finance and Accounting*, 24, 497–509.

Basel Committee on Banking Supervision (2000a, February), "Sound practices for managing liquidity in banking organisations."

Basel Committee on Banking Supervision (2000b, September), "Principles for the management of credit risk."

Basel Committee on Banking Supervision (2001, January), "The new Basel Capital Accord + global package," consultative document.

Basel Committee on Banking Supervision (2002, October), "Quantitative impact study 3—technical guidance."

Basel Committee on Banking Supervision (2003, April), "The new Basel Capital Accord," consultative document.

Baud N., A. Frachot, P. Igigabel, P. Martineu, and T. Roncalli (2000), "An analysis framework for bank capital allocation," working paper, Credit Lyonnais.

Beattie, V., and S. Searle (1992), "Bond ratings and inter-rater agreement: A cross-sectional analysis," *Journal of International Securities Markets*, 6, 167–172.

Beaver, W. (1967), "Financial ratios as predictors of failures," *Empirical Research in Accounting: Selected Studies—1966*, supplement to *Journal of Accounting Research*, 4, 71–111.

Becker, T. (2002, July 25), "Conversion of Chapter 11 cases to Chapter 7 liquidations on rise," Dow Jones Corporates Filing Alerts.

Berger A., R. Herring, and G. Szego (1995), "The role of capital in financial institutions," *Journal of Banking and Finance*, 19, 393–430.

Berger, A., W. Frame, and N. Miller (2002), "Credit scoring and the availability, price and risk of small business credit," working paper, Federal Reserve Bank of Atlanta.

Berger, A., A. Kashyap, and J. Scalise (1995), "The transformation of the US banking industry: What a long, strange trip it's been," Brookings Papers.

Berger, P., and E. Ofek (1996), "Bust-up takeovers of value destroying diversified firms," *Journal of Finance*, 51, 1175–1200.

Berglof, E., G. Roland, and E-L. Von Thadden (1999), "Optimal capital structure and bankruptcy law," mimeo, Stockholm School of Economics.

Berle, A., and G. Means (1932), *The Modern Corporation and Private Property*, MacMillan. Revised edition published by Harcourt, Brace and World in 1968.

Bernanke, B. (1983), "Non monetary effects of the financial crisis in the propagation of the great depression," *American Economic Review*, 73, 257–276.

Bernanke, B. (1988), "Money policy transmission: Through money or credit?" *Federal Reserve Bank Philadelphia Business Review*, 3–11.

Besanko, D., and G. Kanatas (1993), "The regulation of bank capital regulations: Do capital standards promote bank safety?" working paper, Northwestern University.

Besanko, D., and A. Thakor (1993), "Relationship banking, deposit insurance, and portfolio choice," in C. Mayer and X. Vives (eds.), *Capital Markets and Financial Intermediation*, Cambridge University Press, 292–318.

Bevan, A., and F. Garzarelli (2000), "Corporate bond spreads and the business cycle," *Journal of Fixed Income*, 9, 8–18.

Bezard, M. (2002), "Capital economique, allocation coherente et effet portefeuille," working paper, BNP-Paribas.

Bhattacharya, S., A. Boot, and A. Thakor (1998), "The economics of bank regulation," *Journal of Money, Credit and Banking*, 154, 291–319.

Bhattacharya, S., and A. Thakor (1993), "Contemporary banking theory," *Journal of Financial Intermediation*, 3, 2–50.

Black, F., (1985), Discussion of the article by E. Jones, S. Mason, and E. Rosenfeld (1985), in B. Friedman (ed.), *Corporate Capital Structures in the United States*, University of Chicago Press, 262–263.

Black, F., and J. Cox (1976), "Valuing corporate securities: Some effects of bond indenture provisions," *Journal of Finance*, 31, 351–367.

Black, F., and M. Scholes (1973), "The pricing of options and corporate liabilities," *Journal of Political Economy*, 81, 637–659.

Blazenko, G., (1987), "Managerial preference, asymmetric information and financial structure," *Journal of Finance*, 42, 839–862.

Blazy, R., and J. Combier (1997), *La Défaillance d'Entreprise*, Economica–Insee.

Blochwitz, S., T. Liebig, and M. Nyberg (2000), "Benchmarking Deutsche Bundesbank's default risk model, the KMV private firm model and common financial ratios for German corporations," working paper, Deutsche Bundesbank.

Bohn, J., and S. Kealhofer (2001), "Portfolio management of default risk," working paper, KMV.

Boot, A., and A. Thakor (1991), "Moral hazard and secured lending in an infinitely repeated credit market game," *International Economic Review*, 35, 899–920.

Boot, A., A. Thakor, and G. Udell (1987), "Competition, risk neutrality and loan commitments," *Journal of Banking and Finance*, 11, 449–471.

Borio, C. (2003), "Towards a macroprudential framework for financial supervision and regulation," working paper, BIS.

Borio, C., C. Furfine, and P. Lowe (2002), "Procyclicality of the financial system and financial stability: Issues and policy options," working paper, BIS.

Bouyé, E., V. Durrelman, A. Nikeghbali, G. Riboulet, and T. Roncalli (2000), "Copulas for finance: A reading guide and some applications," working paper, Credit Lyonnais.

Boyd, J., and E. Prescott (1986), "Financial intermediary coalitions," *Journal of Economic Theory*, 38, 211–232.

Brannan, S., D. Mengle, C. Smithson, and M. Zmiewski (2002), "Survey of credit portfolio management practices," report, Rutter Associates.

Brigham, O. (1988), *Fast Fourier Transform and Its Applications*, Prentice Hall.

Browne, C., R. Martin, and K. Thomson (2001a, June), "Taking to the saddle," *Risk*, 91–94.

Browne, C., R. Martin, and K. Thomson (2001b, August), "VAR: Who contributes and how much," *Risk*, 99–102.

Calomiris, C., and C. Kahn (1991), "The role of demandable debt in structuring optimal banking arrangements," *American Economic Review*, 81, 497–513.

Carey, M., and M. Hrycay (2001), "Parameterizing credit risk models with rating data," *Journal of Banking and Finance*, 25, 197–270.

Carty, L., and J. Fons (1993), "Measuring changes in corporate credit quality," *Special Comment*, Moody's Investors Service.

Carty, L., D. Gates, and G. Gupton (2000), "Bank loan loss given default," *Special Comment*, Moody's Investors Service.

Chan, Y., S. Greenbaum, and A. Thakor (1992), "Is fairly priced deposit insurance possible?" *Journal of Finance*, 47, 227–246.

Chang, C. (1990), "The dynamic structure of optimal debt contracts," *Journal of Economic Theory*, 52, 68–86.

Chassang, S., and A. de Servigny (2002), "Through-the-cycle estimates: A quantitative implementation," working paper, Standard & Poor's.

Chen, S. (1999), "Beta kernel estimators for density functions," *Computational Statistics and Data Analysis*, 31, 131–145.

Christensen, J., and D. Lando (2002), "Confidence sets for continuous-time rating transition probabilities," working paper, University of Copenhagen.

Cortes, C., and V. Vapnik (1995), "Support-vector networks," *Machine Learning*, 20, 273–297.

Cossin, D., and T. Hricko (2001), "Exploring for the determinants of credit risk in credit default swap transaction data," working paper, Lausanne University.

Cox, J., J. Ingersoll, and S. Ross (1985), "A theory of the term structure of interest rates," *Econometrica*, 53, 385–407.

Credit Suisse Financial Products (1997), "CreditRisk+: A credit risk management framework," technical document.

Crosbie, J. (1997), "Modeling default risk," working paper, KMV.

Crouhy, M., D. Galai, and R. Mark (2001), *Risk Management*, McGraw-Hill.

Crouhy, M., D. Galai, and R. Mark (2000), "A comparative analysis of current credit risk models," *Journal of Banking and Finance*, 24, 59–117.

D'Agostino, R., and M. Stephens (1986), *Goodness-of-Fit Techniques*, Dekker.

Danielsson, J., P. Embrechts, C. Goodhart, C. Keating, F. Muennich, O. Renault, and H. Shin (2001), "An academic response to Basel II," FMG special paper, London School of Economics.

Das, S., and G. Geng (2002), "Measuring the processes of correlated default," working paper, Santa Clara University.

Das, S., L. Freed, G. Geng, and N. Kapadia (2002), "Correlated default risk," working paper, Santa Clara University.

Das, S., and P. Tufano (1996), "Pricing credit sensitive debt when interest rates, credit ratings and credit spreads are stochastic," *Journal of Financial Engineering*, 5, 161–198.

Dasarathy, B. (1991), "NN concepts and techniques, an introductory survey," in B. Dasarathy (ed.), *Nearest Neighbour Norms: NN Pattern Classification Techniques*, IEEE Computer Society Press, 1–30.

Davis, M., and V. Lo (1999a), "Infectious defaults," working paper, Tokyo-Mitsubishi Bank.

Davis, M., and V. Lo (1999b), "Modelling default correlation in bond portfolios," working paper, Tokyo-Mitsubishi Bank.

de Servigny, A., (2001), *Le Risque de Credit*, Dunod.

de Servigny, A., V Peretyatkin, W. Perraudin, and O. Renault (2003), "Portfolio Risk Tracker: Description of the methodology," technical document, Standard & Poor's Risk Solutions.

de Servigny, A., and O. Renault (2003, July), "Correlations evidence," *Risk*, 90–94.

de Servigny, A., and I. Zelenko (1999), *Economie Financière*, Dunod.

Delianedis, G., and R. Geske (1999), "Credit risk and risk neutral default probabilities: Information about migrations and defaults," working paper, UCLA.

Delianedis, G., and R. Geske (2001), "The components of corporate credit spreads," working paper, UCLA.

Denault, M. (2001), "Coherent allocation of risk capital," *Journal of Risk*, 4, 1–34.

Dewatripont, M., and J. Tirole (1994), "A theory of debt and equity: Diversity of securities and manager-shareholder congruence," *Quarterly Journal of Economics*, 109, 1027–1054.

Diamond, D. (1984), "Financial intermediation and delegated monitoring," *Review of Economic Studies*, 51, 393–414.

Diamond, D. (1989), "Reputation in debt markets," *Journal of Political Economy*, 97, 828–862.

Diamond, D. (1997), "Liquidity, banks and markets: Effects of financial development on banks and the maturity of financial claims," working paper, University of Chicago.

Diamond, D., and P. Dybvig (1983), "Bank runs, deposit insurance and liquidity," *Journal of Political Economy*, 91, 401–419.

Diamond, D., and R. Rajan (1999), "Banks, short term debt and financial crises: Theory, policy," working paper, NBER.

Diamond, D., and R. Rajan (2000), "A theory of bank capital," *Journal of Finance*, 55, 2431–2465.

Dichev, I., and J. Piotroski (2001), "The long-run stock returns following bond ratings changes," *Journal of Finance*, 56, 173–203.

Dionne, G., and P. Viala (1992), "Optimal design of financial contracts and moral hazard," working paper, University of Montreal.

Dionne, G., and P. Viala (1994), "Moral hazard, renegotiation and debt," *Economics Letters*, 46, 113–119.

Driessen, J. (2002), "Is default event risk priced in corporate bonds?" working paper, University of Amsterdam.

Duffee, G. (1998), "The relation between Treasury yields and corporate bond yield spreads," *Journal of Finance*, 53, 2225–2242.

Duffee, G. (1999), "Estimating the price of default risk," *Review of Financial Studies*, 12, 197–226.

Duffie, D. (1996), *Dynamic Asset Pricing Theory*, Princeton University Press.

Duffie, D., and N. Garleanu (2001), "Risk and valuation of collateralized debt obligations," *Financial Analysts Journal*, 57, 41–59.

Duffie, D., and R. Kan (1996), "A yield-factor model of interest rates," *Mathematical Finance*, 6, 379–406.

Duffie, D., and D. Lando (2001), "Term structures of credit spreads with incomplete accounting information," *Econometrica*, 69, 633–664.

Duffie, D., and K. Singleton (1997), "An econometric model of the term structure of interest-rate swap yields," *Journal of Finance*, 52, 1287–1381.

Duffie, D., and K. Singleton (1999), "Modeling term structures of defaultable bonds," *Review of Financial Studies*, 12, 687–720.

Durand, D. (1941), "Risk elements in consumer installment financing," working paper, NBER.

Dybvig, P., and J. Zender (1991), "Capital structure and dividend irrelevance with asymmetric information," *Journal of Financial Studies*, 4, 201–219.

El Karoui, N., H. Faracci-Steffan, and K. Sismail (2001), "Non-Markov credit modeling," working paper, CR-Institute.

Elsas, R., and J-P. Krahnen (2002), "Universal banks and relationships with firms," working paper, CFS Frankfurt.

Elton, E., M. Gruber, D. Agrawal, and C. Mann (2001), "Explaining the rate spread on corporate bonds," *Journal of Finance*, 56, 247–277.

Embrecht, P., A. McNeil, and D. Strautmann (1999a), "Correlation and dependency in risk management: Properties and pitfalls," working paper, University of Zurich.

Embrecht, P., A. McNeil, and D. Strautmann (1999b), "Correlations: Pitfalls and alternatives," working paper, ETH Zurich.

Enas, G., and S. Choi (1986), "Choice of the smoothing parameter and efficiency of k-nearest neighbor classification," *Computers and Mathematics with Applications*, 12, 235–244.

Engelmann, B., E. Hayden, and D. Tasche (2003, January), "Testing rating accuracy," *Risk*, 82–86.

Ericsson, J., and O. Renault (2001), "Liquidity and credit risk," working paper, London School of Economics.

Ericsson, J., and J. Reneby (1998), "A framework for valuing corporate securities," *Applied Mathematical Finance*, 5, 143–163.

Ericsson, J., and J. Reneby (2001), "The valuation of corporate liabilities: Theory and tests," working paper, McGill University.

Fabozzi, F., and T. Fabozzi (1995), *The Handbook of Fixed Income Securities*, Irwin.

Falkenstein, E. (2000), "RiskCalc™ for private companies: Moody's default model," report, Moody's Investors Service.

Fama, E. (1985), "What is different about banks?" *Journal of Monetary Economics*, 15, 29–40.

Fawcett, T. (2002), "Using rule sets to maximize ROC performance," working paper, Hewlett-Packard Laboratories.

Federal Reserve System Task Force on Internal Credit Risk Models (1998).

Ferguson, Roger W. (2003, February 27), "Why is a capital standard necessary?" testimony before the Subcommittee on Domestic and International Monetary Policy, Trade and Technology, Committee on Financial Services, U.S. House of Representatives, Washington, D.C.

Fisher, L. (1959), "Determinants of the risk premiums on corporate bonds," *Journal of Political Economy*, 67, 217–237.

Fisher, R. (1936), "The use of multiple measurements in taxonomic problems," *Annals of Eugenics*, 7, 179–188.

Fitzpatrick, P. (1932), "A comparison of ratios of successful industrial enterprises with those of failed firms," *Certified Public Accountant*, 12, 598–605.

Flesaker, B., L. Hughson, L. Schreiber, and L. Sprung (1994), "Taking all the credit," *Risk*, 7, 104–108.

Fons, J. (1994), "Using default rates to model the term structure of credit risk," *Financial Analysts Journal*, 25–32.

Franks, J., K. Nyborg, and W. Torous (1996), "A comparison of US, UK and German insolvency codes," *Financial Management*, 25, 86–101.

Franks, J., and O. Sussman (2002), "Financial distress and bank restructuring of small to medium size UK companies," working paper, London Business School.

Franks, J., and S. Sanzhar (2002), "Evidence on debt overhang from distressed equity issues," working paper, London Business School.

Franks, J., and W. Torous (1993), "An empirical investigation of US firms in reorganization," in E. Altman (ed.), *Bankruptcy and Distressed Restructurings*, Business One Irwin.

Franks, J., and W. Torous (1994), "A comparison of financial recontracting in distressed exchanges and Chapter 11 reorganizations," *Journal of Finance*, 35, 349–370.

Freixas, X., and J. Rochet (1997), *Microeconomics of Banking*, MIT Press.

Friedman, C., and S. Sandow (2003), "Ultimate recoveries," *Risk*, August, 69–73.

Friedman, C., and S. Sandow (2002), "Model performance for expected utility maximizing investors," working paper, Standard & Poor's.

Friedmans, C. (2002), "CreditModel technical white paper," Standard & Poor's.

Fries, S., P. Mella-Barral, and W. Perraudin (1997), "Optimal bank reorganization and the fair pricing of deposit guarantee," *Journal of Banking and Finance*, 21, 441–468.

Froot, K. (2001), "Bank capital and risk management: Issues for banks and regulators," working paper, IFCI.

Froot, K., and J. Stein (1998), "Risk management, capital budgeting and capital structure policy for financial institutions: An integrated approach," *Journal of Financial Economics*, 47, 55–82.

Frydman, H., and A. Kadam (2002), "Estimation of the continuous time mover-stayer model with an application to bond ratings migration," working paper, NYU.

Frye, J. (2000a, April), "Collateral damage," *Risk*, 91–94.

Frye, J. (2000b, November), "Depressing recoveries," *Risk*, 106–111.

Fudenberg, D., and J. Tirole (1991), *Game Theory*, MIT Press.

Galai, D., E. Sulganik, and Z. Wiener (2002), "Investment in real assets and earnings management in banks," working paper, Hebrew University of Jerusalem.

Gale, D., (1993), "Branch banking, unitary banking and competition," mimeo, Boston University.

Gale, D., and M. Hellwig (1985), "Incentive compatible debt contracts: The one-period problem," *Review of Economic Studies*, 52, 647–663.

Galindo, J., and P. Tamayo (2000), "Credit risk assessment using statistical and machine learning/basic methodology and risk modeling applications," *Computational Economics*, 15, 107–143.

Garbade, K. (ed.), (1996), *Fixed Income Analytics*, MIT Press.

Gertner, R., and D. Scharfstein (1991), "A theory of workouts and the effects of reorganization law," *Journal of Finance*, 46, 1189–1222.

Geske, R. (1997), "The valuation of corporate liabilities as compound options," *Journal of Financial and Quantitative Analysis*, 12, 541–552.

Giese, G. (2003, April), "Enhancing CreditRisk+," *Risk*, 73–77.

Gilson, S. (1990), "Bankruptcy, boards, banks and blockholders," *Journal of Financial Economics*, 27, 355–387.

Gilson, S., K. John, and L. Lang (1990), "Troubled debt restructurings: An empirical study of private reorganization of firms in default," *Journal of Financial Economics*, 27, 315–354.

Goh, J., and L. Ederington (1993), "Is a bond rating downgrade bad news, good news, or no news for stockholders?" *Journal of Finance*, 48, 2001–2008.

Golfarelli, M., D. Maio, and D. Maltoni (1997), "On the error-reject trade-off in biometric verification system," *IEEE Transactions on Pattern Analysis and Machine Intelligence*, 19, 786–796.

Gordy, M. (2002), "Saddlepoint approximation of CreditRisk+," *Journal of Banking and Finance*, 26, 1337–1355.

Gordy, M., and E. Heitfield (2002), "Estimating default correlations from short panels of credit rating performance data," working paper, Federal Reserve Board.

Gouriéroux, C., J-P. Laurent, and O. Scaillet (2000), "Sensitivity analysis of values at risk," *Journal of Empical Finance*, 7, 225–245.

Grablowski, B., and W. Talley (1981), "Probit and discriminant functions for classifying credit applicants; a comparison," *Journal of Economics and Business*, 33, 254–261.

Greenspan, Alan (1998), *BIS Review*.

Grinblatt, M. (1995), "An analytical solution for interest rate swap spreads," working paper, UCLA.

Grossman, S., and O. Hart (1982), "Corporate financial structure and managerial incentives," in J. J. McCall (ed.), *The Economics of Information and Uncertainty*, University of Chicago Press.

Haff, H., and D. Tasche (2002), "Calculating value-at-risk contributions in CreditRisk+," *Garp Risk Review*, 7, 43–47.

Hall, C., (2002, October), "Economic capital: Towards an integrated risk framework," *Risk*, 33–38.

Hand, D. (1994), "Assessing classification rules," *Journal of Applied Statistics*, 21, 3–16.

Hand, D. (1997), *Construction and Assessment of Classification Rules*, Wiley.

Hand, D., N. Adams, and M. Kelly (2001), "Multiple classifier systems based on interpretable linear classifiers," in J. Kittler and F. Roli (eds.), *Multiple Classifiers Systems*, Springer-Verlag, 136–147.

Hand, D., and W. Henley (1997), "Construction of a K-nearest-neighbour credit-scoring system," *IMA Journal of Mathematics Applied in Business and Industry*, 8, 305–321.

Hand, J., R. Holthausen, and R. Leftwich (1992), "The effect of bond rating agency announcements on bond and stock prices," *Journal of Finance*, 47, 733–752.

Härdle, W., and O. Linton (1994), "Applied nonparametric methods," in R. Engle and D. McFadden (eds.), *Handbook of Econometrics*, IV, Elsevier.

Harris, M., and A. Raviv (1991), "The theory of capital structure," *Journal of Finance*. 46, 297–355.

Harrison, J. (1985), *Brownian Motion and Stochastic Flow Systems*, Wiley, New York.

Harrison, J., and D. Kreps (1979), "Martingale and arbitrage in multiperiod securities markets," *Journal of Economic Theory*, 20, 348–408.

Harrison, J., and S. Pliska (1981), "Martingales and stochastic integrals in the theory of continuous trading," *Stochastic Processes and Their Applications*, 11, 215–260.

Hart, O. (1995), *Firms Contracts and Financial Structure*, Clarendon Press.

Hart, O., and J. Moore (1998a), "Default and renegociation: A dynamic model of debt," *Quarterly Journal of Economics*, 113, 1–41.

Hart, O., and J. Moore (1998b), "Foundations of incomplete contracts," working paper, NBER.

Henrotte, P., and A. Hyafil (2002), "A performance measurement and risk management framework for financial institutions," working paper, HEC.

Hickman, W. (1958), *Corporate Bond Quality and Investor Experience*, Princeton University Press.

Hoenig, A. (1997), "The search for optimal regulation: The pre-commitment approach," *Federal Reserve of Philadelphia Bulletin*.

Holmström, B. (1979), "Moral hazard and observability," *Bell Journal of Economics*, 10, 74–91.

Holmström, B., and J. Tirole (1989), "The theory of the firm," in *Handbook of Industrial Organisation*, 1, North Holland.

Holmström, B., and J. Tirole (1998), "Private and public supply of liquidity," working paper, University of Toulouse.

Holthausen, R., and R. Leftwich (1986), "The effect of bond rating changes on common stock prices," *Journal of Financial Economics*, 17, 57–89.

Honohan, P. (1997), "Banking system failures in developing and transition economies: Diagnosis and prediction," working paper, BIS.

Hu, Y-T., and W. Perraudin (2002), "The dependence of recovery rates and defaults," working paper, Birkbeck College.

Hull, J. (2002), *Options, Futures and Other Derivatives*, 5th ed., Prentice Hall.

Hull, J., and A. White (2000), "Valuing credit default swaps I: No counterparty default risk," *Journal of Derivatives*, 8, 29–40.

Hull, J., and A. White (2001), "Valuing credit default swaps II: Modeling default correlations," *Journal of Derivatives*, 8, 11–22.

Israel R., J. Rosenthal, and J. Wie (2001), "Finding generators for Markov chains via empirical transition matrices, with applications to credit rating," *Mathematical Finance*, 10, 229–247.

Izvorski, I. (1997), "Recovery ratios and survival times for corporate bonds," working paper, IMF.

Jackson, T. (1986), *The Logic and Limits to Bankruptcy*, Boston, Little, Brown.

Jaffee, D., and F. Modigliani (1969), "A theory and test of credit rationing," *American Economic Review*, 59, 850–872.

Jaffee, D., and T. Russell (1976), "Imperfect information, uncertainty and credit rationing," *Quarterly Journal of Economics*, 90, 651–666.

Jafry, Y., and T. Schuermann (2003), "Estimating credit migration matrices: Measurement matters," working paper, Federal Reserve Bank of New York.

Jain, K., R. Duin, and J. Mao (2000), "Statistical pattern recognition: A review," *IEEE Transactions on Pattern Analysis and Machine Intelligence*, 22, 4–37.

James, C. (1996), "RAROC based capital budgeting and performance evaluation: A case study of bank capital allocation," working paper, Wharton.

Jarrow, R. (2001, September–October), "Default parameter estimation using market prices," *Financial Analysts Journal*, 75–92.

Jarrow, R., D. Lando, and S. Turnbull (1997), "A Markov model for the term structure of credit risk spreads," *Review of Financial Studies*, 10, 481–523.

Jarrow, R., D. Lando, and F. Yu (2001), "Default risk and diversification: Theory and applications," working paper, University of California at Irvine.

Jensen, M. (1986), "Agency costs of free cash flow, corporate finance and takeovers," *American Economic Review*, 76, 323–329.

Jensen, M. (1991), "Corporate control and the politics of finance," *Journal of Applied Corporate Finance*, 4, 13–33.

Jensen, M., and N. Meckling (1976), "Theory of the firm: Managerial behavior, agency costs and ownership structure," *Journal of Financial Economics*, 3, 305–360.

Jones, E., S. Mason, and E. Rosenfeld (1984), "Contingent claims analysis of corporate capital structure: An empirical analysis," *Journal of Finance*, 39, 611–625.

Jones, E., S. Mason, and E. Rosenfeld (1985), "Contingent claims valuation of corporate liabilities: Theory and empirical tests," in B. Friedman (ed.), *Corporate Capital Structures in the United States*, University of Chicago Press.

J.P. Morgan (1997), CreditMetrics technical document.

Kahane, Y. (1977), Capital adequacy and the regulation of financial intermediaries, *Journal of Banking and Finance*, 1, 207–218.

Kaiser, K. (1996), "European bankruptcy laws: Implications for corporations facing financial distress," *Financial Management*, 25, 67–85.

Kane, E. (1989), *The S&L Mess*, Urban Institute.

Kaplan, S., and P. Stromberg (2000), "Financial contracting theory meets the real world: An empirical analysis of venture capital contracts," working paper, NBER.

Kaufman, G. (1994, April), "Bank contagion: A review of the theory and evidence," *Journal of Financial Services Research*, 123–150.

Kavvathas, D. (2000), "Estimating credit rating transition probabilities for corporate bonds," working paper, University of Chicago.

Keenan, S., D. Hamilton, and A. Berthault (2000), "Historical default rates of corporate bond issuers, 1920–1999," Moody's Investors Service.

Keenan, S., I. Shtogrin, and J. Sobehart (1999), "Historical default rates of corporate bond issuers, 1920–1998," *Special Comment*, Moody's Investors Service.

Keisman, D., and K. Van de Castle (1999, June), "Recovering your money: Insights into losses from defaults," *Standard & Poor's Credit Week*, 16–34.

Kempf, A., and M. Uhrig (1997), "Liquidity and its impact on bond prices," working paper, Universität Mannheim.

Keppler, P., and D. Williams (2003), "Credit derivatives: Ready for the test?" Research Study, Financial Insights.

Kijima, M., (1998), "Monotonicities in a Markov chain model for valuing corporate bonds subject to credit risk," *Mathematical Finance*, 8, 229–247.

Kijima, M., and K. Komoribayashi (1998), "A Markov chain model for valuing credit risk derivatives," *Journal of Derivatives*, 6, 97–108.

Kimball, R. (1998, July–August), "Economic profit and performance measurement in banking," *New England Economic Review*, 35–53.

Kliger, D., and O. Sarig (2000), "The information value of bond ratings," *Journal of Finance*, 55, 2879–2902.

Koehn, M., and A. Santomero (1980), "Regulation of bank capital and portfolio risk," *Journal of Finance*, 35, 1235–1244.

Koopman, S., A. Lucas, and P. Klaassen (2002), "Pro-cyclicality, empirical credit cycles and capital buffer formation," working paper, Vrije Universiteit Amsterdam.

Krahnen, J-P., and M. Weber (2001), "Generally accepted rating principles: A primer," *Journal of Banking and Finance*, 25, 2–24.

Kupiec, P., and J. O'Brien (1995a), "Recent developments in bank capital regulation of market risks," working paper, Federal Reserve Board.

Kupiec, P., and J. O'Brien (1995b), "A pre-commitment approach to capital requirements for market risks," working paper, Federal Reserve Board.

Kupiec, P., and J. O'Brien (1997), "The pre-commitment approach: Using incentives to set market risk capital requirements," working paper, Federal Reserve Board.

Kusuoka, S., (2001), "On law invariant coherent risk measures," *Advances in Mathematical Economics*, 3, 83–95.

Laitinen, E., and T. Laitinen (2000), "Bankruptcy prediction. Application of the Taylor's expansion in logistic regression," *International Review of Financial Analysis*, 9, 239–269.

Lando, D. (1998), "On Cox processes and credit risky securities," *Review of Derivatives Research*, 2, 99–120.

Lando, D., and T. Skødeberg (2002), "Analysing rating transitions and rating drift with continuous observations," working paper, University of Copenhagen.

Leland, H. (1997), "Beyond mean-variance: Risk and performance measures for portfolios with nonsymmetric return distributions," working paper, University of California at Berkeley.

Leland, H., and D. Pyle (1977), "Informational asymmetries, financial structure and financial intermediation," *Journal of Finance*, 32, 371–387.

Levitt, A. (1998), "The numbers game," speech by SEC Chairman at NYU.

Li, D. (2000), "On default correlation: A copula function approach," *Journal of Fixed Income*, 9, 43–54.

Liu, J., F. Longstaff, and R. Mandell (2002), "The market price of credit risk: An empirical analysis of interest rate swap spreads," working paper, UCLA.

Löffler, G. (2002), "An anatomy of rating through the cycle," working paper, University of Frankfurt.

Longstaff, F. (1994), "An analysis of non–JGB term structures," report for Credit Suisse First Boston.

Longstaff, F. (1995), "How much can marketability affect security values," *Journal of Finance*, 50, 1767–1774.

Longstaff, F., and E. Schwartz (1995a), "A simple approach to valuing risky fixed and floating rate debt," *Journal of Finance*, 50, 789–819.

Longstaff, F., and E. Schwartz (1995b), "Valuing credit derivatives," *Journal of Fixed Income*, 5, 6–12.

Longstaff, F., and E. Schwartz (2001), "Valuing American options by simulation: A simple least squares approach," *Review of Financial Studies*, 14, 113–147.

Lopez, J. (2002), "The empirical relationship between average asset correlation, firm probability of default and asset size," working paper, Federal Reserve of San Francisco.

Lucas, D. (1995, March), "Default correlation and credit analysis," *Journal of Fixed Income*, 76–87.

Madan, D., and H. Unal (1998), "Pricing the risks of default," *Review of Derivatives Research*, 2, 121–160.

Madan, D., and H. Unal (2000), "A two-factor hazard rate model for pricing risky debt and the term structure of credit spreads," *Journal of Financial and Quantitative Analysis*, 35, 43–65.

Mailath, G., and L. Mester (1994), "A positive analysis of bank closure," *Journal of Financial Intermediation*, 3, 272–299.

Mandelbrot, B. (1963), "The variation of certain speculative prices," *Journal of Business*, 36, 394–419.

Manove, M., J. Padilla, and M. Pagano (2001), "Collateral versus project screening: A model of lazy banks," *Rand Journal of Economics*, 32, 726–744.

Markowitz, H. (1959), *Portfolio Selection*, Yale University Press.

Marshall, A., and I. Olkin (1988), "Families of multivariate distributions," *Journal of the American Statistical Association*, 83, 834–841.

Martin, D. (1977), "Early warning of bank failures: A logit regression approach," *Journal of Banking and Finance*, 1, 249–276.

Matolcsy, Z., and T. Lianto (1995), "The incremental information content of bond rating revisions: The Australian evidence," *Journal of Banking and Finance*, 19, 891–902.

McNulty, C., and R. Levin (2000), "Modeling credit migration," *Risk Management Research Report*, J.P. Morgan.

Merino, S., and M. Nyfeler (2002, August), "Calculating portfolio loss," *Risk*, 82–86.

Merton, R. (1974), "On the pricing of corporate debt: The risk structure of interest rates," *Journal of Finance*, 29, 449–470.

Merton, R. (1978), "On the costs of deposit insurance when there are surveillance costs," *Journal of Business*, 51, 439–452.

Merton, R. (1995), "A functional perspective of financial intermediation," *Financial Management*, 24, 23–41

Merton, R., and Z. Bodie (1992, Winter), "On the management of financial guarantees," *Financial Management*, 87–109.

Merton, R., and A. Perold (1993), "Theory of risk capital in financial firms," *Journal of Applied Corporate Finance*, 6, 16–32.

Minsky, M., and S. Papert (1988), *Perceptrons. An Introduction to Computational Geometry*, MIT Press.

Modigliani, F., and M. Miller (1958), "The cost of capital, corporation finance and the theory of investment," *American Economic Review*, 48, 261–297

Modeling Default Risk (2002), KMV Publishing.

Mookherjee, D., and I. P'ng (1989), "Optimal auditing, insurance and redistribution," *Quarterly Journal of Economics*, 104, 339–415.

Moraux, F., and P. Navatte (2001), "Pricing credit derivatives in credit classes frameworks," in Geman, Madan, Pliska, and Vorst (eds.), *Mathematical Finance—Bachelier Congress 2000 Selected Papers*, Springer, 339–352.

Morgan, D. (1997), "Judging the risk of banks: What makes banks opaque," working paper, Federal Reserve Bank of New York.

Morris, C., R. Neal, and D. Rolph (1998), "Credit spreads and interest rates: A cointegration approach," working paper, Federal Reserve Bank of Kansas City.

Musiela, M., and M. Rutkowski (1998), *Martingale Methods in Financial Modeling*, Springer.

Myers, J., and E. Forgy (1963), "The development of numerical credit evaluation systems," *Journal of American Statistics Association*, 58, 799–806.

Myers, S. (1977), "The determinants of corporate borrowing," *Journal of Financial Economics*, 5, 147–175.

Myers, S. (1984), "The capital structure puzzle," *Journal of Finance* 39, 575–592.

Myers, S., and N. Majluf (1984), "Corporate financing and investment decisions when firms have information that investors do not have," *Journal of Financial Economics*, 13, 187– 221.

Nelsen, R. (1999), *An Introduction to Copulas*, Springer-Verlag.

Nelson, C., and A. Siegel (1987), "Parsimonious modelling of yield curves," *Journal of Business*, 60, 473–489.

Nickell, P., W. Perraudin, and S. Varotto (2000), "Stability of rating transitions," *Journal of Banking and Finance*, 24, 203–228.

Niehans, J. (1978), *The Theory of Money*, Johns Hopkins University Press.

Nielsen, L., J. Saa-Requejo, and P. Santa-Clara (1993), "Default risk and interest rate risk: The term structure of default spreads," working paper, Insead.

Ohlson, J. (1980), "Financial ratios and probabilistic prediction of bankruptcy," *Journal of Accounting Research*, 28, 109–131.

Pagan, A., and A. Ullah (1999), *Nonparametric Econometrics*, Cambridge University Press.

Panjer, H. (1981), "Recursive evaluation of a family of compound distributions," *ASTIN Bulletin*, 12, 22–26.

Patel, N. (2002, February), "The vanilla explosion," *Risk*, 24–26.

Peters, S. (1994), "Why are demand deposits sequential constrained and insured?" working paper, University of Connecticut.

Petersen, M., and R. Rajan (1994), "The benefits of lending relationships: Evidence from small business data," *Journal of Finance*, 49, 3–37.

Pinches, G., and C. Singleton (1978), "The adjustment of stock prices to bond rating changes," *Journal of Finance*, 33, 29–44.

Poitevin, M. (1989), "Financial signaling and the 'deep pocket' argument," *Rand Journal of Economics*, 20, 26–40.

Poole, W. (1998), "Whither the U.S. credit markets?" presidential speech, Federal Reserve of St. Louis.

Prescott, F. (1997, Winter), "The pre commitment approach in a model of regulatory banking capital," *Economic Quarterly*, 23–50.

Prigent, J-L., O. Renault, and O. Scaillet (2001), "An empirical investigation into credit spread indices," *Journal of Risk*, 3, 27–55.

Provost, F., and T. Fawcett (2000), *Robust Classification for Imprecise Environments*, Kluwer Academic Publishers.

Pykhtin, M., and A. Dev (2002, May), "Credit risk in asset securitizations: Analytical model," *Risk*, S26–S32.

Pykhtin, M., and A. Dev (2003, January), "Coarse-grained CDOs," *Risk*, 113–116.

Rajan, R. (1992), "Insiders and outsiders: The choice between informed and arm's-length debt," *Journal of Finance*, 47, 1367–1400.

Rajan, R. (1996), "Do we still need commercial banks?" working paper, NBER.

Rajan, R. (1998), "The past and future of commercial banking viewed through an incomplete contract lens," *Journal of Money, Credit and Banking*, 3, 525–549.

Renault, O., and O. Scaillet (2003), "On the way to recovery: A nonparametric bias free estimation of recovery rate densities," *Journal of Banking and Finance*, forthcoming.

Rissanen, J. (1989), *Stochastic Complexity and Statistical Inquiry*, World Scientific.

Robert, J-J. (1994), "Avis au nom de la Commission des Affaires Economiques et du Plan," Attaché au procès verbal de la séance du Sénat du 27 janvier 1993.

Rochet, J-C. (1992), "Capital requirements and the behaviour of commercial banks," *European Economic Review*, 36, 1137–1178.

Rochet, J-C., and J. Tirole (1996), "Controlling risk in payment systems," *Journal of Money, Credit and Banking*, 28, 733–762.

Rogers, C., and O. Zane (1999), "Saddle point approximations to option prices," *Annals of Applied Probability*, 9, 493–503.

Ross, S. (1976, February), "Options and efficiency," *Quarterly Journal of Economics*, 75–86.

Ross, S. (1977), "The determination of financial structure: The incentive-signaling approach," *Bell Journal of Economics*, 8, 23–40.

Sahajwala, R., and Van den Bergh (2000), "Supervisory risk assessment and early warning systems," working paper, Basel Committee.

Saint-Alary, C. (1990), "Communication sur l'application de la loi du 25 Janvier 1985," *Les Petites Affiches*, 16–25.

Salanie, B. (1997), *The Economics of Contracts: A Primer*, MIT press.

Santomero, A. (1995), "Financial risk management: The whys and hows," *Financial Markets, Institutions and Investments*, 4, 1–14.

Santos, J. (2000), "Bank capital regulation in contemporary banking theory: A review of the literature," working paper, BIS.

Sarig, O., and A. Warga (1989), "Some empirical estimates of the risk structure of interest rates," *Journal of Finance*, 44, 1351–1360.

Schmit, M. (2002), "Is automotive leasing a risky business?" working paper, Université Libre de Bruxelles.

Schmit, M., and J. Stuyck (2002), "Recovery rates in the leasing industry," report, Leaseurope.

Schönbucher, P. (2000), "The pricing of credit risk and credit derivatives," working paper, Bonn University.

Schönbucher, P. (2002), "Taken to the limit: Simple and not-so-simple loan loss distributions," working paper, Bonn University.

Schwartz, G. (1978), "Estimating the dimension of a model," *Annals of Statistics*, 461–464.

Sharpe, S. (1990), "Asymmetric information, bank lending and implicit contracts: A stylized model of customer relationship," *Journal of Finance*, 45, 1069–1087.

Sharpe, W., G. Alexander, and J. Bailey (1999), *Investments*, Prentice-Hall.

Shimko, D., H., Tejima, and D. Van Deventer (1993, September), "The pricing of risky debt when interest rates are stochastic," *Journal of Fixed Income*, 58–66.

Sklar, A. (1959), "Fonctions de répartition à n dimensions et leurs marges," *Publication de l'Institut Statistique Universitaire de Paris*, 8, 229–231.

Standard & Poor's (1999), "Financial institutions criteria," *Criteria Books*.

Stiglitz, J., and A. Weiss (1981), "Credit rationing with imperfect information," *American Economic Review*, 71, 393–410.

Stoughton, N., and J. Zechner (1999), "Optimal capital allocation using RAROC and EVA," working paper, University of California at Irvine.

Stoughton, N., and J. Zechner (2000), "The dynamics of capital allocation," working paper, University of California at Irvine.

Struzik, Z., and A. Siebes (2002), "Wavelet transform based multifractal formalism in outlier detection and localisation for financial time series," *Statistical Mechanics and Its Applications*, 300, 388–402.

Sundaresan, S. (1997), *Fixed Income Markets and Their Derivatives*, South-Western College Publishing.

Svensson, L. (1994), "Estimating and interpreting forward interest rates: Sweden 1992–1994," working paper, IMF.

Tirole, J. (1988), *The Theory of Industrial Organization*, MIT Press.

Townsend, R. (1979), "Optimal contracts and competitive markets with costly state verification," *Journal of Economic Theory*, 21, 1–29.

Turnbull, S. (2002), "Bank and business performance measurement," *Economic Notes*, Banca Monte dei Paschi di Siena.

Van Deventer, D., and K. Imai (2002), "Credit risk models and the Basel accords. The Merton model and reduced form models," working paper, Kamakura.

Vapnik, V. (1998), *Statistical Learning Theory*, Wiley.

Vasicek, O. (1991), "Limiting loan loss probability distribution," working paper, KMV.

Von Thadden, E-L. (1990), "Bank finance and long term investment," discussion paper, University of Basel.

Wang, S. (2000), "Aggregation of correlated risk portfolios: Models and algorithm," working paper, Casualty Actuarial Society.

Webb, A. (2002), *Statistical Pattern Recognition*, Wiley.

Wei, D., and D. Guo (1997), "Pricing risky debt: An empirical comparison of the Longstaff and Schwartz and Merton models," *Journal of Fixed Income*, 7, 8–28.

Weinstein, M. (1977), "The effect of a rating change announcement on bond price," *Journal of Financial Economics*, 5, 329–350.

Welch, I. (1997), "Why is bank debt senior? A theory of asymmetry and claim priority based on influence costs," *Review of Financial Studies*, 10, 1203–1236.

Wiginton, J. (1980), "A note on the comparison of logit and discriminant models of consumer credit behaviour," *Journal of Financial and Quantitative Analysis*, 15, 757–770.

Wilson, T. (1997a), "Measuring and managing credit portfolio risk," working paper, McKinsey.

Wilson, T. (1997b, September), "Portfolio credit risk (I)," *Risk*, 111–117.

Wilson, T. (1997c, October), "Portfolio credit risk (II)," *Risk*, 56–61.

Yu, F. (2002a), "Modeling expected returns on defaultable bonds," *Journal of Fixed Income*, 12, 69–81.

Yu, F. (2002b), "Correlated defaults in reduced-form models," working paper, University of California at Irvine.

Zhou, C. (1997), "Jump-diffusion approach to modeling credit risk and valuing defaultable securities," working paper, Federal Reserve Board.

Zhou, C. (2001), "An analysis of default correlation and multiple defaults," *Review of Financial Studies*, 14, 555–576.

INDEX

ABOUT THE AUTHORS

Arnaud de Servigny, Ph.D., is the European head of quantitative analytics and products for Standard & Poor's Risk Solutions. A popular speaker at conferences and seminars throughout Europe, de Servigny is the author of a number of books and articles on finance and credit risk.

Olivier Renault, Ph.D., works in portfolio modeling in the quantitative analytics and products team for Standard & Poor's Risk Solutions. Prior to joining Standard & Poor's, Olivier was a lecturer on finance at the London School of Economics, where he taught derivatives and risk.